TRANSFORMING
Railways of Central Scotland

From a pioneering intercity route to EGIP

Ann Glen

A Class 385 set on a driver training run from Edinburgh Waverley to Dunbar at Drem in East Lothian on 16 February 2018.
(Ian Lothian)

Produced and designed by Lily Publications Ltd
PO Box 33, Ramsey, Isle of Man, British Isles, IM99 4LP
Tel: +44 (0) 1624 898446   Fax: +44 (0) 1624 898449
www.lilypublications.co.uk E-Mail: info@lilypublications.co.uk

Printed and bound by Words & Spaces, Isle of Man © Lily Publications Ltd 2018

ISBN 978-1911177-371

Contents

The Almond Valley viaduct with a Class 380 EMU bound for Glasgow on 30 April 2018.

EGIP Introduction

The Edinburgh & Glasgow Railway was Scotland's first inter-city line and it continues to be a crucial link joining the ancient capital in the east to the country's commercial hub in the west. Opened to the public on 21 February 1842, it proved transformational and has been the spine from which other routes have been developed. Now EGIP, the Edinburgh Glasgow Improvement Programme that has been electrifying routes across Central Scotland is arguably the most profound railway development in the country since that historic opening took place.

From the outset, the intention of the E&GR company was to form an 'electrified line', meaning that the railway would have the electric telegraph installed along its length. After some experimentation in the interests of safety and the effective operation of the railway, this was completed by 1846. In the summer of 1842 an earlier experiment had involved 'Galvani' – a battery propelled truck that hauled a carriage some distance on the new E&GR claimed to be the first electrically propelled 'locomotive' on any railway in the world.

By 1879 technology for electric traction had advanced sufficiently to be demonstrated in Germany, and was followed within two years by a miniature electric tramway carrying passengers near Berlin. In Britain, Volks Electric Railway was opened at Brighton in 1883 as a tourist attraction, and it continues to run to this day. By 1888, there were test lines in Hungary and Switzerland. In 1890 the first electric underground line was operating in London, and in 1893 the Liverpool Overhead Railway commenced with electric traction. In the USA, the Baltimore & Ohio Railroad had both overhead and underground systems by 1894-5. Further tests in Germany in 1901-3 proved that high speed services were possible using the power of electricity.

In 1903, senior managers from the Caledonian Railway visited the USA to investigate electrification with a view to the Glasgow Central Low Level lines and Cathcart Circle being converted to electric haulage. It was even forecast that within a few years, a system would result in fast journeys between Glasgow and Edinburgh, but the First World War and its aftermath prevented any such investment.

In urban areas where lines were in long tunnels, electrification transformed the adverse conditions for both railway staff and for passengers. It also enabled railways to compete with electric tramways, an increasing threat to their business. On Merseyside, the Lancashire & Yorkshire Railway and the Mersey Railway were pioneers in the period 1903-4. Another was the North Eastern Railway that introduced electric trains on its Tyneside suburban routes in 1904, and soon had two freight lines adapted for haulage by electric locomotives. These showed many advantages over steam locomotives.

While in use for driver training, this Class 385 set was in Edinburgh's Waverley Station on 27 January 2018 prior to returning to Millerhill depot. *(Bruce Peter)*

Abseiling skills were essential when the supports for OLE masts were being installed on the Almond Valley viaduct in February 2016.

The BR Class 303 'Blue Trains', introduced on the Glasgow Suburban network in November 1960, were a breakthrough for electric traction in Scotland. This set is seen passing Kipps at Coatbridge. *(Bruce Peter Collection)*

Rapid progress was being made in Switzerland, where the Bern-Lotschberg-Simplon line, opened in 1913 with its 9 mile long tunnel, was electrified from the outset. By 1940, 77% of the Swiss system was reported as 'electric', when other European railways had only reached 5%. Apart from underground lines and some suburban systems, Britain lagged way behind.

In the early 1950s, dieselisation on British Railways – beginning modestly with shunting locomotives (later Class 08) – was gaining ground. Some BR engineers had hopes that there would be a straight transition from steam to electric at some stage, but it was not to be. There was a lone exception – the electrification of the Woodhead line from Manchester to Sheffield across the Pennines, first mooted by the LNER in the 1930s, had a DC system installed from 1953. In 1954, the North of Scotland Hydro-Electric Board – with its new schemes coming on stream – approached British Railways about electrification possibilities in Scotland. It received no response.

The British Transport Commission's Plan for the 'Modernisation and Re-equipment of British Railways', published in 1954, had proposed several major electrification schemes, including the West Coast main line from London to Crewe. It also mentioned the Glasgow suburban lines, dependent on discussions with Glasgow Corporation. Meantime, as an interim measure, there would be extensive dieselisation on the network, and by 1957 Swindon-built 'Intercity' DMUs were on the Edinburgh-Glasgow route.

From 1960 the electrification of suburban lines in the Glasgow area was a positive step, representing a breakthrough in passenger comfort and environmental improvement. However, at this stage, electrification went no further in Scotland. In 1963 came the Beeching Report, 'The Reshaping of British Railways' that recommended the closure of secondary routes and of many stations, although Scotland subsequently escaped many of the cuts that were initially proposed.

The 1970s and 1980s were times of innovation under a progressive British Rail, with the APT (Advanced Passenger Train) and HST (High Speed Train) capturing headlines. On the West Coast Main line (WCML), electrification progressed and had reached Glasgow by 1974; on the East Coast Main line (ECML), the wires were up in Edinburgh Waverley by 1991.

In 1993, the regional councils of Strathclyde, Central and Lothian, under the umbrella of the Strathclyde Passenger Transport Partnership, commissioned Faber Oscar to investigate electrification across Central Scotland, with the E&G set to play a 'spine' role again. It has taken nearly 25 years to make this solution a reality, but better late than never for the long suffering commuters and other passengers on the congested trains in the region. The Cowlairs incline, shown on the British Railways' gradient profile for driver training as 1 in 41, will at last be subdued by electric traction.

The benefits of electrification have been amply

demonstrated wherever it has taken place – to Gourock and Wemyss Bay in 1967, on the Hamilton Circle and Lanark services in 1974, on the re-opened 'Argyle' line in 1979, and to Ayr and Largs in 1986. Electric trains began running to North Berwick in 1991, and to a re-opened Larkhall in 2005. The Airdrie-Bathgate line followed in 2010 providing an alternative link between Glasgow and Edinburgh, and in 2012 the Paisley Canal route received a 'low cost' electrification scheme.

For the EGIP alliance, the first section to be electrified was from Springburn to Cumbernauld in May 2014. Early in November 2017, the overhead installation on the Edinburgh-Glasgow route was successfully tested thoughout, and it was ready for its new trains. These AT 200 series Class 385s from Hitachi are will be faster, longer and more environmentally friendly than their diesel predecessors. Hopefully, they will give greater comfort and transform the passenger experience on many lines across Central Scotland. Soon the benefits of an electrified railway will extend to Stirling, Dunblane and Alloa. However, the principal target has been the Edinburgh & Glasgow main line, ScotRail's flagship route and the only one in Scotland reported 'to make money'.

The programme, costing £790 million, has been hit by delays, arising from problems with overhead wiring clearances and components, and then by production difficulties at Hitachi's factory at Newton Aycliffe in County Durham. By 1 December 2017, a limited introduction of electric train services at peak hours on the E&G route was possible using some

Kenny Forbes, Foreman, surveys the scene at Millerhill where the first Class 385 set arrived in November 2017.

Siemens Class 380 EMUs from other routes. A full electric service should make journey times of 42 minutes attainable.

To deliver the aims of the EGIP Alliance, a multitude of specialised contractors and a host of talented engineers and technicians have been involved. There has been nothing to compare with this programme in complexity, magnitude and scale of investment since the Scottish railways were built. By any measure, it is an outstanding achievement to have made EGIP a reality.

With the OLE completed, there is fast running at Greenhill where a Class 380 heads for Edinburgh on 30 April 2018. *(John Peter)*

Chapter 1

Choosing a Route and Obtaining an Act

In the early years of the nineteenth century, the Railway Age was dawning in Scotland. About 1816 Robert Stevenson, of lighthouse fame, forecast that 'iron railways' would become the highways of the future, and in 1818, the Highland and Agricultural Society of Scotland offered a prize of 50 guineas for the best essay on the construction of railroads. By 1825, Stevenson was arguing for a public Act for the regulation of railways – legislation that would fix the width of tracks and might also specify the strength of rails and the weight to be carried on four wheels – 'otherwise much confusion will ensue'. Those engineers that he consulted agreed with him; among them was Thomas Telford, the acknowledged father of civil engineering.

The desirability of an inter-city route connecting the historic capital of Edinburgh with the thriving commercial metropolis of Glasgow by an 'iron road', was already being debated. Robert Stevenson himself had a plan for a horse-hauled waggonway in 1817, but it was not built. In 1825 James Jardine, a civil engineer, mathematician and geologist in Edinburgh, came forward with a proposal for a rail link. He believed that the main purpose of railways was to haul minerals and he chose a route that went by Tollcross and Bellshill to Shotts that lay on a coalfield.

Robert Stevenson, engineer and builder of lighthouses, investigated routes for railways in Scotland, realising that options would be restricted by the terrain. *(National Portrait Gallery of Scotland)*

This would have climbed to 790 ft and involved the use of inclined planes. Surveys were made and plans drawn up, but nothing came of the proposal.

By 1831 the Garnkirk & Glasgow Railway had been opened; it was constructed between the city and mineral rich districts of what is now Coatbridge in

The opening of the Garnkirk & Glasgow Railway on 27 September 1831 was a ceremonial event with a Robert Stephenson 'Planet' 2-2-0 locomotive hauling the train. *(After D.O. Hill)*

John Miller, CE was engineer for the Edinburgh & Glasgow Railway and for many other early Scottish lines. *(National Portrait Gallery of Scotland)*

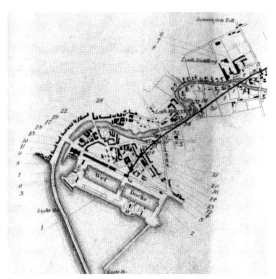

The proposal for the Edinburgh & Glasgow Railway in 1831 also showed a line to the port of Leith. *(Glasgow City Archives)*

Lanarkshire. It used steam locomotives from Robert Stephenson, but was only on the 'Scotch gauge' of 4 feet 6 inches. The engineers were Grainger & Miller, a partnership that was responsible for the majority of the early Scottish 'coal railways' in West Central Scotland – the Ballochney, the Slamannan and the Wishaw & Coltness among others. In 1824 Thomas Grainger had been the surveyor and engineer to the Monkland & Kirkintilloch Railway that carried coal from Lanarkshire to the Forth & Clyde Canal.

His partner, John Miller (1803-1883) was from Ayr and had abandoned law at an early age in favour of land surveying and civil engineering. He soon showed expertise in selecting possible routes, and would prove capable of delivering railways. By 1832 he had achieved membership of the Institution of Civil Engineers; he would become pre-eminent in railway engineering, both through the number of Scottish lines for which he was responsible and for the noble structures that were designed for them. Chief among these would be the Edinburgh & Glasgow Railway, Scotland's first intercity line.

The success of the Liverpool & Manchester Railway, opened in 1830, gave a fresh impetus to the idea of tracks connecting the two Scottish cities and including the port of Leith. By December 1830,

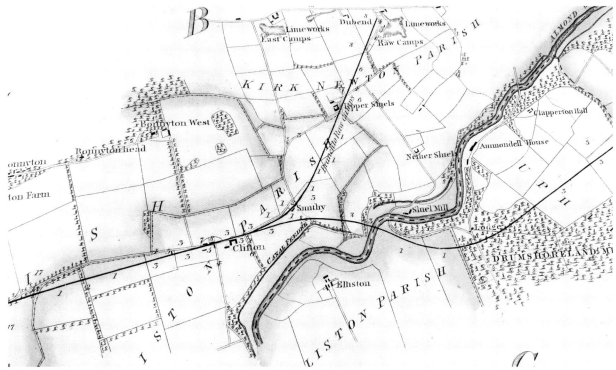

Detail of the 1831 plan, showing the proposed line of the railway near the Almond Valley and a branch to Raw Camps. *(Glasgow City Archives)*

George Stephenson, the 'father of the railways', gave advice to the board of the Edinburgh & Glasgow Railway about a choice of route. *(Wikipedia)*

Grainger & Miller had drawn up a report on the 'Edinburgh, Glasgow & Leith Railway', for which John Miller took the lead. To give the route a start out of Glasgow at less expense, a line that they had engineered earlier would be used – the Garnkirk & Glasgow Railway. This would be followed from its terminus at Glebe Street in the city's Townhead eastwards to a junction near Gartcosh. The new portion would then go north bypassing Slamannan before swinging east to Bathgate. There a branch to Benhar would take off to tap a coalfield, while the main line would continue to the Almond valley. Once across this obstacle, it would go by Ratho and Hermiston to Haymarket. A branch to Leith would

The Edinburgh & Glasgow Union Canal opened in 1822 at Port Hopetoun in the shadow of Edinburgh Castle. The port was named after the Earl of Hopetoun. *(Edinphoto)*

leave at Coltbridge, west of Roseburn. Tunnels were proposed at Ratho Hill and under the Dean estate towards the port. Several viaducts would also have been required across deep valleys, such as those of the Avon and the Almond. To keep a port link in Glasgow, there would also be a line to the Broomielaw with a tunnel going under the Blythswood district – thus joining the principal east and west coast harbours in Scotland.

George Stephenson, the renowned railway engineer, was asked to appraise the two possible routes – the Jardine one of 1825 and the Grainger & Miller proposal. A meeting in Glasgow in January 1831 revealed that access had been refused to the Jardine plan unless £1,500 was put on the table. Stephenson believed that the main purpose of a railway should be 'the expeditious, safe and cheap conveyance of passengers'. The Liverpool & Manchester Railway had proved how very profitable passenger traffic could be – even within weeks of its opening. On the other hand, Scots saw railways as freight carriers and adjuncts to canals and harbours. Stephenson preferred the Grainger & Miller proposal for a railway passing 'through a country extremely favourable' as the summit levels were lower, with 'inclinations sufficiently gentle for the advantageous employment of Locomotive Engines'.

Nevertheless, the attempt to link the cities by rail at this stage was in vain. The fierce opposition of the Edinburgh & Glasgow Union Canal and of the Forth & Clyde Canal companies prevailed. Opened in 1822, the Union Canal was 31½ miles long, and its primary function was to convey coal and bulky goods to Edinburgh. The Forth & Clyde Navigation, completed in 1790 from the Clyde at Bowling to the River Carron's mouth on the Forth, was 35 miles in length, had 36 locks but was capable of taking sea-going vessels of the time. At Falkirk, a flight of 11 locks on the Union Canal enabled barges to descend to Port Downie where the canals met at Lock 16. In 1832, the Bill for an Edinburgh & Glasgow Railway was thrown out by Parliament. Powerful landowners, such as the Earl of Hopetoun, also opposed the railway. He feared that his estate – having lost land to the Union Canal – would now be 'cut to ribbons' by the construction of a railway. Engineers had to be wary of making 'inroads on the privacy of our gentry' and the compensation claims that might ensue. The 1831 plan survives as does the Book of Reference, but the route was by no means a direct line capable of high speeds. Even so, Grainger & Miller were confident about the future of railways and about their own project.

Every year brought the probability of a railway between the cities closer, and it was Glasgow merchants that took the initiative. On 3 December 1835, the First General Meeting of the shareholders of the Edinburgh & Glasgow Railway was held in the Black Bull Inn at Glasgow's Trongate. This was a well known hostelry where a coach left for Edinburgh three times a week – taking about 5 hours on the way. Lord Provost William Mills took the chair; plans were discussed, a company was formed, and subscribers determined to go to Parliament 'next session'.

John Leadbetter (1788-1865), a linen merchant and general agent, trading in Glasgow for many years, was one of the first shareholders and became the chairman of the E&G. He had made a substantial contribution to public life – being on the Trades' Council, the Town Council and a director of the Merchants' House. He drew up a prospectus extolling the value of such a line, emphasising the fact that Edinburgh and Glasgow were 'the only important cities in Great Britain situated a short distance of each other that are not connected by a Railway'. The advantages were set out – the ease of construction across the isthmus between the North and the Irish Seas, where growing populations, forming a large market, were engaged in manufacturing and trade. Nor were the 'picturesque environs and romantic scenery' overlooked – this would attract visitors to the railway and to the steamboats on the firths and lochs. The canals would also have a rôle – for transporting heavy goods, building stone, coal and ironstone, a trade that would be left to them.

The new line would be a strategic element in Britain for 'a Grand Trunk Railway, should this ever be brought northwards … whether by east or west coast' for which the proposed intercity route would 'form the most important feeder'. Raising capital of £550,000 was proposed, but this was not seen as impossible. In selecting a line, 'one of the most eminent English Railway Engineers… shall be employed …to point out the best'. This would give confidence in the public interest, attract affluent English investors, especially in Lancashire, to support the venture, and should ensure the most profitable outcome for shareholders.

Much time was spent in Parliamentary Committees before the Bill for the Edinburgh & Glasgow Railway won approval. In April 1837, John Miller appeared before a House of Commons Committee stating that he had long contemplated a railway between Edinburgh and Glasgow – in fact, he had first 'examined country as a surveyor for Mr Jardine' west of Shotts. As for the Edinburgh & Glasgow Railway now proposed, it was 'determined upon by Messrs Rastrick, Leather and Vignoles' in 1836.

These engineers were 'heavy weights' in their profession that would give reassurance to English investors. John Urpeth Rastrick (1780-1856) was an inventive steam locomotive builder from Northumberland and a judge at the Rainhill trials in 1829 – a year when he exported a locomotive to the United States. Turning to civil engineering, he was associated with the London & Brighton Railway and other lines in South East England. Charles Blacker

John Leadbetter, proponent of railways and the chairman of the Edinburgh & Glasgow Railway Company from 1835 to 1842. *(Mitchell Library, Glasgow)*

Vignoles (1793-1875) on returning from America in the 1820s, carried out surveys for the London & Brighton and the Liverpool & Manchester Railways and rose to be Professor of Civil Engineering at University College, London. George Leather (1804-1885) was a civil engineering contractor with expertise in railways, harbours and bridge foundations.

Engineers in top hats and frock coats are engaged on survey works about 1838 in this vignette by J.C. Bourne

This underbridge, near Broxburn, on the Edinburgh & Glasgow Railway carries the Hopetoun coat of arms as a gesture of conciliation.

Only after this independent assessment, were Grainger and Miller called by the Edinburgh & Glasgow Railway Company to prepare the parliamentary plans and sections. However, John Miller had not been idle. Early in 1833, he had begun 'examining the country more minutely' for a line crossing the Winchburgh ridge, a whinstone outcrop 'always held as a bar against this course'. He made drawings and had sections taken, including 'flying levels'. Rastrick, in the course of several visits, suggested various improvements, advocating a different course at Cumbernauld and an improved terminus at Glasgow.

Appearing before a House of Commons Committee, John Miller described the proposed railway commencing at the North Bridge in Edinburgh, 'near Register House'. He handed in a plan that joined up with the Grainger and Miller line for the Edinburgh, Leith & Newhaven Railway, thus giving access to the Firth of Forth. Sufficient land would be reserved near the Little Mound for a joint depot. From there, the railway would go through Princes Street Gardens and under streets 'by the Riding School and Charity Workhouse' to Haymarket, where Miller recommended a station. Westwards, the construction of the line appeared to be relatively easy towards the city's outskirts.

Negotiations for land acquisition had already begun. Parliamentary Committees tried to ensure that land and property owners would receive adequate compensation when railways crossed their estates, or harmed their possessions. Such compensation (and legal fees) could escalate. In the countryside, land acquisition was based on the value of agricultural land, but there were extra costs to be met. Railways were seen as noisy and dirty neighbours; disturbance arose from construction works, and when fields, roads, or paths were split by the laying of tracks, there was 'the inconvenience of intersection'. This could prevent the movement and watering of livestock. The presence of 'unexhausted manure', where land was taken that could have produced another crop or two, was often an issue. The dumping of spoil, and whether this would be temporary or permanent, led to further wrangling. Finally, there was compensation for the fact of compulsion – as the seller had little choice in the matter.

Acts of Parliament gave railway companies sweeping powers, allowing them to make deviations 100 yards to the sides of their line as shown on the official plan.

To contain compensation costs, Miller disclosed that he always tried to avoid 'domains' as much as possible. It was in such locations that powerful estate owners, assisted by their legal advisers, would try to squeeze as much money as possible out of projects. Miller had rebuffed a suggestion that the line should go along the shores of the Firth of Forth mainly for this reason. Nevertheless, a way would have to be found over the Earl of Hopetoun's property in West Lothian where his estate amounted to 6,500 acres.

By 20 March 1837, capital for the E&GR had reached £747,000 in 2,952 shares. The Provisional Committee now consisted of 52 directors of whom 23 were from Glasgow, 16 from Edinburgh, 5 from Manchester and 8 from Liverpool. The shareholders were mainly business people from the rising middle and emerging professional classes, the occupations ranging from accountants, bakers and bankers to shipbrokers, surgeons and wholesale grocers. Several were listed as 'gentlemen'. Shareholders with Glasgow and West of Scotland interests stood at 16% outnumbering those from Edinburgh and the East, but most had no close local link at all. There was a good representation from England with 42% of the subscriptions coming from Lancashire alone – the biggest investor was a broker from Liverpool with an offer of £153,000. An exotic subscriber was George Peabody, an American banker based in London, remembered today for his philanthropy and support for libraries and academic institutions in the United States.

The sternest opponents of the E&G were again the canal interests led by Robert Downie, chairman of the Union Canal Company. Another canal supporter was John Llewellyn Learmonth, the owner of the Dean estate in Edinburgh, of whom more would subsequently be heard in a railway context. Opponents also included other landowners, the governors and trustees of Heriot Hospital, plus several legal luminaries. They were concerned that income from lands that they owned or administered would decline if the railway dared to cross such areas.

Those opposed to the railway mustered expert opinion to support their stance. Such an authority was William Sawrey Gilpin (1762-1843), an artist who turned to landscape design and had 'an enormous portfolio of satisfied clients'. He spoke for James Maitland Hog of Newliston in Midlothian. That owner had inherited an estate with an Adams mansion and ornamental grounds modelled on Versailles, but such majestic style had fallen out of fashion. Garden designs were now inspired by the romantic and strived for a natural effect. Gilpin found railways 'utterly execrable'. The line proposed would sever the lodge from the house, 'You might as well take a road through his drawing room' but 'hard hearted engineers and flinty projectors of railroads…have no eyes for the picturesque'. Worse, within sight of the house, the E&GR would construct the massive Almond valley viaduct – and whether ornament or eyesore would be debateable.

However, John Miller had investigated the situation. He had discovered that James Hog had a steam threshing mill with a tall chimney in line with the view from his mansion. What then could be objectionable about the occasional passage of trains with steam locomotives on the railway?

By the spring of 1838, the Bill was being considered by a House of Lords Committee and John Miller appeared again.

Q. Is the line before Parliament the best line between Glasgow and Edinburgh?

JM. I have no doubt of it. It would be a line with a ruling gradient of 1 in 880 … to all appearance as flat as that table.

The gentle gradients on the line would ensure that early steam locomotives could be used successfully on it and that high speeds would be attainable.

The mansion at Newliston, designed by Robert Adam, was owned by James Hog, initially a strong opponent of the E&GR.

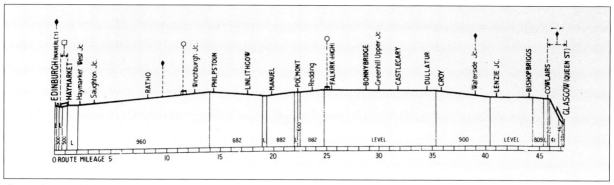

The gradient profile for the Edinburgh & Glasgow Railway – to achieve this outcome to Cowlairs, prodigious effort had to be made with long cuttings in rock, tunnels and impressive viaducts. *(British Rail)*

However, it betrayed a lack of faith in the increasing power of such engines.

Miller was then asked about the rock types, especially the occurrence of hard whin dykes on the route. These were the result of volcanic activity some 300 million years ago, and would be challenging to cut through. By the 1830s, there was increasing knowledge of geology, with particular interest in the distribution of Carboniferous rocks containing the coal measures. The 'Ordnance Geological Survey' was established in 1835 and the following year the first geological map of Scotland had been published. Miller would have been aware of its usefulness to engineers. He reported that since 1837, an employee had been taking bores. With pits dug first, borings going down to 100 to 150 feet took several months, but the work had been completed from one end of

The first geological map of Scotland by John McCulloch dates from 1836. *(British Geological Survey)*

the line to the other. The bores had shown coal seams around Winchburgh and at Callendar near Falkirk. In the Glasgow area, additional information had been gathered from quarries where mainly freestone (fine sandstone) was exposed.

There was concern about the proximity of the E&GR to the Union Canal – when it had been cut, local wells were said to have run dry. The railway followed the canal closely, but in some places it would be carried *below* the level of the canal. Miller had an answer for any damage to the waterway. With money in hand, the cure would be to 'run down a puddle dike, next to the canal'.

There were questions about passenger access at Falkirk. With the line bypassing the town on the south, how would people residing over a mile away reach the station up a steep hill 120 feet higher? Miller had a solution – an inclined plane would go down to the burgh at 1 in 40 for 1¼ miles.

Q. This will be worked by a Stationary Engine? JM. By a horse…if the trade was sufficient, we could work it by a Stationary Engine.

A horse-gin was a low cost solution used in threshing mills and in lifting coal from small pits.

Attention then turned to the principal works on the line. The Almond valley viaduct, of 36 arches 65 feet high with 50 feet spans, would be 'a very beautiful work when finished', and although 'the largest work' was not 'an engineering impossibility'. A tunnel at Winchburgh would be approached by deep cuttings 'in all, about 4 miles' – a major feat of excavation, mostly in rock, where water would gather. By Linlithgow, the railway would run along the back of small gardens and 'kail yards' – only one or two old houses 'of very inferior description' and the stables at the inn would be taken down. A wall 'planted nicely with ivy' would hide the line. The 'lanes and communications' in the burgh would be 'improved' by taking the railway through on masonry arches. Then would come the Avon viaduct of 21 arches, not as long as the Almond, but 90 feet in height.

Approaching Falkirk, a lengthy tunnel of 530 yards would lie beneath the Callendar estate of William Forbes. As there would be no airshafts for the admittance of light or ventilation (the owner refusing any visible evidence of a railway), the tunnel would be 25 feet high, 'double the height of the engines' – to give a current of air and hopefully clear its interior of smoke. The railway would then have to cross the canal at Tamfourhill, where the Union Canal Company had bought the Glenfuir estate. The crossing would be close to a flight of locks giving access downhill to the Forth & Clyde Canal – and the Union Canal, towpath and a carriage road must be kept open during construction. A complex viaduct of 4 arches would be 'tolerably expensive' and a model of this was displayed.

By Castlecary, the Redburn viaduct of 8 arches would be built. Ahead lay the Croymill Ridge, '226 feet above Leith Docks' and the summit of the line. Here 'a considerable depth of whinstone' would be encountered. *Q. You cut through the whinstone? A. Yes, we do.* A tunnel had been considered at one stage and Miller made it sound simple, but this obstacle would cause serious delays to the completion of the railway. After that, there were extents of 'mountain moss' (peat) to be excavated and prepared for carrying the tracks.

Approaching Glasgow, there was more rock – 'freestone of quality', a sandstone that was quarried at Possil. Once at Cowlairs, an inclined plane would allow the line to descend to a city level through tunnels. It had to pass a strategic point - under the Cut of Junction of the Port Dundas branch of the Forth & Clyde Canal with the Monkland Canal. However, the steep descent at 1 in 42 for 1¼ miles would avoid property purchases and save the company money. With the rails being 69 feet below the Cut of Junction, it also kept the lines clear of canal activity at Port Dundas. The original intention was to have made a station near that harbour but canal opposition prevailed.

Q. How many tunnels? JM. Three. These would be of varying length, the longest at 330 yards passing under the canal with deep cuttings in sandstone and mudstone formed between each. Overall, the tunnels would be 28 feet wide but only 18 feet high.

Q. Why lower? JM. There are no Locomotive Engines to go through and they are double the height of carriages.

Miller was not asked how the tunnels would be negotiated but this stretch would require an inclined plane with a stationary steam engine at the summit. Close to Queen Street, there was quarry waste and he commented, *'We shall open it, cut it and build over again - it is what we call 'cut and cover'.*

The terminus would be positioned at the north end of Queen Street. This was close to the Royal Exchange and the business hub of what is now known as the Merchant City.

Q. Is the termination in Glasgow an exceedingly favourable termination?

JM. Very much so. It is at George Square – only about 1,000 yards from the proposed Depot of the Ayrshire and

The Union Canal, without locks, was followed closely by the E&GR to which the canal company was bitterly opposed. This section is near Park Farm, West Lothian.

Greenock. The Railways will unite there.

Miller omitted to mention that the Ayrshire & Greenock terminus was on the *south* side of the Clyde, but he was correct in judging the E&G station's city centre location as advantageous. Conveniently, chairman John Leadbetter had an interest in property in neighbouring Dundas Street where a sale at a bargain price to the E&G would give the station a flying start.

Miller then gave details about gradients and mileages, The E&G would have generous curves as the only tracks under a mile in radius would be at Cowlairs, at the top of the inclined plane. He explained that this approach to Glasgow would end in 'a small piece on the level'. (Inclined planes to access city termini were not unusual on early railways and were a solution used on the London & Birmingham Railway at Camden in its pre-Euston years). Miller also mentioned the Edinburgh & Dalkeith Railway with its tunnel at 1 in 30. This horse-drawn waggonway, built essentially for coal traffic, was conveying up to 200,000 passengers every year,

The Star & Garter Hotel at Linlithgow lost properties at its rear to the E&GR.

The Edinburgh & Glasgow Railway was carried through the south side of Linlithgow with some difficulty, requiring bridges and cuttings.

and 'breaks' (sic) were no problem – the old stagecoaches adapted for railway use had drag boards attached at the rear. The House of Lords Committee sought further assurances from Miller:-

Q. The danger is in going down? A. Much the same when you are hanging on the End of a Rope, it does not signify much whether you are going down or up.

Q. If it were to give way? A. The Waggons would go down. Q. And the Passengers in them? A. Yes.

Miller did not consider 1 in 30 to be dangerous as vehicles would be 'perfectly under the control of the Breaks'. (The Glasgow tunnels would have a gradient of 1 in 42).

Q. If not applied in time, the Result could be fearful? A. Yes it would be dreadful, no Doubt; 1 in 40 is perfectly safe using a Fixed Engine.

Costs were explored in detail with Miller being asked about 'tolls' on the railway, that is, the fares. The company looked for powers to charge 2d per mile, but might take extra for the use of locomotives and for providing carriages – a sum that should not exceed 3½d a mile. At that time, the mail coaches

This watercolour sketch shows the sandstone quarries at Queen Street. These were known as the Cracklinghouse and the Dovanside quarries. *(Glasgow Forum)*

were charging 16s for the 46 miles between the cities, inclusive of coachman and guard, 'but no such persons would be employed on the railway'. Luggage up to 40lbs in weight would be permitted on trains, but limited in size, as Miller observed, 'a passenger's luggage may be very light but yet be very inconvenient and bulky'.

As Miller was diligent with fieldwork, he could confidently state, 'I have examined every inch of the country'. Earth moving he explained as 'cutting, leading and teeming' that would be done by squads of navvies and horse haulage, giving an average cost of 9½ pence per mile. Labour costs were reported to be 30 per cent less in Scotland than in England. Miller had also allowed for contingencies. Both cutting and filling would be carried out in as close proximity as possible, with the longest 'leads' on the E&G being about 2 miles. The heaviest cutting of over four miles would be around Craigton on the Hopetoun estate where Miller had based his calculations on clay with slopes formed 'at 1½ to 1'. Rock on the line would be cut perpendicular. Whinstone at ¼ to 1 would be the most expensive to remove, but *'you get stone that will make blocks, will make fences (walls), and what will not make fences will ballast the road …there is no waste'.* The rails would be laid on stone blocks. He had calculated that there were 480,000 cubic yards of sandstone and whinstone on the route, the latter notably at Croy.

Q. What about Croy Hill? JM. I suppose you mean the cutting at the 35th mile? This amounts to 470 yards and is 60 feet deep. (Miller had allowed 1s 3d to 1s 6d as an extra outlay per yard to deal with this mass of obdurate volcanic rock).

The questions about costs continued. Q. *What for fences?* (These would be mainly stone walls or dykes) *JM. From 5s to 3s 6d a single yard with 7s to 10s for drainage …a 2 foot square drain will run all the way along the line, the whole is £360 a mile.*

Q. Farm bridges and occupation bridges? JM. The occupation bridges are 74 and vary from £280 to £300 …it depends on the situation. The whole bridges are 12 or 13. The price of turnpike road bridges varies. Culverts and inverted siphons, or water bridges, put a gross of £68,000. The line only crosses three great highways.

(These were the turnpike roads to Bathgate, Linlithgow and Cumbernauld).

Matters then turned to the gauge of the line, a central issue as the prevailing 'Scotch gauge' was 4 feet 6 inches, but 5 feet 6 inches had been used on the Dundee & Arbroath Railway:-

Q. What will the width be from rail to rail?

JM. I do not think it is settled. It is very likely to be five feet and a half. Q. Do you propose to place them on blocks or sleepers? JM. On blocks. Q. All the way? JM. Yes, blocks are 2s 3d, sizes 3 to 3½ cubic feet; allowance for ballasting 8s 4d.

Q. What for laying? 1s a yard or 2s a yard forward? Prices for rails and chairs?

By this stage, Miller was becoming tetchy about such questions, replying, *'If you go on raising issues of what railways cost, you will establish a sum that puts railways out of the question'.*

Embankment slopes would be formed at 2 to 1 with only 30 feet allowed at the top for the tracks; a similar space would be made for the rails in cuttings. Excess spoil would go to create an embankment on a proposed line to Falkirk; otherwise, the earth could be thrown on the banks of the Union Canal.

There was again the vexed question of compensation to be considered. The distances and areas where this was likely to arise had been identified and notices served on owners, lessees and occupiers. The 'assents, dissents and neuters' had been recorded and there was much support for the railway, the 'assents' among owners and lessees thankfully exceeding the 'dissents' 2 to 1. Tenants were even more enthusiastic, over 80 per cent being in favour of the line.

Additionally, there were some special requests to be met. Lord Hopetoun wished to protect the ruinous Niddry Castle from harm. Ancestral links gave him 'a strong feeling of pride' in Niddry – even if it was occupied by 'rooks and jackdaws as tenants'. When the Union Canal had been excavated close by, he had accepted it 'for the good of the country', but the railway in a deep cutting would be worrying. He had concerns too about the Niddry Burn near Winchburgh, a watercourse that the railway would cut through. Miller was asked how this would be resolved – replying by a cast iron siphon at extra expense. This was not seen as a problem as 'we have £45,000 to come and go on'. A bigger issue was where spoil should be put, and dumping it on the Earl's fields was disputed – but four miles of Hopetoun land would have to be crossed with several bridges, 'rather more than three a mile', an unavoidable outlay.

In total, Miller estimated that over £95,000 would have to be set aside to meet compensation claims, and he had allowed an extra 10 per cent if disputes went to jury trials. With the total cost of the E&GR now put at £900,000, compensation would be a considerable element in this total.

Initially the E&G directors had every intention of constructing their line into the heart of Edinburgh. From 'the Haymarket', a 'cut and cover' tunnel would take the tracks eastwards. The grounds of the West Kirk would be crossed on the south side – but Miller stated that the land would not be interfered with, not even the clergyman's garden being disturbed. The Castle Rock would not be touched – or the Wall Tower below it, as Miller was determined to keep any curve through Princes Street gardens 'as flat as we possibly can'.

Another obstacle lay ahead – the Mound. This consisted of builders' waste and spoil from the construction of the New Town, material that Miller believed to be 'as solid as can be'. But there were

Stone sleepers support a pathside at Croy station. Such a system was the initial choice for the E&GR.

water pipes lying 20 feet deep within it. How could a tunnel be made and the water supply protected? His reply was 'just suspend the pipes' and shore them up. The work should take about a week, but would water supplies be interrupted? Not so, said Miller, as the New Town only had water at certain times – and none between 11am and 7pm. Would the Royal Institution (now the Royal Scottish Academy) be endangered by a tunnel just 158 feet away from it? Miller replied, *'Not the least in the world. I was much amused when I heard the danger spoken of'.* The Bank of Scotland, constructed on 'made ground' overlooking the Mound would also be unaffected by tunnel construction.

Princes Street gardens however were vulnerable as the railway would cause 'aggravated encroachment', with a potential to be 'most injurious' to a nursery for plants there. But Miller had an answer, *'We will convert part into pleasure grounds and ornament that part of the railway'.* In addition, seven crossings over the railway were proposed and shrubs would be planted. At that time, the gardens were hardly salubrious as Miller reported a pigsty and a

Niddry Castle, then a roofless ruin, was close to the proposed E&GR and a subject of concern to the Earl of Hopetoun.

Travel by stagecoach took about 5 hours between Edinburgh and Glasgow, the Craig Inn at Blackridge was on the 'quick middle road' via Airdrie.

dung heap close to the raised walks. These were so steep that stairs had been built to allow residents to access the gardens.

Another concern was the view. Would the railway, enclosed by iron railings, be seen from Princes Street or from drawing room windows? The answer was 'no'. Charles Vignoles had earlier been asked about smoke from locomotives, to which he replied, "There is no smoke, the engines consume their own smoke". This was of course wishful thinking but it forced early locomotive engineers to use coke, a relatively 'clean' or smokeless fuel. Asked about noise, Vignoles answered, " Not much, but I am partial to Railways". He even suggested having a band, powered by steam, playing music in the gardens to conceal the clatter of railway carriages.

A hazard going east was the site of the former Nor' Loch. Miller also had a solution for this damp stretch – a concrete foundation with an inverted arch would be placed over the spongy ground to produce a firm track bed. A depot for the E&GR between the Shambles (a meat market), and the Little Mound was likely, but would take up little space. Road access to the site would have to be improved as many carts brought vegetables and fruit to the green market by the North Bridge each day.

A scientific adviser called to support the Bill was Dionysis Lardner, a polymath who edited an encyclopaedia and had strong views about locomotives – comparing the new types to racehorses instead of the slow cumbersome examples on the Stockton & Darlington line. He found fault with Miller's estimates of costs – for working the line, the amount was 'not half enough'. The meagre half acre for a depot at Edinburgh was 'an absurd idea and the Town Council should think again', especially when the Great Western Railway was looking for no less than 33 acres at Bath.

The Liverpool & Manchester Railway was held up as an example for the E&GR to follow. In 1837, the

L&MR was carrying half a million passengers a year and a quarter of a million tons of goods. Miller was asked about his knowledge of this pioneering railway. *Q. Were you ever upon the Liverpool? JM. Yes, I have been upon it many times – every year for the last eight or ten years, I dare say. When we meet we try to get information about the different lines.* He had however cast an engineer's eye over the L&MR where '*the road was laid a great deal too light upon the original railway'*. The rails were lightweight and he would avoid that mistake on the E&GR where 75lb rails would be used

When questions turned to stage coach traffic, information for 1837, showed that 124 coaches were running between Edinburgh and Glasgow each week, with over 69,000 passengers carried a year. Travelling at 8mph, a coach would take 18 passengers on an uncomfortable 5 hour journey, the charges being 13 shillings inside (for 6 people) and 9 shillings outside. Some travellers used their own gigs and horses, estimated at over 135,000 a year, many coming from places that the E&GR could serve.

An alternative was canal transport. Swift boats on the canals had been introduced in 1832 and carried 56 passengers – a response to any rail threat. Sailing at night, they were towed by two horses. The passage

> ### MERCURY LONG COACH,
> *Between Edinburgh and Glasgow.*
> **FARES REDUCED,**
> *Inside to 14s.—Outside 9s.*
> JOSEPH BAIN & COMPANY, respectfully inform their Friends and the Public, that the MERCURY continues TO RUN from the CROWN HOTEL, EDINBURGH, and MAIL COACH OFFICE here, by Airdrie and Bathgate, every lawful day at 9 o'clock morning. The Mercury for years has been noted for a safe conveyance, and for punctuality in its arrivals and departures. The Proprietors promise every attention to promote these desirable ends, and beg leave to solicit a continuance of that patronage which has hitherto rewarded their exertions.
> Mail Coach Office; Glasgow,
> 4th October, 1808.

In 1838, when the E&GR obtained its Act, a stagecoach proprietor offered reduced fares with a view to retaining business. *(Glasgow Herald)*

took 4 hours from Glasgow to Falkirk, with a fare of 5 shillings in the cabin and 4 shillings steerage – 34,156 passengers were soon being carried yearly. To Edinburgh, the journey took about 12 hours for which 43,108 passengers paid higher fares. A popular innovation from the early 1830s were 'flyboats' taking advantage of a 'soliton wave' to glide at 10mph over the shallow canal waters.

A key witness at this concluding stage was chairman John Leadbetter who dealt in facts – in 1801 Glasgow's population was 77,421, a number that had trebled to 232,263 by 1831. Over the same period, Edinburgh's population had doubled from 82,666 to 165,332. Transport over land had to respond and he believed railways were the answer. As a Trustee of the River Clyde Navigation, Leadbetter also had an understanding of mercantile interests, explaining how improvements at Glasgow harbour had led to a six-fold increase in revenue in 15 years, reaching £37,503, but that the Forth & Clyde Navigation was doing even better, earning over £63,743 in 1836. The canal owners were accumulating funds without paying a dividend – resulting in £10 shares trading at £580 to £600. The canal carried over 190,000 passengers a year and 356,150 tons of freight – and its directors were resolutely opposed to a railway and to losing their markets.

Meanwhile, the Garnkirk & Glasgow Railway was showing what railways could do by way of handling freight, mostly coal, and by attracting passengers for an 8 mile jaunt out of the city. Although the Monkland Canal was conveying 400,000 tons of coal from Lanarkshire to Glasgow each year, the G&GR was hauling a third of that tonnage and taking a growing number of passengers –119,000 a year.

Robert Ellis, the secretary of the Union Canal Company also gave evidence. In recent years, the Union Canal had averaged only £4,600 in profits. If the railway took away £8,600, consisting of £3,500 in passenger fares plus the balance for goods receipts, there would be insufficient funds to pay the interest on the canal debt of £5,000. He accepted that boats going city to city had to negotiate no less than 15 locks, taking an age, but it was peaceful – there was 'No Noise and Smoke, and occasional Sparks as on a Railway'. He worried about horses being 'put in panic' on the towpath by locomotives in close proximity, pointing out that erecting screens would be insufficient protection.

The site for the Glasgow terminus at Queen Street had already been secured through Leadbetter's foresight, and it was a bargain. There was land speculation on the margins of the Merchant City, and at Whitsun 1838, a triangle of land at Dundas Street, the old feu of Bailie Crauford's mansion, was sold. The 'six roods and two acres by two roods' had once been farmed as runrig and the site was close to the St Enoch Burn (now in a sewer under Buchanan Street). There was also a stance in North Hanover Street. On 2 March 1837, the E&GR acquired these areas with John Leadbetter playing a key role in the purchases. The land soon became the company's station site and accommodated a tunnel mouth. What had been Rottenrow Loan was subsequently transformed by the railway's presence into Cathedral Street, thereby changing the look of the whole district. (Note: A rood was a quarter of an acre).

The Bill evidence and other matters occupied three sessions of Parliament with large demands on time for the witnesses, calling for 'caution and deliberation with untiring perseverance in order to secure a project so beneficial to Scotland'. It was the third attempt at securing an intercity route. John Leadbetter attended the Parliamentary Committees

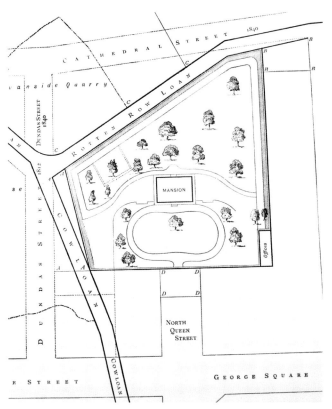

The site for Queen Street station, Glasgow, covered the feu of Bailie Crauford's former mansion and shows the proximity of quarries. *(Regality Papers, Glasgow City Archives)*

faithfully, the journeys to London taking a minimum of four days by coach, and only convincing him of the desirability of constructing railways. For John Miller, whose home was in Edinburgh, the preferred route was by coach to Glasgow, then by steam ship to Liverpool where he could access the nascent railway lines and thus reach London. Once a rail network was in place, direct 10 hour journeys would become feasible.

At the third attempt, the Act for the E&GR was obtained on 4 July 1838. A piece of silver plate to the value of £500 was the shareholders' gift to John Leadbetter for his perseverance. It was now over to the directors and their chosen engineer to make the Edinburgh & Glasgow Railway a reality.

Stagecoach travel over turnpike roads, often with poor surfaces, was hazardous and time-consuming. *(ScotCities)*

Chapter 2

Building the line

With the Act for the Edinburgh & Glasgow Railway finally obtained, on 9 July 1838 the directors held their first meeting. Only six were present to hear the company's lawyer John Ballantyne announce that the Bill had received the Royal Assent. He then outlined the powers given to the directors and the requirements now laid upon them. John Leadbetter of Glasgow was appointed chairman with John Learmonth from Edinburgh as his deputy. Directors were expected to hold £1,000 worth of stock in the company. Two committees were set up, one for Edinburgh and the other for Glasgow, an arrangement that would lead to tensions and disputes.

Calls for funds were made immediately with £5 demanded on each share. Contact was being made with banks in Glasgow and Edinburgh, but also establishments in Liverpool, Manchester and London. Inevitably loans would have to be sought to keep the project on course. A meeting of shareholders was set for 15 August and no time was to be lost in appointing an engineer 'to proceed with the execution of the work'.

The 'greatest importance' was given to an agreement with the Glasgow & Ayrshire and the Glasgow & Greenock Railway Companies 'as to the width of the rails to be used by them' – if the gauge was compatible, trains from Ayrshire and Renfrewshire would then be able to travel to Edinburgh once a junction was formed. But the Ayrshire line's directors hedged their bets until the E&G settled on its own gauge.

A design for the corporate seal was chosen and allocations of 250 shares were proposed for those persons who had assisted the company. On 16 July as a gesture of thanks, 'respected townspeople' organised a public dinner, but who should be sent? A Glasgow lawyer seemed an ideal choice until his involvement with canals was remembered. The E&G would prove to be very much a Glasgow initiative on the back of the city's ambitions and wealth.

The directors determined to appoint an engineer resident in Scotland 'who would be on the spot when required' and who would prepare working plans and superintend the work. But there was a caveat – 'an eminent Consulting English Engineer' would oversee the project. John Miller was therefore appointed engineer with John Ulpeth Rastrick as consultant - he was then occupied with the London to Brighton line, but had advised on the best route for the E&GR. The directors were anxious to know what Miller's charges would be – £5 a day if away from home, or £4 a day when engaged on company business in his office. A fixed salary, possibly amounting to £900 a year (if two-thirds of his time was spent on E&G business), was ruled out. His 'ordinary assistants', would receive £1 per day and seniors 30 shillings but what recompense should 'superintendents' out on the line receive? There were many uncertainties to resolve.

Miller had already stated that tackling the most difficult works should be done first as these would take the longest time to complete. His priorities at this stage were the cutting at Croy Mill near Cumbernauld and the tunnel at Glasgow. Advertising for contractors should be done immediately and with plans in preparation, notices for contracts were placed in both Glasgow and Edinburgh newspapers.

On 15 August, the 'First General Meeting of Shareholders' took place in a hall at Glasgow's Black Bull Inn. There were 4,705 shareholders in attendance with interests ranging from just 5 shares to over 500. John Leadbetter took the chair and to much acclaim received his gift of silver plate. He warned that some opposition had yet to be overcome – both Lord Hopetoun and James Hog of Newliston being mentioned as stern opponents of the railway.

The shareholders were told that John Miller had been given the 'superintendence' of the line based on

The coat-of-arms of the Edinburgh & Glasgow Railway Company displayed the arms of both cities; this example was on a Rule Book. (National Records of Scotland)

his local knowledge and experience of railways. The Dundee & Arbroath, 'now just about completed' was testimony to his 'prudence and professional talents'. He was 33 year old, and was 'to secure in all cases of Difficulty & Importance, the advice of the most eminent English Railway engineers'. Rastrick was then named, but in deference to Lancashire shareholders, Joseph Locke was also appointed. His name was well known to English investors, as he had been active in the construction of both the Liverpool & Manchester and the Grand Junction Railways. Soon he would take charge of the Lancaster & Carlisle Railway over Shap, plus the Caledonian over Beattock. With such engineering talent, shareholders were assured that the E&G would be 'executed on the most approved principles'.

John Miller then explained the portions of the E&G that would take the most time (and expense) to construct – the tunnel at Glasgow, the cutting at Croy Mill, with the tunnel at Callendar at Falkirk and the embankment at the River Almond now added. A notable omission was the tunnel at Winchburgh. With advertisements for contractors 'pushed forward', work was due to begin in September 1838 and take three years to complete by 1 July 1841. As 'preliminary arrangements' had been made with proprietors, possession of lands and property could be immediately obtained.

Questions arose about directors' responsibilities for portions of the line 'to prevent mistakes'. With Glasgow and Edinburgh Committees there was some unease, with the capital's legal interests requesting that 'a well digested deed' should be drawn up.

The first and major contract was the crossing of the Almond valley that consisted of five elements and was let to the experienced contractor John Gibb & Son of Aberdeen. John Gibb had a long association with Thomas Telford, and had carried out many harbour works, bridges, lighthouses and road projects. At £147,669 his offer was considerably lower than the others, and sadly, this would prove a serious miscalculation. (On this one contract, a sum of £20,000 was already set aside to compensate the Road Trustees and landowners – building railways did not come cheaply).

Over the whole line of railway, there were 20 contracts, excluding stations. The expectation was that the E&GR would be completed by July 1841 – if contracts were behind penalties of £20 a day would then ensue. The Edinburgh Committee took responsibility for the line east of Linlithgow and of the extension between that town and the River Avon – but was not to interfere with the bridge over the river that would be 'under the superintendence of the Glasgow Committee'.

By October, Miller's staff was appointed – a secretary, bookkeeper and clerk. The height and width of tunnels were being reviewed and viaduct widths considered as this would dictate how much ground should be purchased. Miller had nowdetermined upon cuttings 30 feet in width and embankments 33 feet at the track formation levels.

Tunnelling was always a problem, and at Croy Hill cutting the tough whinstone was preferred. Here gunpowder is being used at Linslade in 1837, just as it would be at Croy in 1841. *(Sketches by John C Bourne)*

Tunnels were dangerous and expensive to make – there were three initially on the E&GR. This is a tunnel face at Watford on the London & Birmingham Railway (1837). *(Sketches by John C Bourne)*

Robert Stephenson was the engineer for the London & Birmingham Railway, where John C Bourne's sketches record construction works. *(ICE image)*

Slopes and fencing would also affect the quantity of land bought in some localities. Out on the line no gradients were 'to be made worse than 1 in 880' – the ruling grade that Miller had stated in Parliament. This decision would prove costly but produce a line that was remarkably level for high speed running.

Both Locke and Rastrick came to Glasgow to give advice. They preferred rails of 75 lb per yard – it was agreed that the L&MR had been laid 'too light'. A director of the London & Birmingham Railway warned against the use of 'the vicious form of the elliptical or fish-bellied' rail and advocated the 'double-headed' variety. This heavier rail, a forerunner of the bullhead type, would mean that the E&GR 'would be unrivalled in solidity, security, and economy of maintenance'. Locke favoured iron chairs with wooden keys on timber sleepers to hold the rails in place in preference to stone blocks. However, the latter were chosen. A specific instruction to Miller was to ensure ' the most complete and perfect system of drainage and ballasting'.

The Act left little to chance and the index of 21 pages covered everything from 'Accesses' to 'Works and Writs'. Parliament was concerned that finance for projects of such magnitude should be secure and so £80,000 had been lodged with the Bank of England. Arranging calls for money was specified – a wise precaution as there would be several before the railway was complete. Six directors would make a quorum, meeting in Glasgow or within 10 miles of the railway. Copies of the plans were lodged with Sheriff Clerks, with a fee payable for their inspection by the public.

Land acquisition was a legal minefield; owners might not be traced or land might be entailed – a device to prevent property being sold off to creditors. Prior to the Married Women's Property Acts of the 1880s, when women wed, their property became that of their husbands and this also covered any share holdings. So the E&GR Act of 1838 attempted to exclude all possibilities for fraud – listing married women, along 'with infants, idiots, lunatics and other incapacitated persons', to ensure that compensation would be paid legally to 'Husbands, Guardians, Tutors, Curators, Judicial Factors or Trustees' for any land taken. The marriage of female proprietors had to be proven.

There was much to take up Miller's attention. He had to consider the height and width of bridges over roads and canals, the location of depots and stations, and the limiting of deviations of the line when crossing estates. The company could now take land, enter and set out the line. For obstructing persons employed in construction works – poles and stakes were not to be pulled up or any marks defaced or destroyed – there were penalties of £5 for every offence. Agents and workmen were 'authorised and empowered 'to bore, dig, cut, embank and sough' and

The Bonnymuir Contract of 1839 is the sole survivor of 20 contracts let for the construction of the Edinburgh & Glasgow Railway. Bonnymuir is east of Greenhill near Bonnybridge. *(National Records of Scotland)*

also 'to use, work and manufacture any Earth, Stone, Rubbish, Trees, Gravel or Sand' necessary for making the railway. Stonewalls, surviving along miles of today's railway, were to be built, even although thorn fences cost £1,000 *less* per mile.

Footpaths should not cross the railway 'on the level' without the consent of a Sheriff; persons were forbidden to ride or drive cattle along the line, gardens were not to be taken unless specified in the

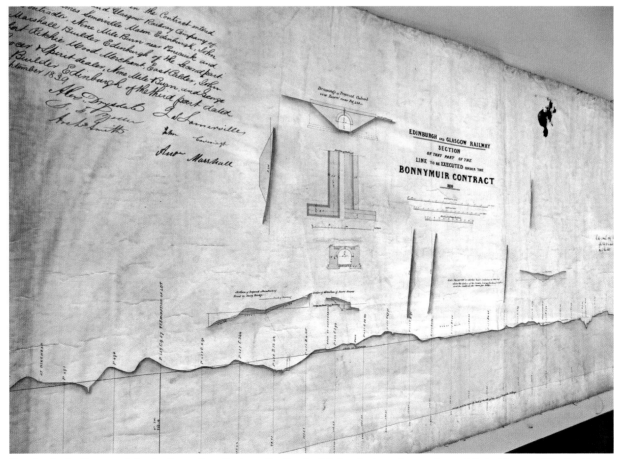

The plan for the Bonnymuir Contract reveals meticulous attention to detail and   shows the requirement for 'cutting and filling' on the E&GR to make the line as level as possible. *(National Records of Scotland)*

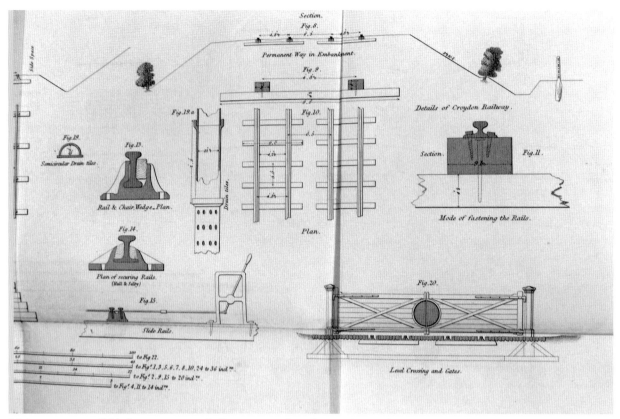

Advice was soon available for every aspect of railway construction – from equipment for navvies to track laying and level crossing gates. (S J Brees, Appendix on Railway Practice, 1839)

plan, gates were to be kept in repair and water pipes protected. Milestones were to be placed at every quarter mile, and there were penalties for persons defacing them. There were environmental concerns too – no spoil was to be deposited on the Hog estate at Newliston, and on the Hopetoun estate only at two approved locations where the material was to be enclosed and planted. There were restrictions on burning waste. Mines under lands purchased were not to be claimed by the railway – but some precautions were taken. Owners within 40 yards of the line had to give at least thirty days' notice of intention to work any seams. If there was any 'injury of the railway', damages would be payable, and no shaft, pit or quarry was to be sunk under the line.

During construction, the traffic on the Union and Forth & Clyde Canals had to be unobstructed, and Turnpike Roads kept open and afterwards repaired if damaged. The pioneering Monkland & Kirkintilloch Railway was given special attention – its lines going beneath a 'Bridge or Viaduct of Two Arches' at 'Garngibber' (Garngaber) that in 'no way would interrupt or impede' its coal trade going to the Forth & Clyde Canal.

By the spring of 1839, there were offers to supply cast iron chairs – at prices ranging from £7 to £5 a ton from the Gorbals Foundry in Glasgow. Some iron works could only produce 30 ton batches of little assistance on a big project such as the E&GR. Rails in quantity were obtainable from John Wilson's Dundyvan Iron Works, near Coatbridge, with its nine

furnaces and large rolling mill. Located on the Lanarkshire 'black band' ironstone, the price at £9 10s per ton was such that no Staffordshire or Welsh producer could match it. Miller believed that Scottish rails were superior as 'no cinder' was used in Scottish blast furnaces, minimising faults in the metal when cast. If rail and heavy items were deliverable by the Forth & Clyde or Union Canals, this was a considerable advantage.

There were 15 enquiries for the Polmont contract alone, varying from £24,449 to £53,800 – these were remitted to Miller to select the best. Invariably the lowest was taken. Such initial activity took up much of the engineer's time, and soon Grainger & Miller were looking for a payment of £1,000 from the E&G's Finance Committee. Eventually in March 1839, £1,000 was paid and Rastrick received £100. The advisability of employing constables to police the line was discussed in order to forestall trouble with navvies, but this would be another expense.

By February 1840 the project was getting into its stride. Access to the site of the Glasgow station had now to be gained by passing below the Cut of Junction of the Port Dundas branch of the Forth & Clyde Canal with the Monkland Canal. For the railway, this was far from ideal as it involved a tunnel with a steep gradient and an inclined plane – but it did bring the line to a city centre location. Most conveniently, John Leadbetter had earlier acquired some land near George Square when the original site of the Crawfurd mansion became available. This generous triangle of land at Dundas Street, extending on the west to the St Enoch Burn plus a stance in North Hanover Street, was on the market. John Leadbetter organised a purchase. By March 1837, the title had already passed to the railway company. The presence of the E&GR would change the whole district.

Miller's reports throw some light on construction techniques. 'Guide mines' for tunnels were excavated, whereby shafts were first cut into the rock, then steam engines could lift out spoil or pump out water. In the spring of 1840, three steam engines and a horse gin were at work at the Glasgow tunnel alone. Over the whole project at that stage there were upwards of 2,000 men, 700 horses and 12 stationary steam engines employed. What greatly facilitated progress was to lay rails and have horse-drawn wagons in action for 'leading and teeming' – to cut and fill, thereby forming the track bed; but would contractors be permitted to use the new rails on site and move these from place to place?

By May 1840, there were eight offers to construct the Glasgow station on the table, ranging from £7,211 to £11,885. Miller had contacts with 'a builder of respectability' who would perform 'with spirit and activity'. There were tenders for turntables of 12 and 14ft diameter with the lowest offers of £89 and £109 from Edington & Son, Glasgow iron founders. These devices were essential as the carriages and wagons had to be turned in order that their brakes could be accessed on the same side of a train.

The balance sheet at June 1840 showed funds of £462,931 were available but £418,339 had already been spent. By 25 August, only 8 miles remained to be let to 'men of skill and experience' who would be prepared to offer a rate 'of little more than £5,000 per mile'. There were 'gratifying reports' from Miller saying that some permanent way had been laid on several parts of the line. With a reduction in the price of iron, rails were being obtained 'on very favourable terms'. Miller mentioned the use of whinstone blocks but also larch sleepers for embankments on the railway. The directors were urging 'a steady, simultaneous advance', but a monthly expenditure of £4,000 had to be faced.

After 'full and deliberate consideration', the gauge had been settled at 4ft 8½ in. This was 'standard gauge', the choice of the 'leading English lines, now approaching Scotland' and would enable integration and a high rate of speed to be attained. Along with other railway companies, the E&GR directors opposed the new Bill for regulating railways, legislation proposed when Gladstone was President of the Board of Trade; the Act for Railway Regulation became law in 1840.

Some contracts were not going smoothly. In September 1840, the contract for the complex viaduct over the Union Canal at Tamfourhill was in difficulties. This was an awkward site bridging the canal, towpath and a turnpike road during construction. When the contractors requested an advance, Miller recommended that £500 be given.

A distraction for the directors was an 'Atmospheric Railway'. This system to propel trains by 'atmospheric power', basically a vacuum, had been developed on an improved plan by 'Mr Whytock of Edinburgh'. A demonstration was held for E&GR directors but they were unimpressed. (Best known is Brunel's installation on the South Devon Railway. However, cast iron pipes, sealed with leather flaps, could not be made air-tight, and the 20 mile long scheme was abandoned).

To give the Glasgow station a presence in a prestigious part of the city, a competition for the design of a gateway was proposed, with 'premiums' offered for the two best designs. Of greater consequence, in Edinburgh, land was bought from the West Church adjacent to Princes Street Gardens in step with the intention to reach Central Edinburgh at some stage.

By November 1840, the tempo was rising and the Dundyvan Ironworks was promising the delivery of 500 tons of rails per month. Miller was asked to investigate the import of coke in quantity from Newcastle. Coke, considered a smokeless fuel, would be the mainstay of the locomotives on the E&GR. Meanwhile, as coal was being taken out from each side of the commodious Falkirk tunnel, William Forbes of Callendar was offered 7d a ton in compensation.

The directors had much to consider – a prospectus for a branch to Stirling had appeared and the E&G would be connected to it. There were pleas from several railway companies to lobby Parliament for a reduction in passenger duty. Then came some reverses – the contractor at Glasgow, could not finish 'without greater expense'. On the Luggie contract at Kirkintilloch, the contractors had resigned when faced with insufficient funds to pay the masons' wages of £30 to £50.

Nevertheless, looking ahead, Miller was requested to report on what stations he would recommend and land at Ratho was bought. Apart from the termini at Haymarket and Queen Street, the principal 'road' stations would be Linlithgow, Falkirk and Castlecary, while there would also be ten 'intermediate' ones. The budget for each station was £500. He was told to accept lighter – and cheaper – rail for use at the stations.

Miller was 'multi-skilled', giving advice about how the company's business should be arranged once the railway opened, and insisting that so complex an enterprise required departments to ensure its proper management. Therefore, a superintendent should take charge of the whole establishment, a secretary of the offices, an engineer of the line, and another of the locomotives and workshops, while a goods clerk would supervise the freight department. As such

The Garngaber viaduct near Lenzie took the E&GR over the Bothlin Burn and the Monkland & Kirkintilloch Railway carrying coal to the Forth & Clyde Canal from the Airdrie area.

expertise would be required before the line opened, staff should be recruited early to resolve 'multifarious details'.

Tenders were soon invited for 'Mason-work of the Offices and Business Chambers at the Glasgow Station' – the lowest offer of £1,237 was accepted, and it conveniently covered joinery and other work. Glasgow became the focus of E&GR operations with its headquarters located there. By 1842, the company had its eye on a valuable property at the corner of Dundas Street and what is now West George Street. This was Dr Wardlaw's Chapel, a handsome building in classical style erected for Congregationalists in 1819; it would eventually become the E&GR head office. (Only in the 1970s, was 'the kirk' replaced by Consort House, the headquarters of the Strathclyde Transport Partnership). In June, a scheme for heating the offices with 'hot water' – an early venture in central heating – was considered but there is no evidence that it was installed.

If the line was to open in July 1841, 'high noon' was fast approaching. Salaries for staff were discussed in April, the 'General Superintendent' would receive £500 a year, the 'Goods' £200, and the 'Coach' £150. Rolling stock was ordered – 120 wagons and trucks, 20 horseboxes, and 10 carriage trucks. First Class carriages 'with a coupé body at each end', cost £445 each. An offer of Second Class carriages, 'with or without brakes' at £275 and £250, came from the Bolton & Bury Railway. Meanwhile, Miller was

experimenting with English and Scotch rails to assess their different strengths and qualities He prepared plans for a 'coke establishment' at Falkirk, and was asked to find a local supplier of the best coking coal – with a view to a smoke-free railway.

With some sections incomplete, such as the Colston contract east of Glasgow, Miller was now looking for contractors of 'ability and experience' to tackle them. The designs for the gateway at the Glasgow station earned a first prize of £60 for a Glasgow team but the design was considered 'too expensive to be executed' and a letter 'on economy in the construction of stations' was read to the directors. Lack of money for investment was to plague the Glasgow station. In April, plans were prepared for a timber passenger shed with truck and carriage facilities alongside. Lowest offers continued to be accepted for this and most other purchases. Some new houses were to be built by the E&GR at Dundas Street – in spite of titles placing restrictions on both height and size.

Thought was now being given to locomotives. In May, a letter from Edward Bury of Liverpool offered to make ten engines 'superior to any yet made by him', thereby avoiding a possible deduction in price for any failings. He suggested that five of these should have copper fireboxes. Bury was an experienced locomotive builder having supplied engines to the London & Birmingham Railway and other companies. There was a conflict of opinion over Bury's four-wheeled types and Stephenson's six wheelers. So a deputation would go to England visiting the principal railways with the engineer 'to enquire into the merits of the different kinds of Engines, Carriages etc', and report before any contracts were placed. They found it difficult to decide and suggested that the E&GR should try both kinds of engine – the directors ordering ten from Bury and ten from Hawthorn of Newcastle. Soon two stationary engines were ordered for operating the incline at Glasgow when an offer of £2,900 from Kerr, Neilson & Company was accepted. The Neilson name would become synonymous with Springburn and with steam locomotive enterprises there.

The directors visited the line on 17 May 1841 and, apart from the Croymill contract, where 'some decided step' would have to be taken with the contractor, they were 'on the whole' pleased with progress. There were questions however over the stability of the large but low arch over the Union Canal where 'part of the centring was entirely out' and 'the arch had sunk somewhat, but less than an inch'. The directors were back on 18 June to 'key' the last arches of the Almond and Avon viaducts – but the works were not ready.

By this date, Miller had rendered his accounts covering July to December 1840 – these amounted to £1,249, for his own time, payments to assistants and other expenses. In his opinion, the target date of 1 July would be missed but by mid-August the railway would be 5/6ths complete, and if the weather was favourable, it might be possible to have the line open in September.

In June 1841 the General Post Office made an enquiry about the E&GR's state. From 1837, railways had been required to carry the Royal Mail. This service became a significant source of income for railway companies and hence when 'Mr Smart, acting for the GPO', asked permission to examine the line 'in reference to the future Post Office arrangements', the directors resolved to give him 'every facility'.

There were concerns about policing of the works, as £30 had been reserved for constables in the event of any serious disturbance. In December 1840, a navvy feud on the Bishopbriggs contract had led to a murder. There was a recommendation that two or three horse patrols should be appointed at Polmont and Kilsyth – otherwise 30 guineas should be paid to the Sheriff to call out local police as required.

Requests for payment kept coming – the Croymill contractors asked for a further payment of £1,500, and at Woodend near Castlecary for £2,000. Where a contractor was in trouble as at Dullatur, a 'requisition' from an arbiter, obliging the contractor to perform as stated, could be served – or the work would be taken from him. Although 'fences' (walls) were going up along the railway at Callendar and Tamfourhill, elsewhere that obligation would have to be 'enforced'.

To push work on, Miller bought an Edington locomotive, 'well furnished and complete'. Thomas Edington & Sons had the Phoenix Iron Works in Glasgow and were building 2-2-2 engines for the Glasgow, Paisley, Kilmarnock and Ayr Railway for which Miller was also responsible. Furthermore, being highly talented, he seems to have designed these locomotives.

If matters were fraught at work sites, there were tensions in the boardroom where the Edinburgh and Glasgow directors were at loggerheads. The former were threatening legal proceedings. The Edinburgh directors complained that they were not given sufficient notice of board meetings – that they then omitted to attend. These were routinely held in Glasgow, but were fixed at times to suit the Edinburgh men; nevertheless, the five-hour journey both to and from Edinburgh was a deterrent. The Edinburgh directors then took exception to decisions made in their absence by the Glasgow men, and would then reconsider these. They argued that the company's carriage works should be in Edinburgh and not at Cowlairs. When they refused to implement the Board's instructions and attempted 'to annul the Resolutions of the recent very numerous General Meeting of the Shareholders in relation to the best mode of managing their affairs', legal proceedings seemed inevitable. They also alleged financial irregularities on the part of the chairman. Ballantynes, the company's Glasgow- based lawyers, were instructed to retain Counsel.

In July 1841, an interdict was granted to John Learmonth, the chairman of the Edinburgh Committee and others, by the Court of Session against John Leadbetter and the Glasgow directors. This was a serious inconvenience at a time when the E&GR should have been approaching completion. The main board was satisfied that this legal intervention was wrong, but for the functioning of the line after opening, there must be unified management. The directors emphasised the 'great importance' they

In 1840 near Cowlairs, Glasgow, 'guide mines' for the tunnel were cut prior to stationary steam engines lifting out spoil – a scene similar to this J C Bourne sketch.

A breakthrough for contractors was to lay rails and haul trains of spoil away with their own or borrowed locomotives – as on the London & Birmingham Railway. (J C Bourne)

attached to the line's completion when at last some revenue would accrue; meantime, there was a ninth call for shareholders to pay up. Loans, varying from £300 to over £4,000 at 5 per cent, were also forthcoming. For the working of the railway, 'the superintendence of a person well qualified for the duty' would be essential, and their eyes fell upon John Miller.

The fitting out of stations began to claim attention, clocks being ordered from Mitchell & Russell in Glasgow – one with a 'double face' for that station and two with single faces for Haymarket. For 'road stations' and other parts of the line there would be '8 spring clocks'. All would have to be maintained by the makers for a year. For many country folk, these clocks would be the first timepieces they ever saw, and they would show local time – Glasgow being some four minutes behind Edinburgh when the sun was overhead at the capital.

A system of 'Booking and Ticketing' was

investigated after a letter was received from 'Mr Edmondson'. Thomas Edmondson, a cabinetmaker to trade, became a stationmaster on the Newcastle & Carlisle Railway. He devised railway tickets that were small cardboard rectangles that could be printed with details of a journey. Such tickets were durable, compared with hand written slips of paper, and could be numbered and dated by a small stamping press when purchased. By the 1840s, Edmondson had patented a machine that produced batches of tickets with serial numbers. Railway companies had to pay for the Edmondson system on a mileage basis. On the E&GR, 'for the use of his Patent' and for the first 20 miles of railway, the charge would be £20 a year, and 'for every additional mile above twenty, ten shillings to be paid for 14 years, being the period of the Patent'. True to form, the secretary of the E&GR was told to 'enquire if these terms could be reduced'. No deal was done and 'a million and a half tickets' were then ordered from McClure & McDonald, Glasgow

Engineers at an embankment site where longitudinal timber sleepers are being laid to spread weight. (J C Bourne)

The Congregationalist Church in West George Street, known as Wardlaw's Kirk, was purchased by the E&GR for offices. (Special Collections, Glasgow University Library)

printers who handled E&G advertising – 200,000 each would go to Edinburgh, Falkirk and Glasgow, with Linlithgow having 160,000 and the others 100,000. Miller was asked to find a machine to put dates on them. Ten sets of cases were bought each to hold tickets for the stations on the line. For the full journey, fares would be 9s, 6s 6d and 4s for 1st, 2nd and 3rd class.

On 24 August 1841, by which time the E&G should have opened, Miller made a lengthy report to the directors about the 'state of the works'. He began apologetically,

"I regret exceedingly that it is not yet in my power to state their final completion…but would have been nearly completed but for the very unfavourable weather which we have had for the last two months". It had been an exceptionally wet summer with heavy rains, causing rivers to flood and burns to overflow. Commencing at Haymarket, Miller described the project contract by contract., beginning with the 6½ miles that took the line westwards over the Water of Leith. Although the contractor had been 'rather backward in finishing work', men and tools would be removed in mid-September.

Then came a complex series of projects and the biggest contract in money value on the line – held by John Gibb & Son. This included two large viaducts, a tunnel and 'very heavy earth and rock excavations'. The Almond Valley viaduct had taken twenty months to reach a stage where one track could be laid and a locomotive had just passed over the structure. Miller praised the 'expedition' shown at the site as 'beyond anything' he had experienced. The Broxburn viaduct, with 6 arches over the Bathgate turnpike road, stood to the west. Massive cuttings in sandstone and whinstone followed. There 1¼ million cu yd had been removed 'with very great exertions' – an average of 40,000cu yd being cut each month. Then came Winchburgh tunnel, 1,100ft in length, and although commenced in November 1838, the excavations had proved very difficult, 'blaes' alternating with hard whinstone. As the entire tunnel had then to be lined with brick, it took two years before the permanent way could be laid. With four locomotives and three fixed engines currently employed on the site, there were hopes of completion by 1 October.

John Gibb wrote to the E&G company in July when penalty clauses of £20 per day would fall:-

'At present we have 350 workmen and 25 horses employed on the different cuttings and tunnel on the line, 80 masons, 100 labourers, 18 joiners, 8 blacksmiths and 20 horses employed on the viaducts and bridges, besides nearly 150 men with a corresponding number of horses, employed in quarrying stone for the viaducts and bridges'.

It was a work force that was 'not small'. Gibb estimated his losses as £40,000 but was urged to continue work at night by the flames of torches.

From 1830 some Royal Mail was carried by rail, and as mail contracts were lucrative, the E&GR determined to replace horse-drawn services. *(Scotcities.com)*

Moving west, most of the contracts were for less than two miles, but an innkeeper's team from Broxburn had drawn a short straw – they were faced with over half a million cubic yards of 'hard cutting, to be carried up and laid out as spoil'. Seven fixed engines were in use, but the contract had been 'much delayed by Lord Hopetoun's interventions'. He objected to deposits of material just 500 yd from Craigton House, a favourite property, and in October raised an action against the E&GR. Then 'slips in the banks of the said railway' had led to further heaps of spoil being formed. These were allowed to remain until January 1842 but must not exceed 1,000 cu yd of 'stuff', and the ground must be restored for cultivation. The problem was the 'wanton and illegal encroachment' of more than double the amount permitted. Nevertheless, the contract was nearly complete, with track laid and 'fences' progressing.

Two more short sections, begun in the summer of 1839, brought the line to Linlithgow, a contract 'nearly finished with tools being removed'. Then came the Avon viaduct. Started in August 1839, the viaduct had been constructed 'in a short time, in spite of the difficulty in obtaining material for it'. There was yet another legal obstacle here as the town's magistrates expected tolls to be paid for the line crossing the River Avon.

An uneventful stretch of just over four miles took

With the E&GR advancing, attention was given to the purchase of locomotives; this four-wheeled type from Bury of Liverpool was one of the choices. *(S.Everard in NBRSG Journals)*

Haymarket station, the original terminus of the Edinburgh & Glasgow Railway, opened in February 1842.

the railway to Falkirk and the Callendar contract. There the 830yd long tunnel, begun in January 1840, was challenging as not only hard rock was present but there was *'very considerable difficulty arising from the old coal measures below and adjoining to it'.* This unusually tall tunnel had just been completed and a locomotive would soon be able to go through. The same contractors were busy at Tamfourhill where the Union Canal was crossed by another viaduct and 274,000 cu yd of spoil removed. The first contractors had given up with only a sixth cleared. The viaduct had been revised – with one 130ft arch, another of 63ft and five small arches, but there had been a serious loss of time owing to the severe frost in winter that stopped all mason work.

West of Falkirk, contract 11 was more hopeful, and 12, where the contractor had been replaced, were now finished 'in a neat and workmanlike manner'. These formed another 4 miles of the E&GR. Then came contract 13 covering the Redburn viaduct near Castlecary that had been finished satisfactorily. Contract 14 was short – less than a mile and a half though its excavation amounted to 130,000 cu yd – and a fortnight would see its completion.

Contract 15 at Dullatur would take the most time

The 36 arch Almond Valley viaduct was the most ambitious structure on the E&GR, meriting this painting by David Octavius Hill. *(Glasgow Museums & Art Galleries)*

on the whole line. This was the notorious Croy Ridge of whin rock. In July, with the works lagging, the E&GR agreed to advance £1,400 plus an extra £600 to Kenneth Mathieson, the contractor's son, to inducehim to remain at the site and enable him to pay wages and other immediate expenses. When an open cutting replaced a tunnel 200yds long, a very substantial excavation had to be made. As work was so slow, it was agreed that a foreman from the Gibbs' contract at Winchburgh, should be appointed 'with the power to engage or dismiss workmen'. An inspector should also be on site and a rate of 4s 6d (instead of 3s 6d) be allowed for rock cutting. The Mathiesons' request for more machinery and tools would go to an arbiter. Of their claim for £1,700, only £1,397 was paid. Eventually part of the site was given to an adjoining contractor and the remainder put under the management of the resident engineer. By the summer of 1841, the obdurate whinstone had been reduced to 15,000 cu yd, but its removal became the key to the line's opening. As autumn was fast approaching. Miller was therefore cautious about the rock cutting:-

'I am afraid that unless the weather should prove very favourable, it will not be taken out in under two months'.

Contract 16 involved a mix of whinstone and freestone (sandstone) cuttings. A small viaduct of 4 arches with 30ft spans over the Moss Water had been built, but with rock yet to be cut, the permanent way had not been laid. On contract 17 of 1¾ miles, the contractor had been replaced and even the new one had been 'rather backward clearing of the 205,000 cu yd of excavation'.

Contract 18 at Claddens was for the 'Garngibber' (now Garngaber) viaduct. Its four arches crossed the Monkland & Kirkintilloch Railway and it was behind schedule. On Miller's recommendation, the resident engineer intervened and was allowed to spend £500 on extra horses and waggons. Progress then became more rapid – the excavation was reduced, masonry finished and much rail laid. On contract 19 (only 1¾ mile long) at Colston, half of the excavation of 233,000 cu yd was in rock. As the work rate was unsatisfactory, a resident engineer had taken charge. A solution was to increase the number of gangers, men and implements and work two or three shifts, but even so, it would take a month to finish. Meantime, 'a locomotive engine' would 'considerably facilitate' this work.

Then came contract 20 extending to 1 mile 640yd, with an open cutting of 125,000 yd, but *'the principal work … is the Tunnel passing under Glasgow … commenced in March 1839. The open cutting is all but finished'.*

Miller explained that this tunnel was divided into three distinct portions, and that the north part had been lengthened by 50 yds. Two large 'eyes' or openings had also been cut, making the tunnel proper 1,099 yd long. With track laying ongoing, the work would take three weeks to complete.

The report ended on a positive note, *'By the first of October, the whole line, with the exception of about 300 yards at Croy Ridge, will be ready for public traffic'.*

Miller then added, *'I am very much afraid that it will be 1ˢᵗ November before the 300 yards will be overcome'.* John Willox, who subsequently wrote a guide to the line accompanied Miller on an engine as far as this site, where *'the rock was literally swarming with workmen, and the continual clank, clank of the thousand hammers, and the all but ceaseless cluck, cluck of the hand-worked jumpers are only diversified by the reverberating roar of hundreds of blasts fired in endless succession, hurling terrific masses of rock high into the air…'.*

If the weather was unsuitable Miller warned that both the Croy Ridge and the rock cutting on the Gibbs' contract might take even longer. According to 'The Investor's Advocate and Journal of Industry', the most rainy season for many years had brought one advantage to the E&GR – 'much of the subsiding and slipping of the embankments, which might otherwise have happened at a future period, has already taken place… and the consolidation of the works has thus been greatly matured…'

Miller's review then turned to the stations; at the contract for the Glasgow station, the station house and passenger facilities were far advanced. The engine sheds and workshops at Cowlairs were being roofed, and the 'fixed engine' for the inclined plane installed in its house. Its 'engineer' was appointed at 40 shillings a week, plus a house and coals. The coke ovens at Falkirk, were complete. At Castlecary, Falkirk and Linlithgow, the station houses were roofed, while Polmont and Ratho 'would be contracted for' shortly. Cast iron tanks for station water supply had been ordered. At Haymarket, the sheds were 'considerably

John Miller devised formidable cuttings in order to make the Edinburgh & Glasgow line as 'flat as possible'. This example is near Niddry in West Lothian.

The viaduct over the River Avon near Linlithgow has tall arches for which stone was difficult to obtain. It reaches a height of 92ft (28m).

J C Bourne's sketches record the scale of tunnelling on the London & Birmingham Railway – the tunnels on the E&GR were shorter but similar techniques were used.

A cast iron milepost from the E&GR, now displayed at Haymarket station.

advanced' and the station house begun, but a temporary booking office would be required for the opening.

After the fact-finding visits to English lines, orders for the 'locomotive engines' had been placed. R&W Hawthorn of Newcastle provided a batch of 6-

A modest viaduct crossing the Luggie Water near Kirkintilloch shows strain from mining at the former Waterside Colliery.

wheeled engines of 'excellent workmanship'. Six out of an order for 12 had been delivered, having been shipped by steam packet from Liverpool. Of 10 ordered from Bury of Liverpool, only one of their 4-wheelers had come. The supply of 'carriages and waggons' was progressing (with 'First Class' judged 'a very excellent job'). Many 2nd class and 3rd class vehicles had been delivered, plus carriage trucks, horseboxes and waggons. The rolling stock was judged sufficient to enable the railway to be run. 'Furnishings' for the line, such as mileposts, were now far advanced.

Miller then suggested that the line be opened in two portions on 1 October – one east and the other west of the Croy Ridge, and that notice should be given to the Board of Trade to that effect. This was disappointing for shareholders – outgoings would simply continue with no serious revenue accruing.

That month Sir Frederick Smith of the Railway Inspectorate came to visit the line. Her Majesty's Railway Inspectorate had been established in 1840 as a result of the Railway Regulation Act of that year. The Inspecting Officers all had military backgrounds – this would become a tradition – though they were appointed by the Board of Trade. A primary duty was to inspect new lines and to ascertain their suitability for passenger trains. They were also charged with investigating any accidents that companies reported and to present their findings to Parliament. Sir Frederic had risen to the rank of general, having taken part in various campaigns in Europe where he became an expert in siege warfare and Colonel-Commandant of the Royal Engineers. John Miller escorted him over the whole line on 25 September when they met chairman John Leadbetter in Glasgow. Sir Frederick 'expressed himself satisfied with the character of the works', and if the unfinished portions were completed to the same standard and certified by Miller, the railway would be in a proper state to open.

Thought was being given to timetables. Trains would start at the same time from both ends of the railway. Passenger trains would set off at 7, 9 and 11o'clock in the morning and at 3, 5 and 7 o'clock in the afternoon. There would be 'luggage trains' for goods at 6am and 1pm. 'Quick trains' would convey 1st and 2nd class carriages and take 2 hours; the best would be the 11am calling only at the three principal

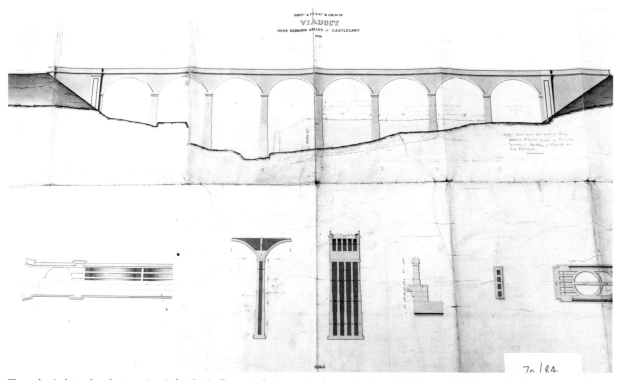

The only viaduct plan that survives is for the Redburn viaduct near Castlecary. It shows Miller's careful design and robust construction details to advantage. (National Records of Scotland)

'road stations' Linlithgow, Falkirk and Castlecary. Where 3rd class carriages were used, these would be 'stand ups', and it later became clear that they would be roofless. Only on 'luggage trains' – carrying goods, calling 'all stations', and taking 3 to 3½ hours – would 'thirds' have seats. There were questions about goods traffic, should only E&G vehicles be employed, or could contractors use their own as on the canals?

Sunday travelling soon became an issue. The carriage of Royal Mail by train was a welcome addition to income for railway companies but there was a problem. The Secretary was therefore asked to ascertain 'the number of Mails which might be required by the Post Office to pass along the line upon Sunday and the hours of departure'. By September 1841, a Commission of the General Assembly of the Church of Scotland was involved; a deputation, the first of many, put pressure on the E&GR directors to desist from 'Sabbath breaking'. Soon presbyteries and other church organisations joined the fray. A public meeting was held in Glasgow on 28 September when synods from Glasgow and Ayr were represented; parishes such as Dunoon and Rothesay were most hostile to Sunday trains having suffered the rowdy effects of 'Sabbath breaking steamboat excursions' for many years. In contrast, the magistrates of Bathgate and Falkirk were in favour of Sunday trains.

By November, a draft of byelaws was being prepared by 'Mr Miller and Mr Ballantyne'. These were submitted to the Board of Trade and subsequently revised. A vexing question had arisen – the extension of the line through Edinburgh's Princes Street Gardens was causing 'strong anxiety' among the directors; soon notice must be given to Parliament of the intention to take the line to the North Bridge.

This was not unconnected with a survey of a 'line of communication with England, a project potentially of value to the company and the nation'. The directors had a preference for an East Coast route and a sub-committee was appointed to consider informing the public whose views regrettably were 'generally erroneous'.

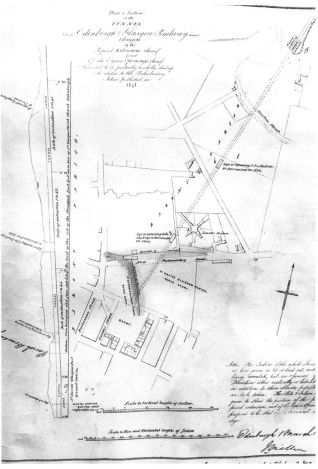

The proposed modification of the Cowlairs tunnel in 1841 with the 'eyes' closed in response to a dispute over compensation with an institution. *(Glasgow City Archives, Mitchell Library)*

On 14 December 1841, it had been agreed that John Leadbetter's site at Queen Street should be purchased for £3,150, a much reduced price. To ease the company's finances, this would be converted to a ground annual of £157 10s, with a feu duty of just over £51 a year. It was a bargain for such a location in the heart of the city. Demands for money kept coming. The Superintendent of the Royal Infirmary in Glasgow requested a donation, citing the number of cases arising from 'accidents & otherwise on the

A viaduct nears completion with the timber scaffolding and formwork for the arches removed while the end embankments are being completed. *(J C Bourne. Sketches)*

The double-beam engine for the Cowlairs Incline was ordered from Kerr, Neilson & Co, Glasgow and cost £2,900. With modifications, it continued in use until 1908. *(The Engineer, 1922)*

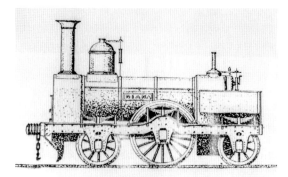

The purchase of Hawthorn six-wheelers completed the initial locomotive stock for the E&GR. *(S.Everard in NBRSG Journals)*

Railway'. The directors sent £25.

By New Year 1842 on the Gibbs' contract at the Almond valley, it was reported in *The Scotsman* that the arches of the viaducts were complete though the adjoining banks had yet to be finished and hundreds of men were hard at work there. A day had yet to be agreed when the line should be opened but a train passed over the whole line on 22 January followed by a directors' inspection on 31 January. Another Board of Trade visit would determine whether the E&GR was fit for passenger traffic.

Just when a date for the private opening had been proposed – 18 February – with public trains commencing on 21 February, there were setbacks. At the Cowlairs workshops, a tank fell and structures below it collapsed causing serious injuries; on examination, the castings, girders and pillars were found to be 'extremely defective'. At Bishopbriggs, there was a damaging collision between two contractor's locomotives. Nevertheless, arrangements for opening were put in place. Public coaches would call at the Glasgow station, posters for the new line were printed while 'tolls' – that is fares – for passengers would be shown on boards at all the E&GR stations.

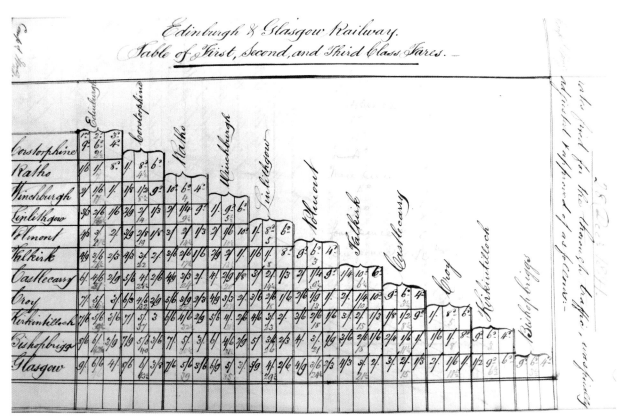

The table of fares for First, Second and Third Class passengers as proposed for the E&GR in 1841. *(National Records of Scotland)*

Chapter 3

Up and Running

By October 1841, the Board of Trade had sent a letter to the directors of the Edinburgh & Glasgow Railway requesting a week's notice prior to the completion of the line when a second inspection would be made. By this stage, Major-General Charles Pasley (later Sir Charles) had replaced Sir Frederic Smith as Inspector-General of Railways. Pasley was a Borderer born at Eskdalemuir in 1780, and during his military career in the Peninsular Wars he too had become an expert in fortifications and sieges. On 12 January 1842 he visited the E&G, examining it 'with great attention'.

John Miller accompanied Pasley on a locomotive that day. As they stopped to look at every object of importance, plus the intermediate stations, the inspection took six hours, a journey that – once the line opened – was only expected to take 'two and a quarter, and eventually two hours'. There had been much progress and 'the laborious cutting (at Croy) through the crag whinstone, about 2,000feet in length' was now complete. On the embankment at the Almond valley, extra support had been given to the up line with the insertion of piling and longitudinal timbers. The termini and stations, 'though not quite finished', had sheds erected that would afford ample temporary accommodation for passengers. The line had been enclosed with stone walls nearly five feet high. Especially pleasing were the viaducts and bridges, 'well proportioned and handsome, but judiciously constructed in the interior parts which do not meet the eye', as the spandrels and wing walls had not been packed with earth or rubbish. The embankments and cuttings though 'very troublesome' to construct were not thought likely to suffer 'slips' as on the many English railways that Pasley had inspected.

The rolling stock was also examined. For passengers, the third class carriages had sufficient height and all had buffers; those for the slow trains, timed to take 3¾ hours on the journey, had seats but those for the 'swift trains' timed for 2¼ hours, had only standing room – Pasley suggested that 'persons in vigorous health will prefer the latter'. Until the embankments were consolidated, he recommended 'very moderate rates of speed' on the line. John Leadbetter met him and both he and Miller gave assurances on this matter. With the Pasley having been impressed with the railway from Glasgow to Ayr, also Miller's work, 'one may reasonably anticipate equal success on this new line from Glasgow to Edinburgh' and the railway could now be opened. (He must have enjoyed his experience on the E&GR as he

When the Edinburgh & Glasgow Railway was opened on 18 February 1842, 'the extensive and arduous cuttings' near Winchburgh – resembling this view on the London & Birmingham Railway – caused amazement. *(J C Bourne, Sketches)*

The Redburn viaduct at Castlecary, now strengthened with rail, straddles the M90.

subsequently asked for a pass, 'in ivory or metal' that he might use on his visits).

Preparations for the opening of the line advanced and arrangements were made to have three public viewings of the tunnels at Glasgow and the one at Falkirk This gave reassurance about the safety of these 'black holes' underground. The interiors were whitewashed and gas-lit giving the opportunity for people to walk through for a modest charge, the proceeds going to charity. This fund had been set up after a calamitous capsizing of a passenger barge on the Paisley Canal. Altogether, £218 was raised – a tidy sum.

John Miller was kept busy, not only having to see to the completion of stations and other matters along

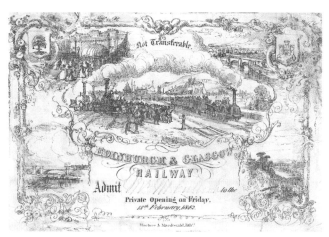

An opening day ticket shows the company's trains and is also decorated with some of the major features on the route. *(Michael Stewart)*

the line, but also being asked to arrange the opening event. This would be lavish and was timed for 18 February. With both committees of directors having composed their differences, a luncheon took place in Glasgow's Queen Street station – although Falkirk was considered. Miller was asked to obtain quotations for the 'collation' from Glasgow hoteliers, and for champagne and wines. In addition, he had to transform the large wooden shed that served as the terminus into a banqueting hall. The rails were covered over with flooring – there were only two lines in and out of the passenger shed – and by hanging curtains on its walls; the public was also invited to view the interior.

On 19 February, 'The Scotsman' reported, *'This magnificent line of Railway was opened yesterday by the Directors and their friends in a style of great splendour'.*

There was extraordinary interest in the event with much excitement in Glasgow and the public schools on holiday – even if, owing to the tunnels, there were few points to view the trains. No similar event of such significance had ever occurred in Scotland – the magnitude and cost of the project and the benefit for the nation were seen as unique.

Tickets had been allotted to civic dignitaries, shareholders and friends, in all 1,100 guests. They boarded little first class carriages, four-wheelers each accommodating 18 passengers in three compartments in well-upholstered comfort. These had to be hauled ten at a time by rope up the 1in 42 incline from Queen Street to Cowlairs. From there, a train of thirty carriages was hauled by three locomotives with a 'courier' engine running in front at a safe distance. Soon heads were 'bobbing out of windows, hats and handkerchiefs were being waved' and onlookers were cheering as the train went past.

Features by the line side were commented upon – the primitive appearance of the old Monkland & Kirkintilloch Railway that was crossed near present day Lenzie, the Croy ridge of tough whinstone with its deep cutting that had much delayed the opening, and the stations at Castlecary, and then Falkirk. Time was lost there before the arrival at Linlithgow, a town on holiday with flags flying. Soon Winchburgh, with its 'extensive and arduous cutting and tunnel', was approached as a prelude to the 'stupendous embankment and viaduct at the Almond valley' where the Gibbs and their men had toiled.

With speed increasing towards Edinburgh, throngs on the roads and in the fields could enjoy a thrilling spectacle as the long train passed by. A military band was playing at Haymarket where the train with the Edinburgh contingent was waiting to leave. Both trains now consisted of 30 vehicles plus three locomotives, but as more time was lost on the return to Glasgow, the banquet could only begin at 5pm (though timed for 2.30pm). The tables were set with white calico cloths while gas lamps with extra jets illumined the shed. A gas pipe outline of a locomotive had been installed behind the top table. Trumpeters signalled the call for toasts that were led by the Lord Provost of Edinburgh who wished prosperity and success to the long-awaited railway.

As chairman of the company, John Leadbetter then spoke. In 1832 he had been greatly impressed by the potential of railways after travelling on the Liverpool & Manchester Railway, and became an enthusiastic subscriber to the E&G scheme. He recalled the intense opposition at three sessions of Parliament before obtaining the Act. In 1835 the probable cost was put at £550,000, but the project was 'much in excess of this', amounting to £1.25 million. 'Care and anxiety' had gone into completing a railway that was 'the crowning triumph … a national work that would add greatly to the prosperity of Scotland'. The E&GR was now part of 'a railway system that was a monument to Britain's science, enterprise and wealth'.

Champagne was drunk 'with great good humour and heartiness' before the Edinburgh party set off about 6pm. There then ensued a delay of over 3 hours at Cowlairs due to the rope on the incline breaking before all the carriages could be drawn up. (Had it been cut by someone hostile to the line? The haulage by a hemp rope on the Cowlairs incline would be a persistent problem for the railway company). After journeying in the cold and dark, it was past midnight when the Edinburgh guests arrived back at Haymarket, but the reporter was impressed with the tunnels and viaducts, displaying 'architectural strength and durability', a testimony to the skill of

construction. For an outlay that was well in excess of forecasts, '46 miles of top class railway' had been made.

There were celebrations elsewhere too – a dinner for the Gibbs' workmen at Broxburn, and festivities at Polmont with dancing on the green.

Following the official opening, train services on the E&G were advertised:-

*'The Public are respectfully informed that the RAILWAY will be OPENED for PASSENGERS on MONDAY the 21*st *February current'.*

The Scotsman 19 February 1842

There were four services out and back between the cities, with the 7am and 3pm calling at all stations, listed as Corstorphine, Ratho, Winchburgh, Linlithgow, Polmont, Falkirk, Castlecary, Croy, Kirkintilloch, and Bishopbriggs. All trains carried first and second class passengers, but the 7am and the 3pm also carried third class. (Corstorphine was later named Saughton, and Kirkintilloch was temporarily on the site of today's Lenzie).

Fares for the whole distance were 8 shillings first class, 6 shillings second class, and 4 shillings third class. Gentry with carriages could have these conveyed on trucks, and pay second class fares. Horseboxes were available – the fare was 15 shillings per horse. For intermediate stations, fares were worked out 'nearly in proportion to the distance'. The 11am and 5pm trains with few stops were 'expected to perform the journey in 2¼ hours, until further notice'.

As the railway system had yet to adopt Greenwich Meantime as standard, the E&G stated that *'The* **Time** *on the* **Railway** *will be* **reckoned by the Railway Clocks'.** Passengers were briefed about travelling on railways - they were requested to take care of their luggage, to have their address marked on it, and to see that it was put on board the carriages – that is on the roofs. Parcels that would be a significant part of E&GR business were conveyed by all trains and delivered by the company. It was hoped that goods trains would shortly commence.

The intention was to run additional trains as the season advanced – at 9am and 7pm from both cities. For some months, there had been negotiations for coaches to operate in connection with the railway at different points. Such 'integrated transport' was developed by the E&G with three services in Glasgow alone – to the city centre near the Trongate, to the Broomielaw for the steam boats, and to the Glasgow & Greenock Railway at Bridge Street.

Immediately under the advertisement for the new railway was a counterblast from its old adversary – the Union Canal – with its 'Great Reduction in Fares' and proclaiming 'ECONOMY – COMFORT – SAFETY' on its passenger boats ('comfortably heated in both cabins') sailing from the cities at 9am and noon. First class from Edinburgh to Glasgow was 3s 6d and

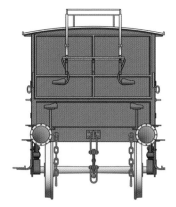

This second class carriage for the E&GR was roofed but unglazed; its wooden seats were arranged in compartments and luggage was carried on the roof. *(Euan Cameron, after A A McLean)*

second class 2s 4d, but it omitted to say how long the journey took – all day.

Business was soon booming with John Miller recommending that extra locomotives be obtained. As ticket sales took off, scales were purchased to weigh gold coins at stations. The coal trade had 'started with some spirit' and 50 extra spring wagons were advisable; more cattle trucks were ordered. To supply the locomotives with coke, 12 additional ovens and a chimney stalk were to be built at Falkirk.

Additional accommodation was sought at Queen Street where Dr Wardlaw's Chapel was again targeted.

In the six months to 31 December 1842 passengers totalled 340,251 – first class showing 51,060, second class 84,061, but third class 205,130 – as single journeys. With patronage growing, total receipts, including goods and Royal Mail (£167), were £59,994. Meantime, a winter timetable had been published in October 1842 with trains at 8am, 11am,

3pm and 6pm, and a luggage train (goods) at 7am, in both directions. It was apparent that Scottish passengers were prepared to tolerate open vehicles at a low cost per ticket.

Early in 1843, a memorial was submitted by John Gibb & Son pointing out the losses sustained by them on the Almond Valley-Winchburgh contract, and 'bringing certain errors in their estimate under the favourable consideration of the Directors'. Their tender had been for £147,669 for the longest and most testing contract, and a miscalculation left the Gibbs £40,000 short. In addition, they had also to deal with 'unforeseen obstructions, unfavourable weather and doing night work' – this earned men a higher rate. The plea was remitted to the former chairman John Leadbetter to see Messrs Gibb, and it was later reported that he had resolved the dispute with an offer of £12,500 to settle all claims. There were also questions about payment deficiencies from the

Initial facilities at railway stations were basic. This is the restored train shed that was originally at Haymarket but is now conserved at the Bo'ness & Kinneil, Railway, West Lothian.

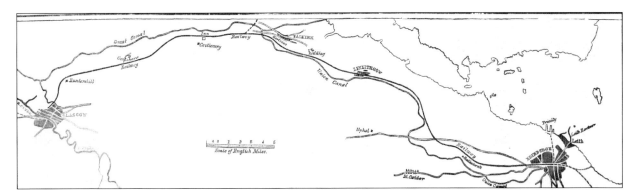

The opening of the E&GR was judged an event of such importance that 'The Scotsman' newspaper produced its first ever map to show the route.

contractor at the Redburn viaduct.

If train journeys offered little comfort, the E&GR directors had plans for refreshment rooms at Castlecary and Falkirk stations. Soon the company was arranging special trains – for the Mechanics' Institute in Glasgow to travel to Edinburgh, for the Highland & Agricultural Society to a dinner in Glasgow. Edinburgh School of Art students were conveyed 'outwards at full fare and back free' with a similar concession for the Edinburgh Temperance Society. Soon there was need for more carriages for third class travel on Saturdays to and from the cities.

The electrically-propelled vehicles of today are not the first to run on the Edinburgh & Glasgow Railway. By the 1840s, there was a fascination with electricity, a force with unrealised potential that both intrigued and alarmed scientists and inventors. The first electric locomotive in the world, named 'Galvani' was tested on the track of the E&G when the railway

had only been open a few months. It was the invention of Robert Davidson, an Aberdeen chemist, who was largely self-taught. It was described as 'an electro-magnetic machine', consisting of a four-wheeled wooden truck in which metal plates were submerged in acid. In spite of weighing five tons, 'Galvani' ran successfully at 4mph for over a mile and a half. Sadly, further testing was cut short by railway employees – they feared for their jobs if it should be successful. While the locomotive was stored in a hut, it was smashed to pieces in a typical 'Luddite' attack. Subsequently, exhibitions were held in both Edinburgh and London where a 'locomotive engine' carrying passengers on a circular track was demonstrated. Robert Davidson took out no patents for his inventions believing that any benefit should be for the common good – but he is without honour in Scotland. (A model of Galvani with an E&GR first class carriage, made by Ron Jarvis, is exhibited in the

The restored Haymarket train shed at the Bo'ness & Kinneil Railway has fine cast iron work.

A medallion was cast in Glasgow to mark the opening of the Edinburgh & Glasgow Railway. It shows the Almond Valley viaduct and the tunnel mouth at the Glasgow station. *(National Railway Museum)*

Guinness Steam Museum in County Kildare in the Irish Republic).

The running costs of Cowlairs incline and the rope's unreliability were continuing worries. There were persistent problems with the heavy hemp rope; made in Newcastle; it was 4,840 yd in length and reported to be 6in in circumference. A description stated that *'the trains are drawn up the incline by an endless rope… carried upon guide pulleys …at a rate usually of 12 miles per hour which is slow motion if the train is light … but this rate may, however, be increased to 20 miles an hour'.*

To attach the main rope, trains waited at the Queen Street tunnel mouth, where a chain and messenger rope was hooked on to the locomotive's front buffer beam. Communication between the great beam engine up at Cowlairs and the foot of the incline was maintained by 'galvanic telegraph' from the outset. The main rope was detached at the top of the incline by the train locomotive increasing its speed and running ahead.

In the summer of 1842, a battery-powered locomotive 'Galvani', invented by Robert Davidson of Aberdeen, was tested for over a mile on the Edinburgh & Glasgow Railway. *(The Steam Museum, County Kildare, Ireland)*

As early as July 1842, a heavier rope was thought to be the answer, but in March 1843 a different solution was suggested – the use of locomotives for banking trains from Queen Street up through the tunnel. William Paton had been appointed locomotive superintendent at Cowlairs, and he was energetic and innovative. Two robust tank engines were therefore built there, with some design input from John Miller. Following the E&GR practice of naming engines, they were appropriately 'Hercules' No.21 and 'Samson' No.22. They had devices to spray hot water on the rails to loosen oil and grease, and cold water jets to wash the debris off. Considered the most powerful locomotives of their day, they came into use in January 1844. Soon their weight caused the light tunnel rails to disintegrate, while the tunnel roof was allegedly damaged by the blast of their exhausts. (Seepage from sedimentary rocks above was deflected by lead sheets conveying water to trackside gutters). This banking experiment was not a success, being given up in March 1847 when enginemen, rope splicers and brakemen were re-employed. One engine was converted for goods haulage, taking from 60 to 100 wagons at night without assistance.

To go down the incline, brake vehicles were used. The train locomotive was detached, then two trucks, each weighing 14 tons, with a brakeman in each, took it down by gravity. As they braved the hot, sulphurous and sooty tunnel, sparks flew from the brake blocks. A mishap at the Glasgow station in July 1844 was reported to the Board of Trade. A train of 11 trucks, loaded with freestone from the quarries at Bishopbriggs, arrived at Cowlairs and was left on a siding until the following morning. A 'break'(sic) truck was then placed by one of the incline locomotives on the main line; this engine then took the train from the siding to the rear of the 'break' truck- the fireman connecting this to the train. The incline engine then descended separately to the station to bring up additional 'breaks' to Cowlairs.

On this occasion, however, the engineman had pushed the train too far forward and the trucks 'had got upon the incline'. The fireman tried to arrest the descent from the one 'break' vehicle, by putting 'scutches before the wheels'. The speed of the train increased, and on emerging from the tunnel, the fireman threw himself off, colliding with a first class carriage on an adjacent line. The train then crashed into the station house, passed through the parcel office, broke through the wall on the opposite side, and 'traversing the carriage way in front of the station house, came against the building opposite, the wall of which was a little injured'. This was in West George Street where trucks and the 'break' were 'piled on each other and much broken'. The fireman was not seriously injured and the driver was dismissed. Buffer stop collisions were not infrequent at Queen Street station.

When the E&GR began to run services, trains were simply sent off from the termini with 'decent intervals' between them. A crucial development that would make railways safer was the electric telegraph. The E&G directors determined to have such a system and engaged Alexander Bain from Caithness, trained as a watchmaker in Edinburgh and an electrical innovator, to have his version on the E&GR. He charged £50 a mile to erect a single line along the railway and his telegraph, using a simple needle device, was installed. The company could then boast of having an 'electrified railway'. However, there were problems and by June 1846, the directors were taking steps 'to have the Telegraph put into efficient working order at *all* the Stations along the Line'. The directors offered Bain £3,000.

There were others experimenting in the same field, notably William Cooke and Charles Wheatstone, who had taken out a patent in 1837, 'for improvements in giving signals and sounding alarms in distant places by means of electric currents transmitted through electric circuits'. Soon railway companies were permitting their lines to be used for experiments. When attempts were made in 1846 to set up the Electric Telegraph Company – aiming to unite the country with a network of electric communications – compensation of £10,000 had to be paid to Bain for his electric clock invention.

The Electric Telegraph Company's Act of 1846 gave it powers to lay wires over public property, including line sides. Soon it acquired the way leave along the E&GR, and Bain's other rights, whereupon his apparatus was immediately replaced with Cooke & Wheatstone two-needle instruments. On the E&GR, in addition to railway activity relating to train movements, personal messages could be sent on paying half a guinea (10s 6d) for 5 minutes. Bain's electric master clocks and an electro-chemical telegraph, a step on the way to fax communication,

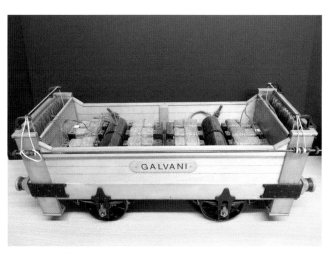

A close-up of 'Galvani', showing the arrangement of batteries in the world's first electrically propelled locomotive. *(Grampian Transport Museum)*

were ground breaking innovations.

Francis Whishaw writing on 'The Railways of Great Britain and Ireland' (1842), described the E&GR with its fir poles 352 feet apart (enthusiasts could judge the speed of the train by these). The wires were galvanised, the insulators earthenware, each pole had a 'mini-roof' to shed rain, and a lightning conductor. Such a system cost £50 per mile. Telegraph wires by the trackside would become an inseparable part of the railway scene. It took just 5 minutes to send a message from station to station. Soon messages could be relayed from Glasgow to London over 520 miles away by rail through the co-operation of seven railway companies, including the E&GR.

The E&GR's 'Rules and Regulations' were issued to employees who had to state that they had read them – or had the rules read to them – before signing the same, and these must be carried with them at all times. All working on the railway must be aware of the terms 'Up'- to Edinburgh, and 'Down' – to Glasgow. The smoking of tobacco was 'strictly prohibited both in and upon the Carriages and in the Company's Stations', the penalty not exceeding Forty Shillings. If a warning to desist was ignored, then removal from the premises and forfeiting the fare

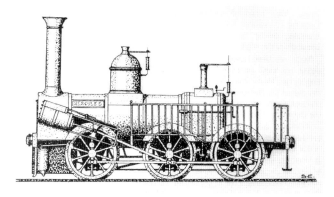

Continuing problems with rope haulage on the Cowlairs Incline led to banking engines being tried between 1844 and 1847. This locomotive is 'Samson'. *(NBRSG Journal)*

would follow. The 'Commission of any other Nuisance in Carriages, Stations or Premises' met with a penalty of £5, a considerable sum. 'For intoxication and riotous conduct', the fine was similar. Humans or animals straying onto the line – which was protected with stonewalls – were trespassing. The E&GR proposed to select police for service on the railway from 'respectable labourers'.

In April 1842, the company advertised for a 'General Superintendent for the Line', to replace John Miller in that role – the appointee was 'To be an Engineer and qualified to take charge of the outdoor business of the Railway'. Alexander James Adie was appointed. He had been apprenticed to the civil engineer James Jardine in Edinburgh, and in 1836 was a resident engineer on a Lancashire line, followed by the Monkland Railways.

In 1844, William Paton submitted a report to the directors about the E&G locomotives and rolling stock. He was frank about their deficiencies; of the company's thirty locomotives, only half were serviceable – some being unfit for traffic and others under repair. They had serious weaknesses – their 'sandwich frames', the outer being timber plated with iron, led to crank axle failures. Moreover, the works were congested, badly lit and poorly equipped. However, with investment, Cowlairs Works would become a pioneering railway centre that combined the construction of locomotives, carriages and wagons for the E&GR and later for the NBR.

Paton was prepared to experiment – unwisely, on an eleven carriage train going down the incline from Cowlairs with one 'break' truck, instead of two. This attained 'high velocity' even before the tunnel was reached. John Miller was in London at the time, and being questioned on his return, stated that only empty trucks or carriages should have been used, and only after the regular workings for the day were over.

On 19 May 1845, a special train of one coach plus engine was hired to run from Glasgow to Haymarket, starting 1½ hours before the regular service. The engine was *Napier* No.18, one of the Bury four-wheelers. It had 'valve trouble' and was losing steam; much time was lost, the train coming to a stand close to Gogar. The driver abandoned the engine, but had no lamps to warn the train approaching from the rear, and had left no word at the previous station, Ratho. The fireman was sent back with a signal to stop the oncoming train, but this was not seen and a crash could not be averted. The coach and passenger were lost. The cause was attributed to the use of a locomotive 'in an imperfect and leaky state', and there had been no inspection of fitness to run.

That November, Paton and the driver were put on trial for culpable homicide and both were found guilty. The Locomotive Superintendent argued that he had warned the management both verbally and in his report that there were insufficient locomotives in perfect order to work the line – the directors'

objective seemed to be getting as much work as possible out of the engines. The judge criticised the E&GR's 'maladministration' for which the directors were personally responsible. Although witnesses spoke 'in high terms' of Paton's good character, his knowledge and ability, he was sentenced to 12 months imprisonment and dismissed; the driver and fireman received nine months, and the 'station agent' and porter at Ratho were sacked. The judge recommended that an inspector 'unconnected with the railway companies' should have 'full powers at all times to examine the condition of engines and the mode of working'. With numerous lines being built, he believed companies would require 'some inducement' to spend money on such inspections.

The E&G directors were clearly shaken by the episode and asked James Aitken of Hill Street Foundry in Glasgow to visit the 'Engine Factory at Cowlairs' and submit a report. This only confirmed Paton's opinion about the inadequacies of both the locomotives and works there. Some engines were 'only fit for short trips or piloting'. Repairs put many out of traffic – from 3 weeks for 'new pistons and general overhaul' to 5 months for a rebuild. The four-wheelers should be converted to six-wheeled locomotives, and two new engines ordered immediately for the 'Quick Trains'. Aitken also gave his views on Cowlairs works – the smithy lacking light and ventilation, the wrights' shop 'a very unfit place' in which to make patterns, and the frequent breakdowns of the 'factory engines' resulting in no power for machines.

Robert Thornton, then in charge of the engines at Haymarket, became interim Locomotive Superintendent (he later became Locomotive Superintendent of the North British Railway). His challenge was again 'working traffic with only half the engines the company possessed' As for the rolling stock, the third class and 'stand ups' were 'in a very bad state' resulting from frequent exposure to rain. For the goods traffic, more vans were advisable and many more mineral trucks.

Furthermore, as the water at Cowlairs and out on the line was 'both bad and scarce' – tender capacities should be raised to 1,000 gallons. Thornton also made recommendations to improve safety – drivers and firemen should be examined on the 'Rules and Regulations'. There should be a daily inspection of the engines before any service was run. He even suggested that the Board had a problem – the directors were 'ever subject to change, and possibly no-one in it possessing either time or qualifications necessary to examine the details.' For his part, the Superintendent should concentrate on repairs and maintenance rather than embark on new construction – such purchases being made from outside firms.

Rules for the qualifications and appointments of 'Enginemen, Guards, Policemen, and others on all

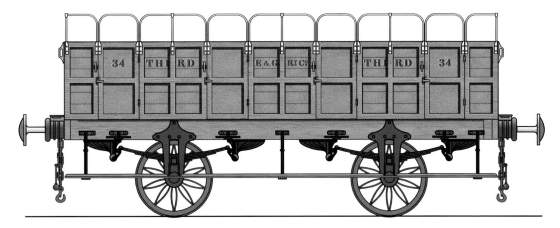

Third class carriages on the E&GR were basic – with wooden seats but no roofs. *(Euan Cameron, after A A MacLean)*

Railways' had been proposed at a 'General Railway Conference' held at Birmingham in January 1841, ('Policemen' were signalmen); nineteen railway companies, all English, were represented. For the E&GR, 'Lord Seymour's Act' for the Regulation of Railways in 1844 was welcomed, as 'raising the standard cannot fail to be beneficial'. Nevertheless, the company engaged in saving money, and 'men-clerks' on £40 a year were replaced by boys at £25. According to an E&GR advertisement in 'The Scotsman', 'WANTED for a respectable Establishment in Town, a YOUTH about 14, who writes a good business hand…' Clerks were only paid every four weeks, but porters (in three teams at the Glasgow station) were paid fortnightly.

On 22 November 1845, 'a Person of Skill and Experience to fill the situation of SUPERINTENDENT' was advertised, as after the accident on the main line, Paton had been dismissed. Meanwhile, A J Adie was holding the post of Engineer with a salary of £1,200 a year, but the Inspector of Permanent Way only received £200 a year. Paton's absence while in prison was keenly felt, but in March 1847 he was reinstated as Locomotive Superintendent and is soon listed as a member of the Institution of Mechanical Engineers. He was sent south immediately to visit 'different railways in England' to examine their methods of working.

The Railway Mania began to sweep Britain in 1844-5 when there was massive investment in joint-stock railway companies that dragged people with money (and many others less wealthy) into a spiral of speculation. From profits arising from factories and mills, the new middle class increasingly had funds available for investment, and government bonds, long thought 'safe' became much less rewarding than railway stock. This was yielding 5 per cent or more making Lancashire investors enthusiasts for railway shares and 'Railway Mania' took off. There were Bills for 110 Scottish schemes in 1845 alone; 'The Railway Shareholder's Manual or Practical Guide to the

Railways of the World' had reached its 7th edition by 1846.

As the speculative 'bubble' grew, there were moves to expand the E&GR's interests. A preliminary notice had been given about a short branch to Kirkintilloch, a flourishing village on the Forth & Clyde Canal but off the main line, plus an extension 'as originally contemplated to the North Bridge of Edinburgh'. Furthermore, a branch to Stirling was under discussion with 'influential Gentlemen of the County'; a committee had been appointed to bring a line to Perth and progress was made with a view to another through Fife. An outcome would be that the traffic on the E&GR would be 'considerably promoted by railway feeders'. There were hopes that satisfactory arrangements would be made with the Edinburgh, Leith and Newhaven Railway, a Grainger project that would give 'a cheap and direct Railway communication with the harbour at Leith'.

Much money went on expenses incurred by the promoters and their support, on paying engineers for making surveys and preparing plans, and in meeting

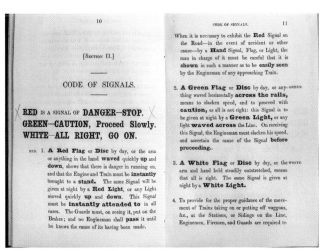

The Rule Book for the E&GR giving information about signalling and other matters, had to be carried at all times – or risk a fine. *(National Records of Scotland)*

It was only in 1911 that this signal box with its clock was opened on the busy and difficult line at Cowlairs. *(Railway Magazine, 1906)*

When the 'Railway Mania' speculation in shares took off in 1845, 'Bradshaw's Railway Gazette' was soon published in several editions. *(Wikipedia)*

lawyers' fees for taking Bills to Parliament – and not on any lengths of track at all. In 1845 Parliament sanctioned Acts for 2,816 miles of railway with capital totalling £40m before the 'bubble burst'. By 1 January 1849, the outline of Britain's rail network had largely taken shape, though little more than half had yet been laid.

In 1846, the E&GR had a Bill in Parliament for the Stirlingshire Midland Junction Railway; this proposed a line leaving the E&GR close to Polmont and running to a junction at Carmuirs near Larbert, thereby making a connection with the new Scottish Central Railway going north. (Joining up with the E&GR at Greenhill would give SCR trains access to Glasgow Queen Street, but this was inconvenient for SCR's Edinburgh services). The Stirlingshire Midland Junction was authorised on 16 June 1846, but was 'absorbed' by its parent E&GR in advance of its construction. Completed in 1850, it was known for its 'Swing Bridge' over the Forth & Clyde Canal at Camelon.

The phase of intense speculation challenged railway companies to make deals that would lead to junctions with 'friendly' lines. If a company met with hostility, it might try to extract running powers over a route. Alternatively, it could stake out territory to claim as its own for the development of a new line, thereby blocking rivals. Directors also opposed schemes that they saw as threatening their interests. The E&GR used all these strategies. 'Plans of all Scotch Railway Bills' before Parliament, and any other Bills that might affect the E&GR, were always carefully scrutinised.

Meanwhile, the E&GR had a wish list of desirable acquisitions involving several railways and the three canals in Central Scotland. In 1844 negotiations began for a take over of the coal railways of the Monklands – the Ballochney, the Monkland & Kirkintilloch and the Slamannan. In December 1845, the Monkland companies handed over their equipment to the E&GR and, prior to altering their lines to standard gauge, working arrangements were approved. Sanction for such amalgamations had to be obtained from Parliament; there were fears about monopoly with traders and merchants concerned about higher charges. Consequently, in July 1846 the E&G's plan for a take-over of the Monklands' mineral railways was rejected – the district was not thought 'sufficiently developed' for such an amalgamation.

On the E&GR, the running of Sunday trains and the carriage of the Royal Mail became inextricably linked. The Railways' Conveyance of Mail Act, (1838), stated that the mail be carried by ordinary or special trains 'as required by the Postmaster General'. As early as October 1841, the E&G directors were concerned that this might compel them to run Sunday trains. The carriage of Royal Mail was lucrative for railways – the conveyance of mail in Lancashire was reported to earn £14 per consignment. Charges were negotiable and early in 1842, the E&G directors offered to carry the mail between the cities for £700 a year, but this was declined – the Post Office stating it should pay the same as for the mail coaches – £198 per annum.

By March 1842 however, the Postmaster General had contacted the E&G directors about the date that a Royal Mail service could begin, and at what hours or times of the day or night. The possibility of trains being run on Sundays now provoked an outcry from church interests with Synods, Presbyteries, Kirk Sessions and congregations protesting – positions supported by many town councils and societies. Petitions carried thousands of signatures and the E&G directors received deputations. John Leadbetter was so opposed to Sunday trains that in August 1842 he resigned as chairman.

Religious controversy was raging in Scotland, culminating in 1843 when over a third of ministers and their congregations left the Church of Scotland to establish their own 'Free Churches' – free from interference in the appointment of ministers. The E&GR's English shareholders were bewildered as many supported Sunday trains. Some Scots were also in favour – among these were the magistrates of Bathgate, Greenock, Leith, Linlithgow and Paisley. Sunday was the only day when people were free from the demands of work, and it gave an opportunity to visit family or to take an excursion. Popular travel times were also Fast Days, the holidays prior to communions, when people did not go to work

A compromise was eventually reached – there would be two trains on a Sunday, morning and evening – 8am and 5pm, times that did not interfere with divine services. This gave the opportunity for both travellers and 'company servants' to attend church. Otherwise, Royal Mail would be carried daily on the 11am trains, calling at Castlecary, Falkirk and Linlithgow. Nevertheless, so vociferous was the campaign against Sunday trains that it caused their discontinuance 'on or after Sunday 15 November, 1846' the only exceptions being occasions of 'urgent necessity or mercy' – and there was no resumption until the company was amalgamated with the North British Railway in July 1865.

For passenger comfort, refreshment rooms were set up at some E&GR stations – one at Castlecary was criticised for taking business away from a local inn while the premises at Falkirk proved too much of a temptation for railway staff. With no renewal of a lease in prospect, the tenant offered to stop selling 'wines, spirits and malt liquor' but it was to no avail – the directors refused. To assist travellers, bells were bought for stations where they were to be rung 'at the starting of trains'.

Passengers had to tolerate 'a rough ride' on the E&GR – over rails laid on stone blocks – a warning ignored when the line was constructed as railways were introducing wooden sleepers. The E&GR did have some larch examples 9ft long laid on

embankments as stone blocks tended to sink into the ground there.

Measures to increase comfort and safety had been set out in the Railway Regulation Act of 1844. Under this law, all carriages had to be 'covered' with roofs to give protection and these must have seats. (Only in October 1846, the 'expediency' of having their fourth class 'standups' roofed was remitted to the E&GR Traffic Committee to pursue 'if they see fit'). Such unglazed carriages exposed passengers to dust and hot cinders, but such hazards were excused by some men as there was 'the opportunity to smoke at their ease', smoking being forbidden in stations and on trains.

For the greater safety of passengers, slip bolts were now placed on the inside of carriage doors to stop these bursting open. To prevent overcharging, railway companies had to provide 'conveyance for third class passengers' at the cost of one penny a mile, at least once a day in each direction stopping at all stations – the so-called 'Parliamentary trains'. The carriages must be 'covered' (roofed) and average speed was to be not less than 12 miles per hour (19km/h). The Act also threatened a state takeover of railways if the private companies failed to co-operate.

In January 1842, the North British Railway, a company that was to feature on the Scottish railway scene for almost 80 years, had been launched. A meeting was held in the E&GR's offices at Haymarket with a view to promoting a line to Dunbar and subsequently to Berwick-on-Tweed. The chairman was none other than John Learmonth, John Leadbetter's old adversary on the E&GR board.

That same month, Parliament received notice of the E&GR's intention to extend its line to the old North Bridge in Edinburgh. This was an eleven arch structure, dating from 1772 that straddled the valley between the Old and New Towns. The directors saw the extension as a potential source of revenue with extra ticket sales and other advantages. In January 1843, costs for the project were estimated at £44,573,

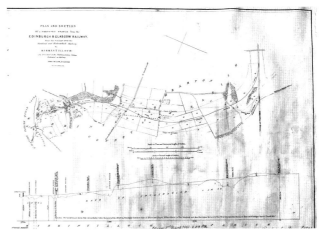

A proposed investment by the Edinburgh & Glasgow Railway was a branch to Kirkintilloch, the coal port of consequence on the Forth & Clyde Canal. *(National Records of Scotland)*

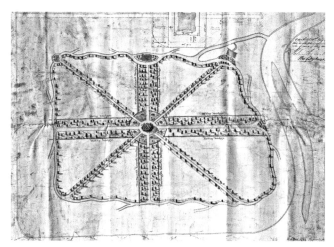

The design of Edinburgh's East Princes Street Gardens resembled the Union flag and property owners opposed the E&GR coming through the site. *(Ask the Archivist, Network Rail)*

including the tunnels required at Haymarket and through the Mound, with £8,000 for a station at the North Bridge, plus £15,000 for land and compensation. With such outlays, some shareholders protested and argued that a station at 'the West End' was quite sufficient.

Tunnelling would be expensive, but John Miller pointed out that a drift mine (now known as the Scotland Street tunnel) had been excavated under St Andrews Square for the Edinburgh, Leith and Newhaven Railway, a line that would commence at Market Street. Miller forecast competition for this central site. On 4 July 1844, an Act for the E&GR's line for *'Public Advantage and Convenience… from its present Termination near the Haymarket to the North Bridge'* was obtained.

In December 1845 the E&GR received an offer from the Guild of Fleshers (butchers) of the Shambles, an insalubrious place, for £16,500. (After a jury trial, the area was later acquired for £11,000) Much more attractive were the sheltered 'green market' stances

under the old North Bridge. Negotiations with the city fathers over acquiring these were slow – they had no wish to part with the sites, but 'any offer from the Directors would be considered'.

The E&GR extension was strenuously opposed by the property owners facing Princes Street Gardens. An Act of 1816 had given the proprietors powers to stop commercial development and to preserve their unobstructed views to the pleasure gardens and castle rock. They feared a serious loss of amenity and a consequent fall in property values. Led by Lord Cockburn, a High Court judge and pioneering conservationist, the residents defended their rights. He forecast that the E&GR would cause ruin in the district:-

'the whole beautiful ground will be given up to railways, with their yards, depots, counting houses and other abominations, at least on the east side…'

Accordingly, there were conditions attached to the Act – the E&GR was not permitted to erect any buildings at its terminus higher 'than Thirty Feet above the Level of the Railway'. This restriction came from the law of 'servitudes and ancient lights' that protected property owners from obstructions being placed in their views. There were objections from the Bank of Scotland, whose Head Office had stood above the Mound since 1806. The 'Station House', limited in height and length, was approved by the distinguished architect William Henry Playfair. Any 'Engine House, Manufactory or Workshop… calculated to create a Nuisance to adjoining Property' was forbidden. Only coke, a relatively smokeless fuel, was to be used by locomotives going through Princes Street Gardens, and on no account must they race there.

The first major work on the extension was the 1,009yd long tunnel east of Haymarket, formed by blasting and brute force. The residents of Princes Street had then to be placated with landscaping,

Falkirk Station features in this painting by David Octavius Hill that dates from 1842 and shows E&GR locomotives in action. *(Falkirk Council)*

plantings and high walls that would make the railway 'undiscoverable' from their drawing rooms. After that lay the Mound between the Old Town and the New. It consisted of spoil from the building of the New Town, and was a route of 'great public accommodation and convenience' across marshy ground, but it had to be cut through with a tunnel of 124yds. William Playfair's Royal Institution of 1826 (now the Royal Scottish Academy) stood on the Mound's north side.

The residual bed of the Nor' Loch, drained in 1763, then planted in 1821 with trees and shrubberies as a pleasure garden, was a 'soft' site where Miller had suggested using concrete. Further east came the Little Mound, where a three-arch masonry bridge allowed the E&GR to meet the NBR tracks end on. Its 'great centre arch' of 65ft was stone built on piled ground and settled 'about 4 inches'.

This structure, linking the Old Town and the New, gave access over the tracks to and from the monument being erected in Princes Street Gardens to Sir Walter Scott, the novelist and poet, one of Edinburgh's most distinguished sons. The title of Scott's first novel was 'Waverley' – and both the bridge and a joint station would soon take that name.

Although the E&GR's lines were reported as finished in May 1846, the joint station was not ready. However, a crowd gathered to cheer on 20 May when a train of NBR carriages was drawn 'from the tunnel at the West Church Manse and rolled slowly and majestically along the valley of the North Loch…' The place where the E&GR met the NBR by the North Bridge was inspected by Major-General Pasley, who reported that the there were two lines of rails, and that both companies had sidings near the junction. The NBR opened its station with due ceremony at North Bridge on 18 June 1846 when a train of fifty carriages hauled by nine locomotives set off for Berwick-upon-Tweed. On 1 August 1846, the E&GR's extension was opened as far as North Bridge, and with the NBR's lines converging there, this site would become the hub for rail traffic in the capital.

The E&GR station building's design, being influenced by Playfair, was neo-classical in style, befitting the city's claim to be 'the Athens of the North'. The whole outlay for this joint station had so far been paid by the E&GR, but the tight-fisted NBR was asked to pay £10,000 as its contribution. Nevertheless, the companies held discussions about refreshment rooms. Points were laid for a goods yard at North Bridge, but access by a steep road was awkward, and there were questions about how to manage through goods traffic with the NBR.

The initial arrangements for passengers were primitive and the E&GR had to make do with a single platform beneath the north arch of the Waverley Bridge. Furthermore, its station building was not yet complete as the contract was behind schedule – it must now be finished 'with the least possible delay'. By February 1847, it was suggested that a small

The old North Bridge at Edinburgh was where tracks of the E&GR met those of the North British Railway in August 1846. *(Ian Smith Collection)*

committee of E&G directors should meet with the NBR 'to consider further management between the companies' with payment of staffs arranged on the basis of ticket sales. The NBR continued to refer to its own station as 'North Bridge', where it avoided 'useless expense in ornamental works', and consequently its Edinburgh terminus was plain, cramped and uninspiring.

A third station was in the offing – premises for the Edinburgh, Leith & Granton (formerly Newhaven) Railway at Canal Street that opened on 17 May 1847. Squeezed out by the E&GR, it was accessed from the north by the steep Scotland Street tunnel. It only had a small site linked by a tight curve to the E&GR – and

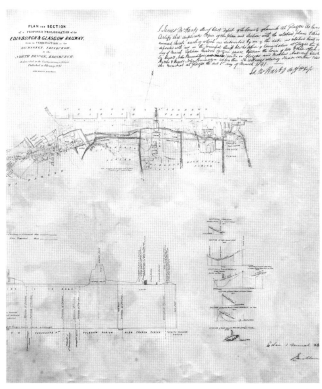

There were complex land ownership issues in taking the E&GR into the centre of Edinburgh as this plan shows. *(National Records of Scotland)*

A view over the E&GR station from the south-east shows the neo-classical building (left) and long train sheds with numerous smoke vents. *(Thomas Begbie)*

compensation of £60,000 was sought from that company for loss of land. The 'switches' of the E,L&GR were laid on ground now owned by the E&GR, and were to be 'removable at E&GR pleasure'.

With business continuing to grow, the intention was to extend E&GR operations in East Princes Street Gardens. There was an obligation on the railway to put the land there in proper order first, but cost was a consideration, 'Delay this as much as possible and object to any interference by the Magistrates of the city' was the instruction from the company's lawyers. Meanwhile, Edinburgh Council was prepared to share the cost of paving drains at the former Nor' Loch.

After a year, there was a realisation by the E&GR directors that expenditure on the railway would have to continue. It was a sobering thought – there was an estimate of £106 a mile for annual maintenance, but should this sum come from revenue and who should do the work? Contractors or men employed by 'the Resident Engineer'? In 1846 Railway Clearing House

expenses for the E&GR had reached £1,300.

In 1847 John Miller's accounts had not yet been settled. For the years 1844 to 1846, these amounted to almost £8,000. With recent project proposals, such as the West of Scotland Junction and the E&G Dumbartonshire line adding an extra £3,800, he was due over £10,460, less a small payment to account. The directors ordered this sum to be paid, while Lord Hopetoun and his tenants would at last receive £1,029 as compensation arising from the construction of the railway.

Locally, the rail network was also growing. Individuals were now permitted to build branches to the E&GR and to carry private railways through the main line by means of bridges or culverts. For road traffic, once 'proper communication' was made by over bridges, the right to cross the railway ceased – though stiles allowing access over the line to church services continued to be a problem.

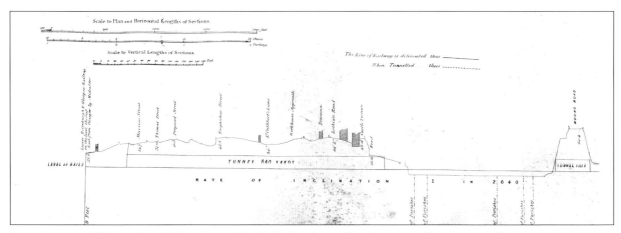

Constructing the E&GR over the 'soft' former bed of the Nor' Loch and tunnelling through the Mound were challenges in accessing the centre of Edinburgh. *(National Records of Scotland)*

Chapter 4

Creating a Network

By 1846 the Edinburgh & Glasgow Railway had achieved its aim of accessing the centre of Edinburgh, and the through station between Waverley Bridge and the North Bridge was taking shape. It was a modest affair, being an iron-framed timber structure supporting a long slated roof with numerous smoke vents. Five sets of rails with little 'turnplates' allowed small 4-wheeled carriages to be reversed. The NBR booking office was at North Bridge, the E&GR one at Waverley Bridge, and their congested goods stations were placed alongside Market Street and Waterloo Place. Relationships were not always harmonious – when the Station Agents at Ratho and Winchburgh were 'poached' by the NBR, the E&G directors 'regretted not receiving communications' on the subject

There was no respite for John Miller. Though he had not been paid for work dating back to 1845 and amounting to over £10,000 and had an account due for £2,000, he was asked to proceed with a parliamentary survey of a line through Strathblane to Ballat, Stirlingshire. Extra station ground was under investigation at Glasgow where a 'Line of Connection' between Cowlairs and Blythswood Holme by the Clyde 'with as little of a Tunnell as possible and with the best possible gradients that can be got' should be devised. A West of Scotland Junction scheme with the Ayrshire & Greenock Railway was to be 'perfected', but a crossing of the River Clyde was proving controversial. Miller had prepared a plan and elevation for a bridge at the Broomielaw, but the Admiralty 'would on no account permit any viaduct to be erected below Glasgow Bridge'. For its part, the proposed Caledonian Railway refused to contribute to a Royal Commission on the subject. Would a Central Station for all the railways in Glasgow ever be possible?

When the Edinburgh, Leith & Granton Railway opened its station at Canal Street in 1847, this was at right angles to the E&G facilities and the EL&GR was now jammed into a small site beside Princes Street, accessed from the north by the Scotland Street tunnel. Trains were hauled up by a cable powered by a stationary steam-winding engine and, as at the Cowlairs incline, special trucks with brakemen on board slowed the descent downhill going north to Scotland Street. The EL&G station, with its two short platforms, some sidings and wagon turntables, was also in neo-classical style favoured by Playfair. He had also devised a plan for West Princes Street Gardens with embankments, drains and walks for which

The first Waverley Bridge had access by tunnels to the Edinburgh & Glasgow Station. The station building is seen (left) and E&GR rolling stock lies in sidings. *(Thomas Begbie)*

estimates were got and grass seed bought.

Uniquely, Central Edinburgh now had three stations within walking distance of each other. Many trains out and back on the E&GR carried through coaches for Leith connecting with steamers to Kirkcaldy and Aberdeen; some trains were also timed for sailings to London. There was freight to forward from 'luggage trains' and questions soon arose between the companies about charges. Mistakes could happen – two bales were sent off to Australia instead of Liverpool.

In Edinburgh, having new railways in their midst excited the attention of the scientific community. A

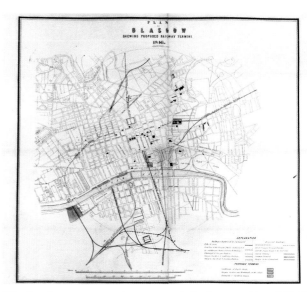

This plan shows a proposed arrangement of railways and termini in the City of Glasgow. *(National Records of Scotland)*

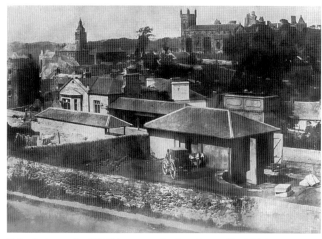

This photograph of Linlithgow station by pioneer David Adamson may be the earliest such image of a railway station. *(West Lothian Local History)*

The original Linlithgow station on its awkward site continues in use.

The swing bridge, taking the Stirlingshire Midland Junction Railway over the Forth & Clyde Canal, received close attention from the Railway Inspectorate. *(Hamish Stevenson)*

request came from the British Association for Geology to have access to the cuttings sections on the E&G and it was agreed to permit tracings of plans to be taken. As railways had brought undreamt of speed, faster than any existing forms of transport, their 'velocity' attracted experiments. An agreement permitted Professor Smith and Captain Cockburn RN

to ride *outside* one of the E&G carriages 'for the purpose of ascertaining by a Machine the Strength of Wind caused by the Velocity of the Train'.

With its Edinburgh terminus now a reality, the year 1847 was a strategic one for the E&GR. By July, passenger numbers had reached 1,069,980 a year – a far cry from the 340,000 estimated in the company's prospectus, and receipts totalled £114,181. In May 1848, congestion on Linlithgow trains led the inhabitants to protest that they needed additional 'travelling accommodation' from Edinburgh – and consequently, a short train was run just for them. The third class was proving the most popular as Scots were prepared to tolerate the discomfort of open vehicles, some without seats – plus the hazards of smoke, sparks and cold conditions – for cheaper tickets.

For the E&GR, business was flourishing. As goods traffic was expanding and revenue increasing, a petition from platelayers for a rise in wages in February 1847 was probably well timed. In March 1848, it was reported that 795 wagons had been repaired in the last six months. To reduce 'wear and tear', the vehicles should be strengthened and have 'Vulcanised India Rubber Buffers and Draw Springs'. When the EL&GR offered two locomotives with tenders for sale at £4,400 – better suited to goods than passenger traffic – these were accepted. An additional six engines were soon ordered from Neilsons of Glasgow. E&GR motive power was clearly deficient as even on the near level route it was disclosed that 9 per cent of the trains were being 'assisted' by pilot engines. Nevertheless, of the 520 trains run on the E&G in March 1847, only 30 failed to keep time, 12 were late 'but not over 5 minutes' and only 2 were 'beyond 15 minutes'.

The E&G directors seemed disconcerted by the costs of running a railway - extra expenses had continually to be met – from liabilities under the Poor Law, prison assessments and taxation to compensation amounting to £1,600 for taking ground at Canal Street Station. They refused to pay full passenger duty, only paying a monthly account under protest. However, a lack of signals at Kirkintilloch with safety implications led to these being 'installed at once' regardless of expense. Having settled further claims for over £4,900 with Lord Hopetoun, the E&GR directors were dismayed when he entered another demand, this time for rock *under* the line that he could no longer access. Near Haymarket, the proprietor of a coach works had a claim for damages arising from the tunnel works - and a judicial offer of £1,500 was made on behalf of the E&GR.

To increase E&G revenue, it was suggested that vacant ground above the tunnel at Glasgow should be enclosed and let for development. When half an acre of land for a station house at Kirkintilloch was given without charge, this was eagerly accepted. A claim arising from 'residential and intersectional damage' on a branch line took 1,000 guineas to settle.

The Railway Mania had waned but during its course the E&GR directors had invested in various promotions. Of immediate interest were the Edinburgh & Bathgate, the Airdrie & Bathgate and the Stirlingshire Midland Junction lines – elements in an expanding network for itself. The latter line went through Falkirk, a strategic place where two canals met at Lock 16 west of the town. The Forth & Clyde Canal was crossed by a swing bridge – its safe operation receiving much attention from the Railway Inspectorate. Thanks to Falkirk's two stations, omnibus links soon developed to Stirling, Perth and the north. The district was set for the expansion of its iron trade in which the railways played a key part – with numerous foundries and ironworks being opened.

There was also a large E&GR holding in the Stirling & Dunfermline, with token amounts in the Scottish Central and the Bo'ness Branch of the Slamannan Railway. The E&GR again proposed purchasing the Glasgow & Garnkirk and the Monkland & Kirkintilloch Railways outright, but such 'takeovers' with a risk of monopoly continued to be opposed by Parliament. The London solicitors acting for the E&GR ran up an account for £2,000 for attempts to buy the Monkland lines and the Garnkirk & Glasgow Railway.

Opposing the Caledonian Railway Bill for its West Coast route cost the E&GR £8,128. Post-Railway Mania, the money market became depressed and the Glasgow Stock Exchange advised against making any calls on shares. If funds became tight, the E&GR directors should try to persuade contractors 'to spread their works …over a longer period', and avoid any new contracts. New Bills should be postponed and branch line proposals withdrawn to cut expenditure. Consequently, the English directors and investors began questioning the competence of the E&G directors to manage 'a concern of vast magnitude' with 'arrangements' for its conduct 'now totally unfit'.

The E&G board's response was immediate – advertisements in the national papers stated that - 'an Officer of very superior qualifications' would be appointed as 'General Superintendent' – a 'mastermind' without divided responsibilities. The choice was John Latham, from the Manchester & Birmingham Railway. After 'most satisfactory assurances', he was given an 'engagement of one year at a salary of £1,000'. Soon Latham's closer scrutiny of costs led to public advertising for stores and double entries in stock books. With James Adie as 'acting Engineer', and William Paton, reinstated as Locomotive Superintendent, this team would manage the E&GR into the 1860s.

A proposed takeover of canals by the E&GR was opposed by the English directors on the E&G board,

The original Summerford viaduct carried the E&GR over the Union Canal at Tamfourhill'. *(J L Stevenson)*

acting they believed in the best interest of shareholders. Why should the railway company purchase rivals that it had defeated? The canal companies had been bitterly opposed to the E&GR, but had now lost most of their passenger traffic to it, while their goods traffic had been dented. But there were other motives at work – the E&GR was concerned that the Caledonian Railway would take over the canals if it did not act. In 1849 the E&GR purchased the Union Canal for £209,000, much to the displeasure of the Lancashire shareholders.

Although the cost of the Edinburgh station and related works was now over £5,000, the E&GR directors felt confident about renting offices at 24 Princes Street for £15 – if the NBR would pay half. They also donated £10 to the Glasgow Royal Infirmary and subscribed to a Mission at Springburn.

With an eye on the Railway Regulation Act of 1844, open carriages on the E&GR were now closed giving an increase in passenger comfort and safety. These basic vehicles were made into parliamentary third class carriages but even so new fourth class ones were being built. Improvements were on the way for second class, with cushions in 'London rib' upholstery stuffed with horsehair, and lamps on order. Windows, as yet unglazed, would be enlarged to improve light,

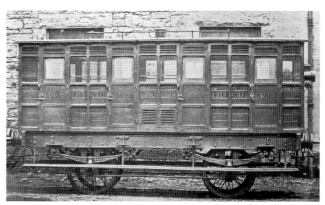

In the latter 1850s, second class carriages on the E&GR had 'improvements', notably glazing and lighting. *(Ewan Cameron, NBRSG)*

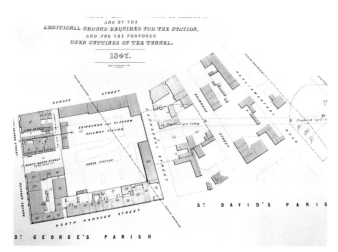

This plan shows additional ground required at Glasgow Queen Street and proposed open cuttings for the tunnel in 1847. *(Glasgow City Archives, Mitchell Library)*

but smoke and sparks proved to be as objectionable as ever. Providing oilcloth or leather blinds was contentious as these made the interiors dark and 'unsuitable for females'.

Passenger experiences could be alarming – when the 10pm train from Glasgow was driven with much force into the passenger shed at Edinburgh, the buffer springs on the first carriage broke and passengers were 'slightly bruised'. It was discovered that the engine had not been coupled 'according to orders'; the train crew was dismissed. When a second class carriage on a train of six vehicles was overturned at Edinburgh 'but with no serious injury to passengers', a doctor wrote that he was willing to attend accidents at Glasgow and on the line for £20 a year. As a consequence of a collision at Corstorphine, the 'Rules and Regulations' were printed in large characters and posted at all stations to alert staff.

Wages on railways were hardly generous. Goods clerks earned only £80 a year and wage rates could go down, as in 1849 when platelayers' wages on the E&GR were cut from 15 to 14 shillings a week with foremen also facing reductions. There were however some positives for employees – cottages for

This early locomotive for the Scottish Central Railway was a 2-2-2 with outside cylinders and double frames. *(Glen Collection)*

pointsmen would be built at Cowlairs, and rents for railway properties would no longer be deducted from wages. A Reading Room costing £293 was provided there and a timber engine shed at £418 was erected; in time, regular contributions to support the Springburn School and its church were also made by the company.

With the railway network growing, there were tensions among the rival companies. Meetings were held in London between the E&GR, the Caledonian and the English companies to resolve traffic questions between the East and West Coast lines where a 'friendly arrangement was desirable'. Questions in dispute would be left 'to the Arbitration of Two Gentlemen, Mr Hudson and Mr Hodgson' – in an effort to preserve peace. George Hudson, of the York & North Midland, was 'The Railway King' responsible for driving forward the East Coast route to Scotland and many English lines, while Richard Hodgson would become the ruthlessly ambitious chairman of the North British Railway. In time, both would suffer bankruptcy.

In Glasgow 'the want of room and inconvenience' at the very basic terminus was now much criticised and the E&G directors realised that steps must be taken to make improvements. In February 1847 a letter was received from a George Square proprietor offering a site between Queen Street and Hanover Street for £18,750 – a price initially refused as 'too high'. But the seller was persistent and early in March stated that 'the offer would not be binding on him after 4 o'clock that day'. The purchase was forthwith concluded. A loan was arranged with Scottish Union Insurance and funds were subsequently raised with a bond on a George Square property.

Through acquiring such property, the E&GR obtained an interest in the Wellington Hotel on George Square, and the company decided to retain Mrs Cotton, its tenant there. The business was troublesome – if the roof leaked or a stove was defective, a reduction in rent was requested. When the E&GR opened, there were only four hotels or inns in George Square near its station – by 1848 there were seven, a likely result of railway influence, one having the prescient name, 'North British Hotel'.

The dangers of railway work had long been known, and in 1841 directors of nineteen English railway companies had met in Birmingham to consider legislation to make railways safer. This had influence on the Railway Regulation Act of 1844. For instance, ticket checking by going along the running boards of carriages was hazardous, and a guard at Linlithqow fell off and was found dazed and injured 3 miles from the station. Ticket platforms, where trains halted, were then erected outside main stations for this purpose – for Glasgow at Cowlairs, and for Edinburgh at Haymarket.

Amalgamations were in the air again. The E&GR continued to eye the 'coal railways' east of Glasgow -

the 11 mile long Monkland & Kirkintilloch Railway, the 6 mile long Ballochney climbing east up from Airdrie, plus the Slamannan that was under construction. Potentially, these were seen as important feeders of minerals and some passengers to the E&GR, but they used the Scotch gauge of 4ft 6in. With a pledge to move to standard gauge, Acts were obtained for that purpose. In April 1847, with only a three-day closure, the track adjustments began, and the coal railways soon formed the Monkland Railway Company. However, the E&GR was again thwarted by Parliament and by the latter company over its amalgamation intention.

In November 1849, the Edinburgh & Bathgate Railway opened with the prospect of tapping mineral rich districts in West Lothian. An inspection by Captain Wynne of the Board of Trade in March 1850 of the Shieldhill branch – possibly in response to complaints – was not complimentary. An old four-wheeled engine struggled on a gradient of 1in 80 and stuck, the train having to be split, whereupon the passenger vehicles were taken forward, 'neither the safety nor convenience of the public being properly catered for'. The return journey, going tender first downhill, was made with the wheels locked.

The E&GR had long fancied amalgamating with the Scottish Central, thereby bringing the opportunity of running trains to Stirling and Perth. The E&G directors worried about the latter company combining with the Caledonian Railway, especially as positive relationships seemed to be forming between the two. Lord Breadalbane, chairman of the SCR, welcomed 'joint arrangements' with both the E&G and the Caledonian. In the hope of a deal with the SCR, the E&GR promoted an Act for the Stirling & Dunfermline Railway in 1846. Subsequently the SCR preferred the Caledonian Railway, with which it would make a junction at Greenhill, and the E&GR deal fell through. Soon the E&G directors were opposing moves for the Caledonian to merge with the Glasgow & Garnkirk and the Greenock lines – with the Caley now being perceived as a persistent threat to E&GR supremacy.

The Cowlairs incline continued to cause problems, by 1847 another solution was being tried – wire rope. Its inventor was Robert Stirling Newall, who was born in Dundee in 1812. When based in London, he developed a machine for making wire ropes with four strands, each strand having four wires. By 1840 he had taken out a patent for wire rope and soon a factory was set up at Gateshead. In February 1847, a 4½ inch wire rope, weighing 15 tons and costing £840, was installed on the long incline at Glasgow. The stationary engines were also altered – but the outlay was not to exceed £2,500. William Paton argued that the installation should be simplified – the complexity arose from two operating speeds –12 and 20 mph – but the lower speed was permanently used and could not cope with 12 loaded carriages. With

R. S. NEWALL & CO. PATENT WIRE-ROPE WORKS, Gateshead-upon-Tyne.

HEMP ROPE		ROUND WIRE-ROPE, of Equivalent Strength.				
Circumference	lbs. Weight per Fathom	Circumference	lbs. Weight per Fathom	Breaking Strain	Working Load	Price per Cwt.
3½	4	1¼	2	2¼ Tons	12 Cwt.	
4½	5	1½	3	5¼ „	18 „	
5½	7	2¼	4	7¼ „	24 „	
6	9	2½	5	9 „	30 „	
6½	10	2¾	6	11 „	36 „	
7	12	2½	7	13 „	42 „	56s.
7½	14	3¼	8	15 „	48 „	
8	16	3½	9	17 „	54 „	
8½	18	3¼	10	19 „	60 „	
9	20	3¼	11	21 „	66 „	
9½	22	3½	12	23 „	72 „	

HEMP.		FLAT WIRE-ROPE.				
Size Inches.	lbs. Weight per Fathom.	Size Inches.	lbs. Weight per Fathom.	Breaking Strain.	Working Load.	Price per Fathom.
4 × 1	16½	1½ × ¼	8	15 Tons.	30 Cwt.	6s. 6d.
4½ × 1¼	20	2¼ × ¼	10	20 „	40 „	7s. 6d.
5 × 1½	24	2¼ × ¼	12	24 „	48 „	9s. 0d.
5½ × 1½	26	3 × ⅜	15	30 „	60 „	11s. 0d.
6 × 1½	28	3½ × ⅜	17	34 „	68 „	12s. 6d.
7 × 1½	36	3½ × ⅜	20	40 „	80 „	15s. 0d.

Signal Cord for Railways, Pits, &c. 14s. per 100 Yards.
Terms—BILL AT 4 MONTHS, OR 2½ PER CENT. DISCOUNT FOR CASH.

In February 1847 a 15 ton wire rope from Messrs Newall was introduced on the Cowlairs Incline. *(Grace's Guide)*

revised gearing, he hoped for 15mph. A steam brake would be fitted to a spare wheel on the crankshaft – to act instantaneously 'as the screw never answered', a worrying disclosure.

Paton suggested alternating the wooden pulleys in the tunnel with more durable iron ones, 80ft apart. Even with haulage modifications, he said 'a deal of time is lost in pushing the Train up to attach the Rope' – as this could not be brought beyond the 'offsets' – lines giving access to the station's goods sheds. He advocated roofing over the departure platform right up to the tunnel, when 'Trains could be set so far into the Tunnel as to be near the Rope'. John Miller proposed opening out much of the tunnel, but the inconvenient incline system would be used for another sixty years.

In September 1847, there was another accident on the incline, this time involving the 11pm goods train from Edinburgh. Twenty loaded trucks were to go to Queen Street, but thirteen empties were also requested. The train went down in two parts, but 'between the bridges, the loaded portion overtook the empty trucks' and the brakemen and guard were knocked down by the impact. Applying the brakes was ineffective and the train raced down the tunnel, struck a wall and entered a store. The guard and one brakeman managed to jump off but the other was fatally injured.

To assist with the policing of the railway by patrolling and protecting the lines, an agreement had been reached with the Superintendent of the Edinburgh County Police. Would this 'enable him to prosecute offenders against the Company's Rules and Regulations'? The E&GR had to find the considerable sum of £1,200 to pay its Police Assessment for Edinburgh and was looking for value for its money.

Though only two Mail trains ran on Sundays, the

Ratho was an original station opened on the E&GR in 1842. It was closed in 1951. A branch to Kirkliston using a low level station had closed in 1930. *(J L Stevenson Collection)*

directors continued to receive a flow of addresses and memorials in protest. The Surveyor of the GPO wrote about the night mail trains – these should depart both termini at 10pm and arrive not later than 12.45am at Edinburgh (an allowance being made for ascending the incline at Queen Street going east), and 12.00am at Glasgow. They would also carry goods, plus first and second class passengers. Traffic that was less controversial was newspapers – such parcels could be put on trains 'up to the hour of Starting of the last Train at night'.

To support the directorate there were now three committees – traffic, finance, land and property. They had much to consider. More carriages were required and both second and fourth class were ordered; one supplier offered twenty-four first class vehicles at £385 each. Note was taken of a warning from the Railway and Canal Commissioners about the 'conveyance of gunpowder' by rail and that special vehicles were necessary.

A survey of a Queensferry branch from Ratho was considered, while the Campsie branch and the 'Wynd Scheme' in Glasgow were claiming attention. The latter was the proposed 'Glasgow Harbour and Monkland Junction Railway' to tie in with the

'Villa tickets' were introduced on the E&GR to encourage house building away from towns and produce patronage as at Lenzie. *(Edinburgh & Glasgow Railway Guide Book)*

Monkland Canal link, and involved forming a junction and railway terminus at Trongate, but the proposal was declined by the E&GR.

With more traffic, dependable water supplies for the locomotives were now a priority; the Edinburgh Water Company charged one penny per 100 gallons, but Cowlairs supplies were free, though piped from an old quarry; some sources were unsatisfactory. Outlays continued – a retaining wall for Cowlairs and a wooden staircase for improved passenger access at Croy were required, but 'considering the increase in Traffic which has already taken place', the goods manager would receive an enhanced salary of £325.

Containing the costs of running the railway was a recurring theme. In October 1847, Latham had conducted a review of locomotive expenditure as this was considered too high. He found that in 156 days, including the mail trains on Sundays, 175,000 miles had been run, but many trains again required two engines. For goods trains, the average load was 25 trucks – giving a total of only 700 tons hauled per day – an amount that should be increased. To encourage economical working, he suggested that premiums be paid to locomotive staff based on costs per mile. Engine drivers would receive 10 to 6 shillings according to the amount of coke used, and foremen would have bonuses of £5 to £20 for good performance.

The locomotive account covered engine drivers' and firemen's pay, wages to works staff, plus oil, tallow, waste and 'general charges', but heavy repairs – with no mileages run – greatly inflated the total. New express engines had performed poorly – being as expensive for repairs as old ones. Paton had removed the complex gear from four engines and substituted 'common valves that answer better'. Repairs were being done at night 'under very disadvantageous circumstances', and there would be no improvement 'until a new Class of Engines is on the Line, suited to the traffic and high speeds now called for, combined with regularity'.

A priority was to place the workshops on 'an Equality with other Railways' as it was 'next to impossible to work the premises effectively and at the same time economically'. With a lack of accommodation for locomotives and stores at Cowlairs, perhaps 'an establishment for repairs' should be set up in Edinburgh. Sharp, Stewart & Company, Manchester, offered to make six engines with inside cylinders for £2,320 each, including tenders – two in two months, the others in four, to ease the position.

In spite of the motive power deficiency, special events received attention; if the Grand Lodge of Scotland could guarantee 200 passengers, then they would be carried from Edinburgh to Glasgow and back at the single fare. The desire of Glasgow and Edinburgh citizens to explore each other's cities brought a surge in traffic, especially at the Glasgow

Fair in July, that called for three additional morning and evening trains out and back over three days. The competitors at the Highland & Agricultural Society shows were allowed free transport for implements and stock 'if the same as before'.

With Anglo-Scottish services via the North British and East Coast companies now possible, the term 'Express Train' appeared, and the E&GR adjusted its timetable from 7 June 1847 to suit. Passengers on the 5.20am from Glasgow, calling at Falkirk only, Edinburgh at 6.43am, Berwick at 8.15am, Newcastle at 11.30am and York at 2.20pm, reached London at 9pm. Another train leaving Glasgow at 10am for York served First Class only. The 2.15pm from Glasgow connected with a service arriving in London at 8am the following morning. In addition, the 5.20am enabled passengers to reach Manchester at 6pm and Liverpool at 8pm the same day. Such travel possibilities were ground breaking for Scots. An E&G clerk was sent to London to learn Railway Clearing House business, and hand written paper tickets were out – Latham was authorised to agree a licence for Edmondson's system of ticketing for the company.

By 1847 the principal English railway companies had announced that they would use Greenwich Mean Time, a decision endorsed by the Corporations of Liverpool and Manchester. On 30 November the chairman of the E&GR wrote to the Lord Provosts of Glasgow and Edinburgh on GMT adoption. This move made sense of timetables nationwide, and was readily accepted. Hitherto, the E&GR had used time from the Edinburgh Observatory that was four minutes and some seconds ahead of Glasgow.

A rival company was coming ever closer. In 1845 the Caledonian Railway had obtained its Act of Parliament for a route from Carlisle via Annandale, Beattock and the Clyde valley into the Central Lowlands. The E&GR directors were unnerved by the prospect of this 'central route' into Scotland - surely two coastal routes east and west would be sufficient? Worse, the CR branches from Carstairs would be like a two-pronged fork aimed at the E&G termini. Although the CR was seen as 'most objectionable', the E&GR board should 'maintain friendly feeling and not resort to open warfare' with the newcomer.

The Caledonian plan showed that E&GR tracks would have to be crossed in the area of Castlecary – the site of a Roman fort and of a later castle. In April 1847, the E&GR faced another encounter with that company – the proposal for a Caledonian and Garnkirk Junction line giving access to a Glasgow terminus near Port Dundas. Remarkably, the E&G directors showed 'indifference' to this CR route passing between their Cowlairs tunnel and the canal branch above, but asked for 'protective clauses'. The construction involved draining the canal and some astute engineering where a relieving arch in masonry east of Buchanan House marks the spot.

By October 1847, it was agreed that the CR would

The E&GR began using Edmondson tickets in 1847. These had a date stamp to prevent fraud and were in use on BR until 1990. *(EdinPhoto/Michael Stewart)*

An aerial view of a strategic railway location where the Caledonian Railway (now WCML) burrowed under the E&GR in 1848 near Greenhill. *(Google)*

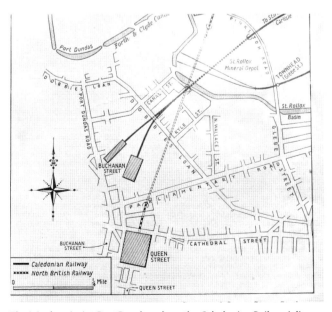

The 'pinch point' at Port Dundas where the Caledonian Railway's line from Buchanan Street station crossed the tunnel of the E&GR, and both passed under the Forth & Clyde Canal. *(Railway Magazine, 1951)*

A view west over Princes Street Gardens in the 1850s shows trains approaching the tunnel under the Mound with the National Gallery of Scotland above. *(EdinPhoto)*

pay £50 for ground at Castlecary when works were due to commence. The lines of both companies would come close at Greenhill, a place that would become strategic for Scottish railways – once the Caledonian tracks appeared and the Scottish Central Railway was completed.

By February 1848, the E&G directors had received a letter from Captain Harkness of the Railway Inspectorate *'ordering (that) the crossing of the Caledonian Railway Company's Castlecary Branch under the line should be effected by the construction of a cast iron arch resting upon masonry piers'.* A temporary lateral deviation from the E&GR rails would be *'laid off in a regular and easy curve'* – but lack of trust by the E&GR was evidenced in having the Court of Session appoint an engineer *'to see the above carried out'.*

In March 1848, 'Dress of Servants' to ensure 'cleanliness and respectability' was discussed by the

E&G board as this would also distinguish their staff from other companies' personnel at joint stations. It was suggested that 'every Servant should have some portion of his dress uniform' and sketches of E&G uniforms from the 1850s survive.

A decline in passenger numbers became a worrying trend that year. Was the novelty of the new railway wearing off, or was competition from other lines having an effect? 'Travellers for pleasure' were reported to be sampling new routes. Were E&G fares too high? It did not help that its stations were described as 'uncomfortable and chaotic'. The opening of the Scottish Central Railway in October 1848 had an effect on train times and more traffic loss was feared. Even so, with passengers showing a preference for through trains, arrangements were made for SCR services to run direct to Glasgow Queen Street.

Thought was continually being given to reducing the cost of maintaining and working railways in Scotland – maintenance was reported to have reached £1,112 per mile each year. With stone blocks on track beds on the way out, creosoted sleepers lasting 10 to 15 years would be used. There was discontent among staff when wages were cut – men at Cowlairs proposed a reduction in their hours of work, and booking clerks at the Glasgow station resigned.

Meanwhile, John Miller continued to look for payment of £10,460 and had a lawyer (a Writer to the Signet, no less) acting for him, but the E&GR directors were unimpressed – even his recent account for £2,547 would not be settled 'until it is convenient for the company and positively not now'. He complained that 'proper notice' had not been given 'as to the Engineering Arrangements lately entered into' by the

Uniforms of staff – a guard (left) and a porter (right) - on the Edinburgh & Glasgow Railway in the 1850s are depicted in these watercolour sketches. *(Special Collections, Glasgow University Library)*

company. Consequently, he would act only as a consulting engineer for E&GR projects, and aligned himself increasingly with the Glasgow & South Western route via Dumfries to Carlisle. Miller retired from engineering at 45, a wealthy man with a mansion at Polmont. He purchased two country estates and in 1868 became Liberal MP for Edinburgh.

In December 1848 a violent storm raged across Central Scotland when 'a large portion of the poles and wires of the Electric Telegraph Company were brought down at the viaduct over the river Almond, which occasioned the interruption in communication by telegraph to Glasgow'. Although the system was vulnerable to gales, snow and ice, thanks to the railways, the telegraph soon covered the whole country, and 'for the transmission of intelligence' had overcome 'both space and time'.

Early in 1848 came bad news for the E&GR – Caledonian Railway fares from Edinburgh to Glasgow via Carstairs were slashed – although the Caley route was 8 miles longer and had some steep gradients. This was the start of a 'price war' between the companies with the CR first class single ticket cut to two shillings, and the third to one shilling. Soon there were complaints about E&G trains omitting stops – at Croy, Falkirk or Linlithgow, as the 'present competition' would not allow calls to be made at 'road stations'. Journey time had become an issue – the E&G had one express taking 1½ hours, though the Caley's best was 2 hours 40 minutes. Fare cutting soon began on the E&G for through tickets between the cities. Consequently, receipts shrank and the E&G directors' response was to pay no dividend, funds being reserved 'to defend our right if invaded'.

In September 1849, Queen Victoria travelled over the E&GR for the first time en route from Balmoral to Osbourne on the Isle of Wight. The royal family set off by coach, then at Coupar Angus, after a wait of 20 minutes, boarded a first class carriage of the Scottish Midland Junction Railway. The train ran to Perth, then by the Scottish Central through Stirling, and latterly by the E&GR to Edinburgh. There the NBR had erected a stand for 600 guests to witness the royal progress. While appreciative of the crowds that had turned out to see her, the Queen was disappointed that the tunnels now hid 'the beautiful town'. The East Coast route proved popular with the royal family and many journeys were made over it and the E&GR to and from Balmoral.

By 1851, the E&GR had drawn up 'Rules and Regulations' for its employees – and they faced a penalty of five shillings if these were not carried when on duty. Men were to obey instructions promptly; incivility, rudeness or the use of 'improper language' could bring a fine or dismissal. Intoxication was a sacking offence. Employees were expected to be 'neat and clean' and to report 'occurrences affecting the safe and proper working of traffic'. Strictest obedience must be given 'by Officers and Servants to Danger and Caution Signals' – responsibility for these resting with those who exhibited them. All orders and instructions should be in writing if possible – any order received verbally must be repeated 'to ascertain that it has been properly understood'.

The relationships between the Scottish railway companies could be tense – apparent cordiality being quickly replaced by suspicion and animosity. An example was the relationship between the Edinburgh & Glasgow and the North British companies. In 1853 tensions led to a Court of Session case that disclosed that the E&G had been doing deals with the Caledonian Railway Company, seen as the NBR's

The sketches of E&GR uniforms also show possibly a senior porter (left) and a policeman, (right), a term also used for a signalman. *(Special Collections, Glasgow University Library)*

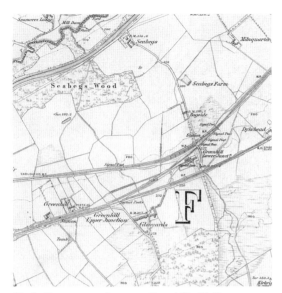

Rival railways came close near Greenhill with the Edinburgh & Glasgow line associated with Greenhill Upper, soon followed by the Caledonian and the Scottish Central at Greenhill Lower. *(Map Room, National Library of Scotland)*

A Goods Superintendent on the E&GR. By 1854, goods revenue was in excess of that from passenger trains. *(Special Collections, Glasgow University Library)*

fiercest competitor. It seemed that an amalgamation between the E&G and the CR was in the air as they had joint arrangements for ticketing with shared purses. This was stoutly contested by the NBR. A legal decision then prohibited the CR from using the station 'at or near the North Bridge' as its terminus in Edinburgh. This was stated exclusively to be the joint property of the E&GR and the NBR, an episode that resulted in the CR establishing its own station on Lothian Road at the west end of Princes Street. Parliament refused to sanction any amalgamation between the CR and the E&GR. To achieve a joint working arrangement, the CR had been prepared to

pay two-thirds of the Parliamentary expenses.

Tourism was growing and in 1850 Black's 'Economical Tourist of Scotland' had appeared in several editions. By 1860, the E&GR was offering sixteen tours of the Highlands in the summer months. These were designed to meet different levels of ambition and income. Tour 1 had tickets available for four days and featured the Trossachs, Loch Katrine and Loch Lomond. From Glasgow, the tourists travelled by rail, steamer (cabin class) and outside on a coach for 17s 6d, and from Edinburgh for 23s. From 1858, Callander could be reached by rail, and a tour in the Southern Highlands, cost 30s for a week,

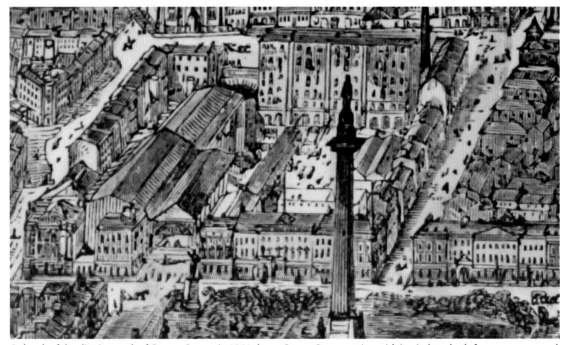

A sketch of the district north of George Square in 1864 shows Queen Street station with its timber sheds for passengers and the tall granary at the goods yard. *(T.Sulman/Special Collections, Glasgow University Library)*

In 1850, to improve E&GR motive power, 2-2-2 locomotives were purchased from Beyer, Peacock of Manchester. These soon proved their worth on the main line. Some continued as NBR engines into the 1900s. *(Euan Cameron)*

returning via Dunkeld. The longest excursion lasted 14 days, cost 79s (coachman's and guard's fees not included) and by using the canals got as far as Inverness and Fort William. The E&GR gave support to local regattas at Helensburgh and Dumbarton carrying 'racing boats' on the roofs of its carriages but drew the line at an event on Loch Lubnaig.

In 1852, a railway impasse was resolved when the Stirling & Dunfermline Railway, a progeny of the E&GR, was opened throughout. Making investment in the S&DR had seemed an attractive proposition, but it was left in isolation from its parent company when the deal with the Scottish Central Railway fell through. However, its tracks did reach Alloa in 1850,and shortly Tillicoultry was connected – though the E&GR refused to work the system, leaving the S&DR to acquire three locomotives and rolling stock of its own.

By 1854 it was clear that joint working arrangements could be advantageous to railway companies. Even better was for a local group to form a company, promote a line, raise funds, construct it and then find an established partner willing to operate its traffic; this saved the expense of having to purchase locomotives and rolling stock, or to pay staff. The 'parent company' should then get a generous share of the profits for its trouble. An example adopted by the E&GR was the Alva Railway, a short branch via Menstrie from the S&DR at Cambus.

Elsewhere, the E&G was active – the E&G's Campsie branch was set for expansion along the Blane Valley route at a cost of £35,000 of which the E&GR was prepared to subscribe £15,000. Campsie Glen, with its waterfalls and inn was proving a popular excursion venue. The Glasgow, Dunbarton & Helensburgh Railway was progressing with a pier requested at Helensburgh. Meanwhile, the rival Caledonian & Dumbartonshire Junction Railway was being carefully watched.

By 1855 freight receipts were in excess of passenger receipts and improving the Glasgow station for goods traffic – by opening out and widening the tunnel up to Cathedral Street – was considered. This would have enabled the doubling of the goods sidings, potentially raising the volume handled to 1,000 tons a week, or 50 extra wagons a day – but the existing station could not accommodate these all at once. The solution proposed was to take a line out of the tunnel to Parliamentary Road and construct a new goods yard there. The estimate of the cost was £54,000 for land and works, but the opportunity was not grasped. The answer was more sidings at Cowlairs. With the Scottish iron industry booming, special wagons to convey pig iron and to transport large coal were bought. Soon more ballast wagons and cattle trucks were on order. As goods traffic rose, weighing machines were installed at stations.

In 1854, the E&GR directors could report that the plant of the Stirling & Dunfermline Railway was now their property, and two years later, the Stirlingshire Midland Junction Railway was formally transferred to the E&GR, thereby ensuring a link to the SCR at Larbert. In July 1858 the S&DR was finally vested in the E&GR, a timely move as by then Alloa's coal traffic was flourishing. With the takeover of the plant and rolling stock of the Monkland mineral lines proposed, a further step was taken towards that long desired amalgamation.

With over a decade having passed since the E&G opened, an inspection of bridges and tunnels showed that these were mostly in 'a very sound and durable state'. Viaducts had been pointed – though parapets might need repair before long 'as engines shake the work'. West of the Almond valley viaduct, there had been heavy repairs on the neighbouring 'Turnpike Road' viaduct, where 'weakness had been sorted' – not the only occasion that it would need attention. Several overbridges with elliptical arches had 'sunk a little'. New rails were being laid in the Cowlairs tunnel, a task done at night to minimise disruption to train services. In 1855 to cut costs, there was a suggestion that contractors be invited to tender for the

Cowlairs station began as a platform where tickets were checked but survived as a station until 1964. *(R W Lynn)*

maintenance of the line from Haymarket to Falkirk.

The letting of advertising space at stations for £100 a year was agreed, but no advertisements were permissible in second and third class carriages. A daily newspaper, 'The North British Mail', was now sold at Glasgow Queen Street. Improving the 'look' of the line led to the notion that a garden be placed *over* the railway in Edinburgh's Princes Street. With tidiness on the agenda, stone blocks left lying by the railway since 1852 (when replaced by wooden sleepers) would now be removed. Prizes were offered to foremen who 'display taste and neatness in the appearance of their respective districts' and the E&GR supported an annual soiree for employees.

With railways becoming more safety conscious, insurance for employees was under discussion. Paton asked about insurance premiums for guards, who had proposed that half should be paid by the E&GR. No decision was taken. In 1858 The Railway Benevolent Institution was set up to provide support for railway staff, both active and retired, and to assist their dependents by preventing and relieving poverty, but there was initial reluctance for the E&GR to participate. However, by 1860 employees' contributions were on the pay sheet. Commendably, the E&GR tried to provide 'light work' for an injured man.

An insurance company had a scheme for passengers that the E&GR did join, the company paying one-third of the cost of a claim for injury or loss. As a safety measure an early version of a communication cord – a 'rope and bell' system between carriages and locomotive – was offered and the E&GR agreed to fit up its carriages, vans and engines. Exotic travel possibilities were appearing – the NBR was considering booking passengers to Dunkirk and Paris via Peterborough.

An improved station at Glasgow was desirable and estimates were obtained – the roof to cost £3,780 and the walls £400 – but the outlay was unacceptable, and instead the roof interior would be whitewashed and the urinals ventilated – at an expense of just £95.

(However, a ladies waiting room at Edinburgh was thought appropriate).

A traversing machine for use at Glasgow was investigated and Messrs Stevens in London could supply points for £250. By 1855, the purchase of the West George Street Chapel was still incomplete, and another offer of £14,100 was made. With the congregation showing reluctance to quit, there would be £600 extra for vacating by Martinmas (November), but only £300 for removing by Whitsun (June) 1856. (Chapel members were also given E&GR ticket concessions – though Free Church ministers going to their Assembly in Edinburgh were refused). When the chapel became the E&G head office, 'being sent fur tae gang tae the kirk', could indicate a reprimand or worse, for railway employees.

In the 1850s 'villa tickets' were an E&GR incentive to property developers to build at any of its stations that were not in towns – potentially to assist in promoting its passenger business. Lenzie, first known as Kirkintilloch, then Campsie Junction (the location where the Campsie branch took off from the E&G main line), was a favoured spot. (It was alleged that this attracted those who were slow to pay their bills as it was beyond the reach of Glasgow's Sheriff Officers). The number of villa tickets on offer was dependent on the value of the proposed property – the more valuable the villa, the more tickets could be got, but if a house had already been built, its owner did not qualify. Pleas for villa tickets continued to come to the directors well into the 1860s – when most were refused.

The E&GR could take justifiable pride in its safety record but this would be shattered by the events on the evening of 13 October 1862. A collision took place between two passenger trains in a cutting at Craigton west of Winchburgh. Only one line was in use as repairs had been ongoing when the two trains, one from Glasgow for Edinburgh and the other from Edinburgh for Perth via Larbert Junction, met head on. Fifteen people were killed and thirty-five injured, many severely. A passenger was able to reach Linlithgow to summon help, and a telegraph message alerted the railway management, a special train with staff and medical assistance being sent that night.

The line was cleared and returned to use the following day. A Board of Trade enquiry followed and the cause was ascribed to human error when the sequence of trains on the single line became confused. Compensation to passengers was in excess of £40,000, settled without quibble by the E&G board.

(Footnote: There have been six serious accidents on the E&GR – most attributed to human error, two to malpractice in operations, and one to vandalism)

There had been a shift in E&G locomotive policy in 1856 when Beyer Peacock became a preferred supplier of locomotives – 'splendid express passenger engines' that in rebuilt form survived into the twentieth century. In 1861 William Paton resigned and received a pension of £170 a year – some recompense for 'what he suffered in the service of the Company'. In September, his successor was William Steel Brown from the Great Northern Railway, but his tenure at the E&GR was brief owing to illness to which he succumbed. In1864. Samuel W. Johnson from the Manchester, Sheffield and Lincolnshire Railway was appointed Locomotive Superintendent while William Stroudley, who would later serve the London, Brighton & South Coast Railway, was made manager of the E&GR's works. Stroudley introduced changes to the building and repair of locomotives and rolling stock, plus 'the stationary engine and rope for working the Glasgow Junction' – he had discovered that this 'only stood still for 12 hours on a Sunday'. The first steel rails were laid on the E&GR in 1864.

The E&GR supported railway expansion, lending £5,000 to the Dunblane, Doune and Callander Railway, and making positive responses to the Inverness, Perth and Dunkeld Company – no Bill would be opposed by the E&GR. In August 1860 to promote rail travel, a 'Railway Enquiry Officer' was sent to London, and tickets for travel overnight to an International Exhibition there were advertised at £1, with first class by day at £4.

That year, a branch was opened to Grangemouth docks and worked by the E&GR. In 1862 the company absorbed both the Glasgow, Dunbarton & Helensburgh and the Caledonian & Dumbartonshire Railways. Cowlairs, busier than ever, was considered a station, with extra sidings, a coal platform and a 'signal tower'. More locomotives were ordered, and both engines and rolling stock were now insured.

Passengers were receiving more consideration with the E&GR also setting aside a generous amount for their insurance. Season tickets and 'pleasure party' rates were available. There were left luggage facilities at stations, and bookstands at Glasgow and Helensburgh. The E&GR now had an interest in the Queen's Hotel, George Square; when 'hot water baths' were introduced, the lessee sought compensation for loss of custom during their installation. Such was the traffic at Edinburgh that engineers were advising that three tunnels be made in the Mound.

The CR and the E&GR kept trying to arrange an amalgamation – they drew up a Thirty Year Agreement in 1863 – but Parliament refused to unify their lines on three occasions, the last in 1864. Each then looked for candidates elsewhere, and in June 1864 the E&GR signed up with the Monkland Railways to progress an amalgamation. On 5 July 1865. 'An Act to amalgamate the Monkland Railway Company with the Edinburgh & Glasgow Railway Company' was sanctioned. It took effect on 31 July. The following day, both were swallowed up by the NBR that thereupon gained access to Glasgow, to Clydeside and the West of Scotland. Overnight it gained the clout that went with this large and lucrative network.

The E&GR timetable book for 1864 shows just how much its network had grown – in addition to the E&G main line, its passenger sections – the Helensburgh Section, Campsie Section, Grangemouth Branch, Bathgate Section, Stirling & Dunfermline Section, were listed. There followed those lines served by E&G goods trains, including the Wilsontown Section. That year, the E&GR had run over 644,742 train miles – over half of these with passenger services. It had 102 locomotives, 290 passenger vehicles and over 3,000 assorted wagons and vans. This pioneering intercity railway company would be sadly missed, as its successor would discover.

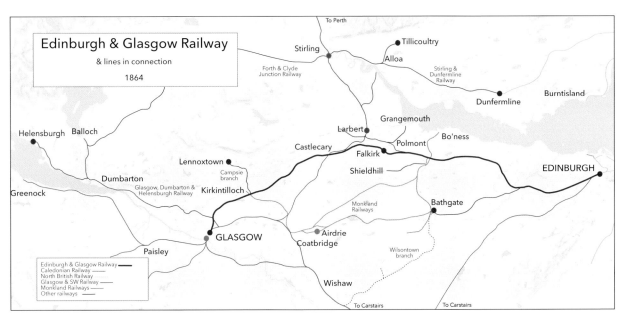

A map based on the Edinburgh & Glasgow Railway and its 'lines in connection' in 1864 on the eve of the amalgamation with the North British Railway. *(National Records of Scotland)*

Chapter 5

New Regimes

After the reorganisation of the Scottish railway companies in the mid-1860s, the Caledonian Railway acquired the Scottish Central Railway and the Scottish North Eastern as its partners. This gave the CR a trunk route that continued the West Coast main line all the way to Aberdeen. Had the Caley been successful in its quest for the E&GR, it would have been well on its way to forming a national rail network in Scotland with controlling interests radiating from both Edinburgh and Glasgow. It was not to be, and by winning the E&GR, the North British not only entered the latter city but also accessed the Lanarkshire coalfields, Clydeside docks and shipyards, and links to several west coast resorts.

The E&GR main line, joining the country's two major cities, was a route of the first importance, carried the most traffic and was very profitable. This acquisition fitted the aspirations that the NBR's ambitious chairman Richard Hodgson had for that company. In 1862 it had already taken control of the Edinburgh, Perth & Dundee Railway, thereby expanding its influence northwards.

On 16 July 1865 'Extraordinary General Meetings' were held in Glasgow and in Edinburgh by the NBR – the shareholders being carefully listed. The first name on the proxy list was 'Richard Hodgson'. All administrative and financial matters would henceforth be handled by the NBR's head office in the capital. All books and documents pertaining to the E&GR were to be sent to Edinburgh, together with staff information – names and duties, length of service, wages and salaries. On or after 1 August, traffic receipts were lodged in the name of the NBR and only its seal would now count.

The E&GR managers and senior staff were either dismissed or demoted. These actions caused immediate resentment and weakened the NBR's

The crest of the North British Railway combined the coats-of-arms of Berwick-on-Tweed with Edinburgh; a mosaic at 'The Booking Office' on Waverley Bridge.

capacity to run the E&G and its associated lines. Thomas K Rowbotham of the NBR became general manager, John Latham of the E&GR only being employed until February 1866. Samuel Johnson, the E&G Locomotive Superintendent, was to stay but 'take all necessary instructions' from the NBR's William Hurst. In 1866 Johnson moved to the North Eastern Railway, and from 1873 to a brilliant career with the Midland Railway. The E&G engineer, James Deas was retained for the E&GR and Monkland sections – as an associate of the NBR's James Bell. By 1869, Deas had had enough of the NBR and joined the Clyde Navigation Trust.

In September 1865, at an E&G shareholders' meeting, some redress was attempted, 'Payments to the company servants as compensation for their loss of situations' were discussed with the general manager, secretary and others to share a total of £11,600. Forthwith, an interdict was served by some stockholders preventing any such payment – there would be no 'donations, gifts or presents' to any of the E&G officials. When all claims were met, any balance would go to preference or ordinary shareholders.

Out of the amalgamation negotiations, five Scottish companies emerged – the Caledonian, with its West Coast main line focus and Lanarkshire interests, also had extensive connections in the Highlands through the Callander & Oban; by absorbing the Scottish Central and the Scottish North Eastern, its influence now extended to Aberdeen. The Glasgow & South Western's dominance was in Ayrshire, and it had a line via Dumfries to Carlisle. The Great North of Scotland Railway, head quartered in Aberdeen, served the North East. From its base in Inverness, the Highland Railway with its long single track routes would become a life-line to remote communities. The North British administered from

A Monkland Railways goods engine No. 296, built by Neilson & Co in the latter 1850s, passed to the North British Railway and survived into the 1880s. (NBRSG)

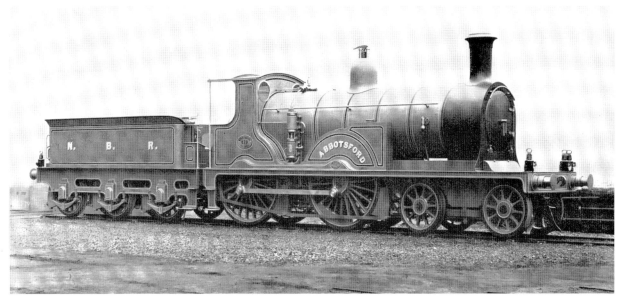

The express 4-4-0s designed by Dugald Drummond and first built by Neilson & Company in 1876 gave outstanding performances. *(J F McEwan Collection)*

Edinburgh now had a mileage of 452.6 miles, and would be hungry for more.

Although the NBR was in Glasgow, in Fife and had reached Carlisle, such expansion came at a heavy price. It had meant cutting expenditure severely on maintenance and on rolling stock. Even so, the directors were considering the reconstruction of the inadequate Waverley Station by holding a competition for a design – won by one of their engineers, Charles Jopp – but possibly costing £90,000. Such a sum could not be raised as by the autumn of 1866 the NBR faced a funding crisis. The failure of the Overend Gurney bank in London had precipitated a financial collapse when the whole economy went into recession and railway stocks were badly affected.

It was soon revealed that the NBR's modest dividends of 2% had been paid out of capital to support the company's share price in the stock market. When a new company secretary 'blew the whistle', the scandal broke. To satisfy an over-ambitious but unscrupulous chairman, it emerged that the accounts had been falsified for years – and the NBR board was guilty of deception. These disclosures infuriated E&G shareholders who believed they had been duped and argued that *their* company should have taken over the NBR, and conferred the E&G name, or a new name, on the whole enterprise.

The anger, especially among Glasgow shareholders that 'their railway', a well run and profitable company, had been amalgamated with an imprudent, indifferently run and financially embarrassed outfit, was intense. Worse, a new board for the enlarged company had only two former E&GR directors to the NBR's thirteen – being outnumbered 6 to1. For the NBR, severe retrenchment was to follow with a decade of penny pinching, and there was the continuing problem of the deficient termini at both Edinburgh and Glasgow. For years, the new board saw any capital expenditure as 'pernicious'. Sunday trains were reinstated – excused as a service to the 'poorer classes', but a useful revenue stream. Decisions had to be made about uniforms and comparisons showed how mean the NBR was - some men only receiving coats and others no garments at all. The least generous practices were maintained.

In 1869 came the jolt of competition for the NBR when the Caledonian Railway opened its Mid-Calder

Drummond rebuilds of E&GR Beyer Peacock 2-2-2 locomotives of 1856 transformed their appearance. These had been 'regulars' on the E&G route. *(Euan Cameron)*

Queen Street station's arched roof of malleable iron and glass, completed in 1878, was largely hidden from view by other properties owned by the NBR. *(J L Stevenson Collection)*

line for passengers in July – bringing a surge in the number of trains between Glasgow and Edinburgh to 54. The CR line closed a gap in its network – a line between the cities that at 46¼ miles was a mile shorter than the E&G intercity route. Although rising to over 700ft, the new line was relatively straight and the Caley's best trains could cover it in 1 hour 10 minutes. It also tapped mineral fields for coal, ironstone and oil shale, and soon had numerous branches. Furthermore, the CR announced its intention to open an Edinburgh terminus at Lothian Road that would compete for Glasgow traffic. So with passenger comfort and safety at Waverley having been overlooked for years, suddenly improvements there became 'imperatively necessary' – but only £50,000 would be spent. By the following year, the NBR Chief Engineer James Bell had a plan available including a new iron beam bridge to replace the masonry one at the Little Mound. An exchange of land with the town council gave the railway the green market in lieu of the former Canal Street station site, and expansion at Waverley could begin.

Penny pinching showed in reluctance to install the block system with interlocking signals and points throughout the NBR network; this was much criticised by Board of Trade inspectors. By 1874.only 25 per cent of the NBR network had been so protected and accidents were caused by its absence – the most serious at Manuel Junction that year when two trains were in collision. To raise funds, old engines and other materials were sold for scrap and lowest prices found for coal – 2,000 tons per month were required for its locomotives (at about 25p per ton).

Although the financial clouds hanging over the NBR were dissipating by the latter 1870s, the flagship route of the E&G had persistent problems – a requirement for fast running was nullified by speed restrictions owing to mining subsidence. Moreover, the 'detentions' of passengers on NBR's trains of 'comfortless shaking six wheelers' led to adverse comments in the press and angry letters of complaint. How should the NBR improve the passenger experience? Railway companies had been challenged in 1872 when the wealthy Midland Railway offered greater comfort by putting third class passengers into second class carriages that were 'upholstered', leading to the accusation that the MR 'pampered the working class'. (It was 1892 before the NBR got rid of its second class vehicles).

April 1873 saw a pioneering venture by the North British – the first sleeping car in Britain running from Glasgow via Edinburgh to London. It was an opulent vehicle but had only six wheels, whereas progressive railways were introducing 'bogie' coaches (with two sets of four wheels per carriage) that gave a much smoother ride. The sleeper failed to win passenger support – and probably the extra charge of 10 shillings was thought too high.

Freight traffic was also problematic for the NBR – cutting expenditure on maintenance had led to the neglect of rails on branch lines and in sidings. Consequently, there were charges for 'demurrage' when goods traffic was held up, causing coal owners to look for compensation for their interrupted trade.

The NBR locomotives had also become outmoded and disappointing performers but in 1875 Dugald

In 1889, the North British Railway attempted to make Queen Street station look festive with palms and draperies for the visit of the Shah of Persia and his son. *(Illustrated London News)*

Drummond, a dour and determined Scot, was appointed locomotive superintendent. He had been at Cowlairs Works briefly in the 1860s under Stroudley. Both men then went to the Highland Railway, and subsequently to the London, Brighton & South Coast. With Drummond's solid experience, a breakthrough in engine design ensued – his 4-4-0s were soon acknowledged as outstanding. In December 1876, Drummond held trials on the Edinburgh & Glasgow route for the continuous braking of trains. The aim was to find the best solution and rival systems were tested on trains of eight carriages with brake vans at each end. Westinghouse won the contest. From 1877, the rhythmic 'thump' of air pumps on NB locomotives was a sound that characterised its stations. By 1882, Drummond had been lured away by the rival Caledonian Railway and Matthew Holmes took over.

A proposal to remodel the Glasgow terminus soon appeared. From George Street, Queen Street Station was accessed by a narrow passage where passengers had to fight their way to the booking office. Once in possession of a ticket, they found the second and third class carriages standing in the entrance to the tunnel mouth. There were just two narrow platforms where throngs of passengers jostled amid the luggage. At the summer peak of the Glasgow Fair in mid-July, crowds were alighting or boarding in the filthy tunnel – despite the difficulties and dangers there. In the decade to1873, the passenger 'footfall' at Queen Street had risen from 1½ million to over 3 million a year, with 'multitudes in the height of summer', over 30,000 travelling on the

Helensburgh line for the Clyde Coast resorts alone.

As Queen Street station was so severely criticised for its inconvenience and hazards by the city magistrates, by the police and the public, in August 1874 came an ambitious proposal. An improved station was mooted plus a new underground line going west. The NBR board delayed making a decision – despite the attraction of having their various lines merging at one major station with 'all platforms upon a level with George Street-George Square'..

Only in 1878 was a cheaper 'in house' scheme to reshape the existing station the choice. The solution was devised by James Carswell, an NBR engineer with experience in both railways and iron construction.

The enlargement of Queen Street Station necessitated the widening of the tunnel mouth. While this was in course of completion, on 18 August 1879 there was a collapse causing complete blockage at the station. Trains were diverted to the College station and there were many delays. Nevertheless, by 1881 the efforts at Queen Street had produced 'a most satisfactory station', although a new booking office and waiting rooms were postponed – until these could be afforded. A sore point with Glasgow's Provost and Magistrates was the goods traffic at Queen Street. From the station's commencement, there were complaints about the inappropriateness of a grain store at the corner of North Hanover Street, and there was further dismay when this was replaced with a granary seven storeys high.

In 1882, the NBR completed its Strathendrick & Aberfoyle Railway, thereby reaching a tourist hub for

The wire hawser on the Cowlairs Incline had to be replaced every 14 months or so. Here 'splicers' are making repairs while brake trucks to control descents are in the background. *(Glen Collection)*

Centre On the Cowlairs incline, trains were assisted by means of a rope attached to the front buffer beam of the locomotive; here a Holmes 4-4-0. 'West Highland bogie' is making the ascent. *(Hennigan Collection, NBRSG)*

the Trossachs. This was achieved from the Forth & Clyde Junction Railway, a rural line going west from Stirling that the NBR had operated from 1856. Local services expanded at Waverley station in 1884 when the Edinburgh Suburban & South Side Junction Railway, a 12½ mile circular route south of Arthur's Seat and Salisbury Crags, was opened. It ran through both leafy suburbs and industrial districts. An island platform was made on Waverley's south side – the

Lower Shale mining in West Lothian told on structures on the E&GR such as the Broxburn viaduct that has been greatly strengthened.

inner circle going east via Portobello and the outer west through Haymarket. (The 'Sub', yet to be electrified, is a useful avoiding line for freight trains). On the Firth of Clyde, the NBR now had a fleet of steamers sailing from its railway pier at Craigendoran.

With the Glasgow & South Western Railway, the North British inherited a half-share in the proposed City of Glasgow Union Railway in 1864. Begun as a goods link between the two companies, it had the first rail bridge across the Clyde. By 1875 it had only reached Springburn on the city's northeast side, but many branches and spurs ensured its value for freight traffic. (The north portion now carries passenger trains from Queen Street Low Level).

In the 1880s the Glasgow City & District Railway was projected, and in 1882 it was authorised as an independent company. This underground line, built to link the NBR suburban routes east and west of the city – between College on the High Street and Stobcross – was just over 3 miles long, but would relieve congestion at the Queen Street terminus. Its low level station had four platforms A, B, C and D – to avoid confusion with those numbered on the high level. Construction of the railway, by cut and cover plus tunnelling, was complex arising from the geological mix that was encountered – from running sand to boulder clay and rock. At the peak 22 tunnelling faces were in action. Nevertheless, being below street level, it cost the NBR relatively little for property acquisition. A through station was created at College, renamed High Street, and the line opened on 15 March 1886 – an underground railway akin to London's Metropolitan routes – and was immediately amalgamated with the NBR.

The station at Charing Cross provoked protest in what was then an upmarket residential district. The locomotives and the lengthy tunnels soon led to complaints about the smoke, steam and lack of ventilation. To reduce the problem, no goods trains ran on the line and Charing Cross station roof was opened out. When there were protests over the absence of light in the carriages, electric lighting was provided by means of a conductor rail on the tunnel walls.

In 1889 there was a visit to Scotland by the Shah of Persia, the main purpose of which was to see the Forth Bridge then nearing completion. The Shah also visited Clyde shipyards and travelled on the NBR to Glasgow where he was received by the Lord Provost and magistrates at the improved Queen Street station – made festive with draperies, flags and pot plants.

By 1894 with the advent of the West Highland Railway, the Glasgow, Dumbarton & Helensburgh Railway via Maryhill and Westerton connected Queen Street station both with that tourist line and with growing suburbs. The downside was that the West Highland services led to increased numbers of trains arriving and departing from the busy high level station.

Meanwhile, on the E&G, the NBR hoped to run a train every hour between the cities, and its locomotives were proving capable of taking expresses through in 60 minutes. However, there was keen competition from the Caledonian Railway with its fast trains and superior passenger accommodation. The NBR had serious difficulties in operating the E&G – the working of the Cowlairs incline always being a headache. A new general manager was appointed in 1891 – this was John Conacher who came from the Cambrian Railways with a sound reputation for his competence. He was dismayed by what he found – Cowlairs, where down trains were backing up for brake wagon descents, and Queen Street where departures were constantly held up. Tests with locomotive-hauled trains convinced him that this was the way forward, but in his view this would not be enough. He had a radical proposal – that the E&G from Bishopbriggs west should be quadrupled – this would mean massive rock cutting – with a second tunnel being driven between Cowlairs and Queen Street.

For six years the board considered Conacher's recommendations, and with a worsening operational situation by September 1898, the directors took the step of adopting his plan. Parliamentary powers would be sought in 1899. Sadly, the railway was never quadrupled and a decade was to elapse before rope haulage ceased. A lasting tribute to Conacher may be the second but hidden tunnel portal. The directors had concerns about locomotive braking power, fearing that an engine and train might plough into crowds on the narrow concourse in Queen Street station. Such an event did occur when a locomotive on an express from Edinburgh got out of control and crashed into the public bar. Thereupon, the engine was given a nickname – that of an American lady temperance reformer. 'Buffer stop collisions' at Queen Street would feature regularly in accident reports.

The notion that the E&G route would be a fast line became an illusion – it was beset by speed restrictions as subsidence from mineral workings negated its gentle grades and easy curves. Sustaining high speeds from end to end was impossible and the route gained notoriety for poor timekeeping. Although mineral traffic was a significant source of income, the fact that the E&G crossed Central Scotland's coalfields came at a cost to the NBR – coal owners looked for compensation if the railway expected minerals to be left untouched under the tracks. There were also workings for fireclay and ironstone to consider, and later shale mining for paraffin oil, became an issue.

When a mineral working was approaching a line or likely to go under it, the railway company expected a survey done 'to the satisfaction of its engineer'. When minerals were to be left untouched, the owner could claim compensation. A crucial point on the E&G was the viaduct at Castlecary where a deposit of fireclay

In 1890 there was severe congestion at Waverley station and its approach lines after the opening of the Forth Bridge. Only in 1895 did the enlarged tunnel at the Mound come into use. *(Davidson Brothers)*

had to be purchased for £1,350 by the NBR. A pillar of coal under the Maryhill line resulted in a claim by the Summerlee Iron Company for calcined ironstone and coal, plus an allowance for avoiding the pillar, and a landlord's royalty of £40. These were charges that the NBR could have done without.

Many Edinburgh-Glasgow services were timed to suit east coast expresses either arriving at or leaving Waverley station. These were known as 'facility' trains and later their performance became linked to poor time-keeping on the difficult Waverley Route – served by the Midland Railway to Carlisle and by the NBR from that city northwards – with knock-on effects for trains on the E&G. Although there were 60 trains a day on the route, passenger dissatisfaction was evident in letters of complaint – fares were too high, services slow and timings inconvenient. Confusion and congestion especially typified Waverley station.

In March 1890 came the opening of the Forth Bridge that only made matters worse at Waverley. However, trains from Glasgow could now head east for Fife at Winchburgh Junction, and trains from Edinburgh west at Saughton Junction, along new stretches of track to Dalmeny. In April the difficult Glenfarg route opened giving the NBR its own line north to Perth. The reconstruction of 'the new Waverley station' was signalled in February 1896 when tenders were invited 'for the Roofs, Footbridges and Relative Works'. There was an outcry when more land was taken from Princes Street Gardens, and there was further tunnelling at the Mound. The station, set in the valley of the Nor' Loch, had again to be as unobtrusive as possible, though a height of 42 feet above the rails was now permitted. The new Waverley would have an extensive roof of steel girders, lead gutters and glass where McLellans were again in action, but only a low profile – so different from most city termini with soaring roofs and grand entrances.

At the same time as work was in progress at Waverley, the old North Bridge was being replaced.

The NBR 'Scott' class were versatile engines dating from 1909. Here 'Kenilworth is being turned at Haymarket in LNER years.

Agreement was reached with the Town Council whereby the NBR contributed one-third of the cost for a new structure of cast iron and steel on massive masonry piers – the central one going through the NBR's new offices. On the west side, the Waverley Bridge of 1873 had to go – much as it pained the NBR directors to agree to its removal after only twenty years of use – but a new design allowed additional lines to be accommodated there. The Waverley station project was not completed until 1903.

For goods traffic in 1901, the NBR opened Cadder marshalling yard, located between Bishopbriggs and Lenzie on the E&G route. It was an early British example of a hump shunting system. A push from a yard locomotive propelled wagons up an artificial hill from which tracks took the vehicles, now uncoupled, by gravity to the desired sidings to form a new train. Cadder was over a mile long, and had 45 tracks in two large yards – up and down – on either side of the E&G main line. These were capable of holding 2,000 wagons and vans. Two shunting engines were employed round the clock with a third on standby. It took staff only 10 to 15 minutes to handle trains of 55 wagons, 'the average number of trains marshalled in 24 hours is 250 …or 6,000 wagons'. A yardmaster

supervised 70 staff, most working with hand signals and hand-operated points. As the E&G was 'heavily occupied' by day with passenger trains, two signal boxes regulated access. Cadder's peak was at night – from 10pm to 6am when coal traffic predominated. This relieved Cowlairs and Sighthill of mineral traffic blockages that had long frustrated colliery owners and shippers.

In May 1903 royal visits to both Edinburgh and Glasgow – the first of King Edward VII's reign – entailed journeys over the E&G route. The royal train left Dalkeith station for Glasgow Queen Street on 14 May, a dull day not showing the terminus 'to picturesque advantage'. The NBR had tried to brighten the premises with 'pines, palms and flowering plants', and although the station was closed, 'a few hundreds of railway servants' had 'comfortable and advantageous lodgement on the roofs of several corridor carriages in a side lye'. After a busy day of engagements, the royal party rejoined their NBR train at Maryhill station.

In 1904 investment went into Eastfield shed built on a green field site by Cowlairs. It became the NBR's largest depot in the west supplying engines for the E&G trains and suburban services. Bigger and stronger locomotives capable of handling heavier and faster trains were a priority, and the first NBR Atlantics appeared in 1906. These majestic 4-4-2 locomotives were placed on the prime routes – to Aberdeen, to Carlisle, to Perth and on the E&G – and later superheated boilers improved their potential.

In the 1900s, passenger trains on the E&G were basic. At this stage, there were no special carriages on the route, and the journey was thought too short for restaurant cars to be deployed. In 1905, the Caledonian Railway introduced its Grampian Corridor Expresses – with magnificent 12-wheeled carriages, 'luxury travel at the ordinary fare', hauled by powerful blue locomotives on its Glasgow-Edinburgh-Aberdeen services. The NBR was soon losing business and had to respond. New coaches with side corridors

Heavier 'block' trains of corridor carriages required more powerful locomotives – and in 1906 the NBR introduced 4-4-2 Atlantics on its premier services including those on the E&G expresses. *(The Locomotive Publishing Company)*

were therefore constructed for block trains – sets of fixed formation – that at last brought the NBR some praise.

In December 1907 the decision was finally taken to work the Cowlairs incline with banking engines and tests were carried out. On 31 October 1908, rope haulage was finally given up when six 0-6-2 tank locomotives of a robust design took on the task. By August 1909 the incline rope was removed. Soon the stationery engine was scrapped, and the classic engine house at Cowlairs was converted to an electrical switch room.

With tensions increasing between Britain and the German Empire both on the high seas and in Africa, in 1912 the government formed a Railway Executive Committee consisting of the general managers of the major companies. This was to co-ordinate rail services in the event of war when the government would take over the railways, with existing managements carrying out its policies. The conflict began on 4 August 1914 and traffic on the NBR for freight and 'specials' immediately intensified with many expresses withdrawn. Territorial battalions were mobilised and there were numerous troop trains on the main lines. Railway employees enlisted in such numbers that an embargo had to be applied – otherwise the rail system could not have been run. Soon essential materials for repairs to engines and rolling stock were becoming scarce.

By December 1915, the protracted reconstruction at Queen Street was nearing completion. The West George Street frontage had been adapted to form the main entrance with parcels facilities on the west side – parcels being an important part of railway business from the earliest days. In January 1917 many NBR stations were reported as closed in order to save manpower. Fares went up 50 per cent and Glasgow-Kings Cross trains ceased to run. For the war effort, massive quantities of freight were handled – coal traffic peaked at 42.5 million tons – bringing further expansion to Cadder yard. Stock had to be

Smoke and steam characterised the interior of Queen Street station where tank engines simmered at the buffer stops. A view from 1960. *(Postcard & Covers)*

From 1908, trains from Queen Street were assisted up the Cowlairs incline by banking engines. Here a former NBR banker looks up to the task in 1960'. *(Postcard & Covers)*

augmented to support the war effort and seventeen new locomotives – mainly for freight – were built at Cowlairs works.

The NBR, now with the largest network in Scotland, was the liaison between Scottish Command and the other Scottish railway companies. The idea of

Eastfield shed, constructed for the NBR in 1904 and destroyed by fire in 1919, was rebuilt. Under the LNER, this large depot could hold 200 engines. *(R W Lynn/Hennigan Collection)*

The LNER introduced stronger 4-4-0 locomotives known as 'Improved Directors' on E&G services and these received Scott names.
(W E Boyd/Glen Collection)

'control offices' with traffic districts clustered round a 'headquarters' emerged. This system was installed first in the 'Central District' at Edinburgh where its HQ had telephones and telegraph links to signal boxes. Head codes, using lamps to help identify locomotives, were introduced. Far from being 'over by Christmas' the conflict continued for four years and the losses were devastating. A bronze war memorial in Waverley station carries 775 names to honour the memory of North British railwaymen. The war and its aftermath took a heavy toll on the railway companies and on their communities.

Post-war, there were arguments for keeping state control as the railways were so depleted, with maintenance postponed and investment minimal. There was a further reverse for the NBR when a fire at Eastfield shed in June 1919 destroyed several locomotives. While an amalgamation of the private railway companies was favoured by the government, the NBR board was totally opposed to this 'unconstitutional action'. William Whitelaw, chairman of the NBR, argued strongly against the low and unfair levels of compensation on offer. Notwithstanding, a Railways Act of 1921 resulted in thirty-seven private railway companies being merged from 1 January 1923 to form the 'Big Four'. These were the Great Western, the London & North Eastern (LNER), the London Midland & Scottish (LMS), and the Southern Railways.

In Scotland, two companies appeared – the LNER taking charge of East Coast routes by absorbing the North British and Great North of Scotland Railways, and the LMS receiving the Caledonian's West Coast main line and network, plus the Glasgow & South Western and Highland Railways. Some found 'London control' irksome, although the LNER had a decentralised system that gave Scotland a general manager and local directors. There was some satisfaction when William Whitelaw was appointed chairman of the LNER, a position he held until 1938. Otherwise, it was 'all change' with new uniforms for employees and new liveries for the locomotives and rolling stock. However, joint operation was inherited on some lines, such as the Kilsyth & Bonnybridge (opened in 1888), and continued so under the LMS and LNER.

On the E&G route, the NBR Atlantics were providing top link power and the 4-4-0 superheated Scotts (1912) were also regulars. On branches and sidings, new NBR freight 0-6-0s kept company with rebuilt veterans from the 1880s. By 1924, Nigel Gresley, Chief Mechanical Engineer of the LNER, was well aware of NBR motive power deficiencies, and a Great Central design was modified for use in

In 1928 'The Queen of Scots Pullman' began running from Glasgow Queen Street to London Kings Cross. Here LNER A3 No.2567 Sir Visto, a Glasgow built engine, climbs Cowlairs bank with the train in 1929. *(W B Yeadon)*

Scotland. These 24 'Improved Directors', class D11, were strong 4-4-0s that were able to handle heavy coaching stock; they received names from Scott novels. When new Gresley coaches in varnished teak appeared, NBR carriages were displaced to secondary lines or branches. From now on, new locomotives would come from Darlington, Doncaster or outside builders, and not from Cowlairs – its last engine was constructed in 1924, and repairs and overhauls became its staples.

The LNER had been the leading coal railway in Britain, hauling over 100 million tons a year, but its industrial heartland in North East England suffered serious depression, especially after the Wall Street crash of 1929, bringing the company 'perilously close to bankruptcy'. Nevertheless, its board was determined to maintain East Coast services and passenger numbers in the face of West Coast competition – so prestige locomotives and glamorous trains captured public imagination, offering superior levels of comfort. 'The Queen of Scots Pullman' was introduced in May 1928 when 8-car all steel Pullman carriages ran from Kings Cross via Leeds and Harrogate to Edinburgh and Glasgow. By the mid-1930s, the service was speeding up with the latest A1 and A3 Pacifics running the E&G section – its most prestigious service ever – at a supplementary fare. For many of these splendid engines and their crews, Haymarket shed was 'home'. Soon Gresley V1 and V3 tank locomotives were regulars on suburban services while the 4-4-0 'Shires' were widely used on secondary routes where 60mph was the top speed.

Freight was in sad decline – the business recession caused a severe slump in trade reflected in declining goods and parcels traffic – and there was increasing competition from road haulage. Local hauliers were exempt from regulated rail freight pricing and could offer lower charges, while passengers were wooed away by bus companies with flexible routes, better frequencies and cheaper fares. The LNER fought back – there were advertisements promoting 'road rail containers' – demountable boxes carried on flat wagons – that could even take household removals. Cheaper fares were advertised at 'off peak' times.

Other economy measures were tried – colour light signalling cut the cost of maintaining and staffing many signal boxes and there were new installations at Waverley and other stations. To save on motive power and staff, the LNER tried Sentinel steam rail cars on some rural branches, and stations were closed – Gogar and Winchburgh went in 1930. Engineering works were limited – in 1933 the flight of locks on the Union Canal near Falkirk were infilled. In 1938 there were introductions of loudspeakers at Queen Street and Waverley stations 'for directing passengers and making announcements as the occasion arises'. Such occasions certainly came with the outbreak of the Second World War on 3 September 1939.

The railways were again under government

In the post war 1950s, there were new locomotives, such as this B1 BR No.61342 on trains on the E&G from Queen Street. *(Postcard & Covers)*

A Swindon-built DMU passes Cadder yard in 1962 – with a V2 on a freight train in the background. *(D Bowman/ K Jones)*

A Class 303 'Blue Train' leaves the tunnel at Queen Street Low Level in 1961. *(Postcard & Covers)*

control with a new Executive Committee managing the companies as one unit. All signage at stations that might assist an invader was removed, and troop trains had top priority. The mass exodus of children from cities likely to be under aerial attack was organised. Over three days, trains took 178,543 evacuees to safe rural locations and Central Scotland's lines bore the brunt of this movement. Station lights

An impressive line-up of BR steam locomotives at Haymarket shed in 1954 shows (l to r) A4 No.60004 William Whitelaw, A4 No.60016 Silver King; A3 No. 60093 Coronach; A4 No.60024 Kingfisher and A3 No.60097 Humorist. *(Harry Knox Collection)*

were dimmed and switched off if air raid sirens sounded. Air raid precaution (ARP) wardens were on patrol to ensure that no lights were visible. For railway staff, there was fire watching for incendiary bombs, and training in fire fighting and rescue duties. Everyone carried a gas mask. While glass was removed from some station roofs, Queen Street and Waverley were too extensive – steam and smoke from below and city soot from above was the 'black out' there. Office windows had gummed paper strips – to prevent shattering by bomb blast. Platforms now had canteens and food trolleys for service personnel in transit.

In addition to major stations, railway yards, depots and key junctions were vulnerable. Instructions were given to limit glare from the fire doors of steam locomotives – and moonlit nights when rails shone were hated by enginemen. Edinburgh and Leith were subject to hit-and-run raids, but the worst destruction came with the Clydebank blitz of March 1941 when much of the town and its infrastructure was destroyed. As most industry in Central Scotland was rail connected, damage to the rail network and to

A deviation on the E&G was made when the Summerford viaduct was removed and a new concrete bridge opened in April 1961. *(R C Nelson)*

factory sidings was always a threat.

Railway advertisements asked 'Is Your Journey Really Necessary'? Few 'non-essential' trains ran and those that did were very congested. As months passed, people were allowed to travel to the countryside to help on farms producing food for the nation – foods being rationed to ensure 'fair shares'. With petrol also rationed and cars laid up in garages, passenger numbers rose. Prior to D-Day, the allied invasion of Europe on 6 June 1944, the railways were under great pressure moving lengthy troop trains and freights conveying equipment and munitions; many of these ran through the Central Scotland network.

This phase of intense usage concealed the true picture of Britain's railways. When VE Day came in May 1945, the railways were seriously rundown. Old engines and equally old vehicles had been kept running in response to the national emergency. The Scottish network emerged worn out but largely unscathed by the conflict.

With the Labour Party in government, 'nationalisation', or state ownership of the private railway companies, was seen as inevitable. This took place on 1 January 1948, but the hope of transformation proved a delusion as inadequate investment continued.

The problem of steam operation on the E&G was accentuated at Glasgow with the bottleneck at the two track Cowlairs tunnel. The 1 in 42 gradient required most trains to be assisted out of Queen Street with an extra engine on the tail. After the short inter-city trips on the E&G, there was much 'unremunerative mileage', involving the disposal of engines and rolling stock both at Queen Street and Waverley. Steam locomotives might stand for some three hours on shed or in a yard for every hour in productive service. But steam was the Railway Executive's choice when the decision to build new

'Standard' class locomotives was taken in 1951. With passenger engines turned out in Brunswick green (it conveniently hid dirt) and coaches in a crimson and cream livery (soon known as 'blood and custard'), British Railways tried to present a new image. E&G services typically had B1, Class 5 and occasional A1 or A3 locomotives as motive power. 1956 brought the end of third class travel – it was 'second' until 1988 when 'standard' took over. Up to the demise of steam, former NBR N15 tank engines could be seen at Queen Street continuing to bank trains up the Cowlairs Incline.

A transformation came to the E&G early in 1957 when diesel multiple units appeared. These Swindon-built sets gave a fast economical hourly service, with extra trains at peak times, between the cities. They not only reduced train movements at Queen Street station but at last the Cowlairs incline could be reliably climbed, thereby transforming time-keeping on the line. Although the sets were rather old fashioned-looking, they were a welcome initiative to improve the passenger experience. The coaches gave a choice of compartments, open saloons and buffet cars, with a guard's van behind the driver's cab. But these DMUs had weaknesses – they were hard used on E&G services, maintenance was questionable, and consequently the sets were withdrawn in the early 1970s.

A proposal to electrify the Queen Street Low Level system was published in 1955, and subsequently in August 1959, the Low Level lines closed for some months. On 7 November 1960, the service of 'Blue Trains', as the North Bank electrics were known, began. They introduced a new era in passenger comfort, speed and cleanliness. The Low Level's re-opening revealed an environment transformed - there were now two spacious platforms, well lit and tiled in pale blue. However, explosions in transformers caused train withdrawals from 19 December for 10 months with steam locomotive haulage resumed. After modifications, the 'Blue Trains' returned and soon proved their worth to the delight of passengers. In appearance, these EMUs were different – industrial designers had styled both the interiors and exteriors, the ends of each 3-coach set having 'wrap round' windscreens. For passengers, the experience of seeing the line ahead in a driver's view was another 'plus'. The 'Blue Train' system soon expanded to form a modern rail network in the city region and beyond.

In 1961 major engineering works took place on the E&G itself when the Summerford viaduct that straddled the Union Canal west of Falkirk was removed. A new alignment for the E&G to the north was set out and a concrete bridge with tall abutments constructed to take the line over Tamfourhill Road. (This is the only instance of a major work on the E&GR being removed).

In 1963 the Beeching Report, 'The Reshaping of

Winchburgh Junction had a distinctive signal box; here a BR Class 27 is on a 'top and tailed' train in May 1978. *(Bill Roberton)*

British Railways' appeared. It was an attempt to make the railways pay by concentrating on inter-city routes and long distance freight. The cuts to the rail network that followed shut secondary routes and branch lines, closed stations and lifted tracks in many parts of Central Scotland. On the E&G, intermediate stations – such as Cowlairs, Dullatur, Castlecary, Bonnybridge and Manuel – were closed. Bishopbriggs and Croy were only saved by ministerial intervention. Generally, the Scottish network escaped the worst of the cuts as strenuous arguments were made for the retention of lines on social grounds. The pruning also affected engineering works – the making of boilers and brake blocks had continued at Cowlairs, but it closed in 1968 with work transferred to BREL (British Rail Engineering Ltd) at St Rollox.

The E&G inter-city services were enhanced in May 1971 when 6-coach trains of BR Mark 2 carriages, topped and tailed by diesel-electric locomotives, Sulzer Type 2s, appeared. These ten year olds, fitted with multiple unit control, became Class 27s, while the Mark 2 coaches of all steel construction were safer and had up-to-date interiors. Once track and signalling installations were modified, the E&G speed limit was raised to 90 mph. It was now possible to reduce journey times dramatically from 55 to 43 minutes. From the termini, trains on the hour called at Falkirk High, whereas those on the half-hour did so at the latter station and Haymarket. In their heyday, these Class 27 hauled trains, gave travellers on the E&G the best service ever. However, with hard usage and indifferent maintenance, the locomotives became unreliable and punctuality declined. Passengers recall leaving Queen Street behind filthy, neglected locomotives belching fumes – only to become stuck in the Cowlairs tunnel with the lights out, and trying to breathe in the polluted darkness.

By 1974 further track and signalling modernisation on the E&G allowed speeds of 100 mph to be contemplated. Trains were soon replaced with Mark 3 rolling stock – these coaches were 'state of the art' being all steel of 'monocoque' construction, with air suspension and disc brakes. They were

Bishopbriggs station prior to 'modernisation' in the 1980s. *(C J B Sanderson)*

Looking east at Croy station with its siding and goods shed in 1954 *(C J B Sanderson)*

designed to run at 125mph. Each set was propelled by a Class 47/7 diesel-electric locomotive with a remotely controlled driver van trailer (DVT) at the other end. This was an adapted coach – and there were questions about this relatively lightweight vehicle's crash worthiness compared with a heavy locomotive. Initially, this push-pull system improved service comfort and reliability, but again there was punishing wear and tear due to intensive usage.

In 1980, the E&G main line through Falkirk High had a lengthy closure owing to works on the adjacent tunnel at Callendar Park. The brick lining on the east side was replaced with reinforced concrete sections while rock bolting was completed at the west end. During this phase, trains used the Grahamston-Polmont route. On 8 December, the reconstructed Falkirk High station, with new platform buildings and footbridge, was opened. It was a time when several stations on the E&G were 'modernised' – for example, Bishopbriggs, Lenzie and Croy. The following year inter-city services were re-introduced between Glasgow Queen Street and London Kings Cross. Running via the E&G and the East Coast Main Line; these high speed train sets (HSTs) were welcomed by passengers. The maximum speed on the E&G is now 100mph.

ScotRail was a name coined in 1983 for the rail network in Scotland when the enterprising Chris Green was managing the BR Scottish Region. He took pride in opening stations – in 1994 Camelon was the thirty-first. Lines were also targeted with passenger services being restored between Edinburgh and Bathgate in 1986.

Class 158 DMUs appeared on the E&G in September 1990, but such sets also ran to Aberdeen and Inverness – ScotRail taking a lead in the introduction of these 'Sprinters' on express services. The employment of such basic units on Scotland's long distance and scenic routes was seen as a backward step. Nevertheless, their use persisted on the E&G, where their cramped accommodation and fickle air-conditioning systems were deplored. For suburban and rural routes, they were matched by Class 156 sets.

Under BR, freight had continued to use Cadder yard, but with the decline of coal traffic and heavy industry, its activity was much reduced. The signal boxes were removed, and in 1990 the north sidings became a 'Green Link' project with tree planting. The passing loops by the main E&G line were retained while the south side was kept as permanent way sidings. From July 2006 to May 2011, Direct Rail Services (DRS) leased the site for wagon maintenance and storage. Then in 2014 Cadder became the construction depot for the EGIP electrification. A new road bridge has been built at Westerhill on its west side for the Bishopbriggs Relief Road – a timely initiative by East Dunbartonshire Council.

Privatisation was mooted in 1991 and implementation began three years later when Railtrack – still in public ownership – was created. In May 1996, Railtrack was sold off to the private sector, despite adverse outcomes being forecast for this upheaval. The break-up of the railways ran counter to their *modus operandi* from the earliest days. It took the network back to the organisational level of the canals where the infrastructure was the property of a company that allowed barges owned by others to pass on payment of a toll. On railways, the track, locomotives, rolling stock and installations had preferably been owned by the same company, and observers argued that this made sense. Many BR managers left, using their expertise to set up companies profiting by the changed 'playing field' for the railways.

The year 1992 saw celebrations to mark the 150th anniversary of the opening of the Edinburgh & Glasgow Railway – the centenary having been missed owing to the Second World War. A special excursion hauled by the former LNER A4 locomotive BR No.60009 'Union of South Africa', renamed 'William Whitelaw' for the occasion, ran from Glasgow Queen Street to Edinburgh Waverley and back. Present on that day was Lord Willie Whitelaw, a descendant of the railway chairman of LNER years. A stop was made

Polmont station with its bay platform (right) for Bo'ness trains. *(T & N Harden)*

at Falkirk High where a statue by the artist George Wylie was unveiled.

By 2001 Railtrack, now a 'spectacular failure', went into administration whereupon Network Rail, a public sector company took over. Meanwhile from 1994, rolling stock had been sold off to the private sector, as were freight operations. On the British mainland between 1996-97, passenger services were franchised with ScotRail plus sleepers, constituting one unit – initially awarded to National Express, later to First Group, and now to Abellio, minus sleeper services. The Anglo-Scottish daytime trains – East Coast, West Coast and Transpennine – are in separate franchise deals.

Since September 1999, Class 170s, known as 'Turbostars', have dominated the E&G and the routes to Aberdeen and Inverness. As passenger numbers have soared, with standing room only on some busy services, these DMU sets have been much criticised. In 2005 when the First Group held the ScotRail franchise, Eastfield shed was redeveloped for these sets, and expansion for servicing and maintenance also took place at Haymarket.

When the Forth & Clyde Canal reopened as the Millennium Link in 2001, there were consequences for the E&G route. A tunnel beneath the railway was constructed at Rough Castle to allow a new cut of the Union Canal to access the Falkirk Wheel. This electrically operated boatlift, now a major tourist attraction, replaces the former staircase of locks at Tamfourhill. In 2003 the E&G got a new station at Edinburgh Park, close to where Gogar had once stood.

Holding the purse strings is Transport Scotland, an arm of the Scottish Government. Some impressive projects have been completed including re-opening the Stirling-Alloa line in 2008, the electrified Airdrie-Bathgate route in 2010 and the reinstated Borders Railway in 2015. AbellioScotRail is currently responsible for the running of services, but it is entirely dependent on rolling stock and locomotive leasing companies (ROSCOs) for its trains.

Network Rail maintains the infrastructure throughout Britain. However, in Scotland, an alliance between Network Rail and the current service operator Abellio began in 2014, and is supported by a formal agreement. This 'joined up' approach takes the railways back to a more coherent past, and it is enabling investment and modernisation on a substantial scale of which EGIP is visible proof.

The 150th anniversary of the E&GR saw an excursion over the route with A4 No 60009 (renumbered 60024 and named 'William Whitelaw') in February 1992.

A new structure on the E&G is the bridge at Rough Castle over the cut on the Union Canal giving access to the Falkirk Wheel. *(John Peter)*

With Pinkston Power Station in view, a Swindon DMU climbs the Cowlairs Incline in June 1957. *(A E Glen)*

A varied line up of diesel power was seen at Eastfield depot in August 1971. *(TOPticl:Digital Memories)*

Eastfield was transformed for an Open Day in September 1972 with CR No.419, the Caley tank from the Scottish Railway Preservation Society, on show. *(TOPticl;Digital Memories)*

A Class 40 on 'The Queen of Scots Pullman' approaching Edinburgh Waverley from Glasgow in August 1968. *(Colour-Rail)*

A Class 47 711 on a push-pull service between Glasgow and Edinburgh passes Greenhill in June 1986. *(J B Peter)*

Class 27s were in charge of expresses on the E&G route when BR 27108 was seen leaving Edinburgh Waverley in the 1970s. *(A.Wass)*

Emerging from the Mound Tunnel, a Class101 arrives at Edinburgh Waverley in August 1971. *(TOPticl:Digital Memories)*

A ScotRail 'sprinter' near Philipstoun in July 1994 on one of the many straight and almost level sections of the E&G . *(TOPticl:Digital Memories)*

Looking south at Millerhill in July 1979 with a Class 25 marshalling a goods train; Monktonhall Colliery is on the right. *(TOPticl:Digital Memories)*

Class 47 715, named 'Haymarket', has pride of place at Haymarket Open Day in August 1985. *(J B Peter)*

Chapter 6

EGIP gathers pace

'EGIP' is the Edinburgh Glasgow Improvement Programme, a comprehensive package that sees a 'step change' in Central Scotland's railway infrastructure. In 2007, the Scottish Government announced its intention to have the Edinburgh and Glasgow and associated diversionary routes, plus lines to Stirling and Alloa, electrified. The programme of works would be delivered by Network Rail and 'alliance partners', among whom Morgan Sindall PLC and Costain have taken leading roles.

Two-thirds of the Scottish population live and work in the Central Lowlands, a region that extends from the Clyde to the Forth. It is here that EGIP's outcomes will be most beneficial for passengers. The core element is the electrification of the former Edinburgh & Glasgow Railway, Scotland's first inter-city line, 45 miles in length. The 'E&G' is Scotland's busiest and most profitable route. It is remarkably level, with easy curves and gentle gradients – apart from the 'ski slope' of 1 in 42 in the tunnel descending to Glasgow Queen Street.

However, the principal problem has been the raising of numerous bridges to accommodate the overhead electrification (OLE) and supporting structures. In December 2011, BAM Nuttall were contracted to tackle bridge works worth £27m. That company had demonstrated its proficiency in adapting over bridges when the electrified Airdrie-Bathgate Rail Link was being constructed, and. they were soon in action at 44 bridge sites in Central Scotland Major projects were the £23 million Carseview Bridge taking the B9124 over the Stirling line and the strategic Larbert Bridge in the town centre.

Routes linking into the E&G spine have also been targeted for electrification, such as Glasgow Queen Street to Cumbernauld and Greenhill Lower. Another crucial line is the alternative inter-city route through Falkirk Grahamston, and the Grangemouth branch of much significance for freight. There is also the mainline to Stirling and Dunblane, where work is ongoing, and the recently re-opened Alloa route.

The completion of the electrified Airdrie-Bathgate rail link in 2010 had some consequences at Haymarket. Only the south tunnel was capable of taking electric trains and there was no effective means of handling 'perturbed working or conflicting moves'. A project on the north tunnel saw Carillion

Transport Scotland Electrification Programme for Control Period 5

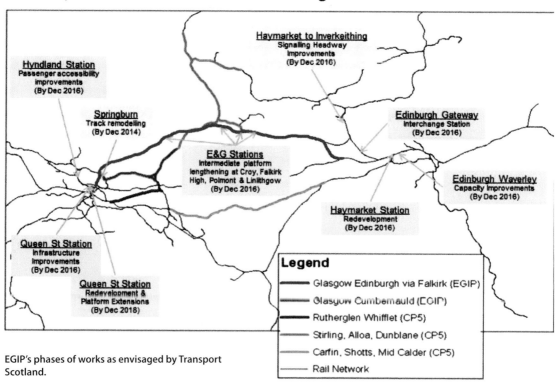

EGIP's phases of works as envisaged by Transport Scotland.

taking a preliminary step towards EGIP. When combined with track lowering and the use of a conductor bar, there was sufficient clearance in the tunnel and no slab track system was required. Commissioning took place in May 2011. Electrification was continued to Newbridge Junction where a short length of masts with catenary was placed on a stub of track close to the Almond valley viaduct.

In July 2012, Transport Scotland announced that EGIP would be phased in as a rolling programme – with some pruning, the result of a review by Jacobs aimed at reducing the costs shown in the initial proposals. There had been plans to take electrification much further – from Polmont to Dunblane, from Stirling to Alloa and from Cumbernauld to Camelon – but these would no longer be tackled at this stage. Fast flyover junctions at Greenhill and Winchburgh – the latter relating to the Almond chord – were deleted and a train depot proposal at Stirling abandoned. Two extra services per hour on the E&G were cancelled, with journey times stretched from 37 to 42 minutes. To offset the reduction in service frequency, train lengths would have to be increased to 8 coaches, with a consequent requirement for longer platforms at both termini and intermediate stations. The modernisation at Queen Street would involve closure for some months, and capacity at Edinburgh Waverley would also have to be augmented with platform extensions and re-openings.

For the revised EGIP, the cost was now put at £650m. However, this was later increased to cover a more extensive redevelopment at Glasgow Queen Street, including track remodelling estimated at £120m. With an allowance for optimum bias and contingencies, this took EGIP to a new budget of £742m.

In January 2014 a fresh business case for EGIP was published by Transport Scotland. With Network Rail managing the scheme, Costain and Morgan Sindall were given five month long 'alliancing' contracts worth £5m to define the scope, programme and target prices. The latter company had impressed at Haymarket during that station's long awaited redevelopment. To accommodate a footfall of 4 million a year, an investment of £25m was delivered on time and below budget in 2013. A new and spacious concourse – an ingenious 'bridge' construction across the lines – with lifts and escalators to all platforms, has been welcomed by passengers.

Costain and Morgan Sindall were subsequently selected to plan and execute the largest element in the EGIP programme – the actual electrification that would use 25kV 50Hz for 156km (96 track miles) from Glasgow Queen Street to Edinburgh Waverley via Falkirk High. Inevitably this phase would have to cover major clearance issues at Winchburgh tunnel,

After a heavy lift by a 1,200 tonne crane, the new concourse at Haymarket station takes shape in September 2013.

The spacious and well-lit concourse - above the tracks at Haymarket - lies behind the original station building.

southeast of Polmont, some infrastructure works at the Glasgow and Edinburgh termini, and platform extensions at Croy, Falkirk High, Polmont and Linlithgow. At a cost of £245m, completion would be due in the latter weeks of 2016. Costain, with its partners Alstom Transport and Babcock Rail, would be responsible for installing the overhead line equipment, masts and wires. This would include placing the OLE system on the notable Almond valley viaduct at Newbridge, probably using a design similar to that on the Royal Border Bridge. Morgan Sindall would be responsible for route clearances, especially on bridges, and for the platform extensions at stations.

The Cumbernauld Line goes Electric

Critical to EGIP's success was electrifying diversionary routes. Of prime importance was the one from Glasgow Queen Street through Springburn to Cumbernauld. This line feeds trains to and from Greenhill – a name of significance for Scottish railway operations since 1848 as it was here that the Caledonian Railway, a West Coast partner, met the Scottish Central Railway's line to Stirling and Perth.

The Cumbernauld electrification became part of

Constructing the new overbridge at Larbert led to prolonged road closure as the work was complex

The electrification of the Cumbernauld line from Springburn was completed in May 2014. Here a Class 334 set is seen at Gartcosh.

The siding north of Cumbernauld station serves as a 'turn back' loop.

the first phase of EGIP delivery; this also included 'infill' works in a triangle where the line north from Motherwell and Coatbridge Central meets a former Caley route near Gartsherrie. With work scheduled at evenings and weekends, 50 kms of electrified railway

– with 1,000 masts between Springburn and Cumbernauld – were delivered by May 2014. The opportunity was also grasped to upgrade the infrastructure with improvements at junctions, such as Sighthill, east of Springburn station, that became double-tracked, while Springburn Junction itself was remodelled to enhance flexibility.

At Cumbernauld, a new station was built with easier access for passengers and longer platforms – a recurring theme at EGIP stations. The line's 'makeover', costing £80m, covered civil engineering, track work, signalling and telecom installations, and it was 'energised' in January 2014. A turn back loop now lies northeast of Cumbernauld station beyond which the line continues to Greenhill.

Twin Tunnel Renewal

An unusual challenge on the Stirling route were the short twin bore tunnels that took the Scottish Central Railway, opened in 1848, under the historic Forth & Clyde Canal, and onwards to Larbert and Stirling. The old tunnels, just 40m long, suffered a rock fall in 2003. Although EGIP electrification at the site had been deferred, tunnel replacement was advisable. BAM Nuttall was appointed the contractor for the £4.5m project and in October 2014, the canal was closed temporarily. The site was on the 'doorstep' of a prime visitor attraction, the famous Falkirk Wheel, the boatlift that connects the Forth & Clyde and Union Canals for the passage of boats. Initially, diversions were set up on the canal towpath and on footbridges, the location being a popular place for cyclists, runners and walkers.

A section of the Forth & Clyde Canal was the focus for the demolition of the old tunnels and the subsequent reconstruction. With the site being on the busy line to and from Stirling, actual rail closure was restricted to the 'window' over Christmas 2014 and New Year 2015 to minimise disruption. Much work was done at night and only a time-lapse video does the renewal justice. With pontoons placed on the canal, coffer dams were inserted to seal off the waterway. Once the basin was drained, excavation was feverish to remove the masonry and expose the railway lines. Abutments were soon poured; then a giant crane lifted the concrete beams for the tunnel roof into position. Soon trains were running again and a replacement aqueduct was constructed on the tunnel top using pre-cast concrete panels. The tight time frame for the contract was honoured thereby ensuring that the Scottish Canals' Easter activities at the Falkirk Wheel in 2015 could go ahead.

Winchburgh Tunnel

Long before any proposed closure at Winchburgh took effect, that tunnel had been making headlines. There were arguments in favour of creating a direct diversionary route, known as the Almond chord,

This aerial view shows the reconstructed tunnel at Carmuirs with the Forth & Clyde Canal above. The Falkirk Wheel, a boatlift, is seen upper left. *(BAM Nuttall)*

thereby allowing trains to run with less interruption during electrification on the E&G – bearing in mind the intensity of its services. The formation of the chord, a line just 3km long, had been part of the original EGIP proposal. (The North British Winchburgh-Dalmeny branch was initially made in 1890 as a consequence of the Forth Bridge opening; its purpose being to carry traffic to and from the west, thus avoiding Edinburgh's approaches). If Winchburgh tunnel were to be closed, then some 20,000 passengers per day would have to be taken by bus between Edinburgh and Linlithgow, a situation that might last three months. Furthermore, there would be no convenient alternative for passengers between Edinburgh and intermediate stations on the E&G, such as Croy, Falkirk High, Polmont or Linlithgow. Services to and from Bridge of Allan, Stirling, Larbert, Camelon and Falkirk Grahamston would also be adversely affected by a prolonged tunnel closure.

Arguments in favour of the Almond chord had been heard in 2008 when services on the E&G were interrupted during the making of the double-lead junction at Newbridge, prior to the opening of the Airdrie-Bathgate Rail Link. By 2015, had the chord been constructed ahead of the Winchburgh tunnel works, it could have carried all the affected trains with minimal loss of journey time on the routes. Network Rail was reported to have designed a chord and begun land purchase for it *before* EGIP was 'de-scoped' in 2012. However, the Almond chord proposal was deleted – Transport Scotland's cost projections giving a total for its installation of £150m. Critics claimed that this figure bordered on fantasy.

With cofferdams inserted in the canal, there was frenetic activity to excavate and construct the new tunnel by Easter 2015. *(BAM Nuttall)*

A Class 170 DMU emerges from the new tunnel beneath the Forth & Clyde Canal aqueduct in July 2015.

ScotRail trains wait at Dalmeny in July 2015 during the diversion arising from the closure of the E&G at Winchburgh.

A team from Austria working on the ÖBB-PORR slab track in the tunnel in July 2015.

Adjusting new track in the west cutting leading to Winchburgh tunnel.

Preparing drainage at Winchburgh where there are problems from a 'loch' forming in an abandoned brickfield alongside the cutting.

1. Holes for spindles
2. ÖBB-PORR slab
3. Elastomeric layer
4. Self-compacting concrete (SCC)
5. Rail support point
6. Long rail
7. Concrete base

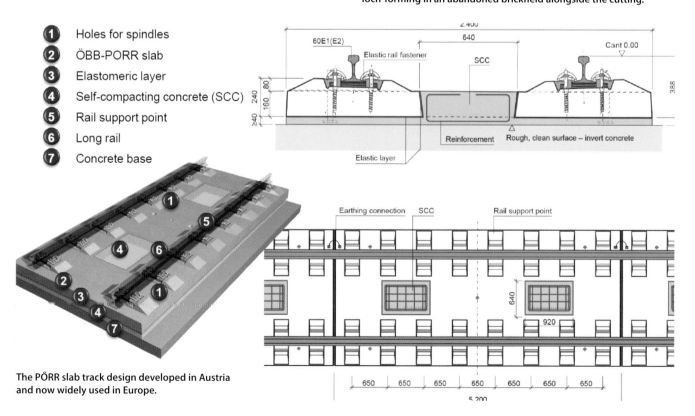

The PÖRR slab track design developed in Austria and now widely used in Europe.

(In time, will this decision be viewed as short sighted?) The chord would not only have served the new 'Edinburgh Gateway' station at Gogar, linking with the trams to Edinburgh Airport, but would also have been a permanent diversionary route for the future. There had been a developer waiting in the wings with plans for 3,500 houses at Winchburgh, and eager to see a station re-opened to tempt commuters to settle there. It was suggested that development funds could have financed a new station).

To ease the inevitable flow of trains through Dalmeny, some headway improvements were made between Haymarket and Inverkeithing with the installation of four-aspect signalling – all aimed at saving time, even if it were only seconds – when the tunnel was shut.

To railway engineers, Winchburgh tunnel was infamous. Surveys showed that there were serious clearance difficulties that would necessitate the lowering of the track bed. In addition to being very wet, the tunnel had a narrow 'six foot' (1571mm) and this would call for a track solution of high fixity. When a 3 month closure was mooted, there was much disquiet. To shut a line carrying 20,000 passengers per day for such a length of time called for re-thinking. By March 2015 Network Rail reported that closure on the E&G east of Linlithgow had been cut to just 6 weeks – from 13 June to 27 July. To meet this new schedule, tunnel work would be done day and night, the aim being to restore services as 'quickly and safely as possible' – in the hope of appeasing passengers, and preparing for the tourist traffic at the Edinburgh Festivals. The cost of the tunnel works would be £17m.

The geology contributed to Winchburgh's drainage problems. The sedimentary mudstone and shale forms a slippery 'soup' when wet, while dolerite, a hard volcanic rock, is impermeable. On the tunnel's west flank lies a loch that has formed since 1955 where abandoned clay pits alongside the line have flooded. At the north cutting, old surface streams are carried over in an aqueduct and a reverse siphon. Pumping is continuous as drainage is such a problem. The long approach cuttings, strengthened in places by masonry, are now wire mesh protected.

The most dangerous and potentially de-stabilising element was lowering the tunnel floor by 200mm – 65m^3 of rock was removed and 2,000m^3 of spoil shifted. Then concrete was poured and 825m of drains formed, with a 'super drain' inserted between the tracks to try to cure the persistent wetness once and for all. Any tight clearances in the tunnel were addressed and interior brickwork was repaired.

The decision was taken to install slab track using an Austrian system developed by ÖBB-Porr. This has been widely used on that country's railways and on other European lines where it has proved its worth.

With the up line completed, the slab track installation continues in the east cutting at Winchburgh in July 2015.

Introduced in 1992, it is especially suited to high speed lines and its 'decoupled elastically supported track slabs' can compensate for any deformations due to creeping and shrinking; these have a life of up to 50 years. For Winchburgh tunnel, 940m of slabs were prefabricated and imported from Austria. (The accompanying section shows how the voids in the slabs were filled with a self-compacting concrete).

A key advantage of the ÖBB-Porr system is its minimal space requirement for width or construction height, hence its suitability for tunnels. There are also positive outcomes for passengers with a reduction in vibration and noise emission when trains are running.

After prolonged planning, the demanding work in the dank tunnel began under floodlights. Air quality was continuously monitored with extraction fans providing ventilation. A communications system, as used in mining, connected radios inside the tunnel as a safety precaution, and as there were potential risks on account of Weils disease carried by rodents, health screening was routine. It was also recognised that continuous working causes strain, and thus shift lengths were limited, with rest days well dispersed. When the slab track was laid, Austrian engineers were present. Once the electric conductor bar was in place and testing done, over 1,000 hours of continuous working had produced a successful outcome on time and below budget. Laser detectors will now monitor any movements in the tunnel structure.

Street names – Station Road, Main Street and Oakbank Place – fixed to the tunnel walls reminded the teams that they were working beneath Winchburgh village. The site compound was sited on land away from the houses, easing the delivery of materials and machines – only vehicles for two concrete pouring sessions went through the village. A priority with all aspects of EGIP has been to keep communities informed with newsletters and 'drop in' sessions, and to negotiate with local authorities for diversionary routes and signage.

Swineburn and Polmont

Swineburn aqueduct carries a small stream across the E&G. Here machines are setting up prior to removing the masonry arch in June 2015. *(Morgan Sindall)*

The new concrete aqueduct for the Swineburn now straddles the E&G line. *(Morgan Sindall)*

Polmont station, one of the original stops on the E&GR, showing the station footbridge and the temporary structure in use when the road bridge was closed.

The new road bridge takes shape on its raised abutments while two Class 170 DMUs pass beneath in July 2015.

Utility challenges at the Polmont road bridge where a variety of essential services had to be reconnected.

With the bridge deck complete, the parapets for the new road bridge at Polmont are lowered into position in July 2015.

Bridges

When the Edinburgh & Glasgow Railway was planned, many bridges taking roads and farm tracks over the line were designed by John Miller, its distinguished engineer. Crossings 'on the level' were unacceptable. These masonry bridges in sandstone have given the E&G character, but electrification meant that extra height was essential to allow the 25kV OLE to be inserted. Accordingly, a rolling programme of adaptation, or in some instances complete reconstruction, was inevitable. A total of 60 structures were on the list. Every bridge site on the E&G was unique and called for special design solutions. Before bridgework could begin there were four years of negotiations with local authorities regarding road closures and the re-routing of bus services.

Most sites required temporary footbridges across the railway and substantial road diversions. Some closures lasted many weeks, if not months, as in Larbert, and were said to have adversely affected local trade. A task of complexity was at Polmont where the bridge at Station Road called for radical reconstruction by Morgan Sindall. Embedded in old structures were an entanglement of utilities that had to be teased out and protected prior to beams for new decks being lowered onto raised abutments. The works took nine months and cost £2.5m.

There was another challenging site at Greenhill where there were two adjoining bridges over several tracks. The bridges were demolished and reconstructed with new decks and parapets simultaneously in a project costing £2.1m, and it succeeded in opening a month early. Described as a great achievement, such accelerated works minimised the length of disruption and were welcomed by local communities. Over many nights, residents' patience near bridge sites was tested by the noise of machines and electric generators supplying floodlighting.

At Drumgrew near Cumbernauld, additional benefits have come to communities as the inadequacy of the local road system has been addressed. The old bridge lay on a section of the B8048, a link road between Cumbernauld and Kirkintilloch, much used by commuters. However, creating the new bridge involved an 8 month road closure. From a railway perspective, Drumgrew was on a hectic stretch of the E&G with frequent trains passing, and therefore much night work had to be scheduled. With a temporary footbridge across the lines – a vantage point from which the reconstruction could be watched – the old masonry bridge was closed early in August 2015.

Taking Drumgrew as an example, with the E&G lines well protected, the old masonry arch was dropped onto the tracks. This then allowed heavy equipment to excavate the abutments. Debris and spoil was taken away from the site by rail – before the

Replacing the Bo'ness Road bridge over the E&G at Whitecross in 2015 involved lifting out the old steel structure before raising the abutments.

Trains continued to run on the E&G line by day and road works were completed in August 2015 adjacent to the Bo'ness and Kinneil Railway.

line was reopened for normal services with minimal delay. Reinforced concrete base units were used for the south abutment, but rock anchors and sheet piles were inserted on the north side. Only then could concrete pouring and waterproofing begin. This was not straightforward as some of the coldest, wettest and stormiest weather of the winter ensued. Nevertheless, to meet the completion target 'all the stops were pulled out', and the new Drumgrew bridge, with its ancillary road works and roundabouts, opened on 15 April 2016.

The conclusion of bridgework on the E&G came at Niddry Castle in February 2017 when a steel replacement footbridge was craned into place – the final bridge structure to be completed after four years of such work. (Meanwhile, at Cadder, the opportunity has been taken to construct a new bridge over the E&G as part of the new Bishopbriggs Relief Road).

In accordance with ORR requirements owing to the proximity of 'live wires', over 100 bridges on EGIP routes have had their parapets raised. The same vigilance has been in evidence along line sides near stations, or on roads and pathways beside the railway where high fencing up to 1.8m has been installed. In some locations, as at Linlithgow, the existing masonry walls have been in part rebuilt and increased in

Greenhill

. A steel bridge over the Stirling line and a masonry arch over the Falkirk Grahamston route had to be removed. With a long footbridge in place, the demolitions were rapid in April 2015. *(Morgan Sindall)*

Reinforced concrete decks were installed on raised abutments where reclaimed stone was used for the masonry. *(Morgan Sindall)*

With parapets in place, the approach roads at High Bonnybridge were remade.

Above: The final parapet for the reconstructed bridge at Greenhill being positioned. The distance is from Carlisle. *(Morgan Sindall)*
Insert: Watchful eyes as the telecom links across the new bridge at Greenhill are re-installed in July 2015.

Drumgrew

The old road bridge for the B8048 at Drumgrew also carried a water main over the E&G. Work began in October 2015. *Morgan Sindall)*

With the E&G tracks protected, concrete pouring for the south abutment is seen in progress at Drumgrew. *(Morgan Sindall)*

Piling by night for the north abutment takes place at Drumgrew. *(Morgan Sindall)*

Owing to the presence of springs, a cofferdam was installed to secure the bank on the E&G's north side. *(Morgan Sindall)*

With the overbridge complete, a Class 170 heads for Glasgow on the main line in April 2016.

Construction works were mainly short possessions at night, - otherwise, trains continued to run on the E&G as seen at Drumgrew in November 2015.

Major road improvements were achieved through the EGIP bridge works - as shown in this aerial view of the work site at Drumgrew. *(Edward Z Smith)*

Park Farm

This bridge lies on a minor road east of Linlithgow. With the track protected with mats, the old structure was removed in December 2015. *(Morgan Sindall)*

Soon work had begun on the abutments and cills and concrete beams were in place. *(Morgan Sindall)*

The new Park Farm bridge with its high parapets photographed in February 2016 prior to its completion.

Philipstoun and Niddry

The old masonry bridge at Philipstoun was once alongside a station closed in 1935.

Using the tested formula, a new cast concrete structure was soon placed on the raised cills built on the old masonry abutments. (*Morgan Sindall*)

In the cutting nearby, netting was spread to reduce the risk of landslides from the slopes. The radio mast is for railway telecom purposes.

At Niddry Castle, this footbridge was the last crossing on the E&G to be tackled. This shows the old structure prior its removal on 1 January 2017. (*Morgan Sindall*)

With rapid progress, the new steel beams and parapets were installed at Niddry by February 2017 when a ScotRail Class 170 was seen on the tracks beneath.

With Queen Street High Level closed in March 2016, temporary shelters for passengers were set up.

Unusual trains were soon seen at the Low Level station, such as this Class 156 bound for Oban. *(Bruce Peter)*

Signage at the Low Level platforms alerted passengers to diverted services. *(Bruce Peter)*

height throughout to make the railway boundaries compliant with safety standards for electrified systems. Some 15km of such boundary measures have been carried out.

Queen Street and Tunnel Works

In the summer of 2016 Queen Street station became the focus of intense activity when substantial works were forecast for the Cowlairs tunnel, making the closure of this major terminus inevitable. Extra trains would have to run through the Low Level station, with questions being asked about its ability to cope with the likely influx of traffic.

'Welcome to your new train timetable' announced ScotRail/Abellio in a booklet to cover 20 March to 7 August 2016 – when Glasgow Queen Street High Level station would close for 20 weeks. Work would then proceed on the station area covering 'essential renewals, maintenance and preparatory enhancements'. These related not only to the tunnel accessing the station, but also to the platforms within its Victorian train shed. That structure of malleable iron and glass presented aesthetic and heritage issues for the project.

To ease the flow of traffic around Queen Street, longer distance trains to and from Aberdeen and Inverness were diverted to Glasgow Central High Level, while all other services that in normal circumstances would start or terminate at Queen Street High Level now ran from its Low Level platforms. Passengers had to be shepherded to Platform 8 if westbound, and to Platform 9 if eastbound. ScotRail staff were well briefed to cope with the throngs at peak times at street level, where temporary shelters were arranged – an impressive marquee was placed by North Hanover Street for Platform 8 passengers ("Is it for a celebrity wedding?" asked a passer-by), and a more modest covered walkway at Dundas Street for queues for Platform 9. It was a daunting logistical exercise leaving little room for any glitch. The diversions saw the lines around Partick station reach a new level of intensity with tight headways and the passage of non-stop trains to such unusual destinations as Alloa, Stirling and the West Highlands. The line through Airdrie and Bathgate proved an invaluable link with Edinburgh via the Low Level station.

Prior to the closure of the High Level station a diversionary route had to be developed for incoming Edinburgh via Falkirk High services among others. This led to a phase of unrelenting engineering exertion by night at Anniesland, west of the city centre, in order to create a rail connection between the Glasgow North electrics, running from Glasgow Queen Street Low Level via Partick, and the route of diesel services from Queen Street High Level via Maryhill. The latter line had been re-opened in 2005 when a mile-long spur to a new bay platform at Anniesland was formed.

The EGIP solution at Anniesland was a new junction where the west portion of the Maryhill line was double-tracked, electrified and re-signalled to prepare for an invasion of traffic that would normally terminate at Queen Street High Level. The main contractor was Morgan Sindall with Babcock supplying rail services. Much of the work was done at night testing the patience of local residents; a 56 hour 'disruptive possession' had to be arranged in November 2015 when a single lead junction was installed. In addition, 350m of new track was laid, and a link made to the bay platform at Anniesland. As two signalling centres – Edinburgh and Yoker – were involved, the commissioning of the project was not straightforward. Nevertheless, the Anniesland diversionary investment was signed off at Christmas 2015 – after almost a year of effort and at a cost of £15 million. A longterm benefit will be its usefulness as a diversionary route.

At this stage, intensive works were also carried out on the eastern part of the E&G lines. At Haymarket East Junction, three sets of points were replaced at Christmas and New Year 2015/16. This location is one of Scotland's busiest rail sections but access to Haymarket depot is restricted. The project, costing £7m was carried out by the AmeySersa/Network Rail Alliance, but encountered the deluges of Storm Frank making working conditions 'desperate'. In advance , forty-four panels of track to form the new switches and crossings were delivered on tilting wagons. Two Kirow cranes placed the panels in position while an array of machines - tampers, laser bulldozers, road-rail machines and elevating platforms - were alsoon site. Men and machines toiled on until a six-hour 'window' was left for installing the overhead line equipment (OLE) and signals to match the new situation. This investment now provides more flexibility on the approaches to and from Haymarket station.

From March 2016, the tunnel works at Queen Street became the focus of engineering services, including lighting, drainage and ventilation – round the clock

Holding the EGIP works together at Queen Street required regular meetings for contractors and engineers in the collaborative programme.

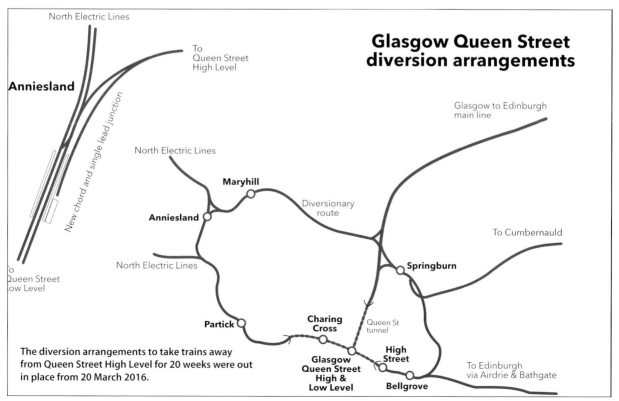

The diversion arrangements to take trains away from Queen Street High Level for 20 weeks were out in place from 20 March 2016.

A view west from Haymarket station over the E&G main line to junctions at Haymarket East and West with the ScotRail depot far right.

Although EGIP was making impressive advances, a crucial project had yet to be tackled – the internal remodelling of Queen Street High Level station where growing passenger numbers were topping 20 million. To accommodate longer trains, platforms had to be lengthened and this also required adjustment to the throat leading to the tunnel on the Cowlairs incline. This would receive new slab track and be prepared for electrification.

The tunnel already had a concrete track bed, a PACT system installed in 1974. PACT was paved concrete track that used a continuous ribbon of concrete to which the rails were fixed using Pandrol type clips. It was produced by McGregor Paving and was seen by BR as most suitable for tunnel applications. In the 1970s, several tunnels in Central Scotland were given this treatment. In the Cowlairs tunnel, the slab had shown deterioration and though various methods were tried to prolong its usefulness, after decades in a damp situation replacement was essential.

The approach to Queen Street High Level is not easy with the 918m long tunnel on a gradient of 1in 42. It took the Edinburgh & Glasgow Railway under a branch of the Forth & Clyde Canal and into the centre of the city. The fact that the tunnel was double-tracked enabled the phasing of project packages from a range of specialist contractors to proceed under Morgan Sindall's direction, one line at a time.

Before the track renewals could begin, there was substantial activity at the tunnel's north end near Cowlairs where track and points were renewed. Conveniently located was a yard at Sighthill where road-rail vehicles, equipment and materials could be located. At Queen Street, the track at the tunnel throat was redesigned to take seven-car units. This involved 2,000m³ of platform demolition and the building of 642m of platform walls. Preparatory to the station's later reconstruction, there was major excavation into the concourse beyond the buffer stops, the voids being filled with polystyrene blocks

and temporarily surfaced. New track totalling 615m was installed, plus seven switch and crossing units fabricated off site and laid on timber sleepers.

Turning to the tunnel, with the feasibility of extracting the concrete slab tested, Story Contracting were appointed for its removal plus the construction of the new slab base. A first step was to lift the rails on the old slab track on the up line, reserving the down line for trains taking waste away and bringing in materials – one in and one out each day. Old tunnel cabling had to be stripped out and drainage adapted to enter a sewer to reduce water flow. Just as at Winchburgh, lighting, ventilation and communication systems had to be set up.

Core drilling followed before concrete saws cut the old slab track into sections. Remote hydraulic breakers then produced a total of 10,000 tonnes of concrete pieces ready for removal by trains hauled by RailFreight locomotives – these took away 400 tonnes at a time. In addition, there was a train every day for the station works, with access complicated by the presence of both on-track and off-track machines and other equipment in the tunnel. Special care had to be taken at all times with the braking of machines owing to the severe tunnel gradient.

With the concrete base stripped out, the sandstone and mudstone, out of which the tunnel had been excavated, was soon exposed. To accommodate overhead electrification, the floor of the tunnel was generally reduced by 1500mm prior to the installation of the new base slab. There were ingenious solutions for the supply of concrete by road vehicles – by dropping consignments from the Cathedral Street bridge, and by the use of two 'eyes' that had once served as construction accesses when the tunnel was cut –subsequently being ventilation shafts for steam and smoke from locomotives.

The new slab track uses the same PORR system as in Winchburgh tunnel, and specialists from Rhomberg Sersa were again present for its installation. They were also responsible for laying the switches and crossover within the Cowlairs tunnel.

The initial works at Queen Street station itself not only incorporated revised track and platform layouts but also saw the raising of masts for the OLE and its wiring. Big excavations were made in the concourse area beyond the buffer stops in preparation for the radical reconstruction of the southern portion of the station. The voids were then infilled with polystyrene slabs and surfaced for pedestrian use.

Edinburgh Gateway

While Queen Street High Level was the scene of upheaval, another EGIP project was taking shape near the eastern end of the E&G. This was the Edinburgh Gateway interchange, a new station at Gogar on the route between the capital and lines to Fife and the north, and seen as a substitute for a rejected

A Kirow crane, carrying the new crossover, emerges from the tunnel at the Forth & Clyde Canal east of Anniesland in September 2015. *(Morgan Sindall)*

Construction at night - trackwork being lifted into place by another Kirow crane in September 2015. *(Morgan Sindall)*

Anniesland

The partially completed track on the new spur running south towards Anniesland station.

Job done – the new line in action with a Class 170 approaching Anniesland in April 2016.

Left: An aerial view over Anniesland station showing the track arrangement with the spur (left) and the North Bank route veering right. (Morgan Sindall)

Above: A line side view of a diverted service approaching Anniesland station on the new line from the north in April 2016.

The removal of the old concrete slab track in the tunnel began with cutting and drilling in April 2016.

Chunks of concrete from the up line await removal by trains using the adjacent down line at night. *(Morgan Sindall)*

Queen Street tunnel was another wet one – especially when the tunnel floor was being lowered. *(Morgan Sindall)*

Edinburgh Airport Rail Link. This elaborate tram train interchange with its escalators and lifts aimed to connect passengers travelling by train with tram services to and from Edinburgh Airport. The contractors were Balfour Beatty, the cost £41m and the station opened in December 2016.

Platform Extensions

EGIP will have new Class 385 trains from Hitachi – these are AT200 electric-multiple units with coaches of 23m length. All stations, where such trains on the E&G services call, has had their platforms extended to accommodate sets potentially of 8 coaches. Croy was tackled successfully at an early stage, but such work was not always straightforward. For example, at Falkirk High, substantial mining remediation had to be carried out, as there had been a colliery close to the station. Linlithgow and Polmont each presented their own challenges, the first having a high elevation relative to the town, and the latter being partially in a cutting.

Millerhill   A New Depot for New Trains

With the advent of the Class 385 units from Hitachi, a new electric train depot is essential for vehicles seen as an East of Scotland fleet. A logical choice was to use part of the extensive Network Rail's Millerhill railway yard. Morgan Sindall set to work on the 7 ha site where the former Edinburgh & Hawick Railway of 1848, a branch of the North British Railway, once ran. A portion of a Millerhill station survives at its south end.

In 1962, the 'state of the art' Millerhill yard was opened beside the modern Monktonhall colliery. The yard's main purpose was to service coal trains from the then active Lothian coalfield and to re-establish a freight route using the arduous Waverley Route to Carlisle. However, the plan for this 'superyard' did not last long as the latter line was closed in 1969 as part of the Beeching cuts. Millerhill continued to handle local coal traffic – but Bilston Glen colliery shut in 1989 and was followed by Monktonhall in 1997.

Since then, Millerhill has been providing lay over, maintenance and servicing for general freight trains run by DBCargo, and this depot will continue to handle freight. Adjacent is Network Rail's own facility for track engineering and maintenance, with a yard supplying much of the Scottish network with ballast.

In 2012 Midlothian Council gave planning permission for a new depot building at Millerhill plus a train wash, 190m long, and other facilities. It is here that Class 385 trains will be stabled, cleaned, serviced and maintained each day. The yard itself has four centre platforms or aprons with seven roads; each road being capable of holding 12 carriages – 84 in total. All the platforms are 305m long. There are two bi-directional lines feeding these roads, but only one in and out of the depot itself towards Newcraighall – raising the question about its adequacy at such a strategic point.

In addition to carriage washing, the yard arrangements include CET (controlled emission toilet) removal facilities. Special attention has been given to drainage with a two-layer system installed – in a deep trench, there is a 375mm carrier pipe and on top,

Queen Street

Road-rail vehicles (RRVs) were invaluable but had to be well secured in view of the severe gradient in the tunnel.

It was down to bedrock at the Cowlairs mouth of the tunnel where the central drain was also having attention in June 2016.

Work taking place on the tandem crossover in the Queen Street tunnel

Looking towards Queen Street station from the tandem crossover in June 2016. (John Cassidy)

The generous dimensions of the Queen Street tunnel portal at the north mouth are revealed here.

The ŐBB-PORR slab track was positioned on top of a concrete base with an elastomeric layer in between. *(Morgan Sindall)*

The ŐBB-PORR team that was proud to be laying the system in the tunnel at Queen Street in May 2016.

The self-compacting concrete being poured into prepared openings in the slab track.

A mobile concrete tanker could also move on rail in the tunnel.

Concrete being fed from a road tanker at street level above a former 'eye' in the tunnel on a Glasgow street in June 2016.

With platforms dismantled, Queen Street station became the focus of track lifting and bulldozing in April 2016.

The excavation of the concourse in June 2016 reveals old buffer stops (right). *(John Yellowlees)*

The Cathedral Street bridge was a means by which supplies could be fed to station work sites - here concrete is being poured. *(Bruce Peter)*

The void in the excavated concourse was filled with polystyrene blocks. *(Bruce Peter)*

An overview shows where RailFreight locomotives, working at night, took out spoil and brought in supplies. *(Bruce Peter)*

A view from the tunnel mouth shows the great arch of the station roof and a support being constructed for the new signal gantry.

Here comes the tamper – having gained access via the new slab track on the up line.

Track laying in progress at the station throat in May 2016 .
(John Cassidy)

A Kirow crane lifts a section of the signal gantry into place in May 2016.

The signal gantry soon stretched across the station throat; the longer platforms with the new track layout were being completed on 31 May 2016.

there is a 225mm filter pipe. This has a sealed membrane to catch all the run off water from the road surfaces and to minimise any possible contamination.

Staff facilities are of a high order. There is comfortable accommodation for train crews, plus engineering, cleaning and clerical staff. It is expected that some 60 people will be employed, servicing and re-stocking the trains overnight. There will be ample staff car parking. Nor has the traditional shunter's bothy been forgotten – there is one. Thus begins a new chapter in Millerhill's long association with railways.

Eastfield Depot

Eastfield depot will have a new role for electric units. The existing train shed has been enlarged to accommodate longer sets and the platforms for servicing have been lengthened. The whole depot has been electrified and four new roads and platforms have been constructed. At the east end the head shunt has been extended into the adjacent cutting. These preparations have been made in order to stable trains conveniently for Queen Street services.

With ticket gates lined up and OLE supports at the platform ends, the concourse prepares for normal service on 30 July 2016.

Electrification

For EGIP and its engineers and contractors, there have been delays and reverses along the way. In addition to the attention to the railway's infrastructure – the bridges, platform extensions and the tunnel works, the core of EGIP has been the preparation for electrification. This began with ground investigations at line sides – to ascertain

Electrification at Queen Street

Using an elevating platform on a road/rail vehicle, the wires for electrification are raised at Queen Street on 30 July 2016.

The RRV manoeuvres in the station where OLE installations were kept to a minimum to preserve the character of the Victorian train shed.

The wagon with the drums of cable at the mouth of the tunnel.

The Queen Street tunnel with the conductor bars in place and a 'drip shield' installed to disperse percolation through the sedimentary rocks above.

Edinburgh Gateway

This shows the tram-train interchange at the new station intended to serve Edinburgh Airport. *(John Peter)*

The ticket hall at Edinburgh Gateway in May 2017. *(John Peter)*

Edinburgh Gateway station viewed from the west. *(John Peter)*

The escalator link from the railway station to the tram stop.

A ScotRail service from Fife calls at the east platform at Edinburgh Gateway where passenger numbers have been disappointing.

Platform Extensions

Work in progress on platform extensions at Linlithgow station in November 2016.

Preparations at Croy station with platform supports under construction.

The lengthened Platform 12 at Waverley station in December 2017 with a Class 380 unit.

The former taxi rank in Waverley station where extensions to Platforms 5 and 6 will be made

This aerial view shows the long platforms for train servicing at the new ScotRail Depot at Millerhill; the yard for Network Rail and other freight use is top right. *(Whitehouse Studios)*

Millerhill

With the old freight yard cleared, concrete sleepers and a stock of ballast appeared by March 2017.

Foundations being prepared for laying rail in June 2017.

With RRV assistance, the wires go up in August 2017.

Finishing touches being applied to the platforms when the concrete panels were sealed in August 2017.

With a 'forest of steel' for the overhead wiring completed, a Class 385 train was in sight as a gantry was checked in December 2017.

At Eastfield depot, an extension was under construction at the ScotRail diesel shed for the electric trains in October 2017. *(Morgan Sindall)*

A ScotRail DMU at the remodelled and electrified Eastfield shed in March 2018.

whether rock, peat, soil or colliery waste was present. In all, circa 3,000 foundations of varying types – depending on the ground conditions – were constructed to provide a secure base for each of the masts. Only then could masts be lifted into position, followed by the installation of cantilevers and booms to support the OLE wiring configuration.

On the E&G itself, all this had to be done on an active and busy railway with trains at 15 minute intervals on weekdays – only Sundays brought lower frequencies. Therefore, EGIP has essentially been a 'night shift' project, and much constrained by the length of possessions between the last train at night and the first in the morning.

The materials and equipment for the OLE have come from stockpiles at Cadder yard, near Lenzie; this was selected at an early stage as the nerve centre for EGIP. Versatile road-rail machines with platforms for installing the wiring and an impressive wiring train have been based there. Wherever work has been ongoing, expert teams have taken the OLE forward through EGIP territory – in fair or foul weather – putting up thousands of metres of aerial earth wire, catenary and contact cabling.

Supplying the Electricity

The electrification programme has required a new feeder station at Greenhill that has three 25Kv feed supplies provided by Scottish Power Energy Networks (SPEN) from Bishopbriggs. In addition, new trackside cabinets have been set up at Gartshore, Polmont and Newbridge, all supporting the extensive electrification project. The whole system is controlled from Cathcart.

A view west over Eastfield depot in April 2018 showing the extensive provision for servicing electric units. The Edinburgh & Glasgow route is to the right.

Electrification in practice - with the portals and wiring in place, a Siemens Class 380 EMU crosses the Avon viaduct west of Linlithgow in April 2018. *(John Peter)*

The Shotts Line

The western portion of the Shotts line between Holytown and Midcalder Junction was also scheduled for electrification. This former Caledonian line branches off the West Coast main line at Uddingston Junction, but was electrified as far as Holytown to serve trains on the Argyle Line of the Strathclyde network. In 2016 BAM Nuttall was selected to raise or reconstruct bridges on the Shotts line with Carillion Powerlines Ltd providing the masts and wiring installations. The investment of £160m in this 74km of railway would provide the fourth electrified route linking Scotland's largest two cities. It would also be expected to bring many benefits to passengers in

Jimmy McKay with a supply of steel components at Cadder yard in June 2016.

Fixing plates for mast supports on the Broxburn viaduct in September 2015.

Preparing for a night's work on the OLE – loading masts at Cadder yard in October 2015.

North Lanarkshire and West Lothian in places where mineral wealth had long since been exhausted and where the daily 'commute' to work was now typical. Improved rail transport with increased capacity and better reliability would be welcomed.

In December 2017 came an announcement of further work on the Shotts line when Carillion Powerlines received a contract of £11.6m for upgrading nine stations This would cover platform reconstructions to accommodate the Class 385 trains, lighting renewals, CCTV and information systems. There had been questions about Breich station's

The interior of the 'inflatable store' at Cadder yard, with drums of cable (left) and insulators (right).

minimal usage but it was reprieved; both it and Livingston South are to be rebuilt.

Queen Street Station

EGIP also covers the reconstruction of historic Queen Street station. In 1842 it began as a terminus for the Edinburgh & Glasgow Railway. The High Level station, where the E&G services and long distance trains arrive and depart, is outdated and inadequate. The station site is a sensitive one, being close to George Square that is Glasgow's civic 'heart'.

In recent years, Waverley station, the eastern terminus of the E&G, has received substantial refurbishment and enhancement of its facilities. These include better track layouts, new and lengthened platforms, and 'state of the art' signalling. For passengers, escalators – especially at the Waverley Steps – and lifts, plus new glazing on the vast roof, have transformed the station. The advent of longer trains also has consequences at Waverley where platform 12 on the west side has been lengthened both for ScotRail Class 385s and for Virgin East Coast new Azuma trains. Additional platforms 5 and 6 are being constructed on former car and taxi parking.

Now it is Queen Street's turn to be transformed. Obtaining powers under the Transport and Works Scotland (TAWS) Act for the reconstruction was a protracted process and only in August 2017, the initial stages towards improving the congested terminus could begin. Preparations involved the

Key elements in the wiring train are the elevating platforms. *(L McEwan)*

Electrification - out on the line

A mobile crane lifts a gantry into position in May 2017. *(L McEwan)*

Drums of cable are conveyed and tensioned by this special vehicle.

A wiring train undergoes servicing at Greenhill while insulating cable is being drawn out in January 2017.

After the noise of excavations and piling, to see a wiring train in action was a relief to communities. *(L McEwan)*

A Class 170 DMU on an Edinburgh service heads for Linlithgow where a £650,000 investment raised the historic line's sidewalls with masonry to match, as the overlay shows.

closure of the George Square entrance and the opening of a ScotRail ticket office in a former pub in Dundas Street. Bus stops and taxi ranks were relocated with restrictions put on walking routes through the station.

The removal of Consort House, an office property from the 1970s, together with an extension of the Millennium Hotel, will allow a major expansion of the station. A glass atrium will form its new frontage and bring its presence onto West George Street. This will significantly increase the concourse area, improving accessibility and passenger amenities. For the first time, it will also show the handsome Victorian roof of the train shed to advantage. The redevelopment also includes further platform extensions for longer trains, a new ticket office and staff accommodation. The plans have been described as 'absolutely necessary' and an enhancement of the cityscape.

New Trains for a New Era
The Class 385 trains from Hitachi are part of their AT (aluminium trains) series.

The cab-end and inter-vehicle gangways rather spoil their looks, but 'facilitate the best use of passenger space' and provide flexibility to suit loadings. As end-to-end journey times are seen as crucial, the sets are capable of 100mph running. With 7 coaches in a set, seating capacity is expected to be at least equivalent to a 6-car Class 170 DMUs at

present on the line. The new trains have to meet a minimum of 15 seconds for door opening, and have short dwell times in stations. Abellio ScotRail has bought 234 vehicles from Hitachi, comprising 46 three car EMUs and 24 four car units. These purchases will give flexibility as the coaches can be configured in a variety of formations. To cover the E&G services, 21 trains will be required and Hitachi will be responsible for their maintenance with facilities at Craigentinny for this purpose.

The first four car sets from Japan appeared in the summer of 2016, with the remainder being built at Hitachi's Newton Aycliffe factory in County Durham. A press viewing of a train took place at Glasgow's Shields Road depot in December 2016 and was followed by driver training on the Gourock-Wemyss Bay route.

The subsequent introduction did not go smoothly as there were issues with the OLE equipment having to meet a new EN TSI – European Technical Standard for Interoperability. This relates to fixed installations, their electrical safety and earthing, always challenging for engineers when faced with Britain's restrictive loading gauge. There were also questions about the distance of OLE wiring from platform edges and of pantographs – from tall men with golf umbrellas to passengers with helium balloons. Such concerns had cost implications and it appeared that the TSI regime was being made more demanding here.

New 385 EMUs for ScotRail emerge from the Hitachi factory at Newton Aycliffe in October 2017. The cabs have the curved windscreens that caused the optical distortion of signals, delaying the introduction of the new trains.

The first electric service for passengers took place on the Edinburgh & Glasgow route on 10 December 2017. Here Siemens Class 380 114 is seen at Falkirk High on the first run that day.

Class 356 EMUs from Northern Rail came to the rescue when 10 trains were hired for ScotRail's use in April 2018. They appeared in a livery carrying the ScotRail logo.

The removal of 1970s buildings in West George Street will allow a radical improvement at Queen Street station.

An artist's impression of the new façade of Queen Street station seen from the Dundas Street-West George Street corner.

Before entering service, the plan was for the new units to log 2,000 miles of fault free running. Drivers from DB Schenker were carrying out this work. Then in February 2018 came warnings about the curved windscreens causing reflections from signals at night – resulting in questions about the applicable light. The problem had become apparent on runs between Glasgow Central and Paisley Gilmour Street, a route where an abundance of signals was encountered. Earlier there had been comments about the small size of the windscreens – reported to give greater impact resistance – that had been used. Whether this was a problem or otherwise, by April Hitachi announced that new windscreens would be fitted to the Class 385s. Before any trains would enter service, rigorous testing - with ScotRail, the regulatory authorities, and unions - would follow.

Conclusion

It is just over 125 years since the Edinburgh & Glasgow Railway opened its Glasgow station in grand style at Queen Street. That early railway brought about a transformation in economy and society for much of Central Scotland. EGIP has also been complex and wide-ranging; it has taxed its engineering teams and the many communities that have faced disruption along its line sides.

However, this major investment in electrification is long overdue. On completion, EGIP will usher in a new era for the railways of Central Scotland, giving not only speed, but also resilience and reliability to venerable routes. For instance, there will be a 20% reduction in journey times between Edinburgh and

Queen Street station's interior will be enhanced by a large, well-lit concourse with longer platforms. The fumes and noise from DMU motors, such as this Class 170, will cease.

Glasgow while offering passengers 30% more capacity. The new ScotRail trains are not only faster and quieter, but are also estimated to provide 7,500 extra seats per day on the very busy E&G services. In addition, the electric sets are more environmentally friendly than any that have hitherto run on the route. With trains that are faster, quieter, cleaner and greener, what's not to like?

EGIP Key Facts

138 single track kilometres of new electrification between Glasgow Queen Street and Newbridge Junction

2936 mast foundations

2370 overhead structures

60 overline bridges or structures reconstructed to allow for electrification

70 sets of parapets increased to 1.8m for public protection

11 station platforms lengthened to accommodate 8 car train sets

3 redeveloped stations – Cumbernauld, Haymarket and Queen Street

A new station at Edinburgh Gateway

A new depot for electric trains at Millerhill and modifications at Eastfield depot

On the Shotts Line, 19 bridges were re-decked; there were 4 demolitions, 1 new build and 9 parapet sets were increased in height. The station at Livingston South has been completely rebuilt.

At Stirling, with its heritage station, the electrification process will challenge engineers.

At Alloa, masts were in place as a prelude to electrification in April 2018. *(Ian Lothian)*

Acknowledgements

EGIP, the Edinburgh & Glasgow Improvement Programme, has been a project with multiple facets, and therefore the assistance of many people and organisations has been essential to make this book possible.

First must come Morgan Sindall PLC for their welcome sponsorship that has enabled the investigation of archives and the recording of the stages whereby the railways of Central Scotland have been transformed by electrification. The author wishes to thank Mark Conway, Nigel Fullam and Richard Wild for their help in arranging site visits, and for the co-operation of Alex Blair, Melanie Workman, Kenny Forbes, Stephan Jackson and many others in making these successful.

There has been extensive research relating to the Edinburgh & Glasgow Railway and its successor, the North British Railway, in the National Records of Scotland. Staff have given both advice and help when investigating documents and plans.

Thanks also go to Andrew Boyd for reading the typescript and commenting thereon, and to members of the North British Study Group for their assistance. The author has welcomed support from Abellio ScotRail, while John Yellowlees, ScotRail's Honorary Ambassador, has taken an interest in the project throughout. Roger Querns of Network Rail and his staff have also given much help.

Hamish Stevenson is thanked for lending his extensive collection of photographs relating to the 'E&G', while Bill Lynn has contributed station images and Harry Knox a selection on Haymarket Shed. Bill Roberton has assisted with line side images. An insight is gained into the Edinburgh & Glasgow Railway's character through the drawings of early carriages by Allan Rodgers and of locomotives by Euan Cameron, both of whom are thanked for their unique contributions. Richard Kirkman has redrawn maps of relevance to EGIP. Both BAM Nuttall Ltd and Macrete Ireland have provided photographs, especially relating to the Carmuirs tunnel.

The aerial views taken by Tony Gorzkowski of Whitehouse Studios and by Edward Z. Smith greatly enhance the record kept of recent works on site. As the EGIP projects were on an active railway, most of the programme was carried out at night, and consequently the night photography by John Cassidy and Laurie McEwan is much appreciated.

From the Royal Archives at Windsor Castle excerpts from Queen Victoria's Journal have been copied and are reproduced here with the gracious permission of Her Majesty Queen Elizabeth. Staff at the National Records of Scotland and the National Library of Scotland, especially at the Map Library, are also thanked for their assistance and for allowing the reproduction of images.

In comprehending the civil engineering of the early railways, J C Bourne's 'Drawings of the London & Birmingham Railway' (1839) has been invaluable. These sketches shed light on the construction techniques subsequently used on the contracts for the Edinburgh & Glasgow Railway. It would become a 'spine' round which the early Scottish main line network grew.

The National Railway Museum, through the Science & Society Picture Library, the Special Collections at the Library of the University of Glasgow, the J F McEwan Collection at East Dunbartonshire Archives, Glasgow City Archives and Glasgow Museums and Art Galleries, have kindly allowed the use of several images. Some Colour-Rail photographs are reproduced with permission. Staff members at Glasgow's Mitchell Library, Edinburgh Public Library and Airdrie Library have also assisted research. James Burnett, Geoff Corner, Ewan Crawford, Bob Gardiner, John McGregor, Robin Nelson, Stuart Sellar, David Shirres, Andrew Stephen, Michael Stewart, Peter Stubbs and Jim Summers are also thanked for providing information or photographs. The North British Railway Study Group Journal has been a commendable source of information and images, some of which originated in now historic issues of 'Railway Magazine' and other publications.

Professor Bruce Peter has shared material, arising from his researches relating to British Rail, and has helped with the selection of images. To explore the Edinburgh & Glasgow line, John Peter offered transport on many occasions and has prepared the extensive selection of images for this book. Photographs without credits have been taken by the author and are her copyright.

Every effort has been made to trace the copyright holders of images and apologies are offered to any who have been overlooked or found untraceable.

LE TOURNEAU
EARTHMOVERS

ERIC C. ORLEMANN

MBI Publishing Company

First published in 2001 by MBI Publishing Company, Galtier Plaza, Suite 200, 380 Jackson Street, St. Paul, MN 55101-3885 USA

MBI Publishing Company books are also available at discounts in bulk quantity for industrial or sales-promotional use. For details write to Special Sales Manager at Motorbooks International Wholesalers & Distributors, MBI Publishing Company, Galtier Plaza, Suite 200, 380 Jackson Street, St. Paul, MN 55101-3885 USA

Library of Congress Cataloging-in-Publication Data Available

ISBN 0-7603-0840-3

On the front cover: The LeTourneau L-1800 is the second largest diesel-electric drive, front-end loader currently in production today, right behind its bigger brother, the L-2350. This L-1800 working just north of Gillette, Wyoming, in October 1995, is equipped with a 45-cubic yard combination bucket for loading both coal and overburden material. *ECO*

On the frontispiece: The SL-40 Electric-Tractor was the largest of the diesel-electric drive loaders built by R. G. LeTourneau Inc., and it incorporated rack-and-pinion systems. This SL–40 is pictured working in Birmingham, Alabama, in January 1966.

On the title page: Working in a western Wyoming coal mine in October 1998, this L-1400 is loading a 170-ton capacity Euclid hauler, equipped with a high-volume coal body. The L-1400 is equipped with a special 30-cubic yard rock bucket, and is powered by an 1,800 gross horsepower Cummins diesel engine. *ECO*

On the back cover: *Top:* The improved version of the LT-360 was powered by no less than eight 635 gross horsepower, Detroit Diesel 16V-71, 16-cylinder engines. This gave it a monstrous 5,080 horsepower.

Bottom: The LeTourneau Gorilla V makes its way across the Atlantic. Its being transported on the back of a gigantic semi-submersible transport ship, heading out to its first working contract in the North Sea. As of 2001, the Super Gorilla class of jack-up rigs are the largest self-elevating drilling platforms in service around the world.

Edited by Kris Palmer
Designed by Two Poppie's Design
Printed in China

CONTENTS

ACKNOWLEDGMENTS

It's been an ambition of mine for some time now to present the LeTourneau story in words and pictures. Since 1994, I have had the great fortune of working with LeTourneau, Inc., photographing mining and logging equipment throughout North America. I've captured these machines at work in about every type of weather condition imaginable. Seeing a picture of an L-1800 front-end loader is one thing. But to actually be on a working unit in the field is another thing entirely. It's a tough job, but somebody has to do it.

As you can imagine, a book project of this size and scope would have been impossible without the help and cooperation of LeTourneau, Inc. Many individuals have gone to great lengths to unearth information and find answers to seemingly endless questions. When viewed individually, all these pieces of information don't add up to much. Put them between the pages of a book, however, and the collected and distilled information makes up a fascinating and thorough historical document.

For gladly offering their time and expertise in this endeavor, I would like to express my sincerest gratitude and thanks to Martha Glasgow, Bridget Carpenter, Dale Hardy, Bill Rodgers, Paul Kelsey, Mark Barr, and Gary Palmer. I would also like to thank Henry S. Witlow, of LeTourneau University, for allowing me to research the vast historical archives concerning R. G. LeTourneau held in safe keeping at the university.

Keith Haddock, Philip G. Gowenlock, Ron Ketron, and Charles Apacki (deceased) deserve special recognition for their numerous articles, books, and research efforts concerning the preservation of LeTourneau history and machines. Without the dedication of these four individuals, much of the company's history would have remained buried and eventually been lost forever.

A special thanks to Ed Akin of California for allowing me unlimited access to his vast collection of LeTourneau equipment.

Last, I would like to pay tribute to the many LeTourneau staff photographers and employees who have chronicled the company's events and machines through the decades. Although there were quite a few people who took photographs of the various activities of the firm since the early 1930s, a few artists have accounted for the vast majority of all images taken. They are George Sommer, Dave Flint, Bob McCarty, Ralph Fairchild, Maurice Jensen, Wayne Furgeson, Bob Bird, Charlie Walls, Jerry Hall, George Hollis, Lenny Mobbs, and Brad Campbell.

—Eric C. Orlemann
Decatur, Illinois, 2001

Many individuals are so closely connected to their inventions that one cannot mention the product without discussing the person who invented it. Thomas Edison developed the light bulb. The Wright brothers built the first airplane. And Henry Ford pioneered the assembly-line production of the automobile. The list goes on and on. These individuals stand out in the annals of modern industrial history. Inventors, tinkers, industrialists, they go by many names. They put a human face on the raw material that has become an innovative product. It's that human face that we can all identify with on a personal level. And like these other industries, modern earthmoving has its own revolutionary inventor. That person is none other than Robert Gilmour LeTourneau, the dean of high-speed, mobile earthmoving equipment.

Better known as R. G., LeTourneau was born on November 30, 1888, the fourth of seven children, in Richford, Vermont. The son of a successful building contractor, R. G. was a restless and somewhat rebellious youth during his early years. He and his father, Caleb, never saw eye to eye on many matters. His dad would always have a ready list of chores for R. G. to perform. From chopping wood, to hauling water, young LeTourneau always felt that he was being singled out from the rest of his brothers for the heavy work as some sort of punishment for his perceived behavioral misdeeds. On one occasion, at the age of 12, he was shoveling snow and got the idea of building a V-shaped plow with curved sides. He figured by hitching it to the back of a heifer, it would save him several hours of backbreaking work shoveling it by hand. The plow worked well enough until the heifer kicked it and LeTourneau practically into the next county. (This incident underlay R. G.'s decision never to power a piece of earthmoving equipment with an animal.) His crude V-snowplow was the first invention of his life. It would not be the last.

R. G.'s mother thought of him as a restless, inquisitive, ambitious, and determined youth. His brothers, on the other hand, saw him as restless, destructive, willful, stubborn, and fanatically determined to amount to nothing. His father read R. G. countless Bible passages describing the inevitable fate of rebellious boys like himself. When the maligned son dropped out of school at 14 to work at a foundry in Portland, Oregon, his family thought his fate was sealed. While employed at the iron foundry, R. G. studied mechanics via an international correspondence school course. Though he never finished the program, he learned the finer

points of steel—knowledge he would soon put to further use. At the age of 16, in 1905, LeTourneau became a devout Christian. From this point on, he would dedicate his life to doing the Lord's work as he saw it.

After his stay in Portland, LeTourneau moved to San Francisco, where he learned the welding trade, along with the basics of electricity. In 1909, he moved to Stockton, California, were he worked in numerous manual trades, especially those pertaining to earthmoving and lumbering. In 1917, he eloped with Evelyn Peterson, whose brothers, Ray, Howard, and Buster, would play important roles in R. G. LeTourneau's evolution as the premier builder of earthmoving equipment in the United States and around the world.

R. G. suffered through a host of personal and business misfortunes early in his life. He suffered a broken neck in a racing car accident, which—although it did not paralyze him—left him unable to fully straighten his head. He almost died in the flu epidemic of 1918. In fact, the doctors gave him little chance of survival. In 1937, a head-on car collision that killed five people left him almost dead with a broken arm and both legs broken and shoved up through his hips. But his stubbornness and his faith in God saw him through. In business dealings, he made millions, he spent millions, but not for personal gain. Never one to surround himself with the trappings of wealth, he spent much of his money on Christian philanthropic activities, as well as for research and design in his business. He lived in modest houses and drove everyday automobiles. He loved to design and build machines. And he loved serving God. That was R. G. LeTourneau in a nutshell.

R. G.'s legacy continues to this day. His fantastic engineering designs, such as the innovative electric-wheel motor, and the massive offshore jack-up marine rigs, are all still in production today. His philosophy of ever larger earthmoving equipment is embodied in the latest front-end loader design from LeTourneau, Inc.—the monstrous L-2350. Along with his ideas for earthmoving machinery, the technical institute that he and his wife, Evelyn, founded in 1946 is alive and well in 2001, though it's had some name changes. It was founded as LeTourneau Technical Institute of Texas, and was renamed LeTourneau College in 1961. Since 1989, the school has been called LeTourneau University, which better reflects its standing as an accredited nondenominational Christian school offering two- and four-year-degree programs.

R. G. LeTourneau poses next to one of his diesel-electric-drive creations in 1957. Note the product line designation on the side of the machine, based on the phonetic spelling of R. G.'s name. The "An AR-GEE Design" slogan was used only for a short time.

R. G. LeTourneau made one of his last public speeches on April 12, 1967—the G. Edwin Burks Lecture at the Earthmoving Industry Conference, Central Illinois Section, Peoria, Illinois (sponsored by the Society of Automotive Engineers). Titled "Progress in Earthmoving," the speech gave R. G. a chance to reflect on his years in the earthmoving field, and to speculate on where new technologies would take the industry. Yet once he got behind the mic, R. G. quickly strayed from the written version of the speech conference attendees received. We have no written record of what he actually said, but that was the essence of R. G. LeTourneau. He never followed a script in life. He made it up as he went along. R. G. attributed all of his success to God, and never looked back on any of the failures, which he believed were just teaching tools to get us to our ultimate goals in life, whatever they may be.

Contained within these pages is a sampling of many of R. G. LeTourneau's greatest achievements. Included with these are the machines built by Marathon LeTourneau, and LeTourneau, Inc., the companies that were the direct heirs to R. G. LeTourneau, Inc. What is not covered are the earthmoving products that were sold under the LeTourneau-Westinghouse name after R. G. LeTourneau sold them to Westinghouse Air Brake Company in 1953.

A single book of this size could not properly cover all of R. G. LeTourneau's vast range of mechanical designs and inventions. Thus, the main emphasis of this book is the earthmoving machinery carrying the LeTourneau name. It also covers many of his one-off and military-type designs, plus logging and offshore platforms. LeTourneau had many other ingenious inventions beyond earthmoving, such as the Tournapass, the LeTourneau steel and pre-formed concrete houses, and so on, that are beyond the scope of this book. Most of the great LeTourneau earthmoving creations have been mentioned, but a few have been left out to make room for others. I believe that what is contained within these pages represents R. G. LeTourneau's most interesting and important contributions to the earthmoving industry.

Most of the images contained within these pages were the work of LeTourneau staff photographers and employees who have worked with the company in its various forms over the decades. Those that were from other sources are identified as such. Though every attempt has been taken to showcase the best color images produced over the years, a few of the color photos taken in the 1950s have lost their proper coloring due to the unstable chemical makeup of the transparency film being made at the time. They have been included here because of their historical significance, and in many cases they represent the only known surviving color images of that particular piece of equipment.

There was a time in the 1930s and 1940s when the name LeTourneau carried almost as much weight as Caterpillar, the earthmoving giant. Although the industry has changed considerably over the years, the company that a restless man from Vermont built with ideas and determination is alive and well in Longview, Texas, serving the earthmoving industry as LeTourneau, Inc.

Many people thought R. G. LeTourneau was a true innovative genius. Others thought he was simply crazy because of his far-out designs and religious zeal. But one thing is for sure: R. G. LeTourneau was the first, and foremost, larger-than-life character in the earthmoving industry. And he was also the last.

R. G. LeTourneau introduced his 6-cubic-yard Highboy semi-drag scraper in 1929. It featured a spring-activated tailgate, and a cable and sheave control arrangement operated by a Power Control Unit (PCU) mounted on the towing tractor. This restored Highboy scraper, carrying serial number 35, is from the introductory year and is attached to a 1928 Caterpillar Sixty tractor. Both are owned by Ed Akin of California ECO.

CHAPTER 1

The San Joaquin Valley was California's heart and soul in the early 1900s. Its rich and fertile soil and rolling fields were an agricultural oasis of plenty for those with the know-how and equipment to best utilize it. This area of California had given rise to the earliest Best and Holt steam traction engines and harvesters. It is here where the first tracked tractor was born. And it would also be the starting place for a famous earthmoving equipment inventor by the name of Robert Gilmour LeTourneau.

LeTourneau had first come to Stockton, California, in 1909. As a young man, he worked many odd jobs until landing at the Superior Garage in 1910. Here he learned automobile mechanics and would eventually wind up owning half of the business. During World War I, he worked at the Mare Island Navy Yard in California as a maintenance assistant. After the war, he returned to the Superior Garage in 1918 only to find out that his partner had bankrupted the company. To help pay his part of the debt to the creditors, LeTourneau took a job in 1919 fixing a rundown Holt 75 tractor at the Whitehall Ranch. After the repairs were finished, the owner requested that LeTourneau take the tractor and a scraper down to a 40-acre section of his property and level it for irrigation purposes. If the tractor was still running after a week, the owner would pay him his repair bill in full, plus one dollar for every hour worked. LeTourneau accepted the offer. After making some repairs to the owner's scraper, LeTourneau commenced work on the land. The one week became two, then a month. LeTourneau was no longer an automobile mechanic, but a land leveler.

In January 1920, LeTourneau sold his Saxon automobile and used part of the proceeds to buy an old 1915 Holt tractor. Then he rented from a friend named Ira Guy an old Schmeiser "Landleveler" tractor-pulled scraper. Ira Guy let R. G. LeTourneau rent the scraper and allowed him to pay for it by doing repair jobs for him. LeTourneau took his tractor and scraper outfit to an area in the San Joaquin Valley known as the Islands. There he put his outfit to work on the Elsolio Ranch. Operating the tractor and scraper required two men. One would drive the tractor, while the second would ride on the back of the scraper and work the air controls of the cutting blade. The latter job, however, was no plum. Riding on a bone-jarring scraper, blinded by the tractor's dust all day was the sort of job a worker did reluctantly, and for as few hours as possible. And that was the problem. LeTourneau wanted to work his outfit longer in the hopes of earning more

money to pay off his debts. The scraper operator did not like the idea of staying on past his shift, which he seldom did. LeTourneau thought that there had to be a better way.

While riding on the old Holt one day, LeTourneau's mind wondered back to his days at the Mare Island Navy Yard, and the work he used to do with electric motors. As he thought about it some more, he remembered a place where a lot of old Navy generators and motors were being sold off as war surplus at junk prices. Then it hit him: If he could adapt a generator to his tractor, it would be able to power electric motors on the scraper. They would control the scraper's functions, and he would control the motors from his tractor. The end result? No need for a second operator.

Within two weeks of his original idea, working mostly at night, LeTourneau had modified the rented scraper by welding electric motors and rack-and-pinion gears on it, which moved the blade up and down. He also welded a generator to the Holt's frame that powered the motors on the scraper. He put the outfit back into the field, and to his astonishment, it worked! In fact, it worked even better than he had envisioned it would.

LeTourneau put his one-man outfit to work, day and night. After he was through with the Elsolio Ranch job, he moved on to other land-leveling contracts. After taking on a job laying 4,000 feet of cement pipe, he returned the rented scraper, with the electric motors still attached, to Ira Guy, since he would not be needing it during the pipe-laying contract.

In May 1921, LeTourneau bought his first house at 122 Moss Avenue in Stockton. It was a small house on an acre of land, with a single barn. Soon the barn would become his machine shop, and the acre of land his open-air factory and assembly yard. This would be R. G. LeTourneau's first official business address.

After losing a major earthmoving contract in the fall of 1921, LeTourneau made ends meet by pulling out stumps with his old Holt 75 during the winter months. As the spring of 1922 approached, LeTourneau had found that his welding and repair business was on the upswing—so much so, that he needed to hire additional help. One of these people was his brother-in-law, Ray Peterson. Ray would also have his younger brother, Howard, help out after school.

A large land-leveling contract that LeTourneau had previously bid on at Bellota finally came through for him. But there was one problem: he had no scraper. He quickly went back to Ira Guy's place to rent his Schmeiser with his electric motors. But to his dismay, Guy told him that he had already rented it to one of LeTourneau's competitors. Worse, the electric motors were still attached to it. Guy told LeTourneau that there simply wasn't another scraper to be had in the area. Guy suggested that instead of LeTourneau taking his electric system off of Guy's scraper, that he instead install the generator setup that was on LeTourneau's tractor, on his. Though LeTourneau was not happy about the whole situation, a paying job was a paying job. This would be LeTourneau's first sale of a piece of earthmoving apparatus.

Once he was finished with this job, LeTourneau still had a land-leveling contract to get started on, and no scraper to do it. After surveying his shop yard, LeTourneau realized that he had the scraper he needed all along, in the bits and pieces of scrap iron and steel scattered around his establishment. With the help of his brother-in-law, Ray, LeTourneau drew up a set of crude plans in the dirt of the driveway. All the project needed now was LeTourneau's welding talents and his trusty oxy-acetylene torch. Within a few weeks, they had a scraper of their own.

R. G.'s first scraper was based on what the industry referred to as a full-drag scraper. As LeTourneau put it in his autobiography, *Mover of Men and Mountains*, this scraper design "was a sort of mongrel drag scraper, part Fresno, part conventional scraper, part scoop. It had so many belts and pulleys that [he] had to go through a check list, like a pilot before take-off, to know which button to press."

With his Holt tractor again rigged up with a generator, LeTourneau could now fulfill his earthmoving contracts. And like the outfit before it, this new design needed only one operator. But this time, he owned the entire rig.

Shortly after putting his new scraper to work, LeTourneau started on a new design that resembled a semi-drag scraper. Referred to as the "Gondola," it was fabricated by brazed welding, the first piece of earthmoving equipment ever to use this type of assembly technique. Before this, all earthmoving implements were of riveted steel plate. With two 10-horsepower electric motors to control the raising and lowering of the scraper's front bucket edge, and an electric winch to raise the rear of the bucket to dump it, the 6-cubic-yard Gondola was another success story for LeTourneau. After completing the Gondola in July 1922, LeTourneau put it right to work on land-clearing contracts that lasted the rest of the year and extended into the early winter months of 1923. In the spring of 1923, LeTourneau had earned enough extra money during the winter to buy a brand-new Holt 75, Model T-8 tractor.

This Full-Drag Scraper was the first such piece of earthmoving equipment built by R. G. LeTourneau from the ground up in 1922. Designed with the help of his brother-in-law, Ray Peterson, it featured electric motors controlling the functions of the scraper, which were powered by a separate generator mounted on a Holt tractor.

R. G. LeTourneau's 12-cubic-yard Mountain Mover from early 1923 was the third complete scraper unit design to be completed. It featured scraper-mounted electric-motor controls and was of a telescoping-bucket design. The Mountain Mover is the oldest surviving scraper unit built by R. G. LeTourneau, and is currently on permanent display at the LeTourneau University in Longview, Texas.

With a bigger tractor, LeTourneau was able to address some of the design weaknesses in the Gondola by building a bigger scraper, which he called the "Mountain Mover." The Mountain Mover was a 12-cubic-yard machine utilizing an auxiliary bucket that nested in the leading unit. As the scraper filled itself, earth would push the telescopic bucket rearward, which would double the capacity of the scraper. Each bucket section measured 12 feet wide and 4 feet long. The LeTourneau Mountain Mover and the new Holt 75 tractor proved a compatible match, and helped put a few extra dollars into LeTourneau's business—which he needed because completing the Mountain Mover had taken all of his money. But lack of funds never seemed to be an obstacle to R. G. One way or another, he would find a way to build his designs. To make the Mountain Mover, he had melted down the bronze curtain rods in his house because he couldn't afford any more tobin bronze welding rods. R. G.'s resourcefulness would be a hallmark trait that served him well as the years went by.

LeTourneau's fourth scraper design was an ambitious concept referred to as the Electric Self-Propelled Scraper. Built in late 1923, it was a five-bucket telescoping scraper design, with four big steel wheels, each powered by its own secondhand electric car motor. One electric motor steered the front wheels, and two more electric motors powered the telescoping buckets. A Navy surplus generator was welded into the front of the machine, which was powered by a Locomobile auto engine removed from a wrecked car chassis. With a 12-cubic-yard capacity and a top working speed of 1 mile per hour, it was a very productive, if slow, machine. It was the earthmoving industry's first self-propelled scraper, electric or otherwise. This self-propelled scraper worked from late 1923 to mid-1925 on an assortment of land-leveling contracts, including levee work along the San Joaquin River, west of Tracy, California, and near Patterson, south of Modesto. In the spring of 1925, LeTourneau converted the self-propelled scraper into a tractor-pulled unit by removing the electric-powered

The 12-cubic-yard Electric Self-Propelled Scraper, built in 1923, was the earthmoving industry's first such machine that could load and unload itself under its own power. Each wheel contained its own electric motor. The five telescoping bucket scraper unit was controlled by two electric motors, while the steering was managed by one. All were powered by a generator driven by a Locomobile auto engine mounted in the front of the unit.

wheels and replacing them with a set of nonpowered crawler track assemblies. The combination worked out surprisingly well.

After the successful conversion work on the self-propelled prototype, LeTourneau built a new, four-bucket telescoping, crawler-mounted scraper that attached to the front of a Holt 75 tractor. By the end of 1925, he had constructed two more units, but these were designed to be pulled, not pushed, like the early one-off model. All of these land-levelers were known as Tracked Telescopic Scrapers. Initially, LeTourneau's tracked scrapers, along with the rest of his creations, were hurt rather than helped in the marketplace by their unique and innovative designs. Contractors were unwilling to take a chance on some newfangled invention, even though it seemed to work.

But the more R. G. LeTourneau worked his machines, the more earthmoving contracts came his way. No one could move dirt faster than R. G. He was now considered more an earthmoving contractor than a land-leveler for hire, capable of bidding on some of the larger highway contract jobs. In the spring of 1926, LeTourneau received his first major contracting job, building a highway through Crow Canyon and across the Dublin Mountains, between Oakland and Stockton. Other big contracting jobs were to follow. Some were very financially successful for R. G. LeTourneau's company. With others he barely got away with the shirt on his back. But through all of them, R. G. kept working his scrapers, and building new earthmoving tools like no one had ever seen before. When machine tools were not available to build his new creations, he would design his own. From advanced welding techniques to building his own machine tools, LeTourneau could do it all, and then some.

LeTourneau had a busy year in 1926, both as a contractor and as a builder of new pieces of earthmoving equipment. R. G. was able to add Caterpillar Sixty tractors to his machine roster, which were far superior to the old tiller-wheeled Holt 75 units. He built an implement called a Rooter, which we now call a ripper, designed to rip hard soil and rock without the need for explosives and extra powered loading shovels. He built his own bulldozer blade and mounted it on one of his tractors. Operated by an electric power cable control unit, this bulldozer blade was the first of its kind. Like his earlier scrapers, these items were used for his own job contracts initially. But soon other contractors would be knocking on LeTourneau's door to buy his innovative and timesaving earthmoving equipment designs.

In 1928, LeTourneau built his first 15-ton-capacity, gravity-dump hopper wagons, which rode on massive steel wheels. In the fall of that same year, R. G. built his first cable-controlled scraper unit and cable power control unit, which would simply become known as the PCU. This 6-cubic-yard scraper design differed in many ways from LeTourneau's earlier creations. Gone were the electric motors that controlled the actions of the scraper. In their place were a series of steel cables and levers, controlled by an engine-driven, tractor-mounted two-drum winch, the PCU. Built from an old Hudson automobile differential and the steering clutches from a Caterpillar tractor, it proved very efficient, as well as reliable, in operation. LeTourneau also eliminated the crawler tracks: now his scrapers would run on steel fabricated wheels. The combination proved so successful that R. G. went into limited production of the setup for use on his Oroville, California, highway contract.

More LeTourneau equipment designs would come to fruition in 1929. In the first part of the year, LeTourneau's master mechanic, Jack Salvador, built the company's first "Sheepsfoot Roller" tractor-pulled compactor. By midyear, R. G. LeTourneau had designed an extra-heavy-duty steel, 12-cubic-yard rock wagon referred to as a "Chariot" because of its resemblance to the Roman horse-pulled device. These cable-controlled dumping rock wagons were built to withstand the tough working conditions created by power shovel loading. Further improvements were made to the scraper designs as well. A new 6-cubic-yard semi-drag scraper called a "Highboy" was introduced, featuring a spring-activated tailgate. With all of the new equipment designs and job contracts, R. G. finally decided to incorporate his business. On November 19, 1929, R. G. LeTourneau Grading Machinery officially became R. G. LeTourneau, Inc.

Even with the Great Depression at hand, 1930 would prove just as busy as the previous years. LeTourneau produced an improved semi-drag scraper called a "Lowboy," which differed from the Highboy mainly in the design of its tailgate. The Lowboy featured a cable-operated arrangement, suspended from a

roller-mounted carrier. The capacity was 7 cubic yards, which was the same as later editions of the Highboy. In all, LeTourneau fabricated 29 Highboy and 43 Lowboy scrapers.

As business increased, both in equipment building and earthmoving, it became necessary to expand operations with a second plant by late 1930. Located in northeast Stockton, at the corner of Roosevelt and School, LeTourneau built a second manufacturing facility entirely of welded steel structures and iron sheeting, the first of its kind in the world. An old streetcar was brought in to serve as the main drafting room.

Starting in January 1931, R. G. mobilized his equipment for the largest earthmoving contract he had ever been awarded—building the Boulder Highway. This road-reconstruction and extension project was crucial to the completion of the Boulder Dam, now known as Hoover Dam. Though R. G. LeTourneau was able to complete his part of the job on time, it was almost a financial disaster for his company. But with the hiring of a bookkeeper, and a few well-timed earthmoving contracts, company creditors allowed it to continue business. In 1932, after the completion of a Carmel, California, highway project, R. G. LeTourneau decided to liquidate the contracting part of his business altogether and devote all of his time and factory output to designing and building earthmoving equipment.

R. G. LeTourneau, Inc. offered seven basic products in 1932 for the heavy earthmoving contractor: the 7-cubic-yard Lowboy scraper; a 12-cubic-yard chariot-type dump cart; bulldozing blade attachments for large Caterpillar and Allis-Chalmers tractors; a rear tractor-mounted cowdozer designed for the Caterpillar Sixty; a cable-controlled rooter; sheepsfoot rollers in units of one, two, three, or four roller combinations; and power control units in single-drum configuration for bulldozers, rooters, and dump wagons, and a double-drum type for the Lowboy scraper.

In mid-1932, LeTourneau replaced the Lowboy scraper model with an improved unit called the Model A "Carryall." This model would be the first of a series of Carryall scrapers that would establish R. G. LeTourneau, Inc., as the premier earthmoving equipment builder in the world. The Model A utilized a rear endgate, which, when pulled forward through the scraper bowl by cables, would eject the material out the front end. The Model A rode on four steel wheels and was initially rated at 7.5 cubic yards.

In 1932, R. G. LeTourneau was trying to get the attention of some contractors by mounting pneumatic rubber tires on one of his Carryall scrapers. He often did this in transporting units during delivery. Once at a job site, the tires were removed and replaced with the original steel units. LeTourneau felt that a rubber-tired scraper would be far superior to a steel-shoed one, if only he could convince someone to try it. In August, a contractor by the name of Nick Basich, of Basich Brothers Construction Company, was working on a job in Imperial Valley, California. LeTourneau talked Basich into trying out his rubber-tired scraper free of charge. If he didn't like it, all he had to do was drop it off

at his company's main offices, and LeTourneau would send a truck to pick it up. As it turned out, the Model A Carryall—shod with the largest truck tires LeTourneau could lay his hands on—was more than three times as fast as the steel-wheeled units. Basich was so impressed that he bought a set of tires for the unit that had steel wheels, and ordered an additional rubber-tired unit to go along with the one R. G. had sent out to the job site. Thus was born the industry's first rubber-tired scraper.

In late 1932, an improved Model B Carryall was introduced. The Model B was the first LeTourneau scraper design to feature an apron, a cable-operated device that helped retain larger heaped loads in the scraper's bowl. The Model B came standard with steel wheels, but pneumatic tires were optional. At 12 cubic yards, it was the company's largest scraper yet.

Business kept on growing for LeTourneau. In 1933, he was granted patents on two types of dozing blades, referred to as the "Bulldozer" and "Angledozer." Built for a variety of large tractor models, they were chiefly targeted at the Caterpillar Tractor Company's range of crawler machines. The relationship between LeTourneau and Caterpillar would broaden even further in 1934, when R. G. LeTourneau introduced the Model J Carryall. The Model J was designed specifically to match the drawbar pull of Caterpillar's latest tractor offerings, the RD6 and RD7. The Model J was rated at 6 cubic yards for the RD6, and 7.3 for the RD7. It was the company's first scraper design to be fitted with a rear-mounted push block for tractor assistance with loading. Shortly

Though R. G. LeTourneau did not necessarily invent the bulldozing blade, he was granted patents on two types of blades referred to as the "Bulldozer" and the "Angledozer" in 1933. R. G. LeTourneau had been manufacturing bulldozing blades for Allis-Chalmers and Caterpillar tractors since 1932. The Caterpillar RD6, shown in 1937, is equipped with a LeTourneau B6T Bulldozer with rear-mounted cable PCU.

The R. G. LeTourneau Buggy was introduced in 1934. Available in two capacity sizes of 24 and 30 cubic yards, the Buggy could be equipped with either 8 or 16 tires, depending on its intended use. When not being used as a dumper, the slide-out dump box could be removed and the trailer could be utilized as a 20-ton-capacity flatbed equipment hauler

The Model J Carryalls, introduced in 1934, were very popular scraper units and were available in three standard sizes: 6-, 8-, and 12-cubic-yard capacity. This tandem Model J12 Carryall configuration in 1935 was made possible by a four-drum PCU mounted on the rear of the crawler tractor, which allowed the operator to control the loading and unloading functions of two scrapers.

after releasing the Model J Carryall, LeTourneau introduced an even larger 12-cubic-yard Model Y Series for use with Caterpillar's big RD8 tractor. Both the Model J and Y were equipped with pneumatic rubber tires as standard equipment.

One more invention of note during 1934 was the pneumatic rubber-tired LeTourneau Buggy. With two models, rated at 25 and 30 cubic yards, the Buggy was a two-axle design, supported by eight balloonlike tires in standard form, with 16 as an option. In operation, the upper portion of the Buggy would slide backward via cable over the stationary floor body, pushing the load rearward and discharging it out the rear end of the unit. But tire problems would plague the Buggy. It was dropped not long after it was introduced, with only 39 units built.

In late 1934, LeTourneau reached a series of agreements with the Caterpillar Tractor Company, under which Caterpillar would represent R. G. LeTourneau, Inc. equipment in all of its domestic dealerships, as well as some of its foreign affiliates. Excluded from this deal were military contracts, which R. G. LeTourneau would handle personally. This was a winning arrangement for both

companies. Since Caterpillar really only built bare crawler tractors at the time, offering LeTourneau earthmoving attachments allowed it to provide its customers with one-stop shopping for all of their earthmoving equipment needs. For its part, LeTourneau got something he had only dreamt about—representation in an established dealer and service network. At the time, it was truly a match made in heaven.

As business increased, the logistics of shipping equipment built at two different LeTourneau plants in Stockton started to weigh heavy on the bottom line. To get closer to the eastern markets, LeTourneau decided to build a new facility in Peoria, Illinois, located close to Caterpillar's main assembly plants. The company purchased a 23-acre lot in northeast Peoria, right next to the Illinois River, in early 1935. By March of that year, groundbreaking commenced on the Peoria site. While the main plant was being built, a temporary outside assembly area was set up so equipment building could start immediately. On April 15, 1935, the first piece of equipment to be fabricated in Peoria, a Model J-12 Carryall, was completed. By December, the facilities

The Carryall was regarded as the finest towed scraper of its time. In 1940, R. G. LeTourneau introduced the Model LP, which was one of the most popular units ever produced in the 15-cubic-yard-heaped class. The company sold thousands worldwide, especially to the armed services. This single-bucket Model LP is shown working in 1942 on a highway project located in Illinois, and is being pulled by a Caterpillar D8.

LeTourneau Carryall scrapers played an important role in various branches of the military during World War II. From building roads and runways, to clearing beaches, R. G. LeTourneau scrapers facilitated operations against the Axis powers. This restored 4-cubic-yard-heaped, single-bucket Carryall Model D and 1945 Caterpillar D4 tractor are both authentic military-issue equipment and are part of the collection of Ed Akin of California. ECO

were finished and ready to commence full production. To oversee the Peoria operations, R. G. appointed his brother-in-law, Howard Peterson, as plant superintendent. (Howard left LeTourneau in 1936, and established the Peterson Tractor Company in San Francisco, which became one of Caterpillar's premier dealerships in the Bay Area.)

With the LeTourneau-Caterpillar alliance came a change of color. In 1936, the rusty red LeTourneau color was replaced with Caterpillar Hi-Way Yellow. New models were also introduced, which included a 35-cubic-yard LeTourneau Cradeldump, a 4.7-cubic-yard Model R-5 Drag Scraper, and three sizes of two-wheeled, tractor-towed utility cranes. Bulldozer and Angledozer blades and PCU controls were produced for Caterpillar tractor models ranging from the RD4 all the way up to the RD8. Push-block attachments were also built for mounting on the RD6, RD7, and RD8.

But the real stars in the LeTourneau product lines were the tractor-drawn Carryalls. The Carryall scraper line consisted of two general types—single bucket and double bucket. Carryall scrapers that had a "U" letter in their nomenclature were double-bucket designs; all others were either single-bucket or drag scrapers.

The first double-bucket Carryall was the 24-cubic-yard Model U-18, first introduced in 1936.

From 1936 to 1940, quite a few Carryall models were introduced, in capacities ranging from 4 to 30 cubic yards in heaped capacity. In July 1938, the company changed all of the model range designations. New single-bucket scraper model lines were the Model E (formerly YR-15), the F (YR-13), the K (YR-12), the L (JR-8), the M (JR-6), the G (G-6), and the Z (Z4). Double-bucket designs included the Model AU (U-20), the BU (U-12), the CU (U-9), and the DU (U-6). Some of the more popular Carryall scrapers introduced in 1940 were the Models LP, LU, and LS.

In the late 1930s and throughout the 1940s, the Carryall was the dominant scraper choice in the industry. Most of these models were designed to be drawn by crawler tractors. But R. G. LeTourneau always felt that his Carryall had much more potential. He felt that the crawler tractor was the weak link in his vision of the future of high-production earthmoving. At first, the crawler tractor was the only suitable power source capable of handling his designs. But that would soon change in 1938, when R. G. would again rewrite the book on earthmoving with his legendary Tournapull high-speed tractor.

The Super C was the most popular C Tournapull model offering. Equipped with a standard 15-cubic-yard-heaped Model LP Carryall, it was a favorite among contractors, as well as the armed services during World War II. This Super C is part of the Ed Akin collection of LeTourneau equipment. ECO

CHAPTER 2

For R. G. LeTourneau, Inc., the late 1930s through the 1940s was a time of great growth, both in product offerings and production output. The company's scraper lines and tractor attachments were selling in ever increasing numbers. With the war in Europe and the Pacific, military procurement of the company's equipment offerings demanded stepped-up production, which required greater manufacturing capacity. New plant locations followed in Toccoa, Georgia, in 1939; Rydalmere, Australia, in 1941; Vicksburg, Mississippi, in 1942; and Longview, Texas, and Stockton-on-Tees, England, in 1946. All of these plants were top producers for the company, except the facilities in England. Because of various production and labor problems, that location never really ever achieved full manufacturing status. To cut the company's losses as quickly as possible, LeTourneau closed the plant by the end of 1947.

In 1946, R. G. and his wife, Evelyn, founded the LeTourneau Technical Institute of Texas, which would become the breeding ground for many of the firm's future design engineers. The Technical Institute's educational focus was to provide for the teaching and training of skilled mechanics, design and technical engineers, and production specialists. Located in Longview, Texas, on the grounds of the old Harmon Hospital facilities, it would give students, many of whom were returning military servicemen, hands-on experience designing, building, and testing all forms of industrial equipment. The institute was officially dedicated on February 25, 1946, with the first classes starting on March 27.

But with the growth of LeTourneau's business came a downside. Caterpillar was starting to see LeTourneau not as an ally, but as a competitor. Both companies wanted to cover certain segments of the market. In February 1944, R. G. LeTourneau officially announced the end of the alliance of the two earthmoving powerhouses. By May 1944, Caterpillar declared that they were going to start production of bulldozers, PCUs, pull-scrapers, and rooters of their own design. The sense of competition between Caterpillar and LeTourneau went back at least to 1938, when LeTourneau introduced its historic, rubber-tired Tournapull scraper.

The Tournapull

In mid-1937, R. G. LeTourneau started the design work on a high-speed, self-propelled tractor/scraper. Consisting of a single-axle tractor connected to a Carryall scraper, it would be the industry's first such machine to ride on rubber tires all around. The rubber tires would give the unit far more speed and maneuverability than crawler tractor–towed scrapers then currently in wide use. The only things holding R. G. LeTourneau back until this time were suitable tires and a transmission. The tire problem was addressed in late 1937, when Firestone molded a specially requested set of tires to R. G. LeTourneau's exact specifications. Then a six-speed transmission, designed by LeTourneau and Ray Peterson, which contained the final drive, friction steering, and acted as part of the tractor's main frame, was built as a single unit. This was connected to a big V-8 Caterpillar D17000 Series diesel engine, which produced a respectable 160 gross horsepower. With the major drivetrain components in place, fabrication of the first prototype "Tournapull" could begin.

In March 1938, company employees slid open the doors of the Peoria assembly plant and drove the first self-propelled, rubber-tired scraper—the Model A Tournapull—into the factory yard for the very first time. With its big Cat diesel engine protruding from the tractor's front, and a rather boxy-looking experimental Z25 Carryall scraper in tow, the A Tournapull was far from a thing of beauty. But it was the first step in an earthmoving revolution. It wouldn't take long for others in the industry to perceive that the Tournapull was the wave of the future in high-production earthmoving.

After several months of field-testing the first prototype A Tournapull, R. G. LeTourneau released a small number of improved machines equipped with the Series TU Carryall scrapers. Referred to as A1 Tournapulls, the first unit was built in July 1938 and shipped from the Peoria plant the following month. Only a handful of Tournapulls were built with the TU Carryall scraper before it was replaced by the HU Series in September 1938. These units still utilized the A1 Tournapull tractors, and all were destined for work on the Hansen Dam project near San Fernando, California.

No sooner had the last A1 Tournapulls equipped with the HU Carryalls been shipped, when a further-improved A2 Tournapull was introduced. This model featured many improvements to its inner workings to increase overall reliability in the field, which was far from stellar. The A2 Tournapulls were also combined with a new RU Carryall. Though having the same 30-cubic-yard heaped capacity as the HU Carryall, it was a far more robust and reliable design. The first of the A2/RU machines started shipping in December 1938.

The Model A Tournapull was the earthmoving industry's first rubber-tired, self-propelled scraper design. Key features were its big 160-horsepower Caterpillar D17000 diesel engine, a LeTourneau six-speed transmission, and a prototype 25-cubic-yard Model Z25 Carryall scraper. The first Tournapull was unveiled in March 1938, and is pictured here in May of that year equipped with a four-drum PCU and a second towed Model U-20 Carryall. This combination was for testing purposes only around the Peoria plant grounds and was never intended for serious production. The prototype A Tournapull tractor was eventually utilized on the LeTourneau Cane Harvester in December 1938, and was referred to as the Tournapush.

Sales for the A2 Tournapull in 1939 were slow. Though contractors were impressed with the Tournapull's production capabilities, there were still many mechanical gremlins that had to be exorcised from the design. Most of these involved the transmission, the source for most of the model's failures in the field.

To help increase the loading speed of the A2 Tournapull, in April 1939 one unit was equipped with specially made prototype Firestone tires. These balloon tires, which were completely smooth, were far taller and wider than previous designs. Designers hoped the new tires would raise the top speed of the unit from around 17 miles per hour, to about 25 miles per hour. They did. By early December 1939, the production version of these 30x40 Series tires—along with heavier-duty and wider rim assemblies—were ready for installation on the latest Tournapull—the A3.

Outside, the A3 Tournapull looked much like its previous siblings, except for the tire and wheel package. But the model also featured further mechanical improvements designed to further alleviate reliability concerns. This unit was originally equipped with the RU Carryall scraper, but in late December

1939, a much larger unit, identified as an NU Carryall, rolled off the temporary assembly line at the new Toccoa, Georgia, plant. Rated at 42 cubic yards heaped, it was the largest scraper of its day. This unit was originally attached to a special A3 Tournapull equipped with a rear-mounted power control unit (PCU). This special A3/NU unit was tested in earthmoving duties around the Toccoa plant, working on housing developments intended for workers at the factory. For some reason, the rear-mounted PCU never became standard fare on the A3. All other A3 units were equipped with front-mounted PCUs.

In April 1941, R. G. LeTourneau took the wraps off another version of the company's largest tractor/scraper offering, known as the A5 Tournapull. The A5 Tournapull departed from previous A Model designs in that it was powered by two Cummins Diesel HBIS600 engines, mounted side by side. Together, these powerplants gave the A5 Tournapull 400 gross horsepower. Each engine had its own transmission and final drive assemblies, connected by hydraulic couplings. The A5 was originally paired up with the NU Carryall. This proved unsatisfactory because the A5 had a wider wheel track than the NU scraper.

These two Tournapulls from February 1940 show the size comparisons of the company's two largest models at the time, the A3 and the B3. The A3, which was first introduced in December 1939, was equipped with a Caterpillar D17000 diesel and a 42-cubic-yard-heaped NU Carryall. The B3, first released in July 1939, was powered by a GM Detroit Diesel and pulled an 18-cubic-yard-heaped SU Carryall. Only three B3 units are listed as being produced.

The Model A5 Tournapull was the company's first twin-engined tractor unit. Designed by R. G. LeTourneau with the aid of one of his brothers-in-law, Buster Peterson, the A5 was powered by two Cummins HBIS600 diesels. The engines were mounted side by side and were rated at 400 gross horsepower combined. Introduced in April 1941 and equipped with a Model NU Carryall, it is shown here in January 1942 attached to a massive prototype Model OU Carryall, rated at 60 cubic yards heaped.

To address this problem, an even larger scraper unit was designed and built, known as the OU Carryall. This scraper unit was first mated to the A5 Tournapull in January 1942. Rated at 60 cubic yards, it was the largest scraper ever built by the company up to that time. But the pairing of the A5 and the OU was only a temporary match. The company had a much more refined model in the works known as the A6 Tournapull. Another twin-engine design, it would be ready to roll in March 1942, equipped with the massive OU Carryall. The A6 utilized the same drivetrain setup as the A5, but unlike the latter it was housed in a much more attractive sheet metal design, making the unit look like a single tractor, rather than two separate units tied together. Though few A6 Models were built because of wartime production requirements, the A6 Tournapull tractor itself appeared on a few other machines of note built by the company. One of these was the A6 Tournatruck from May 1942, and the proposed military

The Model A6 Tournapull replaced the A5 design in March 1942. The A6 was powered by the same twin-engine layout found in its predecessor, including the R. G. LeTourneau–designed four-speed powershift Tournamatic transmission. The complexity of the automatic transmission led to many reliability problems with the A6, and was one of the main reasons, along with wartime production needs, that this giant was produced in very small numbers. This A6 is equipped with the massive OU Carryall in November 1942.

The last of the twin-engined Tournapulls built was the Super A7 from late January 1943. Built at the Peoria plant, it featured the same powertrain setup as the A5 and A6. Its main mechanical features included throttle steering, speed selection by control valve, and a four-speed fluid clutch transmission. The top speed was 20 miles per hour. Equipped with a Model NU Carryall, it is showcased here parked next to a Model D1 Tournapull with a Q Carryall at the Peoria plant in February 1943.

Land Battleship from mid-1942. The Land Battleship consisted of two A6 Tournapull units, connected front and rear, carrying a mocked-up gun turret with a fake 155-millimeter howitzer in place. Tested in September 1942 at the Toccoa plant, it sparked little interest among military officials.

The last try at building a twin-engined Tournapull with a fluid clutch transmission design, like the A5 and A6, was the Super A7 from late January 1943. Built at the Peoria plant, it essentially had the same drivetrain and power ratings as the previous A6 built at the Toccoa facilities. The Super A7 Tournapull tractor had an even cleaner sheet metal design than the A6, with drilled steel plate radiator grilles, and a tapered lower front chassis under the nose. Though shown at the factory equipped with an NU Carryall scraper, it would never go into full production. With wartime needs weighing heavily on factory production, and a crippling flood of the Peoria factory in May 1943 by the Illinois River, which temporarily cut production in half, there was no capacity, let alone raw material, to build the Super A7 Tournapull. In the end, only one was ever constructed.

The one-and-only Model B1 Tournapull was built in October 1938. Looking nothing like its bigger brother, the Model A, the B1 was equipped with a Model BU Carryall, rated at 12.5 cubic yards heaped. It is shown at work here at the Peoria plant's testing area in January 1939.

It wasn't long after the B1 started testing that the Model B2 Tournapull arrived on the scene. Built in March 1939, it featured a Model SU Carryall rated at 18 cubic yards heaped, and a rear-mounted PCU. Its cab and engine were completely enclosed in sculptured sheet metal, resembling the trucklike designs of the time. Only one was ever built.

This rare image of the Model B4 and B5 Tournapulls was taken in June 1940. The B4 on the right was powered by a Caterpillar D13000 diesel engine, while the B5 on the left was equipped with a Cummins diesel. It is believed only one of each model type was ever built and tested.

The Model B6 Tournapull looked much like the B4 unit, and both were powered by the same Caterpillar D13000 diesel engine. The B6 featured a redesigned tractor frame and a semienclosed operator's cab. Introduced into testing in late June 1940, it was equipped with a Model LU Carryall rated at 19 cubic yards heaped. In December 1940, the Model B8 replaced the B6. The models resembled each other, but the B8 was powered by a single Cummins HBIS600 diesel engine rated at 200 gross horsepower.

The A Series Tournapull was suspended for a time until 1945, when LeTourneau engineers started experimenting with electric motors for controlling the cable functions of the Carryall scraper's apron and bowl. Unlike the tractor-mounted PCU cable controls, the new design had electric motors mounted on the scraper itself, eliminating the PCU attachment entirely. The first A Tournapull to be tested with this experimental design was the Vicksburg-built Model A8 in September 1945. This experimental test tractor was followed by the A10, A12, A13, and A15 Tournapulls, all in February 1946. In January 1947, LeTourneau started field-testing the A18 Tournapull. With its long nose and narrow front end, the A18 was a big and brawny machine, with a

rather menacing-looking radiator grille. It was also equipped with a prototype Model E-50 Carryall scraper, capable of handling a 50-ton-capacity payload. Though this model was only an experimental test unit, it would pave the way for future electric-scraper-controlled A Tournapulls.

In 1948, the company introduced two limited-production models of the A Tournapull. Referred to as the Model A19 Roadster (October) and the A20 Roadster (June), both units featured electric scraper controls. The A20 Roadster Tournapull was also the company's first limited release of its Tournapower drivetrain, which consisted of an Allison V1710 engine designed to run on liquefied petroleum gas (LPG), in this case, butane, and a

The Model C was the company's most successful Tournapull of the 1940s. Introduced in May 1940, it was powered by a 90-gross-horsepower Caterpillar D4600 diesel engine, mated to a four-speed Fuller transmission. The scraper unit was an 11-cubic-yard-heaped Model LS Carryall. Pictured is the first C1 Tournapull to come off the line.

In November 1940, the company introduced a souped-up version of the Model C in the form of the Super C Tournapull. The Super C could be equipped with a Cummins or Buda diesel engine rated at 150 gross horsepower, or a Hercules diesel with 124 horses.

Tournamatic transmission. These limited-production machines were replaced in April 1951 with the A21 Roadster and the Super A23 Tournapull. Only the Super A23 could be equipped with the Allison-Tournapower drivetrain. Now, both models featured a single cast radiator design, with crossed metal screen supports. These units would be the last two A Tournapull models offered that were totally designed and built by R. G. LeTourneau, Inc.

Just after the release of the first production A1 Tournapulls, LeTourneau was readying another slightly smaller range referred to as the Model "B." The first of these machines was the B1 Tournapull built in October 1938. The B1 Series looked nothing like the A model line. The B1 tractor's operator's cab was completely enclosed, like a truck's, with the engine protruding from the front. In this design, the PCU was mounted on an extended frame, in front of the radiator. The B1 was tested with a

Model BU Carryall at the Peoria plant, but production was limited to this single prototype machine.

In March 1939, a Model B2 Tournapull, with SU Carryall, was introduced into testing in Peoria. This model featured a rear-mounted PCU for controlling the scraper functions. The operator's cab was more trucklike in its overall look and design. While the B1 had a long nose, the B2 had a snub-nosed look, with the operator situated in front of the drive axle. In the B1 design, the operator sat over the drive axle. Again, only one of this type was ever built.

The B3 Tournapull would follow next in July 1939. The B3 was more conventional in its design approach. It featured a rear-mounted PCU, as well as a Detroit Diesel engine. Like the B2, it was tested with the SU Carryall. Other prototype Tournapull models to follow the B3 were the B4 and B5, both in May 1940.

Beginning in late 1944, R. G. LeTourneau, Inc., started to produce various one-off experimental Tournapull tractors and Carryalls that featured electric motors mounted on the scraper for controlling the functions of the unit by cables. This setup replaced the tractor-mounted PCU. One of these prototypes was the Model 3-6 from March 1945. Note the electric-motor controls and power lines mounted on the scraper unit.

Another one of the experimental Tournapull designs that utilized electric-motor scraper controls was the Model 20-8 Electric Scraper, with S202 Carryall. Built in May 1945, it featured a very contemporary Buda diesel–engined tractor unit that would hint of designs yet to come.

The Model A18 Tournapull was another step in the evolution of the company's electric-control scraper program. Introduced into prototype testing in January 1947, it was the 5,000th Tournapull tractor to be manufactured by R. G. LeTourneau, Inc. With its supercharged 300-gross-horsepower 8DCS-1125 Buda diesel engine, and its big 50-ton-capacity E-50 Carryall, the A18 prototype was one of the meanest-looking Tournapulls ever put into iron.

The Model A19 Roadster Tournapull, introduced in October 1948, actually made it into limited production. This A19, equipped with a 25-ton-capacity E-25 Carryall, is shown working in September 1950 on the Oahe Dam project in Pierre, South Dakota. The A19 was replaced with the A21 Roadster in April 1951.

The first R. G. LeTourneau-designed Tournapull to feature the Tournapower drivetrain was the Model A20 Roadster. Introduced in June 1948, the A20 featured a 450-gross-horsepower Allison V1710, 12-cylinder engine, set up to run on liquid butane fuel. This engine was mated to a four-speed Tournamatic transmission.

The B4 was mated to the SU Carryall, and was powered by a Caterpillar D13000 diesel engine. The B5 featured an LU Carryall and a Cummins Diesel engine. On the heels of these two prototypes was the B6 in June 1940. It used an LU Carryall and a Caterpillar D13000 diesel.

Maintaining its brisk pace, the company released the Super B8 Tournapull in December 1940. The B8 was essentially the B6 design, minus the Cat diesel. In its place was a Cummins diesel, rated at 200 gross horsepower. A small number of B8 units were produced, equipped with either the LU or FU Carryall scraper. The B6 and B8 shared the same curved operator's canopy design. Other variations of the B8 included a modified unit configured like a push-dozer, equipped with a rubber-tired rooter apparatus. It was built in August 1941 to assist the A5 Tournapull during

loading operations in its work on the Toccoa, Georgia, airport, near the LeTourneau plant. This unit had been converted to Caterpillar D17000 diesel power. Another B8 oddity was an experimental military light-tank transporter, built in March 1943. It was made up of a standard B8 with oversized tires, hitched to a specially built Tournatruck flatbed. Only one was built.

Starting in June 1945, the Vicksburg plant produced its first experimental B9 Tournapull, with electric-assisted steering. It was quickly followed by the B29 in October of that same year. The B9 was simply a test Tournapull tractor. The B29 was teamed up with a newly designed E25 Carryall scraper, with electric motors controlling the major functions of the scraper bowl and apron. The B29 was powered by a Hercules DFXE, 214-gross-horsepower diesel, mated to a Tournamatic transmission.

The A20 Roadster became the A23 Tournapull in October 1950. Still equipped with the big Allison-Tournapower drivetrain, it featured a more robust front bumper and headlight design, though the grille was the same. The model line would eventually feature a redesigned radiator housing with the Super A23 of April 1951. This early A23 from February 1951 is equipped with a 50-ton-capacity Model E-50 Tournarocker.

In April 1951, the Model A21 Roadster was introduced with the choice of either a 300-gross-horsepower supercharged Buda DAS1125 diesel engine (pictured), or a GM Detroit Diesel 275-gross-horsepower 6-110 diesel. Both powerplants were featured with a Mack Truck–sourced eight-speed sliding gear–type transmission. Though pictured with the 35-ton-capacity (27.5 cubic yards heaped) Model E-35 Carryall, it could also be equipped with the E-25, as well as the larger E-50 Carryalls.

The last of the big A Tournapulls to be designed and built by R. G. LeTourneau, Inc., was the Super A23 from April 1951. Also referred to as the Model A Tournamatic, the last design of this model was released in August 1952, featuring a slightly revised front end with headlights mounted to the sides of the radiator housing. Powered by the same 450-gross-horsepower Allison/Tournapower drivetrain from the previous models, it is shown here equipped with a newly designed P-35 Carryall, which replaced the E-35 unit. The payload capacities were the same as the E-35. This A Tournapull would become a LeTourneau-Westinghouse model in May 1953, if only for a short time.

After testing a small number of Vicksburg-built B29 Tournapulls at the construction site of the new Longview, Texas, facility, LeTourneau engineers went to work on an even more advanced machine design known as the B31. Built at the Vicksburg plant in February 1947, the B31 Tournapull was first shown with the E35 Carryall scraper, which was equipped with electric cable controls. The B31 featured electric steering, push-button electric operator controls, Buda diesel engine, and Tournamatic transmission and differential. It was a great technical achievement for LeTourneau, unless you had to service it in the field. Though the B31 had made great strides over its predecessors, it was still a case of too much new technology too fast. Problems with the Tournamatic transmissions were especially troubling. Its overall complexity did not lend itself well to repairs on the job site.

Designed and built at the Vicksburg, Mississippi, plant, the Model B29 Tournapull made its first appearance in October 1945. The B29 featured electric scraper and operator controls, as well as electric steering. This B29 from March 1946 was powered by a 214-gross-horsepower Hercules DFXE diesel engine with a four-speed Tournamatic transmission, and was attached to a newly designed, 25-ton-capacity E-25 Carryall.

Following in the footsteps of the B29 was the Model B31 Tournapull from February 1947. The B31 was powered by a Buda 6-DCS-844 diesel engine rated at 225 gross horsepower, attached to a Tournamatic transmission. The electric-controlled B31 is shown being push-loaded by an early prototype Model B Tournadozer in March 1947.

Other B Tournapulls that followed the B31 were the B32 Roadster in March 1948, the B33 in June 1948, and the B34 in January 1950. The B34 Tournapull would be the last to be designed and built at the Vicksburg facilities.

Though the A and B Tournapull Series machines never achieved the sales numbers hoped for by the company, this was clearly not the case with the C Tournapull model line. The C Tournapull was without a doubt the company's best-selling unit,

as well as one of the true legends in the history of earthmoving.

The concept of the C-pull, as it was sometimes called, was the same as the A- or B-pulls—a high-speed, rubber-tired, self-propelled tractor unit for pulling Carryall scrapers or related machinery. C1 Tournapull production would officially start at the Peoria plant in April 1940, with the first unit rolling off the assembly line in May. The original C1 Tournapull was powered by a Caterpillar D4600 diesel engine, rated at 90 gross horsepower, mated to a heavy-duty

The Model B33 Tournapull made its first appearance in June 1948. The standard engine choice was a Buda 8-DC-1125 diesel, rated at 240 gross horsepower with Tournamatic transmission. This B33 from 1949 is equipped with a Model E-35 Carryall, rated at 35 tons (30 cubic yards heaped) capacity.

The last of the big B Tournapulls built by R. G. LeTourneau, Inc., was the Model B34 from January 1950. The B34 looked similar to the B33, but had its front headlights mounted to the left of the radiator. This unit from March 1950 is equipped with a 35-ton-capacity Model A Tournarocker, which would be redesignated as the Model E-35.

four-speed Fuller transmission. Each wheel was separately controlled by an individual steering clutch. The first C1 was teamed up with an LS Carryall of 11-cubic-yard heaped capacity, controlled by a rear-mounted PCU on the C1 tractor. The C1 Tournapull was built tough, and with the Cat/Fuller drivetrain, was fairly reliable as well.

To help broaden the appeal of the C-pull, a second model was added in November 1940, called the Super C Tournapull. The Super C-pull differed from the standard C1 model in that it was powered by one of three different 150-gross-horsepower diesel engines—a Cummins, Buda, or Hercules, all with the Fuller transmissions. With more power came a larger scraper unit—in this case, the 15-cubic-yard LP Carryall. The Super C was an instant success in the marketplace, as well as an important tool in fighting the war in Europe and the Pacific during World War II. In fact, some 2,169 C-pulls were built for wartime use, as well as 10,785 Carryalls for both Tournapull and crawler tractor usage.

Throughout the war years, the first two models of C Tournapulls kept pace with both domestic and overseas requirements with few changes. An experimental C3 Tournapull was built in

Introduced in February 1946, the Model C9 was one of a number of electric-control prototype Tournapulls placed into limited service as the replacements for the popular Super C Series. The C9 looked almost exactly like the C10 and C11 model lines. The standard engine choice was a 113-gross-horsepower Buda 6DT-468 diesel. This C9 pictured in February 1947 is equipped with a 16-ton (13.3 cubic yards heaped) E-16 Carryall.

Released in August 1948, the Model C Roadster was the most successful of the electric-control Tournapulls fielded by the company. The C Roadster could be equipped with a 186-gross-horsepower GM Detroit Diesel 6-71, 165-horsepower Cummins HRB-600, or 150-horsepower Buda 6-DC-844 diesel engine, all with sliding gear–type transmissions. Shown at work in 1949 is this C Roadster with Model E-16 Carryall.

August 1944, attached to a special Tournadisc plow, which was utilized at the Vicksburg plant location. In March 1945 the Toccoa plant also began shipping an improved C-5 Tournapull variation.

In February 1946, the Toccoa plant unveiled two prototype C-pulls that now utilized electric motors for scraper control and steering. These models were the C6 and C9 Tournapulls. Both of these tractors were equipped with E16 Carryall scrapers, rated at 16-ton capacity. The Vicksburg facilities also fielded an experimental C-pull in the form of the C10 in October 1945. All of these models would culminate in the production of the C11 Tournapull, the eventual successor to the original C-pulls from 1940.

The C11 Tournapull was first introduced in December 1947, and for the most part, looked much like the experimental C9 test tractor. The C11 featured electric scraper and steering controls, as well as a 150-gross-horsepower Buda diesel engine and Tournamatic transmission and differential. The standard scraper unit was the E16 Carryall. The C11 was joined by another model in the product line in August 1948, in the form of the C Roadster Tournapull.

This Model C Roadster from 1950 sports slightly redesigned sheet metal on the Tournapull tractor, with the radiator housing now just a bit taller than on the previous model. In 1951, this model could be ordered with a Tournamatic transmission. When equipped with the Tournamatic, the Roadster nomenclature was dropped.

A Model C Tournapull from 1953 is shown with a new Model P-19 Carryall, which was capable of a 19-ton (16 cubic yards heaped) load. The standard engine by this time was the 186-gross-horsepower GM Detroit Diesel 6-71.

The Model D Tournapull was primarily designed as an air transportable scraper unit for wartime use in December 1942. This 1945 D4 Tournapull, with its matching 2-cubic-yard-capacity Model Q Carryall scraper and rear-mounted PCU, belongs to Ed Akin of California. ECO

The C Roadster shared most of its basic component parts with the C11, except the transmission choice was a heavy-duty, sliding gear type, not the powershift Tournamatic. But by 1951, the Tournamatic transmission was offered as an option with the C Roadster, as was the E18 Carryall. This was followed by the 19-ton-capacity P19 Carryall in 1952. The C11 and C Roadster sold relatively well for the company and were considered a success in the marketplace, especially the Roadster. But many customers missed the old C and Super C-pulls.

LeTourneau offered the Model D Tournapull to contractors looking for a small scraper unit for working in tight, restricted areas. The D Tournapull was originally designed to military requirements for an air-transportable scraper unit, capable of being drop-shipped from an aircraft into a battle zone. The design started out in September 1942 as the Jeep-Scraper. But it was soon determined that a military Willys Jeep was ill-suited for pulling a Model Q Carryall scraper. The Army Engineers would get the machine they wanted in December 1942, when R. G. LeTourneau

The civilian-production version of the little D Tournapull was the electric-control Model D6 with the E4 Carryall from October 1946. Based on the prototype D5 Tournapull of December 1945, the D6 was powered by a Buda HP-351 gasoline engine, rated at 85 gross horsepower. Wartime D models utilized Continental gasoline engines. The E4 Carryall was rated at 3.7 cubic yards heaped.

R. G. LeTourneau, Inc., produced a variety of specialized Tournapull-based heavy equipment. One such unit was the Model A Tournatwo. The A Tournatwo consisted of two A Tournapull tractor units joined together inline by a specialized hitch. Power was supplied by two supercharged Buda 8-DCS-1125 diesels, rated at 600 gross horsepower combined. Introduced in November 1952, the Tournatwo was designed to push-load large scrapers. The company also produced a 372-horsepower Model C Tournatwo in May 1952.

showed them the model D1 Tournapull, equipped with the 2-cubic-yard-capacity Q Carryall scraper. Weighing in at only 3.25 tons wet, it was just what the military was looking for. Powered by a 45-gross-horsepower Continental gasoline engine, it was simplicity itself. The first prototype D3 and D4 models were also built utilizing the Q Carryall in December 1943.

Starting in December 1945, LeTourneau built the first experimental civilian D5 Tournapull, equipped with the E4 Carryall scraper. Propelled by a gasoline-powered, 85-gross-horsepower Buda engine, its target market was the general contractor. The production version of this machine was the D6 Tournapull with E4 Carryall, introduced in October 1946.

The D6 was a more refined version of the D5, using the same gas Buda engine. Both units featured electric scraper controls, as well as electric steering. Although an upgraded model of the D6 started testing in October 1947 as the D7 Tournapull with E8 Carryall, it was dropped from production in favor of the D Roadster. Introduced in February 1948, the D Roadster was featured with the new 9-ton-capacity E9 Carryall. The engine choice for the D Roadster was the Detroit Diesel 4-71, rated at 122 gross horsepower. The D Roadster was well liked in the field, and despite its small size, sold rather well for the company. This model was also offered with an optional dozing blade, which also proved quite popular with the small contractor.

If the contractor needed a bit more power to push-load his scrapers, R. G. LeTourneau, Inc., offered a highly specialized butane-fueled Super A Tournatwo. Using two A Tournapull tractors equipped with the Allison-Tournapower drivetrain, the Super Tournatwo produced a very respectable 900 gross horsepower. It is shown here working in November 1952 at the Chrysler Proving Grounds in Chelsea, Michigan.

The Model C Tournapull Tractor was another custom-built hybrid, which consisted of a tractor unit and a towed nonpowered dolly unit. Built in June 1951, it was powered by a single 186-gross-horsepower GM Detroit Diesel 6-71 engine. R. G. LeTourneau, Inc., also produced a Model A version in January 1952, which was equipped with a 300-gross-horsepower supercharged Buda diesel. Tournapull Tractors were designed to pull cable-operated Carryall scrapers.

In addition to the four Tournapull Model lines, LeTourneau also tested a series of units that did not fit into any of its standard categories. Most of these experimental machines were built between 1944 and 1945, and were one-off test units. A few of these units were sized like D-pulls, while others were in the range of a C, B, or A Tournapull class. These models included the 3-1 in October 1944; the 3-2, 3-3, and 3-4, all in December 1944; the 3-5 in January 1945; the 3-6 in February 1945; the 3-9 in June 1965; the 3-10 in August 1945; the 3-12 and 3-14 in September 1945; the 20-1 in November 1944; the 20-8 in May 1945; and the 20-11 in July 1945.

All of the experimental machines' designations refer to the Tournapull tractor itself, and not what it was attached to. Some were tested with Carryalls, while others were hitched to Tournacranes, Tournatrucks, and Timber Wagons. But that was the beauty of the Tournapull concept in the first place. The Tournapull design allowed it to be teamed up with all sorts of ingenious attachments and inventions. In addition to the equipment already mentioned, Tournapulls could be paired with Tournarockers, Tournahoppers, Tournalayers, Tournamixers, Tournamules, Tournatractors, and Tournahaulers. Whatever R. G. LeTourneau could design that hauled, mixed, carried, laid, cut, or dumped, the Tournapull could pull it, and in some instances, push it.

The Tournadozers

R. G. LeTourneau's commitment to building more-productive, high-speed-loading earthmoving equipment during the 1930s and early 1940s mainly revolved around his Carryall scraper and Tournapull tractor lines. LeTourneau felt that the crawler tractor was inhibiting his ability to further raise productivity. For heavy bulldozing applications, the crawler tractor had no equal. But as a push tractor for scraper loading, or as the main pull unit for a Carryall, LeTourneau felt that they were slowing production, not increasing it. R. G. imagined a rubber-tired dozer that had the traveling speed necessary to keep up with his Tournapulls, but also a bulldozing blade for general earthmoving applications.

The Tournagrader was an attempt by R. G. LeTourneau, Inc., to broaden its product line and to match its competitors' offerings machine for machine. Built in April 1945, this motor-grader concept never went beyond the prototype testing stage.

R. G. LeTourneau's first experimental rubber-tired wheel dozer was the T-200 Tournadozer. Powered by a 300-gross-horsepower supercharged Buda Super Diesel engine, it first saw the light of day in December 1945.

The most popular Tournadozer by far was the Model C. Beginning prototype testing in September 1946, it would go into full production in January 1947. The original powerplant was a 160-gross-horsepower Buda 6DC-844 diesel. The first production C1 Tournadozer is shown here undergoing tests in March 1947.

The standard Model C Tournadozer was replaced by the Super C in 1949. The Super C was available with three engine choices: a Detroit Diesel, a Buda, or a Cummins. This Super C Tournadozer, equipped with a down-pressure blade, is powered by a 186-gross-horsepower GM Detroit Diesel 6-71. It is working at an iron ore mine near Kewatin, Minnesota, in February 1951.

This Super C Tournadozer working in Morocco in 1951 demonstrates why the dozer's all-wheel drive was so important to its sales success. It is also equipped with the 210-gross-horsepower version of the Buda 6-DA-844 diesel, the standard engine for this model during this time period. GM Detroit Diesel and Cummins powerplants were listed as options.

The largest Tournadozer was the Model A. Released in September 1947, the A Tournadozer was powered by a large Packard 4M 2500 Series marine engine configured to run on butane. Originally rated at 750 gross horsepower, later units were de-rated to 500 horsepower to extend the life of the four-speed Tournamatic transmission. Pictured is a butane-fueled Model A at work in November 1948.

And like so many of his concepts, if he could picture it in his mind, he could build it out of metal. And that is exactly what he did.

LeTourneau started developing his rubber-tired dozer concept in 1943. But due to a combination of wartime production needs and the flood of the Illinois River in that same year, it never proceeded much further than the experimental test mule stage. But after the war, engineers in Peoria returned to developing the tractor that would become known as the Tournadozer.

In December 1945, Peoria plant engineers started testing the first experimental prototype, four-wheeled, high-speed tractor— the Model T-200 rubber-tired dozer. The prototype T-200 consisted of a rear-mounted 300-gross-horsepower Buda Super Diesel engine, a LeTourneau fluid-actuated disc clutch transmission, four-wheel drive, disc clutch and brake steering system, and front-mounted PCU blade controls. The T-200 was the industry's first rubber-tired dozer built from the ground up, and not a modified crawler design with its tracks removed.

Testing of the T-200 led engineers to make design alterations to the basic layout in 1946, including a redesign of the chassis and operating control area with electric controls and electric PCU. A Tournamatic, air-actuated transmission was also installed. This newly redesigned prototype would start full testing in September 1946. It would form the basis of the Model "B" Tournadozer, one of four models of rubber-tired tractors the company had in the planning stages. Other models would include the A, C, and D.

The next tractor to follow the redesigned T-200 into testing was the C Tournadozer. Configured like the T-200, it was a smaller tractor overall, and was powered by a 160-gross-horsepower Buda diesel engine. Classified as the C1, it was built at the Longview plant in September 1946, with the first production units rolling off the assembly line in January 1947. Following on the heels of the C1 was the first limited-production Model B Tournadozer in February 1947, the Model D1 in April, and the rather large Model A in September. The Model A was the largest of the Tournadozers, while the Model D Series was the smallest.

The Model B Tournadozer followed the Model C1. In fact, the first unit identified as a B unit was the redesigned T-200 test tractor, which now had a bit of paint on it, and lettering on the rear engine

The Model B Tournadozer was the second-largest rubber-tired dozer offered by the company. The first Model B was introduced in February 1947, and was in fact a repainted T-200 prototype unit from 1946. Full-production versions would start coming off the assembly lines in September 1947. The standard engine was the 300-gross-horsepower 8DCS-1125 Buda Super Diesel. The unit shown is from May 1948.

cover identifying it as a Tournadozer Model B. But further testing was needed on this model series, and a finalized production unit would not be shown until September 1947. Most of the B Tournadozers were built at the Longview plant, with the exception of the first prototype units and a small number of production units, which were manufactured in Peoria. But the B-dozer was plagued with numerous technical problems, especially in the transmission area. Though LeTourneau engineers worked on the B-dozer's design shortcomings for most of 1948, it would never achieve full-production status. Management decided to stop work on the Model B so engineers could concentrate on improving the overall reliability of the C-dozer line.

The largest of the Tournadozers was the Model A, built in September 1947. The A Tournadozer was designed to push-load the largest scrapers on the market. Equipped with a Packard 4M 2500 Series marine engine, set up to run on butane fuel, it produced an astounding 750 gross horsepower, making it the most powerful dozer in the world at the time. With a four-speed Tournamatic transmission and differential, and air-actuated disc clutches, the A-dozer featured true on-the-go powershifting performance. The A-dozer's top speed was approximately 14 miles per hour, in forward or reverse. Equipped with a 16-foot-wide dozing blade, the A-dozer was capable of push-loading a 30-ton-capacity scraper in 30 seconds—quite a feat in its day.

The smallest of the Tournadozers was the Model D, first introduced in April 1947 as a front-engined machine. In March 1950, a rear-engined Super D Tournadozer was introduced, powered by a 122-gross-horsepower GM Detroit Diesel 4-71 engine. The blade controls were all electric, as they were on all Tournadozers.

The A Tournadozer was officially introduced at the Chicago Road Show, July 16–24, 1948. The industry was taken aback by the size and sheer power of the A-dozer, but its reliability record was, unfortunately, no less shocking. The prototype A-dozers were destroying their Tournamatic transmissions as fast as they could be replaced. In an effort to cut down on the transmission failures, the A-dozer was de-rated to 500 gross horsepower. But like the B-dozer program, the Model A was starting to eat up too much of the company's time and money. Although the A-dozer was tested in numerous working conditions, it would be phased out of production at the Longview plant by 1950.

The smallest of the Tournadozers was the Model D Series, built at the Peoria plant. The first prototype of this model started testing in April 1947. Identified as a Model D1, it was powered by a front-mounted gasoline engine, and featured an electric-motor-driven PCU. But this configuration would be put on the back burner in favor of a rear-engined design called the Super D Tournadozer. Release of full-production Super D Tournapulls would commence in March 1950. The Super D looked like a smaller C-dozer, and was powered by a rear-mounted Detroit Diesel 4-71 engine, rated at 122 gross horsepower. The transmission was an improved Tournamatic, and blade controls were electric-motor driven. Because of the amount of

R. G. LeTourneau, Inc., tried to market a front-end loader attachment for the Super C Tournatractor, called the TournaDiggster. Built in June 1952, it was developed jointly by R. G. LeTourneau's Machinery Division and Dempster Brothers, Inc., of Knoxville, Tennessee. Hydraulic cylinders controlled the boom and the forward crowd of the bucket attachment. But the leaky hydraulic system was not to R. G. LeTourneau's liking, and the project was terminated.

engineering time that had been put into the Tournadozer program early on, the Super D avoided many of the mechanical bugs of its predecessors and sold rather well because of it.

Of all the Tournadozer models produced, the Model C was by far the most popular in the industry, and became R. G. LeTourneau, Inc.'s hands-down bestseller. While the Model A- and B-dozers were just a bit too big for the Tournamatic transmission, the C Series, initially rated at 160 gross horsepower, was just about right. The C-dozer was originally equipped with the Buda 6-DC-844 diesel engine. But in January 1949, an improved model referred to as the Model Super C Tournadozer was introduced with two additional engine choices. These were the Detroit Diesel 6-71 rated at 186 gross horsepower, and the Cummins HRB-600 with 165 gross horsepower. The Super C was the best of the Tournadozer breed, and could attain a top speed of 19 miles per hour. Its power output and maneuverability made it the perfect platform for mounting or pulling additional attachments. Some of the more popular options included a comfort cab, an Angledozer blade, root rake, V-type snowplow, tree stinger, side boom crane, a Tournaskidder, and a pulled E16 Carryall scraper. Versatility was the Super C-dozer's middle name and contractors the world over purchased the model by the thousands.

New Opportunities

In the early 1950s, R. G. LeTourneau's interest in spreading the Christian Gospel took on new proportions when he decided to build an industrial missionary settlement in Liberia. LeTourneau firmly believed that many underdeveloped countries could improve their economic standing if they would start using modern heavy equipment to help them better utilize their own natural resources. The Republic of Liberia took LeTourneau's message to heart. R. G. LeTourneau was invited to meet with the president of the country and discuss the feasibility of establishing some sort of a development project that would be of mutual benefit to Liberia and LeTourneau's company.

In January 1952, the parties reached an agreement on the establishment of various development projects that could benefit Liberia's social and economic well-being. These projects included road building, logging, and land clearing for livestock, crop, and rubber production. In return, LeTourneau would be granted permission to engage in Christian missionary work. The deal included an 80-year lease on 500,000 acres of virgin jungle for commercial development that would help support all of the missionary work already under way in the area, as well as new missionary projects. This ambitious project, known as Tournata, would be managed by a nonprofit corporation known as LeTourneau of Liberia, Ltd., which was a wholly owned subsidiary of the LeTourneau Technical Institute of Texas.

In late 1953, a similar project was set up in Peru. This industrial development endeavor, known as Tournavista, would be managed by LeTourneau del Peru, Inc., another nonprofit, wholly owned subsidiary of The LeTourneau Technical Institute of Texas. Under this agreement, R. G. LeTourneau, Inc. would be contracted to construct a 31-mile section of the Trans-Andean Highway that would link the Amazon slopes and the Pacific coast. For payment, LeTourneau would receive 960,000 acres of Montana jungle, located on the eastern slopes of the Andes Mountains. The land was to be parceled into lots for sale to colonists and developed for agricultural and logging activities. Most important to LeTourneau, the agreement allowed for the establishment of various Christian missionary philanthropic endeavors in the region, which would be funded by the sale of the property.

Tournavista, along with Tournata, would not only offer benefits for their host countries, but would provide invaluable proving grounds for testing many of R. G. LeTourneau's own equipment designs. In fact, almost every single piece of logging, land-clearing, and earthmoving equipment used on the projects was designed and built by LeTourneau. The benefits the colonies provided for engineering development, however, receded as unforeseen situations arose with these two development programs in the 1960s. By that time, they would become severe financial liabilities for the company.

Although these two philanthropic development projects were similar in nature, they were started under far different corporate circumstances. LeTourneau was a much different company at the time Tournavista was started than it was when the Tournata project commenced. In 1953, R. G. was approached by the Westinghouse Air Brake Company, a division of the Westinghouse Corporation of Pittsburgh, Pennsylvania, with an offer to buy LeTourneau, Inc. Westinghouse saw the established heavy-equipment manufacturer as a sure fire moneymaker in its corporate empire. Westinghouse made an initial offer of $50 million for everything, including all five manufacturing plants. To the surprise of many in the industry, R. G. LeTourneau accepted their offer. He loved selling his machines, and viewed a factory as just one more massive piece of equipment waiting for the right customer to come along. Westinghouse seemed to be just that buyer.

During negotiations, Westinghouse performed a detailed analysis of all the R. G. LeTourneau, Inc. operations and found that they really did not require the Longview or Vicksburg facilities, only Peoria, Toccoa, and Rydalmere. After reaching this decision, they reduced their offer to $31 million. If R. G. LeTourneau was going to sell off his earthmoving equipment manufacturing operations to Westinghouse, what would he do with the two remaining plants? In crafting the final sales agreement, it was decided that LeTourneau would sell Westinghouse the three plants they wanted, and all of the manufacturing rights and patents on existing earthmoving equipment built by the company, including any associated intellectual property involving earthmoving. R. G. would be allowed to keep two plants and continue to operate them as R. G. LeTourneau, Inc. He would be able to retain all engineering patents and work done, or in progress, on his electric-drive wheel motors, as well as any government contracts in effect at the time of the sale. R. G. LeTourneau would be allowed to develop new types of equipment as long as they did not compete with Westinghouse directly and were not of an earthmoving or bulldozing nature. This non-compete clause would remain in effect for five years, starting on the official transfer day of the deal. On May 1, 1953, R. G. LeTourneau, Inc. was out of the earthmoving business for the next five years.

R. G. LeTourneau's earthmoving equipment designs would now be sold by the LeTourneau-Westinghouse Company, a newly formed subsidiary of Westinghouse Air Brake Company. LeTourneau-Westinghouse would take the world-famous LeTourneau-designed Carryalls, Tournapulls, and Tournadozers down another path of earthmoving history. Many in the industry thought that at almost 65 years of age, R. G. would now think about retirement, especially with $31 million in his and the LeTourneau Foundation's hands. But R. G. LeTourneau saw this as another opportunity in life, one that would allow him to undertake further Christian work endeavors, such as Tournavista. It would also allow him the necessary financial resources to further develop one of his greatest engineering accomplishments—the electric wheel traction motor. R. G. wasn't retiring. He was just getting his second wind.

R. G. LeTourneau, Inc., produced the Series T (Model C-6) Transporter in a multitude of working configurations to meet logging, transport, and oil-field drilling and exploration requirements. A single Cummins NRTO-6, rated at 335 gross horsepower, powered the diesel-electric-drive system, with all six wheels driven. This Series T from April 1957 is loaded with two Caterpillar tractors, and carries the short-lived "AR-GEE" model line nomenclature.

For R. G. LeTourneau, Inc., the 1950s was the decade of change for the company. Nothing would be as it was in the 1940s—neither the way the firm would do business, nor the products it would produce and sell. The sale of the earthmoving equipment lines and their associated manufacturing plants would cause the company to go down roads it might not have traveled otherwise. Some of these roads would lead to great fortune and achievement for the company; others simply became expensive learning experiences.

The sale of the earthmoving equipment line for $31 million allowed R. G. LeTourneau to design and build equipment for other industries. These areas included forestry, oil fields, offshore marine, steel, wide-based "floatation" tires, and various military proposals. But of greater importance, it would provide him with the capital he needed to perfect his diesel-electric-drive system.

R. G. LeTourneau had first introduced his radical new electric-drive concept at a special press event held at the Edgewater Beach Hotel in Chicago on November 17, 1950. At this event, R. G. demonstrated his diesel-electric-drive system in a prototype military aircraft tow tractor vehicle referred to as the Tournatow. The Tournatow's diesel-electric-drive system utilized electric-traction motors mounted in the wheel-hub assemblies, an industry first.

Diesel-electric-drive systems had been used for years in the railroad industry and a few special military and mining equipment designs. But LeTourneau's design was different. Instead of mounting the main drive motors on or inside of an axle housing, LeTourneau moved them to the actual wheel mounting. By placing the traction-wheel motors within the hub assemblies themselves, LeTourneau eliminated the complicated extension driveshafts. LeTourneau's design also allowed greater design flexibility in the drivetrain layouts, since the drive wheel assemblies could be mounted in almost any location.

LeTourneau's drivetrain consisted of five major groups—a diesel engine, an AC/DC generator, DC electric-traction motors, electric operator controls, and a dynamic braking system. Primary power came from the diesel engine. The AC/DC generator, mounted inline with the diesel engine, was the main source of current for the system's electric-drive and auxiliary motors. The DC electric-traction motors, mounted in the wheel hubs, drove the wheel assembly through a series of internal gear sets. And the dynamic braking system used the DC motors for regenerative

braking. In this process, the force of the moving vehicle turns the DC motors like generators, which produce power as they slow the vehicle—recapturing some of the energy initially used for propulsion. The heat produced through the regenerative braking process was dissipated through a series of resistance grids. LeTourneau's electric-drive system eliminated the need for a mechanical transmission, torque converter, driveshafts, and differential axles. The elimination of driveshafts, and the individual module design of the electric drive, allowed more radical machine configurations. The drive components could be mounted low in the design, giving the machine a lower center of gravity and better overall balance.

The New Product Lines

The Christian missionary land development projects in Liberia and Peru would prove to be invaluable as the primary testing ground for many of LeTourneau's electric-drive machine prototypes. Since the terrain in these locations was mainly jungle, forestry designs seemed the most logical machines to put into commercial production first. The company's product offerings would include diesel-electric mobile saws, logging arches, tree crushers, tree stingers, log stackers, and transporters.

One of the first forestry machine designs to be put into limited service was the Tournasaw. The first version of this concept, called the Tournasawyer, was built in mid-1944. This design, used a mechanical drivetrain. In late 1951, the first diesel-electric version was built, utilizing traction-wheel motors. The Tournasaw's design was rather simple. A steel-frame structure, mounted on a rear-engined, four-wheel-drive chassis, incorporated an extendable, electric-powered circular saw blade parallel to the ground, which would cut trees off at ground level. An extendable stinger-type steel bar, mounted at the top of the Tournasaw, would apply pressure against the tree itself while it was being cut. This would keep the tree leaning away from the machine while cutting, keeping the Tournasaw and its operator out of harm's way.

Various models of the Tournasaw were built both in single- and double-blade designs. Some of the models produced included the Series 9 in 1952, the Series 13 and Series 14 in 1953, and the Series 15 in 1954. Only 11 Tournasaws were manufactured between 1953 and 1958. The exact number of units built before 1953 is unknown, but it was only a handful at most. The last unit

R. G. LeTourneau is shown here at the controls of his revolutionary Tournatow, the first vehicle to feature electric-traction motors mounted in the wheel assemblies themselves. The four-wheel-drive and -steer tractor is being demonstrated at the Edgewater Beach Hotel in Chicago, Illinois, on November 17, 1950.

The first tree crusher built by R. G. LeTourneau, Inc., featuring diesel-electric drive was the Tree Roller. This slightly ungainly looking piece of equipment was built at the Vicksburg, Mississippi, plant, and is shown at work in late January 1954 in a wooded area adjacent to the main factory.

built was the single-head blade Series 15, which shipped from LeTourneau in October 1958.

Working in conjunction with the Tournasaw was a piece of equipment referred to as a logging arch. The early logging arch, which would also be referred to as a skidder, got its name from its arch design. Usually attached to the rear of a tractor, it would pick up logs by cable from a single end and drag, or "skid," them out of the working area. Before the sale of the earthmoving equipment lines in 1953, Tournadozers equipped with logging arches performed this duty. But after the sale, the company was without a machine to perform this duty. This predicament was solved in 1954, when R. G. LeTourneau introduced the Electric Arch Series YC Model line. The Electric Arch was once again a simplified design with no extra frills to slow it down. It was a rugged and fairly dependable machine, given its electric-drivetrain design. With four-wheel drive and a front, longitudinally mounted, 275-gross-horsepower Cummins diesel, the YC Electric Arch was a real workhorse in the woods. Later versions of the Series YC machines would have an inline, front-mounted engine and extra-stout, square axle housings. In 1957, a slightly smaller Series YD Model was also offered. The Electric Arch sold well and was a success story for the company.

Another device invented by R. G. LeTourneau in 1954 for working in the woods or jungle was the Series 250 Tree Stinger.

The Series G-150 was the second-largest diesel-electric-drive Tree Crusher produced by the company. Originally built in June 1957, it was powered by a single 600-gross-horsepower Cummins VT-12BI diesel engine. In 1960, the G-150's frame was lengthened to accommodate a new engine package consisting of two Detroit Diesel 12V-71 powerplants, rated at 840 gross horsepower combined. The approximate working weight was just a bit over 150 tons, with a 24-foot, 9-inch overall width. The G-150 (S.N. 5851) is shown at work in Pomona, New Jersey, in June 1960.

The largest of all the Tree Crushers was the Series G-175. Introduced in October 1960, it would not go into service until May 1962. Powered by two Detroit Diesel 12V-71 engines, rated at 840 gross horsepower, the G-175 could lay waste to just about anything with its 175-ton operating weight and 35-foot width. Here the G-175 (S.N. 6085) is being unloaded from a barge on the Mississippi River, just down from the Vicksburg assembly plant, for testing purposes.

The three-wheeled Model 34x30 Transphibian Tactical Crusher was custom-built for U.S. Army land-clearing duties in Vietnam. The 34x30 utilized a diesel-electric drivetrain, powered by a single Detroit Diesel 12V-71N engine rated at 475 gross horsepower. Two sets of wheels were supplied—a steel grouser bladed-type (pictured), or foam-filled star-wheeled rollers. Only two 34x30 Tactical Crushers (S.N. 6874/6875) were built.

The Tree Stinger was a towerlike attachment mounted to a LeTourneau-built mobile, powered chassis, such as an LC Electric Tractor or K-600 Tractor. The Series 250 was originally developed from an early prototype model, introduced in 1953, called the AC Push-Pull Tree Stinger. In operation, the operator would position the Tree Stinger's boom in front of a tree trunk and lower a rear-mounted blade on the tractor that would anchor it in place. An electric winch would then force the telescoping center "stinger" section of the boom up against the tree trunk and apply enough pressure to leverage the tree over until the roots broke—a crude but effective means of bringing down a tree, economically, in one piece. R. G. LeTourneau also had a few rack-and-pinion gear-driven Tree Stinger attachments mounted to Army surplus tank chassis for extremely treacherous working conditions. Though only a few Tree Stingers were ever put into service, they nonetheless got the job done wherever they were used.

In areas where the marketable trees had already been removed for lumber, or in thick undergrowth where the vegetation and trees had no commercial value, R. G. LeTourneau would send in his Tree Crushers. The Tree Crusher, also referred to as a Jungle Crusher or Jungle Buster, was designed to flatten everything in its path. A single machine could clear 2 to 4 acres an

R. G. LeTourneau, Inc., built a series of prototype diesel-electric-drive tractors in the 1950s, mainly targeted for use in the forestry industry. One of those designs was the 75-Ton DC Tractor from March 1954. This tractor featured a longitudinally mounted diesel engine behind the operator's cab, and all-wheel drive, as well as all-wheel steering. Only two 75-Ton DC Tractors were built.

hour, depending on forest density and the size of the Crusher. The Tree Crusher can trace its company ancestral roots back to 1948 to a machine called the Mesquite Speed Crusher and Root Cutter, nicknamed the "Mesquiter." Based on a 750-gross-horsepower, butane-fueled Model A Tournadozer, it was equipped with large hollow steel wheels with helical grousers, or blade segments. It also had a large root rake mounted on the rear that would cut the roots off underground as the massive steel-wheeled dozer moved forward, mashing down heavy brush. This machine was built for clearing mesquite-covered land on the King Ranch in Texas.

In late 1953, the company officially took the wraps off its newest concept—the Tree Roller. Built at the Vicksburg facilities, the Tree Roller looked like a steamroller on steroids. The Tree Roller moved on two large steel drums fitted with brush-cutting blades. Propelling the Tree Roller was a diesel-electric drivetrain with traction motors inside the drums. The Tree Roller was tested on some river-bottom acreage adjacent to the Vicksburg plant. In testing, it soon became evident that the unit's center of gravity was too high, making the machine quite unstable as it rolled over larger trees and uneven terrain. In fact, it tipped over a few times during its testing period. The design showed great promise, but it was not yet ready for commercial production.

In August 1953, R. G. LeTourneau, Inc., introduced the Model LC AC Tractor, followed by the LC DC Tractor that November. Both tractor models were powered by a single 186-gross-horsepower Detroit Diesel 6-71 engine, mounted longitudinally behind the operator's area. The main difference between the two, as the names suggest, was that one utilized AC traction-wheel motors, and the other DC. Eventually, 10 of each type were manufactured. Pictured is a DC model in January 1954.

Another limited-production diesel-electric, all-wheel-drive and -steer tractor series was the Model LC22. First built in early 1954, the LC22 featured an inline-mounted engine and generator, set directly behind the operator's cab. The buyer had the option of gasoline, diesel, or liquefied petroleum gas (LPG) engines. A total of 10 tractors were built, all with DC-drive motors. The LC22 shown in May 1954 is a butane-powered unit.

By June 1954, a much more advanced and considerably larger Tree Roller was shipped to Peru for land-clearing duties at Tournavista. Weighing in at approximately 100 tons, it was designed for large-scale jungle work. The 100-ton Tree Roller was long and wide, with a very low center of gravity. Large steel-cleated roller drum wheels were steered by means of articulated mountings, both front and rear. Push-beams in the front and back would knock over a thicket of trees as the machine traveled forward at a top speed of 3 miles per hour. As the Tree Roller advanced, the grousers on the steel drum wheels would start to bite into the base of the trees and climb up them. The weight of the crusher would then push the trees to the ground. Very little could stand in the way of the 100-ton Tree Roller, though large boulders and tree stumps were to be avoided whenever possible.

Even though the large rollers provided relatively good floatation on less-than-ideal ground conditions, wet marshy areas were not to the machine's liking. Getting a machine this size bogged down was a real nightmare. Unfortunately, it happened more times than many would care to admit. The solution was a helper vehicle—a tank-inspired creation called the Crusher Tender.

This Series F-50 Log Stacker (Model A-4) was first introduced in 1956. With its steel forks and curved tusks, it was capable of handling 50 tons of logs with the mast in the vertical position. This was later increased to 60 tons. This F-50 is from March 1958.

The first diesel-electric all-wheel-drive equipment hauler designed by R. G. LeTourneau was the Series T (Model C-6) Electric Transporter, originally built in August 1955. Looking much like the articulated haulers of today, the original Series T was powered by a 335-gross-horsepower Cummins NRTO-6 diesel engine. The payload capacity was rated at 35 tons. The prototype unit is shown here in March 1956 undergoing traction and load evaluation testing.

Designed for land-clearing work, the Model 6-120 Tree Crasher, nicknamed "Queenie," was the first of three different model concepts to utilize six electric-drive wheels mounted with 120-inch-diameter tires. Power was supplied by a single 600-gross-horsepower Cummins VT-12 diesel engine. Built in April 1955, Queenie started operations in August of that year at the Handley Construction Company of Pahokee, Florida. Only one Model 6-120 (S.N. 5247) was produced.

Built on Army surplus tank chassis, it came equipped with a dozing blade, utility crane, and 100-ton line-strength electric winch. The Crusher Tender was just the ticket on those rainy jungle days when your Jungle Crusher was up to its chassis in mud.

The company would soon produce larger and more advanced successors to the 100-ton Tree Roller. These larger machines, now referred to as Series G Electric Tree Crushers, were all built at the Vicksburg plant. The Series G-110, with a 110-ton operating weight, was built in April 1955. In June 1957, the company produced the first of the ultralarge Series G-150 Tree Crushers. Originally powered by a single 600-gross-horsepower diesel engine, its drive system was, of course, electric, with DC traction motors inside the rollers. Measuring 76 feet, 4 inches in length, with an overall width of 24 feet, 9 inches, the mighty G-150 made quick work of a thicket of trees.

R. G. LeTourneau built only one crusher larger than the G-150. The Series G-175 Tree Crusher was built in late 1960. Weighing in at 175 tons in full operating trim, it was powered by a pair of Detroit Diesel 12V-71 engines rated at 840 gross horsepower. The machine's length of just 56 feet is deceptive because the G-175 was not equipped with a rear push-beam structure. Its overall width of 35 feet made it king of the Tree Crushers. Despite its

awesome potential, the G-175 was not put into service until May 1962, when it went to work with JME Fortin of Hull, Quebec, Canada. It was used, along with several other smaller crushers, for clearing more than 1 million acres of forest on the Manicouagan Project, near Hauterive, on the St. Lawrence River in Quebec. Only one G-175 was ever built.

All of the early Series G Tree Crushers were of a two-roller design, including the Series G-50 of 1958, of which only one example was built. R. G. LeTourneau introduced slightly smaller, three-roller wheel designs starting with the Series G-40 in 1960, followed by the Series G-80 in 1961, the Series G-40B in 1962, the Series G-55 in 1963, the Series G-60 and Aluminum A-34 in 1964, the Model 40x40 in 1966 (one built), and the Series G-80B in 1967. The three-roller design proved to be the most popular Tree Crusher type with land-clearing companies the world over.

The most notable of this type of machine was the Transphibian Tactical Crusher Model 34x30, of which two units were built, for the U.S. Army. These units were destined for land-clearing duties in Southeast Asia during the Vietnam War. Shipped from the factory in May 1967, the 97-ton Tactical Crushers served in South Vietnam, clearing wide buffer zones in the jungle around various ongoing U.S. operations for security purposes. But even with their foam-filled, drumlike wheels, the Tactical Crushers would still find that their operating weights were their greatest enemy, as they often got mired in swampy jungle conditions. Finally, the Army gave up on the machines and both units were removed from service in late 1968. They were later sold to a Texas-based company, World Land Clearing, which utilized both machines for large land-clearing duties stateside. As of 2001, both Tactical Crushers were sitting in a contractor's yard in Longview, Texas. Dismantled and partially cut up, they seem destined for scrap.

Between 1952 and 1954, R. G. LeTourneau produced a number of electric-drive tractor concepts that could be utilized for earthmoving and forestry service. After the sale of the earthmoving equipment lines in May 1953, all work on the tractors was shifted toward forestry applications. Many of the tractors were equipped with dozing blades intended for uprooting stumps. Others were featured with root-rakes for knocking down and dozing under vegetation. All of these tractors were direct descendants of the Tournatow program.

The earliest of the electric-drive tractors was identified as simply the AC 4x4. Built in November 1952, this electric four-wheel-drive tractor featured AC drive and electric-steering wheels on all four corners. It was primarily intended as a replacement for the Tournadozer. Only one was ever built. The AC 4x4 was followed by the LC Series machines, starting with the Model LC AC Tractor in August 1953, and was followed by the Model LC DC Tractor in November 1953. The main difference between these two tractor concepts was that one featured AC drive motors and the other featured DC. Both were four-wheel-drive designs with

four-wheel steering. The engines were mounted longitudinally behind the operator's seating area. The engine of choice for both versions was a single Detroit Diesel 6-71, rated at 186 gross horsepower. A total of 20 Model LC tractors were eventually produced—10 with AC drive and 10 with DC drive.

Another variation on the LC tractor concept was the Model LC22 Tractor. On this tractor, the engine was mounted inline with the chassis. It was offered with a choice of diesel or gasoline engines, with the option of butane fuel conversion. The LC22 was DC electric four-wheel drive. As on the earlier LC tractors, all four wheels steered by means of electric motors. The first Model LC22 was shipped to Tournavista, Peru, in early 1954, equipped with a Series 250 Tree Stinger. Other model variations would soon follow, equipped with dozing blades and root rakes. Total production run for the LC22 was 10 units, all with DC wheel motor drive.

The last two four-wheel-drive tractor concepts to be considered for production were the 25-Ton DC Tractor from November 1953, and the 75-Ton DC Tractor from March 1954. In the 25-Ton Tractor design, the engine was mounted longitudinally in the middle of the chassis, with the operator located in the rear portion of the unit, overlooking the engine. The larger 75-Ton DC Tractor utilized larger "A"-sized traction motors, as opposed to the "C" type in the 25-Ton Model. The 75-Ton had its engine module located behind the operator. As with all of the other tractor designs mentioned, electric four-wheel drive and steer were standard fare. Only one 25-Ton and two 75-Ton DC Tractors were actually built.

Another massive land-clearing vehicle manufactured by the company, based on the Model 6-120, was the Model A-6 Crasher from February 1956. The A-6 essentially utilized the same drivetrain configuration found in Queenie, including power output. It was originally built with a front-bucket attachment, then was built with dozing blades mounted front and rear. The last variation, shown here in August 1957, had a massive V-plow dozing blade mounted to the end of the unit with the tandem-drive axles. But in the end, only one A-6 Crasher (S.N. 5322) saw the light of day.

The Series H (Model 6-16) Disc Plow was another one-of-a-kind piece of forestry equipment designed for land-clearing operations. The Disc Plow was powered by a front longitudinally mounted diesel engine. The drivetrain was diesel-electric with six electric-drive wheels. The unit carried a massive six-disc plowing attachment, with each round blade measuring 6 feet in diameter. Originally built in August 1955, the Disc Plow (S.N. 5335) is shown at work in November 1958.

Of all of the forestry equipment offered by R. G. LeTourneau, none made a bigger impact in the marketplace—and to the company's bottom line—than its legendary electric Log Stackers. These log-loading creations were developed to pick up large piles of logs, either on the ground or from the back of a logging truck. The log loaders could stack the logs in designated rows, drop them into chippers, or load them onto trucks. With their steel forks and tusks, they could lift and carry from 25 to 60 tons of logs at a time, depending on the model type.

R. G. LeTourneau first envisioned this type of machine in August 1948. But the prototype "Tournalogger" was scrapped as soon as it was built because its mechanical-drive design proved unworkable. It would not be until mid-1955 that the company would again try its hand at building a log loader. But this time, its drivetrain would be diesel-electric with traction-wheel motors. The first unit built (S.N. 5180) was referred to as a Series F Electric Log Stacker. Rated at 25-ton capacity, it was just what the industry was looking for. Shortly after the first unit was built, the second loader (S.N. 5252) was certified as ready for action in July 1955. After this, there was no looking back for the Electric Log Stacker. Early model introductions included the 25-ton-capacity Series F-25 (Model C-4) in 1955, the 50- to 60-ton Series F-50 (Model A-4) in 1956, the 30-ton Series F-30 (Model C-4) in 1959, and the 17-ton Series FT (Model C-3x2), also in 1959.

Beginning in 1955, through the end of 1960, the company built some 74 Series F Log Stackers, with more to come—many more, in fact. The Electric Log Stacker was the company's first sales success story for the implementation of R. G. LeTourneau's electric-drive design in a mass-produced piece of heavy machinery. It was the company's first electric-drive product line to be counted in the hundreds of units sold. Without a doubt, it was a clear winner for the Texas-based firm.

Another popular LeTourneau offering was its series of Electric Transporters. Produced mainly in six-wheel-drive arrangements, they were designed for tough working environments in the forest and oil-field industries. Available in various chassis lengths to accommodate timber or pipe hauling, they were the company's go-anywhere, do-anything product offering. For oil-field work, the Electric Transporter could be equipped as a flatbed for hauling machinery "floats," tractors, or other heavy equipment. it could also be equipped with a service crane, heavy-duty winches, and a dozing blade. The usual power source was a single Cummins NRTO-6 diesel, rated at 335 gross horsepower. The front tractor power unit steered by means of an articulated chassis, driven by electric rack-and-pinion gears. In fact, these early transporters resembled the articulated all-wheel-drive haulers so popular today in the earthmoving industry. Basic designs offered included the Series T (Model C-6) Electric Transporter in 1955, and the

Series J (Model C-6) Pulpwood Hauler in 1956. Load capacities ranged between 30 and 35 tons, depending on the model type and equipment configuration. The transporters sold quite well for LeTourneau and were well liked by the companies and the operators that used them.

The transporter product line also had the distinction of carrying the company's new trademark name and signature slogan—An "AR-GEE" Design. The slogan was first used in March 1957, but it didn't catch on in the marketplace and was phased out the following year.

R. G. LeTourneau would continue to build limited-production pieces of heavy equipment for the forest industry. One such machine was the Model 6-120 Tree Crasher "Queenie." Built in April 1955, it was delivered in August 1955 to the Handley Construction Company of Pahokee, Florida, for a 1,000-acre land-clearing contract with the U.S. Army's Kings Bay Ammunition Loading Terminal, near Kingsland, Georgia. The Model 6-120 Tree Crasher got its designation from its six electric-powered driving wheels, mounted with 120-inch-diameter tires. The big Crasher was powered by a single Cummins Diesel VT-12, rated at 600 gross horsepower. Equipped with a front-mounted 16-foot-wide dozing blade, it made short work of any thicket of trees. So successful was the Crasher in its basic design execution, it would become the blueprint for future six-wheeled leviathans from LeTourneau.

In February 1956, the company unveiled another vehicle patterned after the Tree Crasher, identified as the Model A-6 Crasher. The A-6 Crasher utilized the same drivetrain layout and specification as the Model 6-120, but was equipped with a large loading bucket mounted on a vertical hoist rack. Its primary purpose was not to dig earth, but to load wood chips and other such material. After testing was completed using the bucket attachment, it was replaced by a pair of dozing blades mounted both front and rear, in March 1956. In this configuration, the operator's cab was moved from the left front of the unit to just past midpoint. It was mounted sideways so the operator could see the operation of the dozing blades, whether going forward or in reverse. After these tests ended, the unit was modified once again in August 1957, when the rear dozer blade was replaced with a massive V-shaped root-plowing blade. Though it worked on some land-clearing projects just east of the Longview plant, it was never sold into private ownership.

Other noteworthy one-of-a-kind forestry creations were the Model C-4 Marsh Buggy, Model C-4 Stump Digger, Series H Disc Plow, Model C-3 Billy Goat, and the Model 6-110 Tree Stomper. The Marsh Buggy, built in October 1954, was equipped with a dozing blade and rode on four oversized, high floatation tires. The Stump Digger, from March 1955, utilized a dual-cab LC22 inline tractor chassis, with a rotating metal-spiked attachment that literally ground stumps into a pulp. The six-wheel-drive Series H Disc Plow (Model 6-16), from August 1955, carried a massive six-bladed disc, mounted in a draft frame, that cut up stumps and loosened

compacted soil. Equipped with either a dozing rooter blade or a bush-hog, the Model C-3 Billy Goat was a three-wheeled, five-tired tractor released in June 1964. Most outrageous among the one-offs, however, was the Model 6-110 Tree Stomper. Built in June 1964, it was designed to crush trees and brush in swampy areas by utilizing the weight of its massive walking shoes. But this mechanized giant was eventually parted out and fed back into the melting furnaces at the company's steel mill.

The first offshore drilling platform designed and built by R. G. LeTourneau was nicknamed the "Scorpion." Fabricated at the Vicksburg shipyard, Hull No. 1 was launched in November 1955, and officially christened on March 20, 1956. Owned by the Zapata Offshore Company, the Scorpion put in many good years of service, until finally being retired in December 1986.

Offshore Drilling Platforms

R. G. LeTourneau often took giant financial gambles in the production of his machinery designs. One of the biggest chances he took was the offshore drilling rig concept for deep-water oil and operated profitably in the open seas, and withstand the awesome forces of the ocean and its weather patterns, presented an extraordinary challenge. For a company the size of R. G. LeTourneau, Inc., a design of this nature in the early 1950s could have been ruinous if it failed. But this company had at its helm a unique motive force—the stubborn, tenacious, willful, and ingenious mind of R. G. LeTourneau.

The company shopped its idea of the self-erecting drilling platform to many of the top oil companies in the industry. All were fascinated by the concept, but none were willing to make a financial commitment. After hearing all that R. G. LeTourneau had to say about his drilling platform concept, the president of Zapata Offshore Company, based in Houston, Texas, decided to take a chance. That same man, George H. W. Bush, would go on to become the 41st president of the United States.

R. G. LeTourneau had made a novel proposal to Zapata concerning his proposed rig. He stated that he would build the offshore platform at his own company's expense, if Zapata would advance them $400,000 with which to begin construction. If the design and building of the platform proved successful, R. G. LeTourneau, Inc., would receive an additional $550,000 payment from Zapata, plus an additional 38,000 shares of Zapata Offshore Company common stock. If the platform project failed in any way before final delivery, or did not perform as promised, Zapata would be refunded its initial investment of $400,000 in full. As Mr. Bush stated in his 1987 autobiography Looking Forward: "Our feeling was that anybody that had that much confidence in himself was worth the gamble." He would also refer to R. G. LeTourneau as "A kind of George Patton of engineering." Most would agree that Mr. Bush's comments were right on the mark.

Building of the first platform hull, Scorpion, commenced shortly after Zapata signed the project's contract on November 11, 1954. By November 2, 1955, the platform was officially delivered into Zapata's hands, as it made its way out of the Vicksburg shipyard and into the Mississippi River. From there it traveled by river to Galveston, Texas, for final outfitting. Moored in Galveston at Pier 12 for its ceremonial christening on March 20, 1956, it would go straight to work off of Port Aransas, Texas, for the Standard Oil Company of Texas. Though the Scorpion had a few mechanical difficulties at first—especially with the electric motors for the rack-and-pinion drives on the giant triangular, open steel-lattice legs—all would be corrected to Zapata's liking. So impressed was the offshore drilling company with the Scorpion, that they ordered another self-erecting drilling platform. Named the "Vinegarroon," it was placed into service on April 29, 1957.

In April 1954, R. G. LeTourneau modified an existing Adams mechanical-drive motor grader with a diesel-electric drivetrain. Referred to as the AC Electric Grader (S.N. 5188), it was powered by a rear-mounted 165-gross-horsepower Detroit Diesel 6-71. It would eventually be shipped to the Tournata missionary project in Liberia, in November 1955.

Military Applications

The military branches had always been strong supporters of R. G. LeTourneau's concepts and designs. Their good relationship would continue long after the sale of the primary earthmoving equipment lines in 1953.

The earthmoving product lines and patents R. G. LeTourneau sold to Westinghouse were for commercial, rather than military, applications. Any military earthmoving machine design program that utilized diesel-electric drive, and was in effect at the time of the sale, remained the property of R. G. LeTourneau, Inc. Even though these machines could not be sold in the private sector, the design and testing data they provided proved invaluable five years down the road, when the company was legally allowed to reenter the commercial earthmoving equipment market.

At the time of the sale, two electric-drive military scraper designs were in advanced states of field-testing. These were the Rigid C-Tow Unit with E-18 Scraper, and the DC 6x6 Tractor with E-16, E-18, and P-19 Scrapers. Both designs started testing in November 1951. The Rigid C-Tow was created for a U.S. Army contract, while the DC 6x6 Tractor was for a different Navy proposal. The Rigid C-Tow was a four electric-drive wheel design, powered by a single inline front-mounted diesel engine. All four wheels steered, since the single-axle tractor unit was mounted in a fixed union with the Model E-18 Scraper unit. The front tractor was also equipped with a rack-and-pinion-controlled dozing blade. Only one example of the Rigid C-Tow was listed as being built. The DC 6x6 design was a two-axle, four-wheel-drive tractor based largely on the Tournatow program. The tractor was designed to pull a scraper unit that also had powered rear wheels,

The Rigid C-Tow was one of the military earthmoving equipment programs that remained under the control of R. G. LeTourneau, Inc., after the sale of its earthmover product lines to Westinghouse Air Brake Company in May 1953. The Rigid C-Tow featured an 18-ton-capacity E-18 Carryall scraper unit, rigidly mounted to the front power tractor unit. The drivetrain was diesel-electric, with all four wheels driven and steered. Originally built in November 1951, the C-Tow was based on a much larger concept machine called the Rigid A-Tow from August 1951. Built at the Longview plant, the A-Tow featured the same drivetrain layout as the C-Tow, but was equipped with Tournapower and an E-50 scraper unit. Only one of each was built for testing by the U.S. Army.

The DC 6x6 E-18 was another diesel-electric-drive scraper outfit built for the U.S. Navy. The electric-tow tractor was powered by a single inline-mounted diesel engine, which powered all six wheels for driving and steering functions. The scraper unit was a Model E-18 Carryall, rated at 18 tons (14 cubic yards heaped) capacity. Originally built in November 1951, it was shipped to the Navy in 1953. Another version of this model featured an E-16 scraper unit. Only one of each type was produced.

The last version of the DC 6x6 Tow Tractor was produced in June 1953. This variation was equipped with a 19-ton-capacity (16 cubic yards heaped) P-19 Carryall scraper unit. The tractor itself now had its main diesel engine mounted longitudinally, in front of the operator. The main design features were its diesel-electric drive and six-wheel-drive and -steer capabilities. Only one example of the DC 6x6 P-19 was ever built.

giving the design full-time six-wheel drive. Two different designs of the DC 6x6 were built. The first one produced had a tractor with its engine mounted inline in the center of the chassis. This design was paired with E-16 and E-18 Scraper units. In June 1953, another variation was introduced with a tractor equipped with a longitudinally mounted engine midway in the chassis. It was teamed up with a Model P-19 Scraper. Though both model types were tested thoroughly by the Navy and LeTourneau, they would not go into limited production. In all, only one of each type of DC 6x6 Tractor/Scraper combination was ever built.

The company continued to design and build military scraper concepts in 1954. In that year alone, four model types were put into testing. The Models D-35 and D-50 were tested in February, the DC-50 in April, and the DC-35 in May. All were prototypes for Army consideration. The D-35 and D-50 were very compact scraper designs, with longitudinally mounted diesel engines. The operator sat over the main electrical generator, which was mounted inline with the engine. The main powertrain was placed behind the front wheels for better balance. The DC-35 and DC-50 powertrain layouts had their engines mounted in front of the leading wheels, which were set back closer to the scraper bowl. All four of these concepts utilized DC electrical-traction motors and all-wheel steering.

These military scrapers also failed to make it into production, with one of each built of the D-35/50 Models, and two of each of the DC35/50. All would eventually work together, along with one DC 6x6 E16 and one DC 6x6 P-19, at a Texarkana, Arkansas, railroad track relocation job that was successfully bid on by R. G. LeTourneau and was under the supervision of the Army Corps of Engineers. The contract called for the relocation of 17.5 miles of track for the Cotton-Belt Rail Line. In January 1955 the scrapers were shipped to the job site, which probably raised a few eyebrows back at LeTourneau-Westinghouse. But since the military scrapers were never intended for commercial sale, and were the property of R. G. LeTourneau, Inc., at the time, there wasn't much they could say about the matter.

The last military scraper built by the company appeared in October 1957, and was simply referred to as the DC Self-Loading Scraper. Designed for the Army, it employed an articulated steering front tractor unit—and not the more complicated all-wheel-steer electric layouts found on the previous scraper prototypes. Again, the Army did not accept the project. But this scraper would have a far greater design impact for the company in the years ahead, during the decade of the Electric-Diggers (see chapter 4).

The DC50 and its slightly smaller DC35 counterpart were prototype scrapers built for U.S. Army consideration. The DC50 was built in April 1954, with the DC35 arriving in May. Both models featured longitudinally front-mounted 450-gross-horsepower Allison V1710, butane-fueled engines, and electric-drive DC motors in each wheel. All four wheels also had full steering capabilities. The total production for the DC50 and DC35 was two units each. Here a DC50 is shown at work on a Texarkana contract under the supervision of the Army Corps of Engineers in October 1955.

Another sort of earthmoving device designed for strictly military purposes was the Army V-Plow. Designed to unearth buried land mines with its massive V-shaped dozing blade, this concept vehicle was built in two, one-off model variations. The first, produced in 1952, was fabricated out of two surplus tank chassis. But early tests showed that when the vehicle encountered land mines, they would cause severe damage to the plowing blade. Another Model II design was built in November 1952, utilizing DC electric-drive wheels. In this design, nicknamed "Pistol Pete," the V-mine plow was reinforced and now rode on four rubber-tired wheels. Power was supplied by an Allison V1710 engine, rated at 500 gross horsepower. But even with this much power on hand, an additional four M46 medium-duty tanks were required to push the unit when the plow was fully engaged. The V-Plow's blade was capable of clearing a 14-foot-wide, 3-foot-deep path, at approximately 2 miles per hour. Tested thoroughly at Fort Knox, Kentucky, for most of 1953, it would never go into production.

The Tournatow Tractor program that revolved around the movement of aircraft on the ground never really got airborne. After the unveiling of the first three prototypes in 1950, only another three model configurations were produced. One model built in 1953 was much like the first prototypes from 1950; it was followed by the Bu-Dock Navy Tow Tractor in November 1954, and then by the Ice-Tow Tractor in August 1956. The Bu-Dock was designed for towing on sandy beaches, while the Ice-Tow was built to tow aircraft on icy runways. Only one of each was produced.

The D35 and D50 electric scrapers were similar in design to the DC35/50 prototypes, but featured single longitudinally mounted Detroit Diesel engines located behind the operator's control area. Both models were built in February 1954 for U.S. Army evaluation, and only one of each was produced. The unit shown is a D35 at work in October 1955, at the same Texarkana job where the DC35/50 scrapers worked.

Only a few Tournatow diesel-electric-drive tractors were tested for use with the U.S. Air Force. This unit, originally built in March 1953, is at work in December 1954 helping a Boeing B-47 Stratojet out of its hanger. With all-wheel electric-drive and -steer functions, the Tournatow AT-4 was ideally suited to the task of aircraft tug.

When the Cold War got into full swing in the early 1950s, the United States gave high priority to building, maintaining, and supplying its many operations in Greenland that made up the Ballistic Missile Early Warning System (BMEWS). To help in this endeavor, the Transportation Research and Development Command (TRADCOM) of the U. S. Army Transportation Corps began testing a number of concepts for transporting cargo across the Greenland Ice Cap. One of the machines tested was the Series TC-264 Sno-Buggy, built by R. G. LeTourneau in June 1954. The Sno-Buggy was a diesel-electric-drive design with four AC drive wheel motors. Power was supplied by a single Allison 12-cylinder engine rated at 400 gross horsepower, modified to run on butane. For floatation on snow, the unit was equipped with eight large 10-foot-diameter, low-pressure, wide-base tires, produced by the Firestone Tire and Rubber Company in molds designed, built, and owned by R. G. LeTourneau, Inc. The prototype Sno-Buggy, along with its matching four-wheel, nonpowered trailer, was shipped to Thule Air Base in Greenland for testing in August 1954. The Sno-Buggy would continue in trial service through the end of the year. Only one example of the Sno-Buggy and its sister trailer were built.

Another long-running military program with LeTourneau was the Corporal Missile Loader. Designed in conjunction with Firestone, which actually built the Corporal SSM-A-17 Guided Missile itself, the Loader was the vehicle that would pick up the missile and transport it to its designated launching site. First introduced in early 1952 as the XM-1, the vehicle had a four-wheel-drive layout with DC electric-traction-drive motors. Features of the early XM-1 included a C-type tow unit equipped with a dozing blade and a cable-operated missile hoist system. Rather crude-looking, the original XM-1 did not perform well in its initial form. A redesign was called for, which included an improved front end and cab unit, and an electrically operated rack-and-pinion hoist design. This model, referred to as the XM-2, was built in April 1954. The last version of the Loader was the production M-2 unit, which first started shipping in November 1956. It featured a more refined front end, along with improved electrical systems. LeTourneau made 21 units of the XM-1 Corporal Missile Loader between 1952 and 1953, 30 of the XM-2 between 1954 and 1955, and 10 of the M-2 variety between 1956 and 1957.

In the early 1950s, the U.S. Army contracted R. G. LeTourneau, Inc., to design and build a prototype vehicle capable of retrieving beached or capsized amphibious landing craft. The company's answer to the Army's perceived problem was the Series MA-31 Landing Craft Retriever (LCR). First shown at the Longview plant on November 29, 1954, the LCR resembled a massive tubular-framed, wheeled gantry crane. The LCR was carried on four 10-foot-diameter tires on steerable wheels driven by DC traction-drive motors. The LCR was capable of wading into surf 8 feet deep in order to retrieve a stricken landing craft or other small boat. The vehicle would raise the vessel with two traveling overhead cranes, each equipped with two electric hoists, capable of lifting a maximum of 67 tons. The LCR was powered by two Detroit Diesel 6-71 engines capable of a combined 460 gross horsepower. The one-and-only Series MA-31 LCR was delivered to Fort Eustis, Virginia. Tests were performed on the unit up and down the Virginian coastline, starting in January 1956. Though the LCR proved somewhat effective in its intended role, the Army, as well as the Navy, decided to pass on such a large single-purpose machine.

The Ice-Tow diesel-electric-drive tractor was designed for the U.S. Air Force for use on icy and snow-covered runways. With its four-wheel drive, it steered by means of a double articulated chassis using a rack-and-pinion gear system. Built in August 1956, only one Ice-Tow was manufactured.

The Series TC-264 Sno-Buggy originated with a request from the U.S. Army Transportation Corps for a vehicle capable of traveling across the Greenland Ice Cap. Unveiled in June 1954, the Sno-Buggy was powered by a butane-fueled Allison V1710 engine. All four wheels were driven by AC electric-traction wheel motors, with eight 120-inch tires mounted in pairs. Only one Sno-Buggy (S.N. 5072) was ever built.

LeTourneau's Squashed Bug

Few of the world's car designs impressed R. G. LeTourneau. One that did, however, was the Volkswagen Beetle. R. G. respected its simple, rear-engined design and reliability. But what he really admired about the "Bug" was its ability to go just about anywhere. Put a set of chains on the rear-drive wheels, and it was as competent as far more complicated and expensive vehicles on most any terrain. Its uncluttered, steel-encased bottom meant that it could be driven in the

It seems that R. G. LeTourneau's 1957 Volkswagen Beetle had seen better days. Luckily, he had just stepped out of it before it met with its final demise.

testing areas and not get hung up on the uneven and often rutted terrain—something his previous cars of choice, mainly Fords, often did. R. G. started driving Beetles in the 1950s and continued with them through most of the 1960s. He usually kept one parked near the main entrance of the plant, underneath the guard tower.

One day, around 1957, while out and about the testing area of the Longview plant, LeTourneau came upon one of his electric-drive machines just sitting idle. This was something R. G. didn't like to see. A machine sitting idle in the testing area usually meant mechanical problems. Unable to pull alongside the vehicle, he pulled his Beetle in behind it and got out to see what the problem was. Just as he cleared the back of the machine to head up to the operator's compartment area, the machine started to move . . . backward! Though R. G. yelled at the top of his lungs at the operator to stop, his voice was no match for a diesel engine's roar. Seconds later the Beetle had been squashed like a bug, so to speak.

Once the operator realized something was not quite right with the way his machine was handling, he got out to see what the problem was. There was R. G. and what was left of his beloved Beetle. It turned out the operator had stopped for only a moment to take a cigarette break. He had never seen the VW pull up behind him, let alone R. G. yelling at him to stop. Luckily, no one was hurt. About the only thing to come of the whole incident was the occasional joking reference from the plant workers on how R. G. lost his VW. It wouldn't be long though, before another Beetle was parked under the guard tower, ready to zip out to the testing area so R. G. could see how his creations were doing that day.

The M-2 Corporal Missile Loader was the last version of this U.S. Army vehicle to be put into production. Designed with Firestone, which actually built the Corporal SSM-A-17 Guided Missile, the M-2 utilized an electric drivetrain with all wheels driven. It was powered by a 375-gross-horsepower air-cooled, Continental Model AO-895-4, six-cylinder gasoline engine. The M-2 was originally built in 1956, with 10 units shipped into service. In all, 61 Corporal Missile Loaders were built, including the early XM-1 and XM-2 variations.

In 1955, the U.S.A.F. Strategic Air Command (SAC) approached R. G. LeTourneau, Inc., in search of a system for removing crashed heavy bombers from an active runway in the shortest amount of time possible. The goal was to find the best method of removing a stricken 200-plus-ton bomber within 20 minutes. LeTourneau's answer to this problem was a pair of ultralarge vehicles referred to as the Series A-A Crash Pushers, Models CP-1 and CP-2. Using the basic design layout of the six-wheel Model 6-120 Tree Crasher, the company built two identical six-wheel-drive tractors with dozing blades and operator's cabs, both front and rear. The 67-ton Crash Pusher, with LeTourneau diesel-electric drive and a big Cummins VT-12 diesel with 600 gross horsepower, had all the power it would need to get the job done. Built in November 1955, the Crash Pushers were shipped to a U.S.A.F. base to begin testing. On December 16, the Crash Pushers, Fantabulous I and II, made short work of a downed Convair B-36 Peacemaker heavy bomber carcass, as they sliced and diced it into small, manageable chunks while clearing the runway. In November 1957, both units were retrofitted with a higher-lifting, narrow V-blade attachment that was specifically designed to make contact under the wings of swept-wing aircraft, most notably Boeing's B-52 Stratofortress, giving the Crash Pusher more downward pressure and better traction while working. In 1958, Fantabulous I and II were officially cleared for active duty and became part of SAC's aircraft handling system.

The Series MA-31 Landing Craft Retriever (LCR) was essentially a large mobile gantry crane structure, mounted on electric-drive wheels with 120-inch-diameter tires. Built in November 1954 for the U.S. Army, the MA-31 LCR was designed to retrieve beached or capsized amphibious landing craft. Only one LCR (S.N. 5234) was tested by the military.

The Series A-A (Model CP-1) Crash Pusher was an ultra-heavy-duty, three-axle, diesel-electric-drive vehicle designed for the U.S. Air Force Strategic Air Command to quickly remove crashed heavy bombers from runways. A single 600-gross-horsepower Cummins VT-12 provided power for the unit. Two Crash Pushers were built in November 1955, referred to as "Fantabulous I" and "Fantabulous II." This is Fantabulous I in November 1957, retrofitted with a special V-blade designed to lift and sheer the wings off a downed swept-wing bomber.

R. G. LeTourneau, Inc., built a number of diesel-electric, all-wheel-drive cargo land-trains. The first of these ultra-specialized vehicles was the Model VC-12 Tournatrain. Originally tested in February 1953 with a single-engined tractor unit, it was redesigned in February 1954 with two Cummins VT-12 diesels, rated at 1,000 gross horsepower combined. Pictured in April 1954 is the redesigned unit with seven powered trailers in tow, giving it 32-wheel drive. The company built only one Tournatrain (S.N. 5032).

The Trackless "Land Trains"

During the 1950s and early 1960s, R. G. LeTourneau conceived and built five "land trains" utilizing his electric-drive system. All of the designs employed multiple cars towed inline, powered by electric-traction-wheel motors in various numbers. The first of the trackless electric land trains was the Model VC-12 Tournatrain, which the company tested in February 1953. The Tournatrain consisted of one power unit and three 20-ton-capacity trailers, each powered by four individual electric-traction wheel motors. The 16 drive wheels were powered by a single 500-gross-horsepower Cummins VT-12 diesel engine, mounted in the lead car, or locomotive. After months of testing, the company added a second Cummins engine to the tractor, bringing total gross horsepower up to 1,000. The fuel tank was also doubled in size. These alterations were finished in February 1954. With the unit's extra power came four additional powered trailers, bringing the total drive wheel count to 32. Maximum payload potential was 140 tons. The Tournatrain was designed to be driven over rough, undeveloped land areas that were unsuitable for ordinary cargo vehicles.

On April 15, 1954, the company demonstrated the Tournatrain to TRADCOM officials, hoping to convince them that a trackless electric train with multiple driven wheels was the best way to transport cargo over snow-packed terrain. TRADCOM thought the concept had merit, and LeTourneau developed a prototype over the following months. Testing continued throughout 1955, but TRADCOM never contracted for a Tournatrain, nor did any other buyers come forward.

Although no one purchased the first offering, a private company did contract with LeTourneau for a successor land train. The Model VC-22 Sno-Freighter was custom built for Alaska Freight Lines, Inc., of Seattle, Washington. Its president, Alfred Ghezzi Jr., had made a business proposal to Western Electric Corporation, which was the principal contractor for building the main U.S., Canadian, and European strategic radar defense network. This network would make up the Distant Early Warning system, better known as the DEW Line, employing surveillance stations stretched from the Aleutian Islands, across Alaska and western Canada, and into northern Greenland. The proposed agreement between Alaska Freight Lines and Western Electric called for Ghezzi's company to haul an initial 500 tons of construction material for the radar systems, to be deposited at designated locations along the DEW Line. Alaska Freight Lines would not be paid until the last load of freight was delivered.

To help in the preparation of such an ambitious project, Alaska Freight Lines set up new headquarters in Fairbanks, Alaska, which would be the main staging area for new drivers and equipment. Alaska Freight Lines signed a contract with R. G. LeTourneau, Inc., on January 5, 1955, for a six-unit, off-road freighter, capable of carrying 150 tons of cargo. It would also need to be able to trek through large snowdrifts, cross rivers up to 4 feet deep, and be able to function in temperatures as low as -68 degrees Fahrenheit. LeTourneau's solution to the specified requirements was the 24-wheel electric-drive Model VC-22 Sno-Freighter, also referred to as the Cross-Country Freighter.

The second land-train built by the company was the Model VC-22 Sno-Freighter, designed and built for Alaska Freight Lines. The Sno-Freighter consisted of a powered locomotive tractor with two Cummins NVH-12BI diesel engines rated at 800 gross horsepower combined, and five powered cargo trailers. The one-and-only Sno-Freighter (S.N. 5198 tractor, 5199 thru 5203 trailers) was completed in February 1955, and is shown here traveling in Alaska in March 1956.

Construction on the Sno-Freighter started almost immediately after the contract was signed. Since the vehicle would utilize LeTourneau's electric-drive system, major components were readily at hand. The lead tractor unit would house two Cummins NVH-12BI diesels with 800 combined gross horsepower. This, along with their inline AC/DC generators, would supply the needed power to drive all 24 independent wheel motors. With all the trailers in tow, the unit measured 274 feet in length. By February 17, 1955, the entire train was complete, minus its final paint job. That would take place in late February. The Sno-Freighter's long journey up to Circle, Alaska, officially got under way on February 21, as various loaded railcars started to make their way out of Longview, Texas.

During its working life for Alaska Freight Lines, the Sno-Freighter performed well. In 1955, the Sno-Freighter and its support vehicles were the first such machines ever to be driven north to the Arctic Ocean. Long out of service, the Sno-Feighter today sits alongside the main highway between Anchorage and Fairbanks, Alaska, waiting to be restored into a tourist attraction.

In October 1955, LeTourneau unveiled another multiwheeled vehicle simply referred to as the Side-Dump Train. In this configuration, 18 wheels were driven, with power supplied by a longitudinally mounted Cummins VT-12, 600-gross-horsepower diesel engine, mounted in the front of the lead unit. The main power unit and its two trailers each had a side-dumping body

designed to carry whatever the owner decided to put into it. It was not, however, to be marketed as an "earthmoving" device in accordance with the sales agreement made with LeTourneau-Westinghouse. Though the unit was tested throughout 1956, it was never sold.

The company built another trackless train in 1955 at the request of the U.S. Army. This vehicle was known as the Logistical Cargo Carrier (LCC-1) in Army lingo, or, as the company called it, the Model YS-1 Army Sno-Train. The Army Transportation Corps wanted a large, multipowered wheeled vehicle capable of bringing fresh supplies to its radar installations along the DEW Line. Impressed by test results from the TC-264 Sno-Buggy, and the demonstration of the multiwheeled Tournatrain, both in 1954, the Army felt that a combination of the two would produce the desired results. That vehicle would became the LCC-1. The LCC-1 was made up of a leading power unit and three trailers, all driven by 16 electric-traction wheel motors, with 10-foot-diameter tires. These tires were the same as those utilized on the Sno-Buggy. The combined load capacity for the three trailers was 45 tons. A single Cummins VT-12 diesel, rated at 600 gross horsepower, provided the necessary muscle to power the train. The LCC-1 was just over 173 feet long. By January 1956, the LCC-1 was ready for testing at the Longview plant. In March of that year, it was shipped to the TRADCOM in Houghton, Michigan, for further testing in snow conditions. After its stay there, it was dismantled and shipped to Greenland for further testing and resupply duties on the ice cap by TRADCOM. As of 1998, the LCC-1, which had been retired by the military from active service decades ago, was in storage in a contractor's yard in Fairbanks, Alaska, awaiting an uncertain future.

Introduced in October 1955, the Side-Dump Train was a bulk material hauler. Power was supplied to the diesel-electric-drive system by a front, longitudinally mounted 600-gross-horsepower Cummins VT-12 engine. All 18 wheels were driven by individual electric-traction motors. The Side-Dump Train was strictly a one-off creation.

The lead power car of the LCC-1 housed a single 600-gross-horsepower Cummins VT-12 diesel engine, which, along with its inline-mounted generator, supplied current to 16 traction-wheel motors. The Army ordered only one LCC-1 (S.N. 5270 tractor; 5271 thru 5273 trailers).

The Model YS-1 Army Sno-Train (also referred to as the Logistical Cargo Carrier [LCC-1], its official military designation) was built in January 1956 and was designed to supply radar installations along the D.E.W. Line. The total load capacity for all three trailers combined was 45 tons. The overall operating length was 173 feet.

The last multipowered wheeled-train design to be built by R. G. LeTourneau was the Model TC-497 Overland Train MkII. The Overland Train was the final expression of what TRADCOM and R. G. LeTourneau had envisioned as the ultimate cross-country land freighter. The Overland Train was designed not only to cross snowy Arctic terrain, but also arid desert sands. The massive vehicle looked as if it drove straight out of a science fiction novel, designed to handle anything the earth or the moon could dish out. The design was packed with the latest in powertrain technology. Past train configurations relied on diesel-electric drivetrains. The Overland Train utilized turbine-electric power. In fact, it used four Solar 10MC gas turbine engines, rated at 1,170 gross horsepower each. One engine was located in the forward command control car, which utilized its powerplant when disconnected from the rest of the train; it was not in use when coupled with it. The actual drive turbines were located at the rear of the train. The first of these cars had one drive turbine; the second car had two. Total power output available for driving the Overland Train was 3,510 gross horsepower. This supplied power to 54 traction-drive motors, mounted with 10-foot-diameter tires, the same as those used on the Sno-Buggy

The largest of R. G. LeTourneau, Inc.'s trackless land-trains was the gigantic Model TC-497 Overland Train MkII. At 572 feet in length, it holds the world's record for the longest vehicle ever built. The Overland Train was turbine-electric powered, with four Solar 10MC gas turbine engines on board—one in the front tractor, and three in the last two power trailers at the end of the train. Total output was 4,680 gross horsepower, but only 3,510 of this was actually utilized for driving the train as a whole unit. In all, there were 54 drive wheels, each with its own electric-traction motor. Introduced in February 1962, the one-and-only Overland Train (S.N. 6017 control car, 6018 thru 6029 trailers) would be the last of the R. G. LeTourneau, Inc., land-trains. Today, the front control-car is preserved at the Yuma Proving Ground Heritage Center in Yuma, Arizona.

and the LCC-1. Along with the control and power-generating units, 10 cargo cars carried a maximum of 150 tons in freight and equipment. The total length of the MkII was a staggering 572 feet. The top speed of the unit was 20 miles per hour, with a cruising range of about 350–400 miles, which could be increased with the addition of the auxiliary fuel cargo cell, bringing total fuel supply up to 7,833 gallons. Full operational weight of the MkII with standard fuel load was 300 tons unladen and 450 tons with cargo.

LeTourneau and TRADCOM engineers completed the specification outline for the Overland Train in 1958. Final design approval came in 1960. Fabrication of the MkII took most of 1961. After preliminary testing at the Longview plant, the unit was officially handed over to Army officials in February 1962. It was

then shipped off to Yuma, Arizona, to start its desert testing program in April of that year. Unfortunately, the Overland Train became obsolete almost as soon as it began testing. During its gestation period, the aeronautics industry had developed large cargo helicopters. With such giant cargo lifters on the horizon, including the massive Sikorsky S-64 Sky-Crane (CH-54A military designation), first flown in 1962, the need for an ultralarge cargo-carrying, land-based vehicle, not requiring roads, evaporated. After all, the big cargo helicopters did not require roads, either. And their overall speeds made the land train seem like a giant snail in comparison. In the end, the Overland Train never got to prove itself. It was soon mothballed with other obsolete military equipment in the hot Arizona desert and eventually scrapped.

The Series L-90 was a real success story for the company, with as many as 31 examples built of all configurations at one time. This close-up view of the lead scraper unit on an L-90 working in California in 1966 shows how this part of the machine was completely self-sufficient. For smaller jobs, the front unit could be disconnected from the other two scrapers and operated as a 30-ton-capacity machine. ECO Collection

Most of the big players in the heavy equipment industry knew that R. G. LeTourneau, Inc.'s five-year moratorium on building earthmovers would expire in 1958. What they did not know was just how the company would reenter the earthmoving marketplace, and what kinds of equipment they would offer. In late January 1957, R. G. publicly announced at the Chicago Road Show that his firm would be getting back into the earthmoving business. Just how, he would not say. But what he did say revealed that these upcoming earthmovers would be built around his diesel-electric-drive system.

Since 1953, R. G. LeTourneau had gained considerable experience with his electric-traction-drive motors in earthmoving applications. The many scraper prototypes built for military consideration provided a wealth of field experience. Though none of these concepts ever made it into full production, the knowledge gained from them was not about to go to waste. Starting in early 1958, R. G. started building the first pilot machines that would form the basis for his new breed of scrapers, to be known as "Electric-Diggers."

In February 1958 the company put two scraper prototype machines to work on an earthmoving contract in San Antonio, Texas, along the San Antonio River. One machine was identified as a 30-ton-capacity Single C Scraper, while the other, a tandem unit, was called a Double C Scraper. This model was rated at 60 tons combined. The Single C consisted of a single-axle tractor front, much like that found on one of the company's transporters, and a rear scraper unit with four driven wheels. A single engine up front supplied power for the complete system. The Double C utilized a similar tractor design, but with a larger engine. This was needed to supply power to the four drive wheels of the rear scraper unit. In all, the Double C had 10 driving wheels equipped with electric-traction motors, all powered by one diesel engine.

It wasn't long before LeTourneau-Westinghouse in Peoria, Illinois, got word of what R. G. was up to in San Antonio. LeTourneau-Westinghouse immediately sent some of its people down to the work site to see for themselves just what they might be up against in the coming months. Once photographs arrived back in Peoria, LeTourneau-Westinghouse immediately filed a lawsuit in Federal District Court on April 7, 1958, against R. G. LeTourneau, Inc. In the suit, Westinghouse asked the court to restrain R. G. LeTourneau from using any of the earthmoving engineering patents and trademarks sold to the company in 1953.

They further insisted that the court restrain the Texas-based company from using the LeTourneau name on any type of earthmoving equipment as a brand or product trade identification. Spokesmen for R. G. LeTourneau, Inc., insisted that they had every intention of living up to the agreement from the original sale in 1953. But Westinghouse had its doubts.

May 1 came and went without much fanfare. But the folks in Longview, Texas, knew that they were free from the legal shackles that had restrained them for the last five years, prohibiting them from building and marketing commercial earthmoving equipment. One of the first things that R. G. LeTourneau did was cut his last ties with LeTourneau-Westinghouse. On May 13, 1958, R. G. LeTourneau announced that he would not renew his personal consulting agreement with the LeTourneau-Westinghouse Company that had existed since 1953. At that time, R. G. had made a personal agreement to assist LeTourneau-Westinghouse as a part-time earthmoving consultant, in addition to his regular duties with his own company, R. G. LeTourneau, Inc. The agreement also stated that R. G. would act as an earthmoving consultant for LeTourneau-Westinghouse only and could not offer his services to any other earthmoving contractor or manufacturer. When this agreement came up for renewal in May, R. G. declined to continue the working relationship, citing his own company's increased activities.

During the month of May, R. G. LeTourneau put another experimental electric-drive machine to work in San Antonio, identified as the Single A Scraper. Utilizing the same six-wheel-drivetrain layout as the Single C Scraper, the Single A was a much larger unit. It looked much like the Single C, but was proportionally larger all the way around. It was powered by a larger and more powerful turbocharged Cummins Diesel engine and carried a claimed 70-ton payload capacity. This machine would provide the engineering basis for the company's first scraper design in its new line of diesel-electric-drive earthmoving equipment. Identified as the L-70, it would mark the beginning of R. G. LeTourneau's famous Electric-Digger series.

The Electric-Diggers

R. G. LeTourneau, Inc.'s first piece of earthmoving equipment was the Series L-70 (Model A-4). First introduced at the American Mining Congress equipment show in San Francisco, it was placed prominently on display in front of San Francisco's Civic

The DC Self-Loading Scraper, built in October 1957, was designed for possible use by the U.S. Army. The experimental scraper used diesel-electric drive and steered by means of an articulated rack-and-pinion gear system. The load capacity was in the range of 20 to 25 tons. Though only a one-off, its basic design would form the foundation for many production electric-drive scrapers to come after May 1958.

This experimental Single A Scraper, at work in May 1958, would supply the engineering foundation for the Series L-70. Based on the Single C Scraper layout from March 1958, the larger Single A featured six-wheel electric drive and a 600-gross-horsepower turbocharged Cummins VT-12BI diesel engine. The payload capacity was listed at 70 tons. Only one unit was built.

The first diesel-electric-drive scraper to be publicly announced after R. G. LeTourneau, Inc., officially re-entered the earthmoving equipment market was the Series L-70 (Model A-4). Unveiled in September 1958 at the American Mining Congress equipment show in San Francisco, it featured a single 600-gross-horsepower, turbocharged Cummins VT-12BI diesel, and four drive wheels, each with its own electric-traction motor. The capacity was 70 tons. This early L-70 (S.N. 5720) was strictly a one-off, experimental show machine.

Auditorium from September 22 through September 25, 1958. The big LeTourneau was impossible to miss. It was the world's largest scraper, with a 70-ton payload capacity and a 50–60-cubic-yard rating. The L-70 was powered by a Cummins Diesel VT-12BI, rated at 600 gross horsepower. This engine powered an AC/DC generator, which in turn supplied current to the DC traction-wheel motors. A key feature of this design was power proportioning, which shifted power away from any wheel that began to slip, and directed it to the wheels with traction. This electric-drive-system layout would become the hallmark of all of the company's electric scrapers, as well as all other types of R. G. LeTourneau earthmovers yet to come.

The L-70 was a four drive-wheel design, with a single-axle power unit up front that housed the engine. Though the L-70 was certainly huge, many thought the design somehow looked "unfinished," especially concerning the operator's station. With its characteristic LeTourneau square-edge look, it was a no-nonsense design built for work and only work. There was nothing aesthetically pleasing in the looks of the L-70. But that was OK with R. G., who felt that cosmetic and streamlined sheet metal only added more weight and cost to his designs. But many in the industry would disagree, especially customers. They had to pay big money for these earthmovers, and look at them all day long, so they wanted machines with at least a little aesthetic appeal.

At the unveiling of the L-70, the prototype carried no real identification to speak of, just large black lettering on the front and sides reading, "Manufactured by R. G. LeTourneau, Inc.,

Longview, Texas." This identification on the machine couldn't have made LeTourneau-Westinghouse very happy, but it was painted on the machine merely to name its manufacturer and where it was made. It was not meant to be the trademark manufacturing name, which would have violated the terms of the sales agreement that R. G. LeTourneau had with LeTourneau-Westinghouse. Though these new scraper designs would eventually be identified as Electric-Diggers, that name did not appear on this machine. Neither did the name "Goliath," which the trade reporters had coined to describe the huge machine. The L-70 was never intended for serious production. Instead, it was used as an eye-opening statement for the earthmoving industry that R. G. LeTourneau was back—and in a big way.

The next scraper models to be introduced followed immediately, with the Series L-130 (Model A-8) appearing in October 1958, and the Series L-50 (C-8) the next month. Each of these designs utilized eight driving wheels and tandem scraper bowls. The L-50 was rated at 55-tons capacity, while the much larger L-130 carried a maximum payload of 130 tons. Up front, the L-50 was powered by a single Cummins VT-12BI diesel, rated at 600 gross horsepower. The L-130 utilized two such Cummins powerplants, giving it a healthy 1,200 combined gross horsepower.

In 1959, the company made "Electric-Digger" its official scraper product name, using it to describe both the L-50 and L-130 in advertising literature and press releases. In 1960, it introduced the trade name "Pacemaker" to cover not only both

In October 1958, R. G. LeTourneau, Inc., introduced the Series L-130 (Model A-8) tandem, diesel-electric-drive scraper. The L-130 was powered by two turbocharged Cummins VT-12BI diesels, rated at 1,200 gross horsepower combined. All eight wheels were driven. The load capacity was 130 tons, and the overall length was 103 feet, 6 inches. This L-130, now referred to as an Electric-Digger, is at work in April 1959. Only two L-130s (S.N. 5729/6015) were manufactured, with the second unit converted into the first prototype L-140 in 1960.

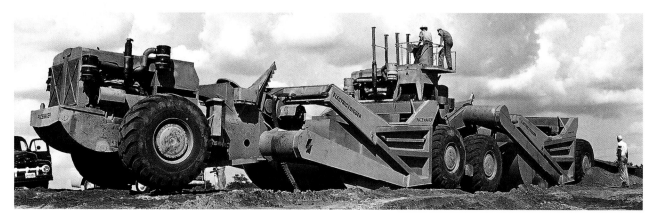

The Pacemaker Series L-140 (Model A-8) Electric-Digger made its first appearance in May 1960. The first unit, which was actually a partially redesigned L-130, was powered by three Detroit Diesel 12V-71 engines rated at 1,260 gross horsepower combined, with a 130-ton payload capacity. In early 1961, the L-140 gained an additional 12V-71 powerplant, raising gross output to 1,680 horsepower. The payload rating also increased to 140 tons. The L-140 was the same length as the L-130 and incorporated the same number of drive wheels. Pictured in August 1961 is a 1,680-horsepower version of the L-140. Three L-140s were produced, including the converted L-130 unit.

The Series L-50 (Model C-8) was introduced in October 1958, the same time as the Series L-130. The L-50 was powered by a single 600-gross-horsepower, turbocharged Cummins VT-12BI diesel engine. The drivetrain was diesel-electric, with eight driving wheels. The payload capacity was 55 tons, and the overall length was 78 feet. This L-50, now referred to as an Electric-Digger, is at work in May 1959, with an L-130 in the background.

The Pacemaker Series L-60 (Model C-8) Electric-Digger took the place of the Series L-50 in May 1960. The L-60 was essentially an L-50 with another engine grafted on. The L-60 was powered by a 420-gross-horsepower Detroit Diesel 12V-71 in the lead tractor, and a 280-horsepower 8V-71 at the rear of the first scraper.

electric-diggers, but all new earthmoving equipment product lines that were starting to emerge from Longview. So, for example, the 55-ton-capacity scraper became the Pacemaker Series L-50 Electric-Digger. The LeTourneau name still could only be used on the company's earthmoving products as a means of identification of the manufacturer, and not as a trade name under which to sell the machines. By late 1964, however, the Pacemaker designation started to fade away in its usage and by the end of 1965, it had slipped from sight altogether.

When the first few Series L-50 Electric-Diggers were put into service, it soon became apparent that a little more power was needed, with a better weight distribution, to make the unit a true self-loading scraper under less-than-ideal working conditions. In May 1960, the company began an upgrade program for the L-50, which included an additional Detroit Diesel 8V-71 engine mounted at the rear of the first scraper unit, above the four center drive wheels. The front-mounted engine was changed to a Detroit Diesel 12V-71. Total gross horsepower output was listed at 700 combined for the two powerplants. The new Pacemaker Series L-60 (Model C-8) Electric-Digger was initially rated at 55-ton capacity, but in 1961, the payload rating was increased to 60 tons. But life for this early L-60 Electric-Digger would be brief also, with the last unit shipping to a customer in February 1962. In all, 11 Series L-50 Electric-Diggers were built, with the last one shipping in June 1960. In the first Series L-60, only 7 machines saw the light of day.

The Series L-130 Electric-Digger also proved lacking in overall balance. First operational in October 1958, the L-130 was a tandem scraper design like the L-50, but larger and more powerful. It was powered by a pair of Cummins VT-12BI diesels with a combined rating of 1,200 gross horsepower. Both engines were mounted in the lead power unit, which also accommodated the operator. Like the L-50, the L-130 had eight independent electric-drive wheels. Capacity was 130 tons for both scraper bowls combined.

By mid-1959, the company had a second L-130 unit, identical to the first, in field testing. The two machines worked next to each other in July 1959 at the Reynolds-Huff-LeTourneau subdivision development near the Longview plant. During these tests, the L-130s proved themselves severely underpowered, as they were not able to load themselves fully without additional pushing help. To correct the problem, the second L-130 was modified in December 1959 with an additional Detroit Diesel 12V-71 engine mounted above the center four drive wheels, between the two scraper bowls. This raised the gross horsepower to a more respectable 1,620. The operator's station was moved to this same midpoint location as well.

By May 1960, the modified L-130 was changed even further when the two Cummins diesels were replaced with more compact and cost-effective Detroit Diesel 12V-71 engines, each rated at 420 gross horsepower. With three identical engines, the L-130 put out 1,260 gross horsepower. This more balanced engine

This prototype Series L-28 (Model C-4) was first put into testing in November 1958. Its diesel-electric drivetrain was powered by a single 420-gross-horsepower Detroit Diesel 12V-71 engine, which supplied power to electric-traction motors in each wheel. The payload capacity was rated at 30 tons (28 cubic yards heaped).

arrangement allowed capacity to be increased to 140 tons, inspiring a new model designation—the Pacemaker Series L-140 Electric-Digger.

The first L-140 built was in fact the second L-130 unit. In early 1961, the L-140 design gained an additional Detroit Diesel 12V-71 engine, mounted midway between the scraper units, next to the powerplant already there. This raised engine output to 1,680 gross horsepower. In all, there were three L-140 units produced, counting the converted L-130. As for the L-130, two were originally built, with the second converted into the prototype L-140. The last L-140 shipped from the Longview plant in June 1962.

In late 1958, LeTourneau began testing a smaller prototype scraper of more modest proportions called the Series L-28 (Model C-4). Rated with a 30-ton payload capacity, and a four-wheel-drive layout, it was aimed toward the smaller- to midsized contractor marketplace. The L-28 was powered by a single Detroit Diesel 12V-71 engine, rated at 420 gross horsepower, mounted in the front power unit. The operator sat atop and to the rear of the engine bay, in a fully enclosed cab. Only the prototype utilized an open-air, steel-tube, wire-mesh design. The first production L-28 shipped in April 1959, and would officially be called a Pacemaker

Series L-28 in 1960. In all, six of these L-28s, including the prototype, were eventually built.

Starting in February 1961, R. G. LeTourneau launched a redesigned version of the 30-ton-capacity scraper called the Pacemaker Series L-28 (Model Hi-C-4). This version of the L-28 featured a redesigned front tractor unit, with the operator's cab mounted offset on the left, just behind the engine compartment. Modifications were also made to the scraper unit, but capacity was unaltered. Eventually, the company would sell 10 L-28 units of this style.

The last of the L-28 Electric-Digger scraper designs was the Pacemaker L-28A (Model Ring-C-4). Built in May 1963, the L-28A looked far more refined than the previous Hi-C-4 Model version, especially in the integration of the engine bay, operator's cab, and access ladders and decking. The main scraper hitch was also redesigned, but capacity and power output remained unchanged. Despite the improvements, the company built only two Model L-28A units.

The original L-28, L-50, and L-130 Electric-Diggers were the first salvo of engineering designs put forth by the company. But with five years of engineering concepts up his sleeve, it seemed

In 1959, the Series L-28 was officially referred to as an Electric-Digger. The following year, it gained the product sales name Pacemaker. This photo from November 1960 shows an L-28 ready for shipping at the Longview plant. A total of six L-28 (Model C-4) units were built in this first series type.

February 1961 would see the introduction of the Pacemaker Series L-28 (Model Hi-C-4) Electric-Digger. The Model Hi-C-4 version of the L-28 featured a redesigned tractor unit with an offset cab. Some minor structural changes were made to the scraper unit, but capacity ratings remained unchanged. The drivetrain was also left intact from the previous model. Eventually 10 of this L-28 model type would be produced.

The last version of the Pacemaker Series L-28 was the L-28A (Model Ring-C-4) in May 1963. The L-28A featured a redesigned tractor unit, as well as an improved scraper unit. The engine type, power, and capacity ratings remained unaltered from previous model types. But in the end, only two examples of the L-28A were ever built.

that R. G. LeTourneau had a new Pacemaker design ready for testing practically monthly. Between 1960 and 1964, the company fielded no less than 22 prototype Pacemaker Electric-Digger Model lines in various configurations of drive wheels and bowl designs. Many of these, especially the three-wheeled designs, looked like something right out of a science fiction magazine. R. G. was having his engineers and designers build his concepts as fast as he could come up with them. Though this might not have been the most cost-effective manufacturing approach, it surely produced equipment designs never before imagined, or seen since, in the earthmoving industry. Pacemaker Electric-Diggers during this time period included the Series L-20, Model C-42, in October 1962 (one built); the Series 29/L-21, Model C-4, in September 1963 (two built); the Series LT-22, Model C-3, in July 1962 (one built); the Series LV-24, Model C-4, in March 1964 (one built); the Series L-27, Model C-3, in March 1960 (one built); the Series LTU, Model A-3, in July 1960 (one built with two different engine configurations); the Series LTV, Model A-3, in January 1962 (two built); the Series LTV-27, Model C-3, in February 1962 (one built); the Series LTC/LC-35, Model C-42, in October 1963 (seven built); the LT/LC-60, Model A-3, in August

1962 (five built); the Series LTV-60, Model C-3, in October 1963 (one built); the Series LTV-60, Model C-6, in October 1963 (one built); the Series L-67, Model C-7, in March 1960 (two built); the Series LTC/LC-75, Model A-4, in April 1963 (five built); the Series LT-110, Model A-6, in August 1962 (one built); and the odd Model A-3 Dozer-Hauler, in January 1964 (one built).

Of all these models, the Series LTC/LC-35, LT/LC-60, and LTC/LC-75 were the most successful, at least as far as numbers built is concerned. All were designed as coal stockpiling scrapers. The majority of the rest of these experimental machines were either shipped to the missionary Tournata, Liberia, or the Tournavista, Peru, projects, or scrapped at the Longview or Vicksburg plants. Although production activity was frantic, Pacemaker Electric-Diggers were making little impact in the earthmoving marketplace. These machines were being followed closely by a large audience in the industry—it just wasn't a paying audience.

In August 1963, R. G. LeTourneau started testing a newly designed Pacemaker Electric-Digger that showed great promise. Called the Series L-45, it was configured much like the original Series L-60 from 1960. The L-45 was powered by two Detroit

The Pacemaker Series LTV-60 (Model C-6) Electric-Digger was an experimental, three-telescoping-bowl, 60-ton-capacity, diesel-electric-drive scraper. Powered by two rear-mounted Detroit Diesel 12V-71 engines, and rated at 840 gross horsepower combined, it featured six-wheel drive. Built in October 1963, only one LTV-60 (S.N. 6237) was ever produced.

One of the more unusual tandem scrapers built by R. G. LeTourneau, Inc., was the Pacemaker Series L-67 (Model C-7) Electric-Digger, in March 1960. The L-67 was a seven-electric-drive-wheel design, with a single-wheeled steering power "tug" unit in front. Two Detroit Diesel 12V-71 engines, rated at 820 gross horsepower together, supplied the power. The load capacity was 60 tons. Just two L-67 tandem units (S.N. 5954/5975) were put into service.

The Pacemaker Series LT-110 (Model A-6) Electric-Digger was very similar to the LTV-60, only much larger. The massive diesel-electric-drive scraper was of a four-bucket telescoping design, rated at 95 tons capacity. Four rear-mounted Detroit Diesel 12V-71 engines capable of 1,680 gross horsepower supplied power for the big six-wheel-drive unit. Introduced in August 1962, only one LT-110 (S.N. 6112) would make it into the iron.

Diesel 12V-71N engines, rated at 475 gross horsepower each. One engine was placed in the front tow unit, while the other was mounted at the rear of the first scraper unit. The L-45 was a tandem scraper design with eight powered driving wheels. The scraper bowls were all-new designs, not carried over from the L-60, with combined capacity a bit under 45 tons. It was a self-loading design that would mark the beginning of the company's most successful run of Electric-Digger Models yet. Though only four L-45 tandem units were built, three would be factory converted to an even larger model, called the Series L-70.

The Pacemaker Series L-70 was first introduced in February 1964. The first three L-70s built were the converted L-45 models, with an additional powered scraper placed between the original machines' tandem scraper units. This would give the new model three Detroit Diesel 12V-71N engines, with a combined output of 1,425 gross horsepower, driving 12 wheels. Maximum capacity of all three scraper units was 85 tons—30 tons each for the rear scrapers and 25 tons for the front unit. In the field, the L-70 Electric-Diggers performed quite well in tough working conditions, even though only seven units, including the conversions, were ever produced. But this was only the start for

R. G. LeTourneau's triple-bowled Electric-Diggers. The best was yet to come.

R. G. LeTourneau would finally introduce a redesigned version of his original L-60 Electric-Digger in April 1964. The prototype was actually built from an earlier model, with the operator's station moved to the rear of the first tandem unit. The unit also had redesigned scraper hitches. The bowls were left as originally designed. The two-engine, eight-drive-wheel configuration remained the same as the original L-60 model. But in October 1964, the company turned out a much improved L-60, sporting the totally redesigned scraper bowls that first made their appearance on a triple-bowled scraper (the L-90) introduced a few months earlier. Normally, the L-60 would be configured as a C-8 Model with eight drive wheels and two engines. But in February 1965, four original L-90 units were sold as special L-60-3 Electric-Diggers, classified as a C-10 Model with 10 drive wheels and three engines totaling 1,425 gross horsepower. Essentially, they were L-90 scrapers minus their third trailing units. Of all the new L-60s originally built, 16 were produced with two engines, and only four with three engines—the L-60-3 units.

Introduced in August 1962, the Pacemaker Series LT-60 (Model A-3) Electric-Digger was a diesel-electric, three-wheel-drive unit. Designed as a coal stockpiling scraper, the LT-60 (also known as LC-60) was powered by two rear-mounted engines—one 432-gross-horsepower Detroit Diesel 12V-71, and one 280-horsepower 8V-71, adding up to 712 horsepower (increased to 795 horsepower in 1965). The capacity was 45 tons, and 67.8 cubic yards heaped. The total production run was five units.

The largest of the coal stockpiling scrapers was the Pacemaker Series LTC-75 (Model A-4) Electric-Digger of April 1963. The LTC-75, later referred to as the LC-75, was one of R. G. LeTourneau, Inc.'s more conventional-looking scraper models. Power was provided by two Detroit Diesel 12V-71 engines, rated at 840 gross horsepower combined—raised to 950 horsepower in 1966. The payload capacity was 65 tons (91 cubic yards heaped), and the overall length was 67 feet, 10 inches. Only five LTC/LC-75 scrapers were manufactured.

The tandem Pacemaker Series L-45 (Model C-8) Electric-Digger was first produced in August 1963. The L-45 was powered by two Detroit Diesel 12V-71N engines, rated at 950 gross horsepower. The capacity for the tandem scraper bowls was 45 tons (42 cubic yards).

Introduced in February 1964, the Pacemaker Series L-70 (C-12) Electric-Digger was a triple-scraper unit with 12 drive wheels. Power was supplied by three Detroit Diesel 12V-71N engines, rated at 1,425 gross horsepower combined. The payload capacity was 25 tons in the first scraper, and 30 tons each for the second and third units, totaling 85 tons (60 cubic yards heaped). The maximum length was 105 feet, 10 inches. Seven L-70 units were produced; this number includes the three units built out of tandem L-45 scrapers, such as this one from April 1964.

The most advanced L-60 design was derived from the Series L-90 (Model C-12), first introduced in June 1964. The L-90 was, without a doubt, the most popular and arguably the best of the Electric-Diggers produced by R. G. LeTourneau in the 1960s. As originally conceived, the L-90 was a 12-wheel design, powered by three Detroit Diesel 12V-71N engines, rated at 1,425 gross horsepower combined. The L-90 looked much like the L-70 it replaced, except that its scraper units featured all-new designs, with each of the three bowls capable of a full 30-ton payload. In January 1966, a special version of the 12-wheel L-90 was introduced, capable of a top speed of 25 miles per hour. To achieve this, an additional 12V-71N engine was added to the rear scraper unit, bringing the total output up to 1,900 gross horsepower. The 90-ton maximum capacity remained unchanged. Other variations of the Series L-90 included an 11-wheel, three-engine

model in November 1964, a 7-wheel model with four engines in January 1965, and an 8-wheel, four-engine unit in July 1965.

Overall, the factory produced 20 of the 12-wheel L-90s, one 11-wheel, four 8-wheel, and three 7-wheel versions. This amounts to 28 units. But things are seldom what they seem when talking about multiunit LeTourneau Electric-Diggers. The factory made two L-90 conversion units in July 1965 for converting two L-60 Models into full L-90 machines. In April 1966, one of the original L-60-3 units was returned to full L-90 status. This would bring the L-90 grand total to 31 factory units. But the company continued to tamper with the L-90s in 1969, modifying four of the 12-wheel L-90s for a sale destined for Japan. Two units were converted to Series L-30 status, both of the two-engined variety, while the other two L-90s were modified into three-engined Series L-60-3 models. So as of 1969, a total of 27 L-90s were listed as being sold.

The most popular of the multibowled scraper units built by R. G. LeTourneau, Inc., was the Series L-90 (Model C-12) Electric-Digger. Released in June 1964, the original L-90 (the Pacemaker name had been dropped by this time) was a 12-drive-wheel design, powered by three 475-gross-horsepower Detroit Diesel 12V-71N engines. The payload capacity was 90 tons (72 cubic yards heaped). Pictured here is one of the first L-90s working in Toledo, Ohio, in late June 1964.

In January 1966, R. G. LeTourneau, Inc., introduced a more powerful Series L-90 Electric-Digger capable of attaining a 25-mile-per-hour top speed fully loaded. To attain this speed, a fourth 475-gross-horsepower Detroit Diesel 12V-71N engine was added to the rear of the third scraper unit. This raised the total output to 1,900 horsepower. The capacity remained unchanged. This L-90 (S.N. 6808), owned by Fort Myers Construction Co. of Cape Coral, Florida, is shown at work in October 1967. It was one of the four-engined, high-powered models.

A variation of the Series L-90 Electric-Digger was the Model C-8, first introduced in July 1965. This version of the diesel-electric L-90 had eight drive wheels, each with its own electric-traction motor. The powertrain consisted of four Detroit Diesel 12V-71N engines, rated at 1,900 gross horsepower. The load capacity was the same as the 12-wheeled-model type. The overall working length was 116 feet. Records show that just four 8-wheel L-90s were sold.

The most powerful version of the newer-designed L-60 was the limited-production Series L-60-3 (Model C-10) Electric-Digger. The L-60-3 units were ordered by the Hunt Paving Company, Inc., of Indianapolis, Indiana. They are shown here getting ready to leave the Longview plant by rail in February 1965.

The Series L-60-3 Electric-Digger was powered by three Detroit Diesel 12V-71N engines that produced 1,425 gross horsepower combined. This supplied power to 10 electric-drive wheels, the most for any Series L-60. The capacity was 60 tons (48 cubic yards heaped). The four L-60-3 Electric-Diggers actually started off as L-90s (S.N. 6500 through 6503), but they were reconfigured to meet the specified requirements of Hunt Paving. The serial numbers remained unaltered.

R. G. LeTourneau, Inc., built an experimental one-off Series L-90 (Model A-4) Electric-Digger in June 1966. This diesel-electric L-90 featured a telescoping scraper bowl with a 90-ton payload capacity. Three large Detroit Diesel 16V-71 engines, rated at 1,905 gross horsepower combined.

After this date, any further changes to these models were made in the private sector. The last full-production, nonmodified, factory-built L-90, shipped from the Longview plant on March 17, 1969, destined for Fort Myers Construction in Florida. It was a 12-wheel, four-engine variety carrying serial number 7073.

The multiple-scraper Electric-Diggers were marketed in numerous ways. They could be configured as an L-30, 4- or 6-wheeled; an L-60, 6-, 8-, or 10- wheeled; or an L-90, with 7, 8, 11, or 12 wheels. These variations might have been advertised by LeTourneau, but they didn't produce all of them. In some cases, various specification sheets, with retouched photographs, depicted machines that never were. As previously discussed, all versions of the L-90 were built. The L-60 was never factory produced in a 6-wheel arrangement, nor in an 8-wheel configuration with three engines. The L-60 was built only in 8-wheel, two-engine, and 10-wheel, three-engine forms. As for the single-bowled L-30 model, very few were ever ordered directly from the factory. Company records indicate that only one L-30, with front-mounted ripper and six wheels, was shipped in October 1966. Two additional L-30s shipped to Japan in 1969 were made from two separate L-90s. In December 1964, the company did show a prototype four-wheeled L-30 with two front-mounted engines. In January 1965, this same unit was modified into a three-wheeled unit, with a single engine mounted on the front single-wheeled tug power unit, and a single engine mounted

The Series 2-B 90 Electric-Digger was one of a small group of experimental scraper designs to feature steel tube frames and telescoping buckets. This model, built in October 1966, was a tandem, two-bucket configuration. The payload capacity was 90 tons. Two Detroit Diesel 16V-71 engines, rated at 1,270 gross horsepower combined, provided power. All eight wheels were driven. No factory serial numbers were issued to these concept machines.

The largest of R. G. LeTourneau, Inc.'s steel tube frame, telescoping-bucket-scraper designs was the gigantic Series 6-B 150 Electric-Digger, also referred to as the Model 6-30. This unit utilized a six-bucket design, with a 7-foot, 6-inch opening width. The maximum payload capacity was a hefty 180 tons. Three 635-gross-horsepower Detroit Diesel 16V-71 engines gave the scraper 1,905 horsepower to drive the four wheels. Built in June 1967, the project was deemed too costly to continue and was canceled. Only one example was built, with no factory serial number issued.

in the rear. Records do not indicate what happened to this machine, but it is probably a safe bet it was utilized in some fashion in an L-60 or L-90 built in that same year. It may have seemed in the industry as though LeTourneau produced far more of the L-30 Electric-Diggers than are mentioned here. In reality, owners were using the front unit of their L-60/L-90 scrapers to work as a stand-alone machine on smaller jobs, which is just what R. G. LeTourneau had intended them to do.

Unfortunately, the success of the larger L-60 and L-90 Electric-Diggers did not translate to the company's other big scraper designs built in 1966 and 1967, including the massive experimental LT Electric-Diggers (see chapter 5). Some of the last designs built by R. G. LeTourneau include the Series L-90 (Model A-4) in June 1966, the Series 2-B 45 in August 1966, the Series 2-B

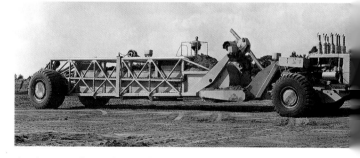

Another experimental one-off telescoping-bucket scraper was the Series 5-B 90 Electric-Digger from September 1966. The scraper bowl was of five-bucket design, and was rated at 90 tons capacity. Two Detroit Diesel 16V-71 engines powered the four electric-drive wheels. The total output was 1,270 gross horsepower.

The last Electric-Digger to be built and sold by the company was the Series SC-35B (Model C-4) Coal Scraper. This model was powered by a single 475-gross-horsepower Detroit Diesel 12V-71N engine. The payload capacity was rated at 30 tons (39 cubic yards heaped). Only two SC-35B scrapers were built and delivered, the first (S.N. 7167) in November 1970 and the second (S.N. 7186) in February 1973. After this, the Electric-Digger scraper program came to an end.

In January 1965, R. G. LeTourneau, Inc., once again tried to add a motor grader to the product line. Identified simply as the Model C-3 Electric-Grader, its three-electric-drive-wheel design was unique for a motor grader, to say the least. By March 1969, the original Model C-3 was retrofitted with a new front end with two drive wheels, making it a Model C-4 with four-wheel drive. This unit (S.N. 6954) was then sold to Fort Myers Construction in Florida. Only one unit was built.

90 in October 1966, the Series 5-B 90 in September 1966, and the rather large, if somewhat unorthodox-looking, Series 6-B 150 (also referred to as the 6-30) in June 1967. All scrapers were of a telescoping bucket design, with the 6-B 150 being the largest. Its six-bucket design was capable of loading a maximum of 180 tons. But these machines were not to be. In the end, only one prototype of each was ever made and none were ever sold.

The R. G. LeTourneau scraper line would finally come to an end with the Series SC-35B Electric-Digger Coal Scraper, of which only two were built. The first shipped from the Longview plant in November 1970, and the last, shipped on February 16, 1973. Both went to Dofasco, located near Hamilton, Ontario, Canada. After this, the book was closed on LeTourneau's electric-drive scraper program.

The first diesel-electric-drive hauler to be designed with electric-traction wheel motors was the Pacemaker Series TR-60 (Model A-4) "Trolly-Dump." Unveiled in July 1959, the truck would finally go into service in April 1960. The prototype four-wheel-drive TR-60 is shown at the Longview plant's testing area in September 1959. Note the rack-and-pinion system for raising the dump body.

The Electric-Haulers

In 1959, R. G. LeTourneau, Inc., tried its hand in off-highway truck design with a model called the Series TR-60 Trolly-Dump. The TR-60 Hauler program can actually trace its origins to a design request proposal from the Anaconda Company, for an all-electric-drive mining truck for use at its Berkeley Pit in Butte, Montana. Because of the long, steep grades coming out of the main pit, the mine operators thought that a trolley power system might be of greater economic value, since mechanical-drive configurations were clearly not performing up to expectations. Never shying away from a customer's engineering challenge, R. G. LeTourneau accepted the design assignment in 1958 with great enthusiasm.

The TR-60 was of straightforward design. It used a chassis with articulated steering, with a single-axle-powered tow-unit in the front, and a single axle in the rear. Each of the four wheels in the diesel-electric-drive system incorporated an internal electric-traction motor, like the rest of the company's earthmoving equipment designs. Rated capacity for the hauler was initially 60 tons. The TR-60 was designed to get most of its power from overhead trolley lines that would be put in place at the Berkeley Pit. To power the truck away from the trolley lines, such as around the loading shovels or at the spoil dump sites, an auxiliary Cummins NRTO-6 turbo-diesel engine, rated at 335 gross horsepower, direct-coupled to a LeTourneau-designed AC and DC generator, was mounted in the front tow-unit. This power source was meant only to maneuver the TR-60 away from the main 600-volt DC power lines on relatively level ground. When the TR-60 was fully engaged with the overhead lines, the truck's power output was rated at 1,600 gross horsepower, or 400 horsepower per wheel motor. During early tests conducted by the mine in April 1960, the TR-60 averaged 1,242 net horsepower, with an average load of 65 tons on board. With increased voltage, this

The Series TR-60 was built with the cooperation of the Anaconda Company, for use at its Berkeley Pit in Butte, Montana. The hauler was powered by an overhead 600-volt DC trolley line, which gave the TR-60 an electrical gross horsepower rating of 1,600. When disconnected from the overhead electrical source, it utilized a single front-mounted 335-gross-horsepower Cummins NRTO-6 turbo-diesel engine. The initial load capacity was 60 tons. Here the TR-60 is at work in the Berkeley Pit in August 1960.

figure climbed to 1,528 net horsepower. In July 1959, R. G. LeTourneau had the first TR-60 up and running at the Longview plant. In August, the front-mounted trolley pantograph was installed and tested at the factory on a specially constructed overhead wire system. By September, the truck was ready for shipping. But a labor strike at the Berkeley Pit delayed delivery until late March 1960. Testing would officially commence on the hauler on April 6, 1960.

Now officially referred to as the Pacemaker TR-60 (Model A-4) Trolly-Dump, the hauler performed well in service on the trolley lines. But off of the lines was another story. With a full load on board, the single 335-gross-horsepower engine was just not up to the task. To make the truck functional off the lines, LeTourneau quickly designed a new front tow-unit for Anaconda's TR-60, with a second engine. The new unit, which shipped from the factory in February 1961, now featured two Cummins NRTO-6 turbo-diesels, with a combined rating of 670 gross horsepower. With this power increase came an increase in payload as well. Using the new tow-unit in conjunction with the original dump body, the revamped truck had a payload of 75 tons.

Miners soon found that the TR-60 was too underpowered when not connected to its overhead trolley line. To correct the problem, R. G. LeTourneau decided to manufacture a new tractor unit for the TR-60, equipped with a new operator's cab and an additional Cummins NRTO-6 turbo-diesel. Here the new tow unit gets ready to depart the Longview plant in February 1961.

It is late February 1961, and the TR-60 is back at work with the new, more powerful twin-engined front tow unit. With 670 gross horsepower to maneuver the truck when not on the trolley line, the TR-60 became a much more productive hauler—so much so, that it was uprated to 75 tons capacity. As productive as the TR-60 had become, the competition eventually caught up and surpassed it. Only one example of the TR-60 (S.N. 5793) was ever produced.

The Pacemaker Series TR-30 (Model C-42) was another attempt by the company to establish a rear-dump, diesel-electric-drive hauler product line. Built in March 1963, the TR-30 was powered by a single 420-gross-horsepower Detroit Diesel 12V-71 engine. Only the front two wheels of the hauler contained wheel motors, with the rear set being nonpowered. The payload capacity was listed at 37.5 tons. Only one (S.N. 6166) was ever produced.

The TR-60 put in a few good years of service for Anaconda, before competitors stepped forth with superior technology. The trolley lines never worked as planned, especially when it came time to move them to accommodate new haul road layouts. Though LeTourneau tried to keep the hauler project alive by offering a non-trolley-equipped model, powered by two Detroit Diesel 12V-71 engines rated at 840 gross horsepower combined, there were no takers. In the end, only one TR-60 was ever built, and it is currently on display in an outside exhibit at a mining museum located in Butte, Montana.

In October 1960, R. G. LeTourneau offered another take on the off-highway hauler with its Pacemaker Series TTR-60 (Model A-3), sometimes referred to as the Double-Dumper. The TTR-60 was one of the company's designs that looked as if something were missing. This hauler was a collection of component modules built around an ejector-type dumping system that pushed its payload out the rear section. As it did this, the front semicircular section of the dump-body would telescope into the rear portion as the front apron would push the load fully through the second segment. The TTR-60 was powered by two Detroit Diesel 12V-71 engines suspended from each side of the chassis. These engines were capable of 840 gross horsepower combined. The hauler was

Built in October 1960, the Pacemaker Series TTR-60 (Model A-3) Double-Dumper was a three-electric-drive-wheel hauler, with a single-wheeled tug unit in the front. Power was supplied by two Detroit Diesel 12V-71 engines, capable of 840 gross horsepower combined. The ejector-type dump box was rated at 60 tons. But like so many other experimental haulers envisioned by the company, only one saw the light of day. There was no factory serial number issued.

designed with electric-powered drive wheels—two in the rear and one in a powered tug module that also acted as the main steering wheel. Capacity for this model was rated at 60 tons. But like so many of the company's three-wheeled designs, it never found favor in the marketplace. Only one was produced.

After two false starts, R. G. LeTourneau would try once again to build a rear-dump, off-highway hauler that was a little more conservative in size and less controversial in design. The Pacemaker Series TR-30 (Model C-42), introduced in March 1963, was a much-better-balanced design than the earlier TR-60. On the TR-30, only the front wheels were powered. There were no drive motors in the rear two wheels supporting the dump body. Steering was made possible by an electric-powered articulated chassis. A front-mounted Detroit Diesel 12V-71 engine delivered a rated 420 gross horsepower. Maximum load capacity was 37.5 tons. The TR-30 actually resembled rear-dump rocker-haulers the company had made years earlier. But again, the earthmoving industry was not impressed. Even when the company advertised the TR-30 Model line as available with full four-wheel electric drive and more powerful 635-gross-horsepower Detroit Diesel 16V-71N engines, there were no takers. In 1966, a Mexican

contractor approached the company about securing 20 of the haulers. Although serial numbers were assigned for all 20 units, the contractor's financing fell through and none of the haulers were built. The one-and-only TR-30 never found a permanent home outside of the Longview plant. The hauler did put in quite a few good years of work shuttling steel odds and ends around the steel plant until falling into disrepair in the 1990s. Finally, in early 2000, the prototype TR-30 was cut up for scrap and melted down in the steel plant's great electric furnaces.

Despite all of LeTourneau's attempts to market a rear-dump hauler, it was actually its forward-dumping model that sold best. The Pacemaker TF-22 (Model C-42) Dutch-Dump was first produced in February 1964 as a special-order design destined for the Netherlands. It had two drive wheels at the rear and two nonpowered wheels in front. The operator's cab sat at the rear of the unit facing forward, overlooking the 22-ton-capacity dump body. The back engine module, housing a Detroit Diesel 12V-71N, 475-gross-horsepower engine, was articulated, enabling the unit to steer from the rear. The TF-22 would dump its payload forward, in clear view of the operator. When the dumper was in motion, it looked as if it were going backward, when in fact it was traveling

Oddly enough, the most popular diesel-electric-drive hauler built by R. G. LeTourneau, Inc., was the forward-dumping Pacemaker Series TF-22 (Model C-42) Dutch-Dump. Introduced in February 1964, the TF-22 was a special-purpose, rear-wheel-drive-only dumper built for use in the Netherlands. The drivetrain consisted of a single, rear-mounted 475-gross-horsepower Detroit Diesel 12V-71N. The rated capacity was 22 tons. Eleven Dutch-Dumpers were produced.

In May 1965, the Series TS-100 (Model A-4) Electric Side-Dump was introduced. The diesel-electric drivetrain consisted of a pair of front-mounted Detroit Diesel 12V-71N engines, rated at 950 gross horsepower combined, and four-wheel electric drive. The side-dumping box could handle a 100-ton payload. It is shown here in June 1965, being loaded by the experimental Orange-Peel Loader. Only one of each concept machine was built, with no serial numbers issued.

The largest of the experimental side-dump haulers was the Series TS-100 (Model A-6) from June 1967. Rated at 100 tons capacity, the brawny-looking hauler was powered by two rear-mounted Detroit Diesel 12V-71N engines, rated at 950 gross horsepower. All six wheels were powered by individual electric-traction motors. Sadly, the Model A-6 of the TS-100 fared no better than the previous A-4 configuration. In the end, only a single A-6 model type TS-100 (S.N. 6869) was manufactured.

forward. Two separate orders were placed for the Dutch-Dumper, totaling 11 units. Five went to the Netherlands in March 1964, with another six going to Amsterdam later in the year.

When it came to designing an off-highway hauler, LeTourneau left no design stone unturned, no matter the consequences. In May 1965, the company tried its hand at a side-dumping hauler. Designs similar to this had been tried in the past, but were usually of a trailer type for hauling iron ore. Identified as the Series TS-100 (Model A-4) Electric Side-Dump (the Pacemaker identification had been discontinued by this time), the hauler was powered by two Detroit Diesel 12V-71N engines, mounted side by side in the front power unit. This combination yielded a healthy 950 gross horsepower. All four wheels were driven by the company's tried-and-true electric-wheel traction motors. The TS-100 was capable of carrying a 100-ton load, which it would dump on the left side of the unit. It was not designed to dump to the right side at all. But like so many of the other fine but misunderstood hauler concepts produced by the company, this prototype would also have no future in the marketplace.

The last hauler concept to be put into iron by R. G. LeTourneau was another version of the 100-ton side-dump, the Series TS-100 (Model A-6). This model differed from the original in that it was now a six-drive-wheel configuration, with the engines mounted in the rear. These engines were the same Detroit Diesels found in the original design, with the same power output. With the engine modules mounted above the rear four drive wheels, and a double-width cab offset to the left up front, mounted above two drive wheels, the improved TS-100 was rather a good-looking hauler. It also resembled a finished product, with sheet metal covering the mechanicals past designs had often left exposed. Produced in June 1967, the TS-100 was to have been shipped to N'Changa Consolidated Copper Mines, Ltd., in N'Changa, Zambia, in July 1967. Company records suggest that the unit never left Longview—the last entry in the shipping log reads "SCRAPPED." This would be the company's last try at building an off-highway hauler with R. G. in the picture. The industry would have to wait until 1985 before another mining truck would roll off the Longview assembly line.

The Power-Packers

In the early 1930s, R. G. LeTourneau was a pioneer in the development and production of the sheepsfoot roller. When R. G. LeTourneau sold the earthmoving equipment lines to Westinghouse, the sheepsfoot roller designs became the property of LeTourneau-Westinghouse. But once R. G. LeTourneau had reentered the earthmoving equipment manufacturing business in 1958, he felt he needed some type of an earth compaction device. Since he was forbidden to make any of his old designs, he made a new one. The early sheepsfoot rollers were a tractor-pulled attachment. R. G. LeTourneau's new concept would combine the tractor and the sheepsfoot tamping drums into one self-contained unit. Thus was born the Power-Packer.

The self-powered sheepsfoot roller made its first appearance in March 1959, identified as the Series M-50 (Model C-4) Power-Packer. The M-50 consisted of an articulated chassis, with two tamping drums mounted in oscillating frames, both front and rear. Each drum unit had an internal mounted electric-

R. G. LeTourneau, Inc., introduced the Series M-50 (Model C-4) Power-Packer in March 1959. The M-50 consisted of four electric internal-motor-driven sheepsfoot compactor drum wheels, powered by a single 420-gross-horsepower Cummins VT-12 diesel engine. Only two M-50 Series types were built (S.N. 5764/5772). Pictured is the second M-50 in May 1959.

In September 1959, the company introduced a revamped version of its Power-Packer, identified as the Series M 50-55. The improved M 50-55 now featured a single 420-gross-horsepower Detroit Diesel 12V-71 engine, along with improved roller drum frame carriers. In August 1961 the frame carriers featured improved spring-mounted drum cleaners, like this unit from 1966. In all there were 35 Power-Packers manufactured of all model types.

traction motor for a total of four. Power was supplied by a single Cummins VT-12 engine, rated at 420 gross horsepower, mounted longitudinally between the two drum pairs. The operator's station could be swung 180 degrees so that the unit never needed to turn around at the end of a run, saving both time and money. The M-50 was essentially always facing forward, ready for work. The company made only two M-50 units before changing the overall design later in 1959.

In September, R. G. LeTourneau shipped the first of four improved Power-Packers, called the Series M 50-55. While it looked like its predecessor, this design featured improved tamping drum frame carriers and wheel motor mountings. Power choice was a single Detroit Diesel 12V-71 engine, rated at 420 gross horsepower.

A more updated version of the compactor was released in March 1960, now referred to as the Pacemaker Series M 50-55 Power-Packer. This was by far the most successful of the Power-Packer designs. New features included redesigned oscillating drum frame carriers and a raised operator's and engine platform, improving the view of the working area measurably. In August 1961, this same model would have spring-mounted drum cleaners installed on the front and rear of the machine. In 1962, power output was raised to 432 gross horsepower, though the engine type remained unaltered. The M 50-55 was simple in design and a solid performer, and for the most part, contractors that used them were quite impressed with their rugged build and reliability. When the last M 50-55 finally shipped in July 1967 (S.N. 6890) to Western Contracting, a total of 33 had been built, including the two M-50 units, and the four M 50-55 units, built in 1959.

In September 1964, the company produced a one-off experimental Power-Packer called the Pacemaker Series M 60-55. This unit, which utilized the same basic chassis and drum mountings as the M 50-55, employed two Detroit Diesel 12V-71 engines, giving the compactor 864 gross horsepower. The M 60-55 also featured a dozing blade mounted to the cab end of the unit. The operator's station had also been mounted to the center, behind the blade and in front of the twin-engine power modules. The M 60-55 was a special-order item only, and the company received no further orders after the first unit was delivered.

The last of the Power-Packer models was the downsized Series M-20, built in April 1967. The little M-20 utilized a single drum, mounted in an articulated steering chassis. Only one electric motor drove the tamping drum. The rear of the unit was supported by two small rubber-tired wheels that were unpowered. A rear-mounted Detroit Diesel 6V-71N, 238-gross-horsepower engine supplied all the power the little M-20 would require. Like so many of the company's other creations, the M-20 was a one-off model, abandoned for financial reasons before production began. Even so, with a grand total of 35 Power-Packers built in total for all varieties, they were considered a minor success for the company.

The first purpose-built diesel-electric-drive tractor designed by R. G. LeTourneau, Inc., to push-load large scrapers was its Series K-100 (Model A-4). Introduced in January 1959, the big electric, four-wheel-drive tractor doubled as a rubber-tired dozer when not assisting scrapers during loading. Power was supplied by a single 600-gross-horsepower Cummins VT-12BI diesel engine.

The Electric-Tractors

The Electric-Tractors built by R. G. LeTourneau, Inc., between 1958 and 1970 were comprised of two basic model types—wheel dozers, and wheel loaders and shovels. Outside of the Electric-Diggers, the Electric-Tractors had more engineering misadventures than any of the company's other diesel-electric-drive earthmoving machines.

Soon after the introduction of R. G. LeTourneau's first Electric-Digger, the L-70 (Model A-4), the company produced a rubber-tired push tractor identified as the Series K-600 (Model A-4). Built in September 1958, the K-600 was intended to be a push-loading tractor for the company's Electric-Diggers. The K-600 tractors were actually developed from the Series T Transporter program. The K-600 was a four-wheel design, with electric-traction motors at all four corners, and a bulldozing blade mounted up front. A single Cummins VT-12BI diesel engine powered the entire unit. But the K-600 never developed to fill the company's push-tractor needs. Instead, only two K-600s were built, and these were used as the chassis for the Series 250 Tree Stingers delivered in November 1958.

An electric-wheel tractor very similar to the K-600 was offered in company literature in November 1958. Called the Series K-275, this tractor was in fact nothing more than a retouched photograph of a Series YC Electric Arch. In reality, the company never built a single K-275 tractor.

The first true purpose-built wheeled push tractor produced by the company was the Series K-100 (Model A-4), which went into service in January 1959. The K-100 utilized the tractor power unit found in the K-600 model types, with the same Cummins Diesel engine. The rear section had a large counterweight box mounted over the two rear-drive wheels, which provided the necessary weight for push-loading or dozing work. Following an established pattern, however, the company produced only one example.

Between 1960 and 1962, LeTourneau produced approximately 11 separate Pacemaker Electric-Tractor designs, both in three-wheel and four-wheel variations. There was even one five-wheel model. Making matters worse, many utilized the same model identification, which was extremely confusing. The first of the Pacemaker tractors from this time period was the Series K-50 (Model C-3) Tug-Dozer, released in April 1960. This was also the first electric tractor to utilize a rear-steering, single-wheeled, powered "tug" unit. Only one was ever built. Other three-wheeled Tug-Dozers included the Series K-53F "Catug," Model C-3, in August 1960 (three built); the Series K-103, Model A-3, in January 1961 (four built); the Series K-53G, Model C-3, in December 1960 (one built); the Series K-53, Model C-3, in January 1961 (four built); and the Series K-103 (new design), Model A-3, in March 1962 (three built).

A few four-wheeled Pacemaker electric power-dozers and tractors were also manufactured alongside the tug-dozers. These included the Series K-50-4, Model A-4, in July 1960 (one built); the

Following the prototype K-100 electric tractor was the Pacemaker K-104 (Model A-4) Power-Dozer. Tested as a prototype beginning in December 1960, the Power-Dozer featured two 420-gross-horsepower Detroit Diesel 12V-71 engines. But again, only one example would be manufactured, and it is seen here in January 1962, with a push-block mounted on it. No serial number was issued to the K-104.

R. G. LeTourneau, Inc., produced a variety of three-wheeled, diesel-electric-drive tractors with the name "Tug-Dozer." One of these was the Pacemaker Series K-53 (Model C-3) from January 1961. The K-53 steered by means of a single rear-mounted "tug" electric-powered wheel unit. The single inline-mounted Detroit Diesel 12V-71 engine put out 420 gross horsepower. The operator's cab was mounted offset on the left side. Four examples of the K-53 were produced.

Series K-54 Hi-C, Model C-4, in September 1960 (three built— two experimental and one prototype); and the Series K-104, Model A-4, in December 1960 (one built).

Of all the early Pacemaker tractors, the Series K-205, Model A-5, introduced in March 1961, was by far the largest and most powerful manufactured by the company. The K-205 was designed from the start to push-load the biggest scrapers on the market. The tractor utilized five drive wheels—four in the front and one in a rear-steering power-tug. Three big Cummins V-12 diesel engines turned out 420 gross horsepower each. With 1,260 gross horsepower on tap, the K-205 could put a massive amount of force to bear with its 20-foot-wide dozing blade. But like all of the other Pacemaker tractors before it, the K-205 was just too radical a design approach for the everyday contractor to consider seriously. Only one K-205 was completed.

As the company's large Electric-Diggers became true self-loading scrapers, the need for a production push-tractor diminished. Instead, engineers set their sights on producing a more modern rubber-tired tractor-dozer that the marketplace would accept. In September 1965, the company introduced the first of this new generation of electric tractors, the Series K-54 Dozer. Gone was the Pacemaker product name, as well as any hint

Another example of an R. G. LeTourneau three-wheel-drive tractor was the Pacemaker Series K-103 (Model C-3) Tug-Dozer. Built in January 1961, the K-103 resembled the Series K-53, but was powered by two Detroit Diesel 12V-71 engines, providing 840 gross horsepower. This K-103 Tug-Dozer, one of the original designs at work in October 1962, is equipped with steel wheels for use in rocky conditions. Just four of the early K-103 Tug-Dozers were built.

The largest of all the Pacemaker diesel-electric-drive tractor-dozers to feature a single rear-steering tug unit was the powerful Series K-205 (Model A-5) from March 1961. The K-205 featured five electric-drive wheels, and three big 420-gross-horsepower Cummins V12-420 diesel engines. The dozing blade alone was 20 feet wide. The overall working weight of the K-205 was 160 tons with counterweight. Though it was the largest and most powerful dozer of its day, only one machine (S.N. 6084) would ever be produced.

The Series T-450A electric-drive tractor was originally introduced in September 1965 as the Series K-54 Dozer. This K-54 diesel-electric-drive tractor was a completely new design, not just an upgraded version from the 1960 model. In January 1966, the tractor was redesignated the T-450A. The tractor featured four-wheel drive, an articulated steering chassis, and a single, rear-mounted 475-gross-horsepower Detroit Diesel 12V-71N engine. This T-450A, working in November 1967, is equipped with a high-volume wood-chip dozing blade. In all, there were four late-model K-54 and eight T-450A tractor-dozers produced.

of a single-wheeled tug power unit of old. This new K-54 design, which shared nothing with an earlier model of the same designation, looked every bit as modern as its competitors in the marketplace. Only the use of rack-and-pinion gear drive for the blade control and articulated steering gave it away as an R. G. LeTourneau creation. The K-54 was powered by a single, rear-mounted Detroit Diesel 12V-71N engine, rated at 475 gross horsepower. Electric-traction wheel motors gave it four-wheel-drive and 98-inch-diameter by 40-inch-wide tires gave it the necessary traction. The company sold four K-54 tractors before changing the model name to the Series T-450A in January 1966. The T-450A was basically the same as the new-generation K-54. The first tractor to ship carrying the new designation left the factory in June 1966. In all, there were eight T-450A units built. In April 1970, an updated Model T-450B tractor, now referred to as a LeTro-Dozer, was introduced with a more powerful 530-gross-horsepower Detroit Diesel 12V-71N engine. Other than component updates aimed at improving overall reliability, the "B" Model looked just like the "A" version. Three T-450B wheel-dozers were eventually put into service. The first T-450B unit, serial number 1032, is still in existence, stored in the back lot of the Longview plant. Its fate has yet to be decided at the time of this writing.

Unveiled in late December 1965, the Series D-300C diesel-electric-drive tractor resembled the K-54/T-450A model, but in a smaller package. The D-300C had the same basic layout as its bigger brother, but was powered by a smaller 320-gross-horsepower Detroit Diesel 8V-71N engine. The original D-300C (pictured with a root-rake) weighed in at 52,000 pounds, while the larger T-450A tipped the scales at 75,000 pounds.

The largest of R. G. LeTourneau, Inc.'s diesel-electric-drive, rack-and-pinion articulated-frame-steering, rubber-tired wheel dozers was the Series T-600A Tractor. Built in June 1967, the first unit would start testing with a 16-foot-wide bulldozing blade the following month. In August 1967, the first machine equipped with a 6-foot-wide push-block was produced (pictured). The T-600A (initially referred to as the K-600A) was powered by a single rear-mounted 635-gross-horsepower Detroit Diesel 16V-71 engine.

Just after releasing the new K-54, LeTourneau introduced a smaller version, designated the Series D-300C. Built in December 1965, the D-300C looked like the K-54/T-450A Model on a smaller scale. Sharing the same design features as its larger brother, it was powered by a Detroit Diesel 8V-71N engine, rated at 320 gross horsepower. The first D-300C shipped to a customer in March 1966. But after a few months of trial service, it was returned to the factory and put in inventory. During that time period, it was rebuilt into a new model called the T-300A in November 1967. When the tractor was finally sold and shipped in May 1968 to Boise Cascade Papers in Washington, it was labeled the T-300C. Thus, the D-300C, T-300A, and T-300C were all the same tractor, serial number 6737.

In December 1966, LeTourneau announced the release of a much larger electric tractor than the T-450A, called the Series K-600A. By June 1967, the first of this new model line was ready to go, but by now it was referred to as the Model T-600A. The T-600A was a four-wheel-drive, articulated steering design, with the usual LeTourneau-built electric-drive system and rack-and-pinion gear controls. A single, rear-mounted Detroit Diesel 16V-71N engine, rated at 635 gross horsepower, supplied the

necessary grunt. The big electric tractor could be equipped with a dozing blade or a push-block. The first T-600A to be equipped with a bulldozing blade started testing in July 1967, while the first unit with a push-block was built in August 1967. Even though the T-600A performed well in early field tests, only three would eventually be produced. An updated version was announced in December 1969 as the Model T-600B LeTro-Dozer. But only one tractor was ever built carrying this designation. It was shipped to AMERON, in South Gate, California, in June 1970, and was used as the main power unit for the company's Pipemobile III mobile precast concrete pipe carrier.

In addition to the electric push and dozer tractors offered by the company, a series of shovel and front-end wheel loaders were also built, with mixed results, starting in 1960. The first front-end loader of sorts was the Pacemaker Series SL-10 (Model C-4) Short Lever Shovel. Built in September 1960, it was based on a modified log-stacker chassis, with four-wheel electric drive and a rear-mounted engine. The concept for the SL-10 arose when a 30-ton-capacity LeTourneau Log Stacker working at Jefferson Plywood in June 1960 was retrofitted with a simple dump bucket, hinged on the two lower tongs of the front-end assembly. This crude but

This Pacemaker Series SL-10 (Model C-3) Short Lever Shovel was the second design to carry the SL-10 designation. This version of the Short Lever Shovel, introduced in December 1960, featured a simplified, if rather large, rack-and-pinion hoist-rack for the rollover bucket handle. Only one of this type was built, with no factory serial number issued.

effective concept seemed workable at the time, so company officials decided to pursue the project further. The front rollover bucket assembly on the SL-10 traveled up and down on a vertical hoist rack, much like a forklift. An electric motor and cable system moved the bucket. From the beginning, the design posed serious problems. After a few months of testing, it was abandoned altogether.

December 1960 marked the return of another design of the Short Lever Shovel, identified as the Series SL-10 (Model C-3). This SL-10 had nothing to do with the previous design. In fact, it looked almost like a simple child's sandbox toy, blown up to life-size proportions. Laid out on a three-wheel chassis, based largely on the drivetrain layout of the Series K-50 Tug-Dozer, it was unlike any other existing piece of earthmoving equipment. A massive pivoting arm attached to the rear of the unit held a 10-cubic-yard-struck rollover dumping bucket. The arm was raised and lowered by means of electric rack-and-pinion gear drive on a 31-foot-tall hoist rack, mounted to the front end of the shovel chassis, between the two drive wheels. It was powered by a single Detroit Diesel 8V-71 engine, rated at 280 gross horsepower, mounted inline with the center of the main frame of the unit. Even though the design looked like a sure loser, it actually worked quite well in testing. This was due in large part to the design's overall simplicity, which was R. G. LeTourneau's main intent in the first place. But by mid-1961, the SL-10 project was put on the back burner permanently.

The Series SL-15 (Model C-3) Electric-Tractor was R. G. LeTourneau's smallest-capacity front-end loader. Introduced in March 1965, the SL-15 featured three-wheel electric drive, and rack-and-pinion hoist, bucket, and articulated-frame steering control. The payload capacity was 15 tons. Power came from a rear-mounted, 475-gross-horsepower Detroit Diesel 12V-71N engine set longitudinally. Only one SL-15 (S.N. 6541) was manufactured.

Next up in size from the SL-15 front-end loader was the Series SL-20 (Model C-4) Electric-Tractor. Three different configurations of the standard SL-20 were produced. The model pictured here was the second type built in April 1965, of which only one (S.N. 6528) was manufactured. This version of the SL-20, built at the Longview plant, was powered by an inline, rear-mounted 475-gross-horsepower Detroit Diesel 12V-71N engine. The bucket capacity was rated at 20 tons. Other models included the SL-20-L from December 1964 (three built at Vicksburg plant), and one Cummins-powered unit (S.N. 6730) with a special rollover dumping bucket attachment made in December 1965.

Between 1964 and 1965, the company made further attempts to build an electric front-end loader product line that would have more commercial value than the oddball SL-10 creations. These new electric-tractor models were the Series SL-15, SL-20, SL-30, and SL-40. All were front-end loader designs, with rack-and-pinion, electric gear drives controlling the loading, dumping, and steering functions of the articulated chassis. All models utilized electric-traction motors and generators designed and built by R. G. LeTourneau, Inc.

The smallest of the loaders was the Series SL-15 (Model C-3), first introduced in March 1965. A three-drive-wheel design, it was classified as a 15-ton-capacity machine. The SL-15 was powered by a single, rear, longitudinally mounted Detroit Diesel 12V-71N engine with 475 gross horsepower. Though the design showed promise, its three-drive-wheel configuration was just a bit too unorthodox for potential customers. Only one would ever be built.

Stepping up in size, the next model in the product line was the Series SL-20 (C-4). The SL-20 was produced in three different configurations—a front-end loader, a front-end loader-and-dozer combination, and a front-end loader with a revolving bucket. The basic Model SL-20 was a four-wheel design, with a bucket

The Double-Cab Series SL-20 (Model C-4) Electric-Tractor was built in March 1966, and was actually the second prototype SL-20 front-end loader, serial number 6528. But the tractor now featured a dozing blade and separate operator's cab mounted on the rear engine chassis unit. The dual-cab unit was shipped to the Quebec Iron & Titanium Corporation, in Sorel, Quebec, Canada, in April 1966.

Manufactured in February 1966, the Series SL-20R (Model C-4) Revolving Bucket Tractor was another specialized design based on the Longview SL-20 program. The SL-20R was designed from the ground up with a 180-degree revolving bucket and operator's cab. Other features included four-wheel electric drive, rack-and-pinion hoist, bucket, and steering control, and a 475-gross-horsepower DD 12V-71 engine. The loading bucket capacity was 20 tons. The unit also featured a rear-mounted dozing blade. Only one SL-20R (S.N. 6765) was produced, and it was shipped to Tournavista in Peru, April 1966.

capacity rated at 20 tons. The base engine was a 475-gross-horsepower Detroit Diesel 12V-71N. All major design features were the same as the SL-15, such as rack-and-pinion gear hoist and dump actuation. The first SL-20-L loader was shipped from the Vicksburg plant in December 1964. On this unit, the bucket could be quickly removed and replaced with a forklift option. Another variation on the SL-20 was shipped to Lone Star Steel in Texas in December 1965. It featured a specially designed rack-and-pinion rollover bucket, as well as a Cummins Diesel V-12 in the rear. Again, only one was built to these specifications.

Some of the SL-20 modifications went way past a minor design or engine change. One of the early SL-20 loaders, built in February 1965, was converted into a double-cab, loader-dozer configuration in March 1966. This SL-20 had an additional operator's cab mounted to the rear engine module, along with a bulldozing blade. In this setup, the operator could utilize the unit as a front-end loader, or change operator stations and use it as a wheel-dozer. Another variation on this loader-dozer model was the Series SL-20R revolving bucket loader. This design featured a front-end loader attachment and cab assembly that rotated a full 180 degrees. The rear section of the unit also had a rearward-facing dozing blade. But unlike the loader-dozer-modified machine, this design did not feature a second operator's cab. Built in February 1966, only one was produced. In all, six SL-20 loaders, including variations, were manufactured.

The Series SL-30 (Model A-4) Electric-Tractor was the first diesel-electric, articulated-frame-steering, front-end loader that R. G. LeTourneau designed and built. Introduced in February 1964, the SL-30 was powered by two rear-mounted, longitudinal Detroit Diesel 12V-71N engines, capable of 950 gross horsepower combined. The bucket capacity was 30 tons. Pictured here is the first SL-30 (S.N. 6307) during tests in April 1964. Only three SL-30 loaders were placed into service, with the last two machines (S.N. 6311/6353) converted into SL-40 tractors in 1967.

In July 1964, R. G. LeTourneau, Inc., started testing a revamped Series SL-30 Electric-Tractor. Its new features included a relocated operator's cab— now behind the front left wheel—and a new mounting for the loader's rack-and-pinion bucket control. In 1967 this SL-30 was converted into an SL-40 machine, with a new front-end loading arm attachment and repositioned engine modules.

The largest R. G. LeTourneau front-end loader to feature rack-and-pinion systems for loading and steering controls was the Series SL-40 (Model A-4) Electric-Tractor. The prototype SL-40 was introduced in November 1964. The loader was powered by two 475-gross-horsepower Detroit Diesel 12V-71N engines, rear mounted side by side, inline with the tractor's chassis. The first SL-40 (S.N. 6347) is shown during testing at the Longview plant in February 1965; it was the only unit of this model with the operator's cab mounted over the front left wheel.

After the SL-20 model line came the Series SL-30 (Model A-4) in February 1964. The SL-30 was configured like its smaller brothers, but utilized larger "A" Series electric wheel motors, as well as two, rear-mounted Detroit Diesel 12V-71N engines with 950 combined gross horsepower. Bucket capacity was rated at 30 tons. The twin-engine module was suspended out the rear of the tractor, behind the back drive wheels, and acted as a counterbalance weight, keeping the loader from tipping forward during loading. Even though seven SL-30s were assigned serial numbers, only three were ever built and placed into service. Company officials decided early in the development of the SL-30

that an even larger loader was needed. Work on the 30-ton loader thus stopped, so engineers could concentrate their efforts on a larger 40-ton-capacity machine.

In November 1964, the first prototype Series SL-40 (Model A-4) Electric-Tractor came off of the Longview plant assembly line. With a maximum 40-ton payload capacity, it was the largest wheel loader model the company would ever make employing rack-and-pinion gear designs for hoist, bucket, and steering controls. With its 19-cubic-yard rock bucket, and twin Detroit Diesel 12V-71N engines, rated at 950 gross horsepower combined, it was considered the world's largest and most powerful wheel loader.

The SL-40 carried its engine modules in much the same way as the SL-30. But in the SL-40 design, they were mounted inline with the chassis, while the SL-30 had them situated longitudinally side by side. After a few months of testing the prototype, company engineers changed the location of the operator's cab. This change showed up on the first production machine in March 1965. In May 1965, an SL-40 was retrofitted with a dozing blade instead of a loading bucket. It is doubtful that the unit ever shipped in this configuration. With just nine SL-40 loaders put into the field, production ended on the model line when the last unit (S.N. 6776) shipped from the factory in April 1966, destined for Tournavista in Peru. Of the nine loaders built, two were actually SL-30 models rebuilt into SL-40 machines in 1967.

The story of R. G. LeTourneau's foray into the realm of front-end loaders and shovels just wouldn't be complete without at least mentioning three concept machines that probably should have stayed on the drawing board. These were the Orange-Peel Loader from January 1964, the Double Orange-Peel Loader from July 1966, and the Series RS-40 Revolving Shovel from June 1966. The Orange-Peel Loaders got their name from the design of the machine's main earthmoving attachment, which was made up of multiple curved blades that resembled the outside of an orange being peeled. The blades' teeth would penetrate the digging surface and then close around the load, engulfing it in an almost-round steel cocoon. It also had the ability to rotate the shovel works a full 360 degrees. The first Orange-Peel Loader was originally designed with three electric-drive wheels, powered by a single diesel engine. But in July 1964, a revamped version of the

In March 1965, the company introduced the first Series SL-40 loader to feature a repositioned operator's cab. The SL-40's bucket was rated at 19 cubic yards, with a maximum payload capacity of 40 tons. The loading bucket itself was 14 feet, 3 inches wide. The total operating weight was 147,000 pounds.

same unit featured four drive wheels and twin Detroit Diesels. In July 1966, a second machine of this type was introduced as the Double Orange-Peel Loader. Unlike the first model, this configuration featured two digging attachments, mounted at either end of a steel-lattice boom structure that rotated a full 360 degrees around the center axis of the chassis, on a rack-and-pinion gear drive column. Both the single and double Orange-Peel Loaders never left the testing grounds at the Longview plant.

One of the last electric loaders designed by R. G. LeTourneau himself was the rather improbable Series RS-40 Revolving Shovel. This shovel design, which reached its final form in September 1966, was like nothing anyone had seen before. Its layout was as unconventional as it was simple. A four-wheel-drive chassis, powered by two rear-mounted Detroit Diesel 12V-71 engines, made up the main foundation supporting a massive 40-ton-capacity, revolving bucket mechanism mounted on a large rack-and-pinion gear drive hoist. Mounted between the two front wheels, the bucket was capable of swinging a full 360 degrees. The operator's station was mounted on the left side of the rotating unit, next to the main support boom, with no cab protection of any kind. Saying that the RS-40 wasn't very operator friendly would surely have been an understatement at the time of its testing. As with the Orange-Peel Loaders, the RS-40 would have no commercial success whatsoever.

R. G. LeTourneau's front-end loader designs during 1960 to 1966 had no impact on the marketplace to speak of. But the valuable engineering experience that the company gained in designing and building electric-drive systems for these creations—especially the SL-40—would help pave the way to a true production, large diesel-electric front-end loader in the not-too-distant future. And on that loader, the company would build its fortunes.

The 950-gross-horsepower SL-40 Electric-Tractor featured diesel-electric four-wheel drive, and an articulated steering frame. The overall length of the loader was 52 feet, 8 inches. In all, nine SL-40 front-end loaders were produced. Seven of these were factory original production, while two were rebuilt SL-30 units upgraded to full SL-40 specifications in 1967.

In May 1965, one of the production Series SL-40 Electric-Tractors was retrofitted with a dozing blade. After a series of factory tests, the machine was returned to its original front-end loader configuration. No SL-40 was ever shipped from the factory equipped with this blade option.

The rather odd-looking Series RS-40 (Model A-4) Revolving Shovel was first tested at the Longview plant in September 1966. Nicknamed the "Big Dipper," it was powered by two rear-mounted Detroit Diesel 12V-71N engines rated at 950 gross horsepower combined. The payload capacity for the revolving dumping bucket was 40 tons. The massive rack-and-pinion loading mechanism was able to rotate a full 360 degrees. This very unorthodox shovel was one of R. G. LeTourneau's most unusual earthmoving designs.

The newly redesigned LT-360 Electric-Digger now rode on eight tires that were 122 inches in diameter. The load capacity was the same as the previous layout, but overall length had increased to 200 feet. The land leviathan was 19 feet, 6 inches wide and 22 feet high at the top of the operator's cab. The maximum travel speed was 15 miles per hour loaded.

R. G. LeTourneau's fantastic designs were considered bold engineering achievements by many, and pure folly by others. One thing you could say for sure is that they were never ignored. The giant freighter and military trains of the 1950s, and the sheer number of earthmoving equipment designs in the 1960s, left many in the industry to wonder what mechanical giants would soon be lumbering out of the Longview plant. That wait was a short one. In 1965, R. G. LeTourneau introduced what would be the largest self-loading scraper ever to load a ton of earth. That machine was the astounding LT-360 Electric-Digger.

For years, R. G. LeTourneau had envisioned massive, high-production, self-loading scrapers that did not require the assistance of additional push-loading tractors to achieve a full load. He saw these scrapers as diesel-electric, with electric-traction-wheel motors, and loading and traveling speeds unmatched by the competition. The lowest cost per yard of dirt was the end goal for these creations, and their size would dictate just how productive they would be. The basic reasoning was this: the bigger the scraper, the larger the loads, the more yardage per trip, the lower the overall costs to the customer. Oh, if it were only that simple. Building the world's largest scraper is one thing, but marketing it was another matter entirely.

The giant LT-360 actually had its origins in a prototype identified as the LT-120. The LT-120 was the first of what would comprise three sections of the LT-360. The LT-120 was powered by four diesel engines. Two 12-cylinder Detroit Diesel 12V-71N engines powered the electric-drive system for the front end of the scraper, while two 16-cylinder Detroit Diesel 16V-71 units powered the rear end. The front two powerplants produced 950 gross horsepower combined, while the rear engines together cranked out 1,270 gross horsepower. Total gross power was thus a very respectable 2,220 horses. All four wheels contained electric-traction motors, powered by four separate generators, one per diesel engine.

The LT-120 scraper utilized telescoping bowl sections that fit into each other. As the scraper lowered its cutting edge, earth would fill the forward fixed section of the bowl. As this filled, the telescoping sections would move rearward. In this way, the entire length of the scraper bowl could be fully loaded to heaped capacity. To unload the scraper, a rear rack-and-pinion drive would push the rear section forward, acting as an ejector apron. As the unit unloaded, each bucket section would nest into the one in front of it until empty. Then the unit was ready to go back to the working cut and start the loading cycle all over again.

The payload capacity of the LT-120 was rated at 72 cubic yards and 120 tons. The scraper's fixed front bowl sported a massive 14-foot, 2-inch-wide cutting edge, one of the largest ever designed for a machine of this type. The overall width was about 19 feet, 6 inches. Though originally equipped with an enclosed operator's cab, it was removed in March 1965 during the unit's early testing period. The look of the LT-120 was pure LeTourneau. Large and powerful, with little thought for aesthetics or operator comfort, it was classic LeTourneau, both good and bad.

The testing program for the LT-120 would continue into April 1965, with the addition of another 72-cubic-yard scraper unit. This additional scraper was identical in design and operation to the first, except for its engine configurations. This tandem unit configuration was referred to as the LT-240. The original LT-120 front scraper controlled all functions of the second, rear unit. Modifications to the original LT-120 machine included the removal of its rearmost Detroit Diesel 16V-71 engine. The fully enclosed operator's cab was now reinstalled, affording some measure of protection to its occupant. The rear towed unit was powered by two 16V-71 engines, rated at 1,270 gross horsepower. The second scraper only had drive wheels at the rear. No power unit was needed in front since it was towed by the lead machine. The total output for this design was 2,855 gross horsepower. But there was still more to come.

After a few weeks of testing, the LT-240 received a total makeover as it was transformed into the first incarnation of the LT-360 Electric-Digger. But there was much more to it than just grafting on an additional scraper unit. More engineering work was necessary to increase both the power and overall structural integrity of the design. The front yoke that attached the front drive unit to the scraper bowl was strengthened around key joint weld areas. The torsional bending and twisting stresses applied to these areas as the front power unit traveled over uneven ground, had taken their toll. As a fix, extra metal bracings were welded into place. In addition, the operator's cab was relocated on the lead scraper unit to a more elevated location mounted at the left rear of the unit. This allowed the operator to better view the operation of the three bowled scrapers during loading.

To make the LT-360, an additional powered, 72-cubic-yard scraper was added between the two existing units. This became

Built in March 1965, the Series LT-120 (Model A-4) Electric-Digger was the first of the scraper units that would combine to make the LT-360. The LT-120 was powered by two 475-gross-horsepower Detroit Diesel 12V-71N engines in the lead power unit, and two 635-horsepower 16V-71 powerplants in the rear. The total output was 2,220 horsepower, and the maximum payload capacity was 120 tons (72 cubic yards heaped).

the second scraper inline, with the rear unit of the LT-240 also becoming the rear unit of the LT-360. The new center unit utilized a four-wheel, two-engine power module to push the scraper unit. This module featured the 16V-71 diesels, which brought the total number of engines of this type to six. Add to this the lead power unit's two 12V-71N engines and you have a staggering 4,760 gross horsepower on hand. The twin-bogie, four-drive-wheel layout of the new center section was also adapted to the original front unit, which was previously only a two-drive-wheel layout at the rear. The third trailing scraper unit would retain its original single-axle, two-wheel-drive design. The LT-360 could bring its massive power output to bear through 12 drive wheels, all powered by internal electric-traction motors. These would carry a scraper that was capable of handling 216 cubic yards of earth that weighed in at a record-breaking 360 tons. No other scraper model had ever carried such a gigantic load. Many in the industry thought it just wasn't possible for such a machine to even exist, let alone work. Again, R. G. LeTourneau had proven to the industry that he was not an eccentric old man, but an engineering genius of the highest order. If R. G. LeTourneau could think of it, he and his engineers would find a way to build it. And they proved this time and time again.

In July 1965, the newly completed LT-360 was given a chance to prove itself in a real working environment. A sizable road construction project was under way on Interstate Highway 20 in east Texas, just west of US 259, 2 miles east of the Sabine River. The working site concerning R. G. LeTourneau was a 2-mile stretch across the Sabine River bottom. A huge area had to be cut through the hills west of the river to get enough fill to raise the roadbed to a level higher than any recorded flood waters. It was estimated that at least 1.6–2-million yards of material would be required to make the fill across the river bottom. Adams Brothers of Athens, and Texas Bitulithic of Dallas—the main contractors for the entire 6.4-mile project—had subcontracted R. G. LeTourneau, Inc., to handle the 2-mile excavation across the riverbed.

Starting on July 5, 1965, R. G. LeTourneau's massive diesel-electric-drive scrapers, push-dozers, and haulers were put to the test. Though R. G. LeTourneau was principally a manufacturer, he saw that bidding on such a high-profile earthmoving contract would give many possible customers a firsthand look at his creations in full operation, proving to them once and for all the virtues of his electric-drive-wheel systems. R. G. was able to put all necessary prototype and production earthmoving equipment available at the Longview plant to work on this one project, including three L-60s, nine L-90s, and the monstrous LT-360. By December 10, their work was done. The job section that R. G. LeTourneau contracted for was finished in record time, with the entire fleet of Electric-Diggers averaging a very impressive 93 percent availability on the job.

The LT-360's performance was impressive to say the least, considering that this machine was still in its design testing phase. The LT-360 was able to load 360 tons of earth in about 80 seconds, with a traveling top speed of 15–20 miles per hour as it traveled to the dumping site. It was able to dump this load in just

By April 1965, the LT-120 had gained an additional powered scraper unit. The combined machine was called the Series LT-240 (Model A-6) Electric-Digger. The extra unit, with two of its own 635-gross-horsepower DD 16V-71 engines (one of which was removed from the rear of the LT-120), gave the LT-240 a total output of 2,855 horsepower. The capacity doubled to 240 tons (144 cubic yards heaped).

The LT-240 received an additional powered scraper unit in July 1965, becoming the Series LT-360 (Model A-12) Electric-Digger—the world's largest self-propelled scraper. The LT-360 was propelled by 12 electric-drive wheels powered by six DD 16V-71 and two DD 12V-71N diesel engines. Power was a staggering 4,760 gross horses; payload capacity was a record-breaking 360 tons (216 cubic yards heaped). The overall working length was approximately 175 feet. The LT-360 is shown at work in August 1965.

After the LT-360 finished its working stay on the Interstate Highway 20 project in December 1965, it was shipped back to the Longview plant for modifications. The third scraper unit was removed to produce a revamped Series LT-240 Electric-Digger, first seen on March 3, 1966. The unit now sported six DD 16V-71 diesels, rated at 3,810 gross horsepower combined, and six drive wheels, shod with massive 122-inch-diameter, 60-inch-wide, wide-base tires.

40 seconds, spreading it evenly 8 to 10 inches deep as each of the bowl's ejectors pushed it out. During the initial loading cycle, the first scraper bowl was filled first, then the second, and then the third. They did not load all at once. With 4,760 gross horsepower pushing and pulling each of the scraper units' cutting blades through the earth at 6 miles per hour, the inertia of the earth as it was being loaded actually caused it to jump into the telescoping bowl sections. And all of this was done without the aid of additional pusher tractors.

During the few months that the LT-360 was in operation on the Interstate Highway 20 project, a few design shortcomings began to appear. Because of the drive-wheel arrangements, the LT-360 simply had an enormous turning radius that made it difficult to position the multibowled unit in more restricted working areas. The 12 drive wheels added rolling resistance that required more power to overcome. Also, 10 of the 12 tires used on the Electric-Digger were 98 inches in diameter and did not provide the necessary floatation for a machine the size and weight of the LT-360 in unfavorable working conditions. After the completion of the contract in December, the LT-360 was shipped back to the Longview plant for additional engineering work to correct these performance shortcomings.

On March 4, 1966, the newly redesigned LT-360 was unveiled at the Longview plant. This revised design featured 8 electric-drive wheels instead of the 12 found on the original unit. All wheels featured larger traction motors and massive 122-inch-diameter, nondirectional, tubeless, wide-base 60.00x68, 72-ply tires,

designed by R. G. LeTourneau and produced by the BFGoodrich Company. The elimination of the rear-drive wheels on the first and second scraper units also helped reduce the turning radius, giving the machine's hitches more clearance in tight turning situations. Providing the necessary power for driving the eight giant wheels were eight 16-cylinder Detroit Diesel 16V-71 engines, producing a whopping 5,080 gross horsepower. In this version of the LT-360, the original front-leading 12V-71N powerplants were replaced with the more powerful 16-cylinder units. Now all engines were of the same type and power rating. This change would also add a bit of length to the unit, as well as other changes in the hitch areas. The original design had an overall length of around 175 feet, while the redesigned model was about 200 feet. The new unit's capacity was unchanged, as were the designs of the telescoping bowls themselves. This version of the LT-360 was the most powerful scraper unit ever produced, as well as the largest in payload capacity. That record stands to this day.

But the marketplace can be very fickle at times, and this was one of those times. Would-be buyers were very impressed with the LT-360's performance specifications. But what worried these potential customers was the immense size of the unit. Its massive width, along with the length of each scraper assembly, meant that the machine would have to undergo an extensive tear-down each time it was transported over any roadway, adding costs and time, as well as a mountain of trucking permit paperwork. The LT-360 was also of little interest to the general contractor because of its limited uses in other working applications. In reality, any

On March 4, 1966, another scraper unit was attached to the LT-240 to make it the revamped Series LT-360 (Model A-8) Electric-Digger. The drive wheel arrangement had been redesigned to improve the maneuverability of the giant in less than ideal working conditions. The person next to the LT-360 in the VW Beetle is none other than R. G. LeTourneau himself.

The improved LT-360 was now powered by no less than eight 635-gross-horsepower, Detroit Diesel 16V-71, 16-cylinder engines. This gave the giant a bone-shattering 5,080 horsepower. There was never a factory serial number issued to the LT-360, nor any of the other experimental LT Electric-Diggers that combined to form it.

The size of the massive LT-360 proved its ultimate downfall. It was just too large and wide to be dismantled and transported on public roads economically. To address this size issue, R. G. LeTourneau, Inc., built the tandem Series LT-300 (Model A-6) Dozer-Digger in August 1966. The LT-300 was composed of a four-engined, four-wheel-drive scraper unit called the LT-180 (built in June 1966), combined with the trailing scraper unit of the LT-360 and with another DD 16V-71 diesel grafted on.

application other than a very large earthmoving assignment, with lots of working area, was too small a job for the LT-360. The machine was just too large for its own good. The LT-360 might have had a chance in the marketplace in the late 1950s or early 1960s, but with so many of the giant interstate road building jobs nearing completion, it was a machine out of step with the demands of the earthmoving marketplace. It was a fantastic engineering achievement, as well as a great publicity maker, but of little value beyond that. This version of the mighty LT-360 would never see a paying earthmoving contract come its way and would spend the rest of its life, in one form or another, at the Longview facilities.

As the company faced leaner times, it tried in vain to interest the marketplace in very large Electric-Digger machine designs. After the failure of the LT-360 as a three-scraper unit, the company tried to promote its engineering and production capabilities in various other creative ways. These efforts included the improved LT-240 and the LT-300. The LT-240 was nothing more than the redesigned LT-360, minus its third trailing unit. In fact, the photography for this version of the LT-240 was shot the day before the model images of the LT-360 were taken. The first two scraper units found in both models were the same. When you look at the history of the LT-120, LT-240, and LT-360, you find that they were made up from only three scraper units. Though they were modified in testing, only three scraper bowls were ever fabricated. So the original LT-120, LT-240, and LT-360 from 1965, plus the redesigned LT-240 and LT-360 from 1966, were all

essentially the same machines. LeTourneau did not set out to deceive the marketplace. They were ready to build any one of the models mentioned. But as time passed, individuals started to count each model as a completed, separate unit, which was not the case. In some ways, this added to the mystique of the giant Electric-Diggers. They seemed to be everywhere in the trade journals, but nowhere to be found in the real world.

The company's last effort to keep the giant Electric-Digger program alive was the LT-300, also referred to as a Dozer-Digger. This unit consisted of two scraper units. The front unit, called the LT-180, was a 180-ton-payload-capacity, 107-cubic-yard, telescoping bowl, four-engine design. All the engines were Detroit Diesel 16V-71 units, rated at 2,540 gross horsepower. The four electric-traction wheel motors and tires were the same as those found on the redesigned LT-360. In fact, they probably were removed from that unit in the first place, but old records neither support nor deny such a thing. What is known is that the powered scraper unit towed by the LT-180 was the third trailing unit of the improved LT-360. It was removed and added to the LT-180 to make it the LT-300. The original LT-180 was built in early June 1966, with the additional 120-ton-capacity scraper unit added by the end of the month.

The third scraper unit from the LT-360 had to undergo some modifications before it became part of the LT-300. First, another Detroit Diesel, 16V-71 engine was added to the rear next to the two existing units. This brought its output up to 1,905 gross horsepower. Also, the hitch and drawbar were modified to better

The Series LT-300 Dozer-Digger was rated as a 300-ton-capacity scraper. It carried 180 tons (107 cubic yards heaped) in the front telescoping scraper-bowled unit, and 120 tons (72 cubic yards heaped) in the rear-powered towed unit. Seven Detroit Diesel 16V-71 engines provided 4,445 gross horsepower combined. Measuring approximately 148 feet in length, it would never leave the confines of the Longview plant's testing area. In the end, only one LT-300 was built. And like all the other concept LT Electric-Diggers, it was never issued a factory serial number.

match the different turning radius of the front-powered control unit. This was further reinforced in August. The total output from this tandem hybrid unit was 4,445 gross horsepower, with a maximum payload capacity of 300 tons.

With the LT-300, the company tried to address some of the logistics problems in the LT-360 design. Though it did not match the triple unit's payload capacity, it came very close to it with a tandem configuration. Measuring approximately 148 feet in length, it was considerably shorter than the LT-360, which the company hoped would improve its overall maneuverability on a work site. The front unit also sported a bulldozing blade, giving the unit greater flexibility in working assignments. With the rear scraper unit detached, it could work alone as a dozing unit on a limited basis. Though the LT-300 was still a very large machine, transporting a tandem scraper design would cost much less than moving a triple unit. Yet, as with the other experimental LT Series Electric-Diggers, the LT-300 would find no home outside the confines of the Longview testing areas.

The designs and overall look of the giant Electric-Diggers were pure R. G. LeTourneau. Because of the modular nature of his electric-drive systems, new concepts could be created in months instead of years. With the elimination of transmissions, torque converters, and long driveshafts and universal joints, the LeTourneau machines could take on any type of powerplant arrangement in their designs, some more pleasing to the eye than others. R. G. never allowed the looks of a machine to hinder the design process. As far as he was concerned, extra metal that did not have a structural purpose was just added weight. What mattered most to R. G. was a design's functionality and its overall production output. The looks of a machine never added one extra dollar to a contractor's pocket by the end of the day, so why spend the extra resources on designing nonfunctional sheet metal? On the downside, this gave the LeTourneau machines a bare-bones industrial look that gave many in the industry the impression that these were works in progress. And for the most part, they were.

The last LT-360 was actually quite dynamic in operation. As it snaked across the landscape with its long and low profile, its modular design seemed to have everything in the right place. The LT-300, on the other hand, looked totally out of harmony with itself. The lead unit of the LT-300, with its two V-16 engines perched high on the upper scraper bowls' structural framework, looked simply like an afterthought. There was no attempt to integrate them into the overall design. The LT-300 looked as if it were designed in a hurry, which it probably was. The LT-300 would be the last of the experimental LT giants. R. G. LeTourneau's scraper leviathans were quickly heading for extinction. After building the massive and unorthodox-looking 6-B 150 scraper in 1967, all large scraper design work would come to an end. There simply was no money left in the coffers to experiment with large machines that were totally nonmarketable. Though many of these designs exhibited great industrial design genius, their total loss, financially speaking, was a bitter pill for the company to swallow.

The L-700 proved to be a very capable large mining wheel loader. Whether working in the sub-freezing conditions of northern Canada, or the hot and humid conditions of South America, the L-700 was a stellar performer. This Marathon LeTourneau L-700 is shown at work in July 1973.

Throughout the 1960s, the equipment lines R. G. LeTourneau was offering were meeting stiff resistance in the marketplace. Though individual models, such as the triple-bowled L-90 Electric-Diggers and various versions of the Power-Packer, sold relatively well, too many designs moved in small quantities. Their overall development costs far exceeded any amount eventually paid in the marketplace, if they sold at all. Too many innovations, as well as a totally unique design philosophy, kept potential customers away. They just didn't trust the technology. Many of these contractors had been burned before on other manufacturers' latest-and-greatest earthmoving creations, and they viewed R. G. LeTourneau's machines as the riskiest of them all.

During this time period, many outside factors started to take their toll on the financial well-being of the company. All of the failed prototypes, the millions invested in the missionary establishments in Peru and Liberia, and changes in the U. S. tax laws, forced R. G. LeTourneau to change drastically. On August 25, 1966, R. G. LeTourneau officially stepped down as president of the company, entrusting leadership to one of his sons, Richard LeTourneau.

The circumstances leading up to R. G. LeTourneau's resignation are examined more closely in the next chapter, since there were actually two forces at work during this time period— R. G. LeTourneau's detrimental decisions for the company, and the creation of an entirely new earthmoving equipment line for the mining industry. Even as the former were undermining the company's finances, the latter were laying the foundation for its future—diesel-electric-drive front-end loaders with hydraulic controls.

The idea of using hydraulic systems in one of its creations was not a decision company management and engineers took lightly. R. G. believed that fluid mechanical systems and controls were far too inefficient and complicated. He was convinced that electric motors were the answer to all machine design shortcomings. Such a complete negative view of hydraulics was shared with few in the company, but that was life with R. G. at the helm. With his resignation as head of the company, however, new voices could now be heard—and what they were saying was, get rid of the gear-driven rack-and-pinion designs, and replace them with modern hydraulic equipment. These voices came from upper management, the engineering staff, the company's dealers, and

sales personnel in the field, and most important, prospective customers in the industry. But the heart of these new designs would stay true to the vision that R. G. had for the development of heavy equipment—they would all employ diesel-electric-powered drivetrains with wheel-mounted electric motors.

The development of the company's new wheel loader program was entrusted to Lloyd A. Molby, a longtime design engineer with the company and graduate of the LeTourneau Technical Institute. He, along with other key company engineers and other experienced designers hired from outside the company, would bring the project to fruition. Referred to early in the loader's design phase as the XL-1, the project would be in full swing by June 1967.

The XL-1 was to be marketed to large open-pit mining operations where large wheel loaders from other manufacturers were finding some success. These included the Hough 10-cubic-yard H-400 PAY-loader from 1964, the 10-cubic-yard Scoopmobile from 1965, and the 12-cubic-yard Michigan 475A Series III and 15-cubic-yard KW-Dart D600, both introduced in late 1965. The LeTourneau offering would compete with the bigger loaders, and had the Michigan and KW-Dart offerings clearly in its sights.

Even though R. G. LeTourneau had built articulated-steering wheel loaders in the past, they never really made a dent in the marketplace. But the new loader would take the best of these early designs, and incorporate it into a creation that would stand out from the rest, not only in technology, but in looks as well.

During the early design phase of the XL-1 program, it was not uncommon for R. G. LeTourneau to stop by Molby's office to check on the progress of the new loader. Even though R. G. was no longer president of the company, he still maintained an office on the premises. R. G. would routinely suggest that the hydraulic controls were not the way to go and that electric motors would save the day. All would listen and as soon as R. G. left, the engineers would get right back to work on the new hydraulic designs. Even though R. G. was an engineering genius, he was wrong on this point. Richard LeTourneau knew this, as did the whole engineering staff of the company.

By March 1968, the first prototype loader was completed. The XL-1 moniker was now abandoned, replaced by the machine's official name, the L-700 LeTric-Loader. Unlike previous LeTourneau loader designs, the L-700 looked like a complete machine, and not a work in progress. It was well thought out,

This front-end loader is the prototype diesel-electric-drive XL-1 LeTric-Loader, in March 1968. The XL-1, which became the L-700 model, was the first wheel loader design to feature hydraulic system controls, instead of the archaic rack-and-pinion-gear designs of the past. The design program began in June 1967 and incorporated little input from R. G. LeTourneau, who had stepped down as company head in 1966 because of health problems.

from its integrated front fenders, which also doubled as control cabinets, to its rear sloping deck cover design, giving the operator a superior rearward view. The L-700 used a diesel-electric powertrain that made do without a transmission, torque converter, or driveshafts and differentials. In their place was a large LeTourneau-designed and built DC generator, mounted inline with the engine, which supplied the necessary power to each of the four DC wheel-mounted electric motors. This simplified design allowed the engine to be mounted low in the frame and just ahead of the rear axle, with the generator extending out toward the rear. This gave the loader a very low center of gravity, translating to better overall stability in working conditions. The powerplant in the first prototype unit was a 16-cylinder Detroit Diesel 16V-71T-N75, rated at 700 gross horsepower. But the most important features were the hydraulic cylinders and systems controlling the loader's digging and steering functions. Instead of using engine-mounted hydraulic pumps, LeTourneau engineers devised an AC electric-motor-driven pump. In the electrohydraulic design, systems could be

placed where power was applied. Valves and tanks could be placed in ideal locations to eliminate extensive hosing and piping, reducing downtime due to hydraulic fluid leaks. It was a marriage of hydraulic and electrical technology that only LeTourneau engineers could have conceived.

The L-700's bucket rating of 15 cubic yards, with a maximum payload capacity of 45,000 pounds, made the 175,000-pound machine one of the largest wheel loaders of its day. In comparison, the Michigan 475A Series III weighed in at approximately 144,000 pounds, while the big KW-Dart D600 tipped the scales at 151,000 pounds. The L-700 was most defiantly a force to be reckoned with by the competition. Its wide track, long wheelbase, low center of gravity, and sheer bulk made it the perfect high-production loading tool for large mining operations.

While the development of the XL-1 (L-700) was nearing its final stages, two additional machine designs were given the go-ahead to proceed to prototype levels. These were the XL-2 and the XT-1, better known as the L-500 and the D-450B, respectively. While the larger loader was intended to be marketed to large mining operations, the L-500 design would be sized for the needs of big quarries as well as smaller mines. The D-450B would handle light dozing and pit cleanup around the main loading shovels, and was intended for all quarry and mining operations. The D-450B was based on L-500 mechanicals, except for its dozing blade. All loading and blade controls for both models were hydraulic, with diesel-electric drive. The machines were designed concurrently to save design time and reduce costs.

By November 1968, the L-700 design was going through some engineering alterations. The prototype machine was now equipped with a fully enclosed operator's cab, with redesigned air-cleaner placement locations behind the cab area. Other than this, the loader looked much like it did in March 1968. It would not be long before the mining industry, as well as the trade press reporters, would get to see the L-700 up-close and in the iron.

During the 1969 Conexpo equipment show, held in Chicago February 16–22, LeTourneau arranged for a special airlift of potential customers and other special VIPs on February 19. They were flown down to the Longview, Texas, testing area to see not only the world unveiling of the big L-700, but also the L-500 and D-450B. All of the machines were put through their paces during the daylong event, and the spectators were surprised by what they saw. All three were well-thought-out, full-production machines, and for the most part, were quite handsome. Things were looking up and the LeTourneau sales personnel in

The prototype L-700 (XL-1) is seen here in November 1968 undergoing performance testing at the Longview plant. Changes from the March prototype included repositioned air cleaners behind the operator's area, as well as a new comfort cab.

The prototype L-700 LeTric-Loader was officially unveiled at a special event at the Longview plant in February 1969. After further testing, the unit was shipped to Lone Star Steel in December 1969 to experience real-world working conditions. The big 15-cubic-yard loader was equipped with a new Waukesha L1616DSI diesel, rated at 725 gross horsepower. The LeTric nomenclature was dropped in favor of a new product line name—LeTro-Loader. The factory serial number for the very first hydraulic-equipped machine was L-700-1027.

During the development of the first L-700, R. G. LeTourneau, Inc., engineers were also hard at work on a slightly smaller loader called the L-500 LeTric-Loader. Unveiled in February 1969, the L-500 was powered by a single, rear-mounted Cummins V1710-C500 diesel engine, rated at 500 gross horsepower. The L-500 looked much like the L-700, just proportioned smaller. The L-500 weighed in at 120,000 pounds (while the L-700 tipped the scales at 175,000 pounds).

The prototype L-500 was shipped to Lone Star Steel in November 1969 for further performance testing. But R. G. LeTourneau, Inc.'s financial situation at the time did not allow development funds for both the L-500 and the larger L-700. The L-500 loader program got the ax with only one unit built.

attendance were enthusiastic. But many months of hard prototype testing lay ahead for the new LeTourneau machines before they would be ready for release into the marketplace.

The L-500 LeTric-Loader and D-450B LeTric-Dozer were finished just in time for the February 19 airlift demonstration. As late as February 5, both machines were awaiting final paint touchup and model nomenclature application.

The L-500 looked much like its bigger brother, the L-700. Weighing in at 120,000 pounds and carrying a 10-cubic-yard bucket, the L-500 was to counter Caterpillar's new 992 loader, introduced in 1968. The 992 was also rated as a 10-cubic-yard machine and weighed in at approximately 119,500 pounds in full operating trim. The prototype L-500 was powered by a Cummins V1710-C500 diesel engine, rated at 500 gross horsepower. Other than the engine, the L-500's layout was basically the same as the L-700's, sized to meet the demands of a smaller loader. The similarity between the two came in handy when the company used an L-700 picture on the specification sheet for the L-500. It did so because the L-500 wasn't yet completed when the product literature was printed. A quick way to tell the two apart is to count the ladder rungs to the top platform step on the sides of the machines. The L-700 has eight steps to the top counting the main platform, while the L-500 has only seven.

The wheel-dozer counterpart to the L-500 was the D-450B. Sharing the same basic diesel-electric-drive layout as the loader, the D-450B was powered by a Detroit Diesel 12V-71N engine, rated at 475 flywheel horsepower. Though the dozer was offered with the Cummins engine found in the L-500, none were ever produced with it. For all intents and purposes, the D-450B was an L-500 with the loader front end removed and replaced with a hydraulic dozing blade. The blade was also equipped with full hydraulic tilt cylinders, both right and left. As with the L-500, the specification sheet on the D-450B featured a picture of the L-700, this time retouched to include a dozer blade. Like its sibling, the D-450B was not completed at the time the promotional literature was made.

Both the L-700 and L-500 would eventually find their way down to Lone Star Steel, not too far from Longview, to continue their prototype testing programs. LeTourneau was able to place the loaders at this facility, if only temporarily, so they could be tested in real-world working conditions. The L-500 would arrive at Lone Star Steel in November 1969, followed by the L-700 in December. The larger loader had gone through a few more upgrades and changes for work at Lone Star. The prototype L-700 was now powered by a Waukesha L1616DSI diesel engine rated at 725 gross horsepower, 25 more than the original Detroit Diesel. The exhaust system was also rerouted from under the rear decking, to on top of it, bringing the engine compartment temperature down considerably. At this time the short-lived LeTric-Loader name was thrown on the scrap heap. The company replaced it with the new name of LeTro-Loader. This name would stay with the loader line for years to come.

This L-700 LeTro-Loader from April 1970 was the first production model to be delivered to a customer. Originally equipped with a 15-cubic-yard bucket, it was replaced with a 23-cubic-yard bucket by the time it was shipped to the Navajo Mine, near Farmington, New Mexico, in May 1970. The engine in the first production unit was the same-type Waukesha diesel engine installed in the prototype L-700 in December 1969. This machine was the second unit manufactured after the prototype L-700 (XL-1).

But just as the engineering side of R. G. LeTourneau was looking so promising with the three new designs, its financial outlook was hitting historic lows. The lack of operating and investment capital would force the company to scale back development of the new designs. There simply wasn't enough money to bring all three designs up to full-production standards. Management decided to cancel the L-500 program, taking the D-450B wheel dozer with it, since it was basically an extension of the smaller loader design. There were fewer competitors in the 15-cubic-yard class, and Caterpillar had gotten an early jump in the 10-yard market with its 992 loader. Thus, LeTourneau's 15-yard L-700 had the best chance for success. All available funds would be put into the L-700 program to resolve reliability issues.

By April 1970, LeTourneau had the first production L-700 ready to go. Looking much like the prototype unit, the production L-700 was easily recognizable by its redesigned circuit control boxes, which doubled as the loader's front fenders. They were now tapered in at the top at a sharp angle to allow the operator a better view of the bucket's working area. This unit would also be equipped with the Waukesha diesel engine. By the following month, the loader would find its first long-term home at Utah Construction & Mining Company's Navajo coal mine, located near Farmington, New Mexico. Equipped with a larger-volume 23-cubic-yard-capacity bucket suited for coal-loading applications, the loader impressed all at the mine with its speed, durability, and productivity.

The L-700 had all the makings of a successful mining machine, but LeTourneau coffers were empty. If the new loader were to establish a presence in the marketplace, it would have to be with the help of an outside firm. In 1970, the Marathon Manufacturing Company entered the picture, marking a new chapter in the life of R. G. LeTourneau, Inc.

The prototype L-1200, shown in April 1979, is undergoing a trail stay at a mining operation so Marathon LeTourneau engineers can gather real-world working evaluation data. The L-1200 was powered by either a Detroit Diesel 12V-149TI, or a Cummins KTA2300 diesel engine, both rated at 1,200 gross horsepower.

Since November 19, 1929, R. G. LeTourneau had led his company as president. Over insurmountable odds in many instances, R. G. pushed his company, his designs, his religious philosophy, and himself to limits almost unheard of, not just for a man heading up an industrial manufacturing company, but for anyone, anywhere. He overcame difficulties in his early years that would have caused most of us simply to give up. He always credited his successes to his partnership with God. Failures were just part of a larger plan by God that would teach the lessons of life. His life's devotion to a Christian lifestyle with testimony was without question. It seemed that R. G. would go on forever. But the one thing that he did not have control of was time. If R. G. was guilty of anything in his later years, it was simply that he got old. His other certain fault was that he never knew when to quit. By the mid-1960s, R. G. LeTourneau's age and his mental capabilities were subjects of concern for everyone else at the company. His leadership had to come to an end, and with it would come changes to the company that he could not imagine.

During 1966, business had slowed down at both the Longview and Vicksburg manufacturing plants. Decreasing orders for the offshore oil drilling platforms, as well as for all of the diesel-electric-drive earthmoving and forestry equipment, were starting to put a financial strain on the company. Though the firm had produced numerous innovative earthmoving machines since 1958, it lacked a well-organized dealer network to move these machines in quantity. All were built as one-offs, or in very small quantities. Also, the designs were quite eclectic, to say the least. What dealers there were, never had a complete line of equipment to sell to a potential customer. Even though the electric-wheel drive had vastly improved in reliability throughout the 1960s, many customers that had gambled on LeTourneau equipment were left with machines in need of constant repair, requiring spare parts that seemed to take forever to be delivered. R. G. was best at conceiving brilliant new ideas and engineering them into reality. But quite often, just about the time one such machine was nearing completion, his interests would switch to another great idea, and off to his drawing board he would go. His short attention span for a single project was well known throughout the company. This led to production of numerous designs, at a cost of millions of dollars, that were never refined to the point of commercial viability.

Another problem that finally could no longer be contained in 1966 was the hemorrhaging of vast sums of capital keeping the agricultural, philanthropic, and missionary activities of Tournata in Liberia, and Tournavista in Peru, in operation. Changes in these countries' governments had made it all but impossible to continue work on these endeavors any longer. The project in Liberia, controlled by LeTourneau of Liberia, Ltd., was dissolved and all properties handed back to the government in mid-1966. The operations in Peru were halted in 1969, when the Peruvian Minister for Agriculture voided the original 1953 contract agreement they had made with LeTourneau del Peru, Inc., making any further investment in the project a lost cause. In the end, the project was abandoned, with all land handed back to the Peruvian government. It was a complete financial loss.

When R. G. LeTourneau had sold his earthmoving equipment line to Westinghouse Air Brake Company, the approximate selling price was around $31 million. Much of the funds received from this sale had been used up over the years in the continued development and refinement of the electric-wheel motor. But vast sums had also been drained away by a false start in marine shipbuilding, initially commenced in 1952, and the projects in Peru and Liberia. Add to this the experimental nature of much of the earthmoving equipment designs at the time, and you have a sure recipe for financial trouble.

As the United States was getting itself ever further mired in the war in Vietnam, the armed forces realized they were running low on 750- and 1,000-pound bombs. When the government approached LeTourneau about the possibility of quickly going into production of these needed ordnance, R. G. saw this as a way to improve the company's financial standing and keep both of its plants and all of their employees working. R. G. took this proposal up with the Board of Directors of the company, which consisted of five men inside the company and three men outside. Their role was to guide company affairs. To make bomb production a reality, the company would need money to gear up for production. Because of the risk involved, the Board of Directors said no. But R. G. had a different take on the matter. Since he controlled 90 percent of the company's stock, which was maintained by the LeTourneau Foundation, he didn't really have to take the board's advice in this matter. Sometimes he would take their advice. In this case, he did not.

In August 1975, Marathon LeTourneau put its first L-800 LeTro-Loader to work. The L-800 featured the same basic drivetrain layout as the L-700A, with one major exception: along with solid-state controls, the L-800 was equipped with solid-state power conversion. The standard engine choices were the 860-gross-horsepower Detroit Diesel 16V-92T, or the 800-gross-horsepower Cummins VTA-1710-C. This L-800 is shown at work in March 1978.

But the U.S. government, as well as the banks that would be supplying the capital, needed a little reassurance. R. G. was 78 years old. If anything were to happen to him, there was no one person who could step in and take control of the company to see that the government's contracts were fulfilled and the banks repaid. To get around this, R. G. appointed one of his sons, Richard, as executive vice president of R. G. LeTourneau, Inc., in May 1966.

To get production of the bomb castings under way required large, expensive, specialized machine tools. The U. S. government agreed to let R. G. LeTourneau, Inc., go ahead and purchase the needed machine tools, for which the government would then reimburse them. In essence, the U. S. government would own the machine tools and would contract R. G. LeTourneau, Inc., for the production of the bomb castings. To get needed operating funds quickly, LeTourneau billed the government for the cost of the machine tools and was reimbursed promptly. But instead of paying off the suppliers of the machine tools, the company used the funds to make necessary payroll and other overdue expenses. When the machine tool suppliers demanded immediate payment, there was simply no money to pay them. This information got back to U. S. government officials, which promptly sent LeTourneau an ultimatum—remedy this problem in 48 hours or else. There had been a few times in the past where

The L-800 was rated with a standard bucket capacity of 15 cubic yards, with a maximum payload of 45,000 pounds. A heavy-lift option raised this amount to 51,000 pounds. The overall working weight of the loader was 185,500 pounds.

New diesel-electric-drive L-800 LeTro-Loaders are seen here on their way down the Longview plant's main assembly lines. This scene was quite common during the late 1970s and early 1980s. When the last L-800 shipped from the factory in October 1985, it became one of 192 units built in total. The L-800 remains the company's best-selling, single-loader model.

the creditor wolves had been scratching at the company door, but this time, they were breaking it down. If something drastic wasn't done quickly, R. G. LeTourneau, Inc., would be bankrupt.

An emergency meeting was called on August 25, 1966. At the meeting were the company treasurer, the company controller, and Richard LeTourneau. Management set out for R. G. the company's dire situation, stressing that 48 hours were all they had. At that point R. G. realized that the only thing that would buy some much-needed time was a change in company leadership. R. G. had suffered a few minor strokes and he knew he was no longer up to the task. His memory would often lapse and his strength was declining. The only thing he could do was resign as president and hand over complete control of the company to Richard.

Richard LeTourneau immediately began working to get the company back on its financial feet. He rearranged management and key department heads. He reassigned his brothers, all of whom worked for the company, to new positions. Roy LeTourneau, who managed the company's sales outlet in Portland, Oregon, was brought back to Longview to head up product development. Ben LeTourneau, who had been managing the Vicksburg plant, was to assume responsibility for all manufacturing operations. Ted LeTourneau was to head up engineering. Of all of the brothers, Ted was the one most like R. G. when it came to engineering design and technical matters. Ted was heavily involved with the engineering of the offshore platforms.

It wasn't long before things started to take a turn for the better at R. G. LeTourneau, Inc. Sales were steadily increasing between 1966 and 1968. The government and various other creditors were patient with the company. They saw that it was making an earnest attempt to turn itself around and meet its manufacturing and financial commitments. But the year of 1969 would not be as kind.

On June 1, 1969, R. G. LeTourneau died from complications from a major stroke that he suffered on March 17, 1969. Though he had not been involved with company activities for over a year, his death was a great psychological blow to the family, and therefore, to the company. At 80 years old, he had been as productive as several men in his lifetime. Always on the go, with ideas and beliefs to share with everyone he met, he was practically unstoppable. The aging process had taken its toll on R. G. in his final years, but with his son Richard at the helm, he was able to see the company he started in 1929 pass to the next generation, if only briefly. His passing seemed to take from the company that bore his name some of the spirit that had made it all possible.

The next event to transpire in 1969, which would have an even greater effect on the company, was a change in U. S. tax laws passed by Congress that year. In essence, the new tax law prohibited a foundation from owning or controlling more than 10 percent of a business. The law was designed to end the practice of sheltering corporate profits from taxation by setting up company ownership in a foundation. R. G. was never motivated to duck taxes, but he had set up a foundation for another purpose. Although R. G. LeTourneau, Inc., was a public company with stock to trade on the open market, R. G. had owned 90 percent of it himself. To keep these funds from being inherited by family members and their heirs and spent on private purposes, R. G. set up the LeTourneau Foundation in 1935 to propagate the Christian Gospel. R. G. then donated all of his stock to it, ensuring that all dividends would be used only for the Lord's work. The money received from this stock was not taxable, and was out of reach for personal use, either by his children or R. G. himself. But the new tax law would change all that. Because of the new law, the LeTourneau Foundation was going to have to sell its stock. Yet the company's low market value, and the liabilities of the Foundation, made this a dangerous move for the company. The best bet for investors was to try to sell the company as a whole.

The company first announced a potential new owner around January 1970. But the investment company that had agreed to purchase LeTourneau—FMI, Inc., of Dallas—actually had another plan. They were going to broker LeTourneau to another company and retain a fee from the completed deal. Once R. G. LeTourneau, Inc., people found this out, they forced the firm to withdraw from the sales agreement in April.

In July 1970, a Houston, Texas, bank, which handled a large credit line for LeTourneau, Inc., contacted the company in the hopes of setting up a meeting with a potential buyer. That buyer, Houston-based Marathon Manufacturing Company, took a keen interest in R. G. LeTourneau, Inc., and after several meetings with management the two firms reached a tentative deal on August 25, 1970. The deal, which was finalized on September 30, 1970, would make R. G. LeTourneau, Inc., a subsidiary of Marathon Manufacturing. Included in the deal were the means of paying off the LeTourneau Foundation's debt, endowment income for LeTourneau College, and a block of stock in the new company.

Initially, the Longview company retained the corporate name of R. G. LeTourneau, Inc., after its purchase by Marathon. But in 1972, the name was officially changed to the Marathon LeTourneau Company, Longview Division. As for the Marine Products Division, which was responsible for the giant offshore

Marathon LeTourneau gave the quarry-sized loader market another try in late 1976, when it introduced the L-600 LeTro-Loader. Its diesel-electric-drive system featured solid-state controls and power conversion, as well as four-wheel drive, just like the L-800. The L-600 is shown working in a quarry in March 1977.

During the 1970s, all of Marathon LeTourneau's diesel-electric-drive mining loaders were considered large machines. But if the L-800 was just a bit too small for your operation, then the L-1200 LeTro-Loader was perfect. With a big bucket capacity of 22 cubic yards, and a payload capacity of 66,000 pounds, the L-1200 was all about high-volume loading productivity. The L-1200 was introduced in October 1978. The prototype unit shown is equipped with Goodyear 65.55x51, 54-ply tires that are 10 feet, 6 inches in diameter.

drilling rigs, its new name would be Marathon LeTourneau Offshore Company, with corporate offices in Houston and manufacturing continuing at the Vicksburg plant. Both entities were subsidiaries of Marathon Manufacturing Company.

Marathon LeTourneau product offerings included LeTro-Lifts, LeTro-Porters, LeTro-Stackers, LeTro-Crushers, LeTro-Cranes, LeTro-Grips, and of course, the LeTro-Loaders. The marine division produced offshore drilling rigs, ships, and barges. The Electric-Diggers scraper line, however, would not make the products roster for the new subsidiary. When R. G. LeTourneau died, his remarkable electric-drive scraper giants passed with him into history.

During the Marathon LeTourneau transition period, the company was selling a good number of Log Stackers. In fact, it was the company's most popular product line. The earthmovers,

on the other hand, were selling in small quantities, due in large part to the fact that the L-700 mining wheel loader was the only model being produced. Company literature offered the L-700 in several variations, such as a wheel-dozer, a pusher, or a compactor, but none of these varieties were ever produced. And with the termination of L-500 series development in 1970, the L-700 wheel loader was all the company could offer.

During the early 1970s, Marathon LeTourneau's main goal with the L-700 series loader was to resolve reliability issues with the machine's diesel-electric-drive system. During 1973, the L-700 became the L-700A model with the introduction of partial solid-state controls, replacing much of the original's older switch gear circuit designs. During this time, only two engine choices were offered—the Detroit Diesel 16V-71T-N75 and the Cummins VTA-1710-C, both still rated at 700 gross horsepower.

When the standard tires on the L-1200 would not do, the customer could opt for massive Goodyear 67x51, 44-ply tires that were 11 feet, 6 inches in diameter. These were the same-size tires utilized on the 24-cubic-yard Clark Michigan 675, though with a slightly lower ply rating. The total operating weight of the L-1200 with these tires was 335,000 pounds. The loading bucket was 18 feet, 10 inches across.

The Waukesha diesel engine option had been dropped with only eight loaders ever equipped with it. In late 1974, a more powerful 800-gross-horsepower Detroit Diesel 16V-71TI-N90 was also offered for the L-700A.

As the new company refined the L-700A, it was only natural that it would evolve into a new model designation. It became the L-800 in 1975. The L-700 series had a solid sales run, with some 76 units built, including the prototype. The L-800 would continue this streak at an even more rapid pace. The first L-800 pilot loader shipped from the Longview plant in August 1975, making its way to the Navajo Mine, near Farmington, New Mexico. As mentioned before, this mine was home to the first production L-700 loader as well.

The L-800 development program actually started with the pilot L-700 loader. The prototype L-700, which was built in 1968, was not sold until July 1973, when it was shipped to Fort McMurray, Alberta, Canada, to the Great Canadian Oil Sands mining operation (now referred to as Suncor). This loader, called the L-700SS, not only featured solid-state controls, but also solid-state power conversion as well—a company first. This system eliminated all mechanical and electromechanical components, greatly simplifying maintenance, while increasing reliability at the same time. This is the same system engineers would use for the L-800. Many consider this machine a turning point in the history of LeTourneau's loader development. Not only was it the first L-700 (XL-1), it was also the first L-700A, as well as the forerunner to the L-800 in the form of the L-700SS. One thing is certain—LeTourneau engineers sure got a lot of mileage out of loader serial number L-700-1027, master group 401-5880, shop number 1.

For a while, the L-700A and L-800 were produced concurrently. Some customers still wanted the L-700A with only partial solid-state controls and the old system for power conversion, while other customers wanted the state-of-the-art system found in the L-800. Both loaders had the same capacity rating, so this was not a factor. During 1975, the company released only one factory-built L-800, with full production commencing in 1976. The L-700A was offered in 1975 and 1976, with the last unit—built as a front-end loader—shipping from the factory in March 1977. By this time, the L-800 was in such demand that the company was having a hard time keeping up with all of the

The L-1200 was ideally suited for loading haul trucks in the 150- to 170-ton-capacity range. The height of the 22-cubic-yard bucket fully raised was 33 feet, with a maximum dump height of 18 feet, 10 inches, when the bucket was equipped with teeth. This loader is working at a Boliden Copper mine, near Gallivare, Sweden, in June 1981.

orders. Of all of the diesel-electric-drive earthmoving equipment developed by the company since 1958, the L-800 was the most popular and profitable machine built up to that time, and by quite a large margin.

It is interesting to note that one of the last L-700 models was not built as a wheel loader at all, but as a modified tractor, called an L-700 LeTro-tow Unit (S.N. 7188). Built for Ameron of California, it was to be incorporated into the design of that company's 250-ton-capacity Liftmobile II, built between June and July 1976. This 78-foot-tall mobile gantry crane structure was designed to pick up 225-ton sections of precast concrete pipe, and transport them in a vertical position. The L-700 tow-unit, which consisted of the rear section of the original loader design, supplied the motive power for the machine.

By 1978, the L-800 was offered with a choice of engines—a Detroit Diesel 16V-92T or a Cummins KT2300-C—both rated at 860 gross horsepower. Weight was up a bit, to 185,500 pounds, as compared to the L-700A's 180,000 pounds. When the last L-800 shipped from the Longview plant in October 1985, some 192 units had been delivered into service around the world. To this day, it is still the largest production run for any single loader model ever offered by the company.

As the L-800 was starting to hit its stride, Marathon LeTourneau introduced a slightly smaller loader into prototype testing in late 1976, identified as the L-600. The L-600 was essentially a downsized version of the L-800. It was also similar in size and appearance to the abandoned L-500 program from 1969. But the L-600 was all new from the ground up, and designed from day one with full solid-state controls and power conversion for its electric-drive system. The L-600 was equipped with a standard 10-cubic-yard bucket, rated at 30,000 pounds, the same as the L-500. The new loader was definitely aimed toward the industry leader in this size class, the Caterpillar 992. The big Cat had carved out an enviable market segment for itself and helped establish the 10-plus-cubic-yard loader as an industry standard. Marathon LeTourneau wanted a piece of the action and thought the diesel-electric-drive L-600 was just the machine to get it.

The L-600 was offered with either a 12-cylinder Detroit Diesel 12V-71T, or a 6-cylinder Cummins KT1150, both rated at 525 gross horsepower. The loader's operating weight was about 130,200 pounds. Like its big brother, it used four-wheel-electric AC/DC drive. In appearance, the L-600 was every inch a LeTourneau design and looked like it had the muscle to back up its performance claims. But the marketplace can be very fickle.

Though the L-1200 was an excellent mining loader, the world economic conditions at the time of its manufacture sealed its doom. There just weren't enough customers in the marketplace willing to take a chance on such a large machine in such uncertain recession times. The last six L-1200s, built between 1982 and 1984, were all shipped to M-K Carbocol in Columbia, South America, painted white. In all, only 11 of the big L-1200 loaders were produced. Ten were equipped with Detroit Diesel power, while only one received the Cummins engine option.

Customers in the large quarry industry had grown comfortable with the Cat 992. They liked its mechanical-drive layout and knew how to fix it, and they were reluctant to commit to a totally different drive system. This, more than anything else, kept L-600 sales figures very low.

The first L-600 prototype spent its early months working at Johnson & Morgan in Pennsylvania. Two more prototype machines would follow before the first production unit was shipped from the factory to Bluestone Coal in Wise, Virginia, in May 1977. The last L-600 left the factory in May 1986. In all, only 26 of the L-600 loaders were built over its production run. Even though the recession of the early 1980s played a big part in the model's low sales, the marketplace was simply not ready for a "small" LeTourneau.

At the American Mining Congress' (AMC) International Mining Show, held in Las Vegas, Nevada, in October 1978, Marathon LeTourneau took the wraps off their latest "big" LeTro-Loader— the L-1200. The L-1200 was the largest wheel loader the company had ever designed. It looked similar to the L-800 model series, but was a much bigger machine in every way. The L-1200 was designed for large open-pit mining operations. With a 22-cubic-yard bucket, rated at 66,000 pounds, it was an ideal match for haul trucks with capacities in the 120–170-ton range.

The L-1200 was powered by either a Detroit Diesel 12V-149TI, or a Cummins KTA2300 engine, both rated at 1,200 gross horsepower. The drivetrain, as with all LeTourneau designs, was diesel-electric, with separate electric-traction motors mounted in each wheel assembly. As with the L-800, solid-state power conversion and controls were the norm. The hydraulic system utilized a high-capacity accessory gearbox, mounted inline with the engine and AC generator, to drive all of the hydraulic pumps. This was the same type of system found on the L-800. The early L-700/700A design used an electric AC motor to power the hydraulic pump. This design was deemed too unreliable and was finally changed in the L-800 Series.

The L-1200 faced two rival wheel loaders that were after the same market niche in the mining industry—the International-Hough 580 PAY Loader, and the massive Clark Michigan 675. Both of these competitors had been on the market, or in prototype testing, for several years. The Clark Michigan 675 started testing in the summer of 1970. The International-Hough 580 got its start in 1971, when the company first previewed an experimental 18-cubic-yard pilot machine. The 580 loader was previewed again in more complete form at the 1975 Conexpo. But it would not be until the 1978 AMC show that a full-production unit was displayed ready for sale worldwide. The machines were comparable in size, with the Michigan the largest of the three. Based on 1978 specifications, bucket capacity for the Michigan 675 was 24 cubic yards, with a 72,000-pound payload rating. Both the International 580 and LeTourneau L-1200 shared the same 22-cubic-yard/66,000-pound load rating. The 675 weighed in at 388,200 pounds, while the 580 tipped the scales at only 289,000 pounds. The L-1200 was right in the middle of these two, with an operating weight of 335,000 pounds. With its two engines, the 675 produced 1,400 gross horsepower, while the L-1200 and the 580 were both rated at 1,200 gross horsepower.

The most significant difference between these three giants was the layout of their drive systems. The Michigan 675 used two engines, two torque converters, and one powershift transmission. The International 580 utilized a single engine, torque converter, and powershift transmission. The LeTourneau was, of course, diesel-electric drive, a distinction that gave the L-1200 at least a fighting chance in the marketplace. It was the one area in which LeTourneau could claim its design was superior to the other two. And they had a point. In the field, the twin-engine layout of the Michigan 675 earned it the nickname, "old double-trouble." The twin torque converters, along with all of the rest of the system's driveshafts and universal joints, were a constant source of complaints in the field. As for the 580, its single, three-speed powershift transmission was its weakest link. Throughout the 580 loader's entire design life, the three-speed transmission was always keeping what was considered a rather good design from achieving greatness. It just wasn't up to the task of hustling a 22-cubic-yard loader around, even though it was the lightest machine of the three.

To be fair, the L-1200 wasn't without its troubles, but these were small when compared to its competition. But the one thing neither the L-1200 nor Marathon LeTourneau could control was the economy. Just as sales were starting to take off for the big LeTro-Loader, the world economy came to a screeching halt in

Marathon LeTourneau tried once again to interest the mining industry in a large diesel-electric-drive, rubber-tired wheel dozer with its D-800 LeTro-Dozer. Introduced in October 1978, the D-800 was intended for use as a high-production land reclamation and coal stockpiling wheel dozer. The big wheel-dozer was originally offered with a Detroit Diesel 16V-92T or Cummins KT2300-C engine, both rated at 860 gross horsepower. In 1981, power output for the Cummins powerplant was increased to 900 horsepower.

This D-800 LeTro-Dozer from February 1980 is equipped with the U reclamation blade, which measures 21 feet, 3 inches across, and 7 feet high. The special optional 50.42x50 Trak-R-Tred steel-cleated tires are intended to be used when the dozer is working in rocky conditions that might cut or puncture regular tires. The reclamation wheel dozer weighed 194,400 pounds.

the early 1980s. Mining companies that had planned major expansions put almost all of their new equipment investments on hold. This not only mortally wounded the L-1200, it also delayed or brought early retirement to many fine pieces of heavy mining equipment from other manufacturers. The world recession, more than anything else, was responsible for holding production of L-1200 loaders to only 11 units.

Three prototype L-1200 loaders were built, including the 1978 AMC show machine. The second machine was delivered in early 1980 to Drummond Coal's Cedrum Mine, near Townley, Alabama, while the third unit would ship from the factory in May 1980 to Kaiser Resources in British Columbia, Canada. The original pilot L-1200 would make a few demonstration stops at various mining operations until finally being sold to CCB of Antwerp, Belgium, in 1982. There it joined another L-1200 already at the site, which in fact was the first production unit of the L-1200, shipped from the Longview plant in July 1980. The last L-1200 produced left the factory in September 1984, destined for M-K Carbocol in

Columbia, South America. Along with this machine, M-K Carbocol operated the last six L-1200 loaders built. At the time of this writing, a few of these units were still listed as operational, with spare parts coming from decommissioned units at the mine.

All of the L-1200s were equipped with the Detroit Diesel engine, except for the unit delivered to British Columbia, which was specified with the Cummins powerplant. All would also find their final homes outside of the United States, except for the second machine built, which was shipped to Alabama. If not for the worldwide recession, surely the L-1200 would have made a significant showing in the marketplace. It seems the worst criticism you could level at the L-1200 program was bad timing, and that, in this case, was beyond the company's control.

During the same 1978 AMC show at which it introduced the L-1200, Marathon LeTourneau also unveiled the wheel-dozer version of the L-800 loader—the D-800 LeTro-Dozer. The D-800 was designed as a high-production reclamation or coal stockpiling wheel-dozer intended for the largest such

The D-800 could also be equipped with a 22-foot, 5-inch-wide coal stockpiling dozing blade that was 9 feet, 4 inches high in the center. As can be seen from this LeTro-Dozer attacking a coal stockpile in July 1981, the environmentally controlled comfort cab was a must for operator comfort and safety. Marathon LeTourneau built a total of 18 LeTro-Dozers, with the last shipping from the Longview plant in October 1985 equipped with a special Cummins KT38-C diesel. This was the only D-800 to be optioned with such a powerplant.

applications in the mining and power-generating industries. Like the L-800 loader, the D-800 was offered with the Detroit Diesel 16V-92T or the Cummins KT2300-C engine, both rated at 860 gross horsepower. By 1981, the Cummins engine had an increased rating of 900 gross horsepower. The drive system was the tried-and-true LeTro-matic AC/DC, four-wheel electric-drive. Two bulldozing blades were offered for the D-800. The blade for reclamation was a "U" type that measured 21 feet, 3 inches across. The coal "U" blade measured 22 feet, 5 inches. The reclamation dozer version weighed in at 194,400 pounds, while the coal version tipped the scales at 193,000 pounds.

The prototype D-800 displayed at the mining show was delivered soon afterward to Drummond Coal in Kellerman, Alabama, on a lease basis. The first production unit left the factory in November 1979, destined for U.S. Borax in Boron, California. After a short stay at this location, it was eventually shipped to the Boardman Steam Plant in Boardman, Oregon, in November 1980. The last D-800 produced left the LeTourneau factory in October

1985, bound for the Mississippi Power Company in Gulfport, Mississippi. In the end, some 18 D-800 LeTro-Dozers were built. After its lease contract was up, the prototype D-800 was returned to Longview, where it sat in the backyard behind the main plant. Over the years, it contributed various parts to other machines, until, in early 2000, the remaining dozer chassis was finally scrapped.

During the D-800's run, it was considered the world's largest production wheel-dozer. The three massive VCON dozers, one V-250 and two V-220s, were all larger than the D-800, but these machines were considered experimental and were discontinued before the release of the LeTourneau offering. Though the D-800 sold rather well over its production run, its numbers were nowhere near what Marathon LeTourneau had hoped for. In the end, the diesel-electric-drive system that worked so well in wheel-loader service, was not the best choice for a wheel dozer of this size and intended applications. It wasn't long before the D-800 joined the rest of LeTourneau's wheel-dozer designs of the 1960s.

Marathon LeTourneau officially unveiled its redesigned Titan
T-2000 Series hauler at the American Mining Congress show in
October 1986. This new Titan truck now featured Marathon
LeTourneau–designed electrical-drive components, replacing most
of the old GM/Delco systems. It also featured a redesigned radiator
front-end assembly, and a completely new operator's cab. This first
prototype unit, shown here at the Longview plant in August 1986
just before shipping to the mining show, was powered by the same
engine as the 33-15D haulers, with the same power output. After the
show, the hauler was placed into service in January 1987.

As Marathon LeTourneau entered the 1980s, its earthmoving equipment was gaining an increasing presence in the world mining market. The company's financial situation had also improved in December 1979, when Marathon Manufacturing became a wholly owned subsidiary of the Penn Central Corporation. But the company still had a very limited earthmoving product line, consisting of three wheel loaders and one wheel dozer. What the company needed was a few more complementary equipment offerings. Their dealers agreed. Management settled on a haul truck. This would enable its dealers to offer present and future customers more complete equipment packages. But designing a complete hauler line from the ground up would be an expensive proposition. Ironically, what helped make this endeavor a reality was the same worldwide recession of the early 1980s that had doomed expansions and product lines across the industry.

The heavy manufacturing sector faced bleak prospects during 1981, 1982, and 1983. These were simply devastating years for manufacturers of heavy mining equipment. The recession spared few in the industry from the pain of escalating interest rates and double-digit inflation. Companies that looked just fine at the end of 1979 were now staring into the abyss of total ruin. For some companies, alliances and joint ventures were a way to keep research and development moving forward, as well as fend off threats from the new emerging powerhouse in the mining equipment sector, Japan. But for others, the only way to survive was a merger or buyout. Marathon LeTourneau was not immune to the effects of these economic times, which caused the early demise of its L-1200 wheel loader and D-800 wheel dozer. But as some opportunities ended, others were created, and those with the strongest bank accounts, or at least credit lines, prevailed. For once, Marathon LeTourneau was in the right place at the right time.

General Motors Corporation had been in the heavy earthmoving equipment business since 1953, when it purchased the Euclid Road Machinery Company. In 1968, because of antitrust concerns raised by the U.S. government, GM was forced to sell its hauler line, as well as the Euclid name and trademark itself, leaving it with only wheel loaders, dozers, and scrapers. The company adopted a new name and trademark in 1968, Terex, and set up Terex Division in 1970. In 1972, it released an entirely new line of haul trucks in the United States, including a 150-ton-capacity, diesel-electric-drive unit designed and built at Diesel Division, General Motors of Canada, Ltd.'s London, Ontario, Canada, plant. Because of the upheaval in the automotive industry in the 1970s, GM had its hands full trying to make desirable small cars to compete with the Japanese imports flooding into North America. By 1980, GM decided it needed to focus all of its energies on the business of building cars, not earthmoving machines.

In August 1980, GM entered negotiations with IBH Holding AG, of Mainz, Germany, concerning the possible sale of Terex Division. GM Chairman Roger Smith, and Chief Executive of the IBH Group Horst-Dieter Esch, signed the purchase agreement in September 1980, making the former GM earthmoving division a subsidiary of the IBH Group, effective January 1, 1981. Under IBH, the company was called Terex Corporation.

The Terex deal with IBH did not include the diesel-electric-drive haulers built in Ontario at Diesel Division, General Motors of Canada, Ltd. Because of the design of the trucks and their relationship to the Canadian locomotive assembly plant, GM decided it was in its best interests to retain ownership in the hauler line. The Terex name was removed from the trucks and replaced with a new label, "Titan."

In 1981, two diesel-electric-drive, rear-dump haulers were offered by Diesel Division—the 170-ton-capacity Titan 33-15B, and the 350-ton-capacity Titan 33-19. All sales came from the smaller model, as the giant, three-axle 33-19 found no takers. In November 1981, the company released an improved version of the smaller truck as the 33-15C, but the ice-cold economy made for slow sales. So bad was business, that for most of 1983, and for all of 1984, no 33-15C trucks were sold. No company wants to retain an expensive product line that generates no revenue, GM concluded.

GM had clearly lost interest in building haul trucks. The only logical thing for the company to do was find a buyer to take the Titan mining hauler off its hands. By late 1984, Marathon LeTourneau had entered the picture and was talking seriously with GM about purchasing the truck line. The two companies signed a deal just before Christmas 1984, transferring all Titan plans, drawings, tooling, and world manufacturing rights to Marathon LeTourneau. The Titan product line officially transferred from GM to LeTourneau on February 1, 1985.

The first Marathon LeTourneau–built diesel-electric-drive 33-15C Titan comes off the Longview truck assembly line in June 1985. The Titan hauler at this time was still largely based on the designs and components of the General Motors Diesel Division hauler. Rated at 170 tons capacity, this Texas-built truck was powered by a 1,600-gross-horsepower Detroit Diesel 16V-149TI, 16-cylinder engine.

Marathon LeTourneau acquired not only the 33-15C and 33-19 truck designs, it also received all rights to the proposed 200-ton-capacity 33-17. But Marathon LeTourneau was only interested in pursuing development of the 33-15C Series, so no effort was put into the 33-17, which only existed on paper, and the 33-19, which was just too expensive to produce, given its limited market appeal at the time.

When the company purchased the Titan hauler line from GM, there were no completed trucks in inventory at the London, Ontario, plant. The last big order of haulers to leave the GM plant was filled in January 1983, and consisted of four 33-15C Titans destined for Syncrude in Northern Alberta, Canada. This allowed Marathon LeTourneau to start building haulers almost

immediately at its Longview plant, without any complications from unsold inventory.

By June 1985, just four months after closing the Titan hauler deal, Marathon LeTourneau was rolling its first diesel-electric-drive 33-15C truck off the assembly line. The first Titans they produced were carbon copies of the GM trucks. The 33-15C was rated as a 170-ton-capacity hauler, and was powered by a Detroit Diesel 16V-149TI engine, with 1,600 gross horsepower. This engine powered a Delco Model 3E-6495 three-phase, four-pole AC alternator. A bank of solid-state, high-voltage diodes rectified the AC current output to DC. This supplied the necessary current for two GM D-79 CFA traction motors, which were mounted inboard within the rear axle structure, not in the wheel

In September 1986, the company shipped an order of Titan haulers classified as 33-15D models. The 33-15D Titans featured more Marathon LeTourneau–built components. All of these trucks were powered by 1,800-gross-horsepower Detroit Diesel 16V-149TI engines. This 33-15D is being loaded at the Goonyella coal mine near Queensland, Australia, in 1988. Only six of this type of the Titan hauler were produced, and all went to the Goonyella mine.

assemblies as in LeTourneau-designed systems. Marathon LeTourneau began production with the Delco/GM system only as a means to get sales started. It would take the Longview engineers a little time to redesign the Titan line for Marathon LeTourneau electrical components.

Now that the Titan hauler line had a new home, with a company that was committed to the needs of the mining industry, potential customers felt more at ease in their consideration of the truck. The improving economic outlook of the mid-1980s was an additional factor in LeTourneau's favor. The perception that things were definitely improving in the marketplace helped jump-start production of the big hauler. The first two Titan haulers, both equipped with 85-cubic-yard dump bodies, were finished in

June 1985 and would eventually find homes at Energy Supply in Indiana. The next order for Titan haulers came from Syncrude Canada. They had been pleased with the trucks supplied by GM and wanted to expand their fleet with an additional nine units, all with 115-cubic-yard bodies. These trucks were shipped from the factory between August and December 1985.

After a slowdown in truck orders, Marathon LeTourneau shipped a special batch of six Titan haulers, identified as 33-15D Models, to the Goonyella mine in South Africa, in September 1986. Though almost identical to the 33-15C, these trucks had several updated and improved components that were intended to increase overall reliability in the field. All of these trucks were equipped with the Detroit Diesel engine, uprated to 1,800 gross horsepower. All dump bodies were rated at 112 cubic yards and were the biggest visual difference between the two model types. While the company was getting these trucks out the door, it was also working on an updated model. This improved Titan hauler would be the T-2000 Series.

The first T-2000 Titan hauler was completed in August 1986, and officially unveiled at the American Mining Congress' (AMC)International Mining Show in Las Vegas in October of that year. The T-2000 was still based heavily on the old 33-15D, but there were very significant changes and improvements throughout the entire design. The T-2000 was initially offered with three engine choices—a Cummins KTTA-3067-C, a Detroit Diesel 16V-149TIB, and an MTU 16V-396TC43, all rated at 2,000 gross horsepower. Payload capacity was between 170–200 tons, depending on application and options. The T-2000 utilized LeTourneau-designed electrical-drive components instead of the GM/Delco system. The main alternator was a LeTourneau 12B unit, while the two main traction motors were LeTourneau G1 drives. All controls were of LeTourneau origin and all were of solid-state design. Even though the traction motors for the rear-drive wheels were now built by LeTourneau, they were still mounted in the center axle housing and not in the wheel assemblies. Also new to the T-2000 Series was an operator's cab that was more driver-friendly than the previous design. The radiator sheet metal was also redesigned to give the hauler a more distinctive look. To cope with the Titan's greater working range, the tire and wheel combination was upgraded with 37.00xR57 radials, replacing the original, smaller 36.00xR51 type.

After the mining show in Las Vegas, the first T-2000 Titan hauler soon found a home in Kentucky at J. Smith Coal Corporation in January 1987. This unit was rated as a 190-ton hauler, with 1,800 gross horsepower. After the first three T-2000 haulers were sold, the trucks picked up more specific nomenclature to better represent their payload capacity. Starting in mid-1987, there were three Titan Hauler Models—the T-2170, T-2190, and T-2200. All three trucks were offered with the Detroit 16V-149TI, with ratings of 1,600, 1,800, and 2,000 gross horsepower. For the Cummins engine option, the T-2170 and T-2190 were offered with a 16-cylinder KTA50-C diesel rated at 1,600, and a KTTA50-C rated at 1,800 gross horsepower, receptively, while the T-2200 utilized a K-2000 powerplant rated at 2,000 gross horsepower.

The first big fleet of Titan haulers, which were T-2200 models, began shipping in October 1987, with solid sales growth continuing through 1988. In January 1989, the Titan truck line went through a minor upgrade with the installation of LeTourneau G-2 traction motors, as well as larger radiators with increased sizes from 41 square feet, to 43.5 square feet. The first hauler of this type was a T-2200 that spent its testing life at the ASARCO Mission Mine in Arizona. So impressed was the mine with the new Titan hauler that it placed orders for a further 19 units.

Starting in the late 1980s, the 240-ton-capacity hauler was starting to establish itself as the truck of choice in the mining industry. Manufacturers such as Komatsu Dresser, Unit Rig, and Wiseda all offered a hauler of this size, and Caterpillar would introduce its challenger in early 1991. To stay competitive in the industry, Marathon LeTourneau felt that it too must field a truck in the 240-ton range. That hauler would be the Titan T-2240.

The T-2240 was based on the proven design of LeTourneau's T-2200. The T-2240 utilized the reliable Detroit Diesel 16V-149TI, rated at 2,200 gross horsepower. Its electric-drive system was the same as those found on other Titan haulers at the time. To support payloads in the 240-ton range, the wheels were increased in size to accommodate 40.00x57,68PR tires. The main frame and suspension were beefed-up to handle the increase in payload. But while all of the competing truck designs now utilized GE traction-wheel motors mounted in the wheel assemblies, the LeTourneau T-2240 still relied on internal axle-mounted traction motors, which drove the rear-wheel assemblies through planetary gears and driveshafts. This was the design the company had inherited in the GM Terex 33-15. No doubt LeTourneau's engineers would have preferred the internal wheel-mounted motors found on the rest of their mobile equipment designs, but the funds were not there for a complete redesign of the drive system.

The first two Titan T-2240 haulers left the Longview plant in March and April 1990, destined for the Westar mining operation in British Columbia, Canada, near the town of Sparwood. This mine, through many name changes, had operated a large fleet of 33-15B and 33-15C haulers, all rated at 170-tons capacity, plus the one-and-only Terex 33-19 Titan, with its world-record 350-ton payload rating. So they were very familiar with the drive-system layout of the T-2240. But because of a downturn in the mining market in the early 1990s, Westar decided to pass on the two T-2240 units, even though they had already shipped. These units would eventually make their way all the way back down to the ASARCO Mission Mine, south of Tucson, Arizona. Both trucks would join the massive fleet of T-2200 units already at the mine and would spend their total working lives at this facility, until being retired in 1998.

The next two T-2240 Titan trucks shipped from the factory in January 1992. These trucks were delivered to Syncrude Canada in northern Alberta for work in the oil sand mining operations just north of Fort McMurray. After a short stay with Syncrude, both trucks were sold to North American Construction, a company that does overburden removal work for Syncrude on a contract basis. At the time of this writing, both T-2240s were still in full operation, though they have had their payload capacities derated to 220-tons capacity, instead of 240.

Competition had increased to such a point in the 240-ton hauler class that LeTourneau found it could not compete with the likes of Caterpillar and Komatsu. These huge companies could offer complete equipment packages, including extended parts

This immaculate, 200-ton-capacity Titan T-2200 hauler is being loaded at the Saraji mine in Australia in 1988. The Saraji Titan trucks were powered by 2,000-gross-horsepower Cummins K-2000 diesel engines, and all were equipped with 133-cubic-yard dump bodies. The first Titan shipped to the Saraji mine in October 1987.

warranties and guaranteed production and availability contracts, that were beyond the means of a company the size of LeTourneau. Without brisk sales, it became too expensive to produce not only the T-2240, but all of the other Titan haulers as well.

After Rowan Companies, Inc., bought Marathon LeTourneau in 1994 (see chapter 9), the Titan product line name was dropped entirely. Under Rowan, only the top three truck sizes were offered; the T-2170 was dropped from the product line. But LeTourneau's hauler technology had fallen behind the times, and the new company, like Marathon LeTourneau before it, could not afford the immense capital needed to modernize its off-highway trucks—especially in light of the thin profit margins in the mining truck industry. In December 1995 and February 1996, LeTourneau shipped its last two truck orders, both T-2200s, to the Iron Ore Company of Canada (IOC), located near Wabush, Newfoundland, Canada. Since then, no LeTourneau trucks have been built.

LeTourneau had always specialized in machines built in small quantities. Even though the company is not actively marketing its hauler line anymore, if one of its customers wanted to add some units to its truck fleets, LeTourneau would be more than happy to build them. Often mining operations have large fleets of a particular type of truck that they are quite accustomed to, both in operation and maintenance. Having the latest and greatest hauler is not as important as having a truck that fits in with the mine's established infrastructure, including its production output, loading shovel sizes, maintenance facilities and practices, and parts inventory.

Though the LeTourneau hauler line became a bit outdated toward the end, the company did try to shake up the off-highway mining truck industry in 1992, when it unveiled a concept hauler identified as the Titan T-3320. At the MINExpo'92 show in Las Vegas, Marathon LeTourneau, as part of its display, had a wall panel illustrating a side view of the concept truck, as well as some brief specifications. Though nothing more than a flat, upright, black-and-white display, it nonetheless caught the attention of quite a few onlookers, as well as the mining trade press—which was the whole idea. The display depicted a 320-ton-capacity hauler of three-axle design. But unlike the tandem-drive Terex 33-19, the T-3320 utilized two forward-set steering axles, with a single-tire-per-wheel mount. At the rear was a single-drive axle with two tires per wheel. The diesel-electric drivetrain could be powered by two Cummins diesels rated at 1,600 gross horsepower each, or one big MTU diesel rated at 3,200 gross horsepower. Model types for these engines were never mentioned. The estimated weight of the truck would be in the neighborhood of 496,000 pounds empty, and 1,136,000 pounds when fully loaded. Standard tires were listed as 40R57 radials, with an option for larger 44R57 sizes, which would have raised the truck's payload capacity to 400 tons. Could a truck as outrageous as the T-3320 actually be built? Many felt that if anyone could pull off such an unconventional design, it was LeTourneau.

Marathon LeTourneau Titan haulers were originally introduced in three model capacity sizes: the 170-ton T-2170, the 190-ton T-2190, and the 200-ton 2200. In March 1990, the company shipped its first 240-ton Titan truck, identified as the T-2240. This diesel-electric-drivetrain giant was powered by a 2,200-gross-horsepower Detroit Diesel 16V-149TI DDEC engine. The standard tires were the 40.00/R57 Series, almost 12 feet in diameter. The special 240-ton-capacity dump bodies were rated at 178 cubic yards.

Four Titan T-2240 haulers were built in all. Two units were originally shipped to the Westar coal mining operation, near Sparwood, British Columbia, while the last two shipped in January 1992 to Syncrude, just north of Fort McMurray, Alberta, Canada. This Titan T-2240 at work in November 1990 is one of the Westar trucks working at the Balmer Pit location.

Throughout 1993, the company did some serious computer design work on the three-axle truck to get it to a point where it could be presented to prospective customers with some hopes of production. As the designing progressed, two model types were envisioned—the original T-3320 rated at 320 tons, and a T-3360 rated at 360 tons. But potential customers gave these daring designs a cold shoulder in the marketplace. Haul trucks with two engines and three axles spelled trouble as far as they were concerned. Historically, three-axle haulers, such as the Terex 33-19 and the WABCO 3200 Haulpak, have promised much, but in reality, their operating costs, especially concerning tires, were always in the red. When Komatsu introduced its 320-ton-capacity

930E diesel-electric-drive hauler in 1995, it crushed any hopes that the three-axle LeTourneau concept would make it into iron.

Even though its three-axle design was dead, LeTourneau did try to keep its big truck program alive by trying to interest a few potential customers in a 320-ton-capacity, two-axle design identified as the T-2320. Since the beginning of the concept truck program, larger engines and tires had become available that made three axles unnecessary. But it was too little, too late. LeTourneau just couldn't get potential customers interested in its big truck proposals. In the end, the T-2320 never made it any further than some engineering drawings. The mining industry had lost interest in these concept designs, and LeTourneau would soon do the same.

The L-1400 was a digging machine of the highest order. With its standard 28-cubic-yard/84,000-pound payload capacity, it could load massive amounts of material extremely fast. The original model's diesel-electric drivetrain could be powered by a Detroit Diesel 16V-149TI engine, or a Cummins KTA50-C, both rated at 1,600 gross horsepower. By 1992, 1,700- and 1,800-horsepower versions had become available. With the installation of either a DD 16V-149TI, DDEC III, or Cummins K-1800 in 1996, the loader would have 1,800 horsepower standard. The L-1400 pictured here is equipped with a 43-cubic-yard, 21-foot-wide combo bucket, designed for loading overburden or coal. ECO

CHAPTER 9

It took LeTourneau quite a few years to hit on just the right type of earthmoving equipment to satisfy the particular wants and desires of the marketplace. The company's diesel-electric-drive wheel loaders were starting to get a reputation as the ideal loading tool in mining operations the world over. The reliability issues that had plagued many earlier electric-drive designs had been addressed and now its machines were just as reliable as the competition's mechanical-drivetrain units, if not moreso.

LeTourneau's clear breakout success story was the L-800 wheel loader. Its popularity in the marketplace helped establish Marathon LeTourneau as the premier mining wheel loader manufacturer. But the L-800 couldn't go on forever. In 1982, Marathon LeTourneau took the wraps off what would eventually become the replacement for the aging L-800 model line. This machine was the L-1000 LeTro-Loader. As the L-700A had done with the L-800, the L-1000 was initially produced alongside the L-800 in its first few years of life. There were several reasons for this, but one of the biggest was the economy. When the L-1000 loader was first announced at the AMC International Mining Show in Las Vegas in October 1982, the world was mired in a severe economic recession. Potential customers existed for a loader the size of the new L-1000, but the lower cost and proven track record of the L-800 still made it the machine of choice. The L-1000 would have to prove itself in the field before customers would switch from the tried-and-true L-800.

When comparing the L-1000 to the L-800, the new loader was a larger machine all around. The standard bucket capacity of the L-1000 was 17 cubic yards, and 51,000 pounds—more than 6,000 pounds greater than the L-800's. This capacity size was perfect for loading haulers in the 150–170-ton range. The overall working weight of the L-1000 was 230,000 pounds, while the L-800 weighed in at 185,500 pounds.

The L-1000 was offered with two engine choices, a Detroit Diesel 12V-149T or a Cummins KT-2300C. Both of these engines were rated at 900 gross horsepower. By the late 1980s, the KT-2300C was replaced with a Cummins KT-38C, which, like the Detroit Diesel offering, was uprated to 925 gross horsepower. The new design reduced a number of the loader's subsystems and components . To simplify maintenance and reduce spare-parts stocks, the L-1000 utilized identical electric motors and drivers, as well as disc-brake assemblies, on all four wheels. All main braking

systems were electric-dynamic, with air-operated caliper discs and no hydraulic components. Other design enhancements included heavy plate reinforcements of the frame and lift arms, and a single belt-driven blower unit that cooled all wheel motors, the AC generator, and the power conversion system. The operator's cab was also redesigned, with the Rollover Protective Structure (ROPS) moved to the outside. This increased interior space and reduced interior noise levels. Air conditioning was now standard fare—displacing after-market systems that bolted to the roof of the cab. The new cab gave the loader a very clean and modern look. But make no mistake, its overall appearance was classic LeTourneau.

The prototype L-1000 would find its first home at Energy Supply in Indiana in the fall of 1982. It would be almost a year before the first production unit would ship from the factory to Maritiki Coal in Kentucky in August 1983. Five more loaders were built in 1983 before production hit full stride in 1984. After this, there was no looking back for the L-1000. The last two L-800s shipped from the Longview plant in October 1985, making the L-1000 LeTourneau's only mining loader . . . but only temporarily.

During the development of the L-1000, the company was also working on a model variation called the TCL-1000. This trailing cable loader, hence TCL, was a special engineering project that involved a wheel loader operated from a mine's electrical power source via a retractable cable. The TCL-1000 was designed with a unique turret-and-reel assembly mounted on the rear portion of the loader. A power cable connected to the reel on the turret was attached to a movable utility pole in the pit, which kept the cable from touching the ground and allowed up to 200 feet of travel in any direction. When the operator needed to reposition the loader, he could insert the loading bucket's lip into a slot in the base and pole assembly, and reposition it. To change job sites, the TCL-1000 would be hooked up to an auxiliary power source and driven to the next working location. This was necessary, as the loader was not equipped with a diesel engine. It was powered by a single three-phase, 7,200-volt, 60-cycle commercial generator and main transformer, which reduced it to a more manageable 480 volts. This power ran to the AC/DC Marathon LeTourneau powertrain, which in turn drove the four DC traction-wheel motors. The TCL-1000 was essentially an all-electric wheel loader on an extension cord.

On paper, this loader appeared to offer cost savings in certain mining conditions. The TCL-1000 had the same payload capacity as the L-1000, which was considered quite large in its day for a machine of its size. Thus, with its high productivity and all-electrical powertrain system, the TCL-1000 seemed like a real operating cost-cutter to any potential customer.

Marathon LeTourneau debuted the TCL-1000 at the same October 1982 AMC International Mining Show at which it announced the coming L-1000. But, as mentioned earlier, the harsh economic recession that embraced 1982 was no environment for offering new mining machines. Potential customers were looking for tried-and-true technology with as little financial risk as possible. The TCL-1000 never had a chance in such a market. Though the loader was put to work in 1983 and 1984 at the Navajo Mine, near Farmington, New Mexico, it would never go into production. The TCL-1000 was just too innovative for its own good. In the end, only one unit was ever built.

As the economy started to pick up in the mid-1980s, Marathon LeTourneau set its sights once again on a larger loader design to replace the discontinued L-1200. Identified as the L-1100, this offering was marketed as the most technologically advanced front-end loader in the world. And for the most part, it was. The L-1100 was certainly a very large machine, with a standard bucket capacity of 22 cubic yards. The payload rating was a healthy

Marathon LeTourneau first introduced the L-1000 LeTro-Loader at the American Mining Congress show in October 1982, but it would not be until July 1983 that the first production unit was placed in the field. As of 2001, the engine choices are 925-horsepower DD 12V2000, and Cummins QSK30 diesels. The standard bucket capacity is 17 cubic yards, with a maximum payload of 51,000 pounds. The working weight is 232,000 pounds. ECO

The Marathon LeTourneau TCL-1000 Trailing Cable Loader was introduced at the same time as the L-1000 in 1982. The TCL-1000 utilized a retractable cable reel system that was hooked into a mining operation's electrical supply. The TCL-1000 was not equipped with a diesel engine and was completely electric powered. The bucket capacity was the same as the L-1000. The operating weight was 240,000 pounds. The one-and-only TCL-1000 is shown at work at the Navajo Mine, near Farmington, New Mexico, in April 1984.

When Marathon LeTourneau discontinued the L-1200, it left a big hole in its product line. That hole was filled in October 1986 when the company officially unveiled the diesel-electric-drive L-1100 LeTro-Loader at the AMC show, along with the first Titan T-2000 hauler. The L-1100 could be equipped with a Detroit Diesel 12V-149T, or a Cummins KTA-38-C engine, both rated at 1,050 gross horsepower. The loader's payload capacity matched the old L-1200, with a 22-cubic-yard/66,000-pound rating. This L-1100 is the first unit built in August 1986, just before it was disassembled and shipped to the mining show in Las Vegas, Nevada.

66,000 pounds with standard lift arms, and 60,000 pounds with the high-lift option. As with the L-1000, two engines were offered, the Detroit Diesel 12V-149T and the Cummins KTA-38C. Both of these 12-cylinder engines were rated at 1,050 gross horsepower. The overall working weight in standard form was 265,000 pounds. When compared with its predecessor, the L-1200, the L-1100 did more with less. It was down 150 horsepower, but had the same rated payload capacity as the other machine. It also weighed 70,000 pounds less than the old L-1200. In service, the L-1100 could run circles around the old L-1200.

The L-1100 was Marathon LeTourneau's most advanced front-end loader. Its diesel-electric-drive system and traction-wheel motors were all built in-house at LeTourneau. Other key features included state-of-the-art electronics and solid-state controls that provided on-board diagnostics and load testing while parked or in operation. Traction was always maintained during difficult working conditions due to the design of the electric-drive system. Computerized nonspin torque was independently applied through each wheel motor. If any one wheel lost traction, power was immediately prorated and distributed to the loader's other drive wheels. This type of traction-control had been used on the company's loaders for years, but never in such an efficient and highly computerized form. Such systems made the L-1100 one of the fastest-cycling, ultralarge wheel loaders of its day.

On the outside, the L-1100 looked much like its little brother, the L-1000. The L-1100 was a bit larger overall, but the design giveaway was the torque-tube that connected the two massive lift arms. The L-1000's was welded to the inside of each lift arm only.

On the larger machine, it was welded to the inside and the outside sections of the arms through cutouts in the steel plating. This gave the loader's front lift-arms extra strength and rigidity to resist the torsional twisting and bending forces it encountered as the 22-cubic-yard bucket penetrated the rock face. Its low center of gravity and wide wheelbase would also help maintain the loader's composure in uneven working areas. The L-1100 was simply the finest front-end loader LeTourneau engineers had ever created.

The L-1100 prototype was first displayed with the pilot T-2000 Titan hauler at the October 1986 AMC International Mining Show in Las Vegas. It was a huge hit. Because of difficult times during the long recession, many in the industry thought Marathon LeTourneau was down for the count. Not so. Though times were tough for the company in the early 1980s, the company never cut back on research and development. They knew that the recession would end and the mining market would once again need state-of-the-art loading machines to maximize their productivity and profits. Lessons learned on the L-1000 were put to the test in the new L-1100. The L-1100 was all the company had hoped it would be. Where the L-1200 had failed in the marketplace, the L-1100 would bring home the gold for LeTourneau.

After the mining show, the prototype L-1100 was shipped to the Addwest mining operation in Kentucky in December 1986. The first production machine was not far behind it, shipping in January 1987 to Newmont Gold in Nevada. Since that time, L-1100 loaders have been delivered into mining operations the world over. You can find them working not only in the United States, but in such places as Alberta, Quebec, Australia, Japan, Columbia, Chile, Brazil, Israel, Newfoundland, Mexico, and Russia. The L-1100 has been one the company's longest-running and best-performing loaders. As of 2001, it is still offered in the product line with the same capacity rating as in 1986, though gross horsepower is now up to 1,200—you can never have enough ponies under the hood, or, as in the case of the L-1100, under the rear deck lid.

When the L-1100 first entered service, there were very few loaders that competed with it head-on. Its closest rival was the International/Dresser 580 Pay Loader, rated at 22 cubic yards. Machines such as the Clark Michigan 675C and the SMEC 180t with larger capacities of 24 and 25 cubic yards, respectively, were not true threats for the big LeTourneau. The 675C had gone out of production in the early 1980s, with the last two units delivered in 1988 from old dealer and factory inventories. The SMEC 180t came out in 1986, the same year as the L-1100, but never really went anywhere. It is reported that only two units were ever put into iron. In October 1990, Caterpillar introduced a large wheel loader targeted at the L-1100's market niche. That machine was the 23-cubic-yard Cat 994. The 994 truly put pressure on Marathon LeTourneau, as sales of its popular L-1100 started to taper off. Every sale of a 994 was a lost sale of an L-1100. Dresser upped the pressure further in 1991 when it released an updated design of the 580, called the 4000 Haulpak. This 24-cubic-yard

Today's LeTourneau, Inc., L-1100 front-end loader is alive and well, and is considered one of the company's finest loader designs. The loader's appearance is virtually unchanged from 1986. As of 2001, the L-1100 is offered with a standard Detroit Diesel 16V2000, or an optional Cummins QSK45 engine, both rated at 1,200 gross horsepower. The operating weight is 276,000 pounds. ECO

In April 1999, LeTourneau, Inc., took the wraps off its first diesel-electric-drive front-end loader to feature digital controls, rather than solid-state designs—the L-1350. The L-1350 can be ordered with a Detroit Diesel/MTU 12V-4000 or a Cummins QSK45 engine, both rated at 1,600 gross horsepower. The overall working weight of the loader is 390,000 pounds. The prototype unit is pictured at the Longview plant with the engineers and designers who made it a reality. ECO

The first L-1350, now repainted white, was delivered in May 2000 to a lignite coal mine in North Dakota. The L-1350 is rated as a 26-cubic-yard/80,000-pound capacity loader, but the first unit was specified with a 45-cubic-yard bucket for coal-loading operations. ECO

machine for a time was able to claim the title of the world's largest-production, single-engined, mechanical-drive wheel loader. The key words here were mechanical-drive. This type of drivetrain layout was used in all of the competing machines thrown at Marathon LeTourneau. The company knew that it was going to have to act quickly to save its market share for its diesel-electric offerings. And that is just what they did, and in a big way.

Just a month after the release of the Caterpillar 994, Marathon LeTourneau quietly put a massive front-end loader into restricted prototype testing at High Power Energy Coal's mining operation in Drennen, West Virginia, on a trial lease basis. That machine was the L-1400 LeTro-Loader. When the L-1400 was first released, it was the world's largest wheel loader, period. Its 28-cubic-yard bucket and 84,000-pound payload capacity was without rival in the industry. No other front-end loader had attained such a lofty capacity rating. LeTourneau had responded perfectly to the competition, sending them back to the drawing board.

The massive L-1400 required some serious horsepower in the rear end. Two big-displacement 16-cylinder engine options were initially offered, a two-cycle Detroit Diesel 16V-149TI, or a four-cycle Cummins KTA50-C, both rated at 1,600 gross horsepower. By 1994, these figures had increased to 1,700 gross horsepower.

In 1996, still more power was available, from an upgraded Detroit Diesel 16V-149TI, DDEC III, or the Cummins K-1800E, both rated at 1,800 gross horsepower. The current L-1400 from 2001 is offered with a four-cycle Detroit Diesel/MTU D4000-16V, DDEC, or a four-cycle Cummins QSK60 engine, still carrying power outputs of 1,800 gross horsepower.

The overall working weight of the original L-1400 was about 410,000 pounds with standard lift arms. To carry this weight, the first loaders were given 49.5/57,68PR tires on 34-57-inch rims. Bridgestone supplied a massive optional 67.5/60-51,84PR tire, mounted on 45.00-51-inch rims. These tires were usually requested by customers in Australia to meet their specific working needs. The smaller standard tire was really not up to the working standards of the L-1400, but at the time, there just wasn't any other cost-effective tire option available to the industry. By 1994, a larger standard 50/80-57,68PR tire and 36-57-inch rim assembly started to become available, which were far more durable. In 1995, an optional 55.5/80-57,68PR tire on a 44-57-inch rim was offered as a larger alternative to the standard tire, but at a price. They were quite expensive. By 2001, the L-1400 was offered with the option of 55/80R57 radials. Through all of these weight gains and tire upgrades, the L-1400's payload rating has remained consistent.

As of 2001, the LeTourneau L-1400 is offered with Detroit Diesel 16V-4000, DDEC, and Cummins QSK60 diesel engines, both rated at 1,800 gross horsepower. The maximum working weight of the loader is 445,000 pounds with standard-lift arms, and 450,000 pounds with the optional high-lift arrangement. This 1,800-horsepower, 28-cubic-yard L-1400 is loading a 200-ton-capacity Titan hauler at a copper mine in Arizona, in October 1998. ECO

The L-1400 model line was officially announced for sale to the mining industry approximately six months after the delivery of the pilot machine to High Power Energy Coal. But it would not be until January 1992 that the first full-production loader shipped to R. W. Miller in Australia. In fact, the next two machines would also go to Australia, though to different customers. The slow sales start for the big LeTourneau can be traced directly to the mild economic recession in North America at the time. This stifled potential sales in the company's home market, but stronger interest in overseas mines helped the company weather the temporary downturn. Of the first 15 loaders built, 9 were for customers outside of the North American mining market.

Every mine that operated the L-1400 was impressed by its performance. Customers that owned both the L-1100 and the L-1400 said that the bigger and heavier machine could run circles around the smaller L-1100. That's saying a lot, since the L-1100 was quite a fast-cycling machine in its own right.

Just as the L-1400 was starting to hit its stride in the mining marketplace, another front-end loader was already waiting in the wings to wrest the crown of the world's largest wheel loader from the mighty diesel-electric-drive machine. This time the new loader was another massive Marathon LeTourneau machine.

The L-1400 was a gigantic loader. The L-1800 is bigger still. This is the prototype L-1800, as it appeared in December 1993 at the Longview plant, equipped with the standard 33-cubic-yard/100,000-pound-capacity rock-bucket.

Pictured here is the first L-1800 front-end loader shipped to a coal mine in the Powder River Basin coal mining area of Wyoming in July 1994. Now referred to as a LeTourneau L-1800, the loader was equipped with a 45-cubic-yard combo bucket for coal and overburden loading duties. ECO

The world mining industry got its first glimpse of LeTourneau's new concept at the 1992 AMC International Mining Show in Las Vegas. At the company's display were preliminary specifications for an ultralarge front-end loader christened the L-1800 LeTro-Loader. Carrying a standard rock bucket rated at 33 cubic yards, with a 100,000-pound load capacity, it was designed to do the jobs once reserved only for hydraulic and cable mining shovels. But this was simply a flat display at a trade show. The proof would be in the real machine. Many thought that this concept was simply wishful thinking. And if such a loader ever were built, it would be years down the road. But Marathon LeTourneau was well under way with the engineering part of the L-1800 design program. Just over a year after the mining show announcement, the L-1800 would become a physical reality in Texas.

Marathon LeTourneau officially announced the L-1800's availability in a news release dated December 10, 1993. Accompanying this release was an image of the L-1800 with a Ford F-150 pickup truck parked next to it, which looked minuscule. The L-1800 was no longer just a bunch of numbers on a piece of paper, but a machine whose physical size matched its claimed credentials. The L-1800 was now the new king of front-end loaders.

The new loader's dimensions and overall size were similar to those of the L-1400. What made the loader an L-1800 was a newly designed frame, larger wheel motors and tires, a greater-capacity bucket, and more horsepower. The new frame was redesigned to handle the extra stress it would encounter handling 50 tons with each loading cycle. The wheel motors were upgraded, larger, and more powerful LeTourneau J-2 heavy-duty type, while the L-1400 made due with smaller L-14B traction motors. Tire and rim

choices were the same as for the L-1400. In most cases, the loader was equipped with the largest tire option available. The engine choices were the same as those offered for the L-1400, but with more horsepower dialed in. Standard power ratings for the L-1800 were 1,800 gross horsepower, with 2,000 available as an option. These ratings applied to both the Detroit Diesel and Cummins offerings. The L-1800 tipped the scales in standard lift form at 440,000 pounds, and at 445,000 pounds with the high-lift option. The high-lift configuration reduced the standard rock bucket capacity to 31 cubic yards with a 94,000-pound payload rating. Any way you looked at it, the L-1800 was one mighty big wheel loader.

Just before the prototype L-1800 loader was put to the test in the marketplace, Marathon LeTourneau was bought by another Texas based industrial giant, Rowan Companies, Inc. Rowan, based in Houston, was a major provider of international and domestic offshore contract drilling and helicopter services, and had purchased many of LeTourneau's massive jack-up drilling rigs in the past. At the time of the sale, Marathon LeTourneau Company was a subsidiary of General Cable Corporation, which was originally part of the Penn Central conglomerate of companies, before being spun off on its own in 1992.

Rowan announced its interest in purchasing Marathon LeTourneau in November 1993, and officially became the owner of the company on February 11, 1994. It promptly renamed its new subsidiary LeTourneau, Inc. To help connect the company with its former heritage, and distance itself from Marathon, Rowan reintroduced the Big "L" global LeTourneau logo. LeTourneau saw its acquisition by Rowan as the best thing that had ever happened to the company. Rowan had a solid reputation in the industry as a fair company that acted with professionalism and integrity in all of its business dealings. The deal would breathe new life into the Vicksburg plant, which had been idle for quite some time, and would guarantee the continuation of the marine group for years to come. For the first time in years, LeTourneau had a parent company that looked after the long-term interests of the company in its many manufacturing areas, instead of looking only at quarterly profit and loss statements.

During this time, the L-1800 prototype was given a thorough workout at the Longview plant testing grounds. Finally, in July 1994, the first L-1800 shipped from the factory to the AMAX Eagle Butte coal mine, just north of Gillette, Wyoming, in the Powder River Basin. Though this machine was tested with a 33-cubic-yard rock bucket, AMAX requested a 45-cubic-yard combo-bucket for both earth- and coal-loading applications. The second L-1800 would eventually ship to Howick Coal in Australia in May 1995. From this point on, there was no looking back for the big LeTourneau.

The L-1800 was given a facelift in the fall of 1996 with a redesigned ROPS cab, giving the loader a much cleaner and modern look. All L-1400s would also get this same cab treatment.

The L-1400 and L-1800 loaders being sold as of 2001 retain the same outward appearance as the machines offered in late 1996. The biggest change has been with the engine choices. For both model types, two 16-cylinder engine models are offered, the Cummins QSK60 or the Detroit Diesel/MTU D4000 16V, DDEC. These engines are rated at 1,800 gross horsepower in the L-1400, and 2,000 gross horsepower in the L-1800. The loaders also weigh a bit more than their earlier counterparts, with the L-1400 coming in at 440,000 pounds (445,000 pounds with high-lift), and the L-1800 tipping the scales at 480,000 pounds (485,000 pounds with high-lift).

Loaders the size of the L-1400 and L-1800 can only be utilized by large mining operations. This narrow market limits sales volume. But despite the limited number of potential clients in the marketplace, both models have sold very well. Their reputation as fast, reliable, high-production loading tools is unblemished. Loaders of this size have the ability to take the place of a mining operation's main loading machine, most likely a cable-shovel, in emergency situations, or when the shovel requires routine maintenance. In this way, production schedules can still be met and truck fleets need not be reassigned to another working location, saving both time and fuel costs.

This rather spiffy-looking L-1800 LeTro-Loader was the second machine built, and was shipped to an Australian coal mining operation in May 1995. It is equipped with a 34-cubic-yard rock-bucket and a 2,000-gross-horsepower Cummins KTTA50-C diesel engine. The tires on this unit are optional 55.5/80-57 Series rubber, which were the largest available in 1995.

The L-1800 is a powerful loading tool in a mining operation's arsenal of machines. This 33-cubic-yard, 2,000-gross-horsepower, Cummins-equipped L-1800 is working at a gold mine in Nevada in October 1998. The air-cleaner box unit on the side of the loader is the LeTourneau KLENZ Air Filtration System, which extends the filters' lives by purging them of dust and dirt particles with a blast of air every 60 seconds. ECO

The L-1800 rides on standard 53.5/85-57, 76PR tires that are almost 13 feet in diameter. Optional units are wider 55/80R-57 radials. In 2001, an even larger tire option was introduced, the 58/85-57. These tires are 58 inches wide and are intended for severe service applications. ECO

To broaden its product line, LeTourneau, Inc., introduced a slightly smaller-capacity machine in 1999, called the L-1350. But the L-1350 is no little front-end loader. It was specifically designed to minimize the cost-per-ton for loading 150–200-ton-capacity trucks. Its 26-cubic-yard bucket and 80,000-pound payload capacity allow the loader to load 200-ton-capacity haulers in five quick passes.

The L-1350 incorporates LeTourneau's first use of digital controls in a loader design. It is also the first company design to do away with the conventional steering wheel and replace it with two joystick hand controls mounted on the operator's seat. No previous machine built by the company ever had as many state-of-the-art computer controls and systems. The L-1350 utilizes the LeTourneau Integrated Network Control System (LINCS) to manage all of the loader's main operating systems, including hydraulics, machine electronics, traction drive, and engine, through the interaction of multiple Remote Control Modules (RCMs) and the Master Control Module (MCM). The entire system is directed by the MCM, which combines rugged industrial hardware with a Pentium-class microprocessor located in the operator's cab. The RCMs are the eyes and ears of the system, monitoring all critical loader functions. Various types of information conveyed include bucket weights, cycle times, preventative-maintenance information, and self-diagnostics. This system replaces most of the solid-state hardware that had controlled all loader functions in previous LeTourneau designs.

As with all LeTourneau front-end loaders before it, the L-1350 is diesel-electric drive with powerful traction-wheel motors at all four corners. The loader is offered with two engine options, the Detroit Diesel/MTU 12V4000 or the Cummins QSK45. Both engines are 12-cylinder, four-cycle turbocharged and aftercooled configurations, rated at 1,600 gross horsepower. The overall working weight of the loader is 390,000 pounds. The L-1350 can almost match the capacity of the 440,000-pound, 28-cubic-yard L-1400, requiring less power and weight to do so. This type of progress in loader design means a more productive machine with lower operating costs for the mines that run them—exactly what the L-1350 is all about.

The first L-1350 was officially unveiled at the Longview plant in April 1999. This loader was equipped with the Detroit Diesel/MTU engine, and was originally painted LeTourneau yellow during testing at the Longview plant. After the loader had completed all of its factory tests, it was sold to a lignite coal mining operation in North Dakota. It arrived at the mine site in May 2000, repainted in white at the request of the new owners to match all the other equipment operating at their facilities.

The L-1350 was seen as a turning point in front-end loader design for LeTourneau, Inc. Its use of digital, rather than solid-state, controls marked a new beginning in the design of LeTourneau's massive loaders. With the MINExpo 2000 mining show in Las Vegas coming up in October of that year, many in the industry thought that LeTourneau would use the L-1350 to highlight these new state-of-the-art digital control systems. The company was bringing a new machine to the show, but it would be an even newer and larger loader than the L-1350. This machine was so large, in fact, that it would surpass the L-1800 as the largest wheel loader in the world. The new behemoth was the incredible L-2350—simply the largest and most powerful front-end loader ever to be put into iron.

LeTourneau had done a remarkable job of keeping the titanic L-2350 out of trade magazines and off the Internet. Even as the loader was being assembled at the Las Vegas Hilton Convention Center, the competition had no clue what LeTourneau was up to, since the loader was wearing L-1800 identification. Only on the opening day of the show would the giant loader's true identity be known. When show attendees first approached the L-2350, they were greeted by a voluminous rock bucket, rated at a staggering 53 cubic yards. This translated to an incredible 160,000-pound, or 80-ton, lift capacity. To put this in perspective, the world's largest hydraulic front shovel, the Terex/O&K RH400, has a maximum dipper capacity of 80 tons. It wasn't long ago that 80 tons was considered large for a cable loading shovel. Machines such as the Marion 301-M, Bucyrus 495B, and original P&H 4100 Series of the 1980s all had working ranges in the 80–85-ton-capacity range. For a rubber-tired front-end loader to even approach such a lofty payload was all but unthinkable to the mining industry. But that was before MINExpo 2000 and the unveiling of the L-2350.

The L-2350 was everything the cutting-edge L-1350 was, but in a much larger size. All of the LeTourneau engineering hallmarks were there, such as diesel-electric drive, massive traction-wheel motors, and digital controls incorporating the computerized LINCS system. The L-2350 is offered with the same two types of engine choices as the current L-1400/L-1800, but with a difference. Both the Detroit Diesel/MTU 16V4000 and the Cummins QSK60 turbocharged and aftercooled engines are rated at 2,300 gross horsepower, the most for any wheel loader in the history of earthmoving. The main engine powers a

In 1998, LeTourneau shipped a special, massive coal-loading bucket to a mining operation in the Powder River Basin of Wyoming. The new bucket was retrofitted to the mine's L-1800 loader, replacing its standard 36-cubic-yard unit. Rated with a massive 55-cubic-yard payload capacity, it was the largest coal-loading bucket ever fabricated for use on a front-end loader. ECO

LeTourneau-designed and -built Model 12C, AC generator, which in turn drives the four Model J2, DC traction-wheel motors. At the show, these motors were mounted in wheels shod with newly designed Bridgestone 58/85-57 tires. But as big as these tires were, they are not the ones that would eventually find their way onto the L-2350. On a separate display, mounted on the right rear tire of the show machine, were the specifications of the tires that were designed specifically for the L-2350. Produced by Bridgestone, the 70/70-57,82PR, mounted on beefy 60x57-inch rims, would be the tire of choice for the big LeTourneau. The 70/70 is the largest earthmoving tire ever made for any type of machine or application. Its size speaks for itself. The 70/70-57 is 70 inches wide, weighs 7.7 tons each, and has a height of 13 feet. Each tire has a capacity rating of 327,500 pounds at 90 psi. They need to carry this much since the operating weight of the L-2350 is a whopping 540,000 pounds, or 270 tons. Compare this to the standard L-1800's 480,000 pounds and you start to get an idea of just how large the L-2350 really is.

In 2000, the L-1800 surrendered its crown as the world's largest front-end loader to another LeTourneau, Inc., diesel-electric-drive machine: the awesome L-2350. Weighing in at a whopping 540,000 pounds, the L-2350 outweighs the former champ by 60,000 pounds in standard form. The new loader is 64 feet, 1 inch (58 feet, 6 inches for L-1800) long, with a maximum bucket height of 43 feet, 9 inches. The prototype L-2350 is shown in late August 2000 at the Longview plant, just prior to disassembly and final painting before shipping to its world unveiling at the MINExpo show in Las Vegas.

On October 9, 2000, at the Las Vegas Hilton Convention Center, the world mining press and show attendees got their first look at the mammoth L-2350. The standard rock-bucket on the loader was a stunning 53-cubic-yard unit, capable of a 160,000-pound payload. The bucket width alone was 22 feet, 4 inches. ECO

But why was the show machine equipped with the 58/85-57 tires instead of the 70/70-57 sizes? Simple—the new tires were not finished in time for the show.

After the mining show, the L-2350 was dismantled and shipped back to the Longview plant, where it will spend most of 2001 going through various prototype-testing programs. Once testing is finished, and all of the loader's new systems meet the company's rigid quality-control standards for productivity and reliability, the loader will be offered for sale to the world mining market. There were a few customers at the show who already wanted to sign on the dotted line, if only LeTourneau would let them. If the response from the show is any indication of the loader's success, it looks like the future of the L-2350 will be very bright indeed.

As technological achievement in mining wheel-loader design, the L-2350 really has no equal in the industry. No competing manufacturer builds, or plans to build in the near future, anything on the scale of the L-2350. Its standard 53-cubic-yard bucket is more than twice as large at its nearest modern competitor's, not counting other LeTourneau-designed machines. Even the mighty 24-cubic-yard Clark Michigan 675C from the late 1970s would be put to shame by the might of the L-2350. LeTourneau has pushed the boundaries of mining front-end loader design like no other manufacturer in the history of earthmoving. It has given the industry an alternative choice to mechanical-drivetrain

The prototype L-2350 is powered by a four-cycle, turbocharged and after-cooled Detroit Diesel 16V-4000, 16-cylinder engine, rated at 2,300 gross horsepower. The optional engine choice is a Cummins QSK60, four-cycle, two-stage turbocharged and after-cooled 16-cylinder unit carrying the same rating as the big Detroit. The controls in the loader are all digital, with joystick hand units replacing the steering wheel. ECO

designs with its innovative electric-drive systems, pioneered by R. G. LeTourneau back in the 1950s. It is this drive system that is the heart of every loader built by the company. And it can only be found on machines bearing the LeTourneau name.

LeTourneau Log Stackers are the standard in the logging industry, known as ultra-reliable, long-lasting machines. The Model 5594, shown at work in September 1998, is rated at 55 tons operating capacity. Its four-wheel-drive, diesel-electric drivetrain is powered by a 475-gross-horsepower diesel engine. The two-wheel-drive version of this stacker is the Model 5592. ECO

R. G. LeTourneau, Inc. put diesel-electric-drive systems for earthmoving equipment into full production in 1958, but earthmoving equipment was only one component of the company's product lineup. The company has continued to market its log stackers and massive offshore drilling platforms, introduced in the mid-1950s. Also of great importance is the production of its own steel from the Longview foundries, which is also sold on the world market. But along with these long-running product lines, LeTourneau has offered various other innovative product groups, especially when it comes to the material-handling industry. In the 1960s and 1970s, the company's many design and product innovations allowed it to diversify and establish itself in various key market segments. By diversifying, LeTourneau was no longer financially dependent on just a few markets. Its revenue base was much larger, and the company was better equipped to withstand market changes.

Since their official launch in 1955, the LeTourneau Log Stackers, once referred to as LeTro-Stackers, have been an incredibly successful line. In many respects, the stackers were the company's best-selling electric-drive product lines during the 1960s and most of the 1970s. Even though the giant front-end loaders are more widely known, the log stackers helped fund the early development of the electric-drive earthmovers. For the most part, the modern LeTourneau Log Stackers look much like the early machines. All have remained faithful to R. G. LeTourneau's original designs. Each Log Stacker uses electric-traction-wheel motor systems and rack-and-pinion gear drive for the rack mechanism that also controls the angle of the main front fork and tusk assembly. The main hoist is cable-operated by an electric motor, as is the articulated rack-and-pinion gear toothed steering mechanism. Unlike a competitor's machine, hydraulic cylinders are not utilized. Although LeTourneau's designs have a dated appearance, their superior performance in lumberyards and mills around the world is without question. The Log Stacker is one of the fastest-cycling and smoothest-operating machines of its type ever built. Its electric four-wheeldrive gets up to speed faster in forward or reverse than the competition. Its cable-hoist design is simple and efficient. It does not carry hydraulic controls that might leak and contaminate the lumberyard. Although the Log Stacker's designs have not significantly advanced since their introduction, their reliability record is the envy of the industry. This impressive reliability and longevity have slowed new sales,

because many LeTro-Stackers built in the 1960s are still in service in many regions of North America. Their simplicity in design has guaranteed them long operating lives. It just goes to show you that a machine can be built too well.

At the time of this writing, LeTourneau, Inc. offers nine models of log stackers, available in two- and four-wheel electric-drive configurations. The capacity ratings range from 35 tons to 65 tons. The largest of these models are the 6592 and the 6594. Both are rated at 65 tons; the main difference between the two machines is that the 6592 is two-wheel drive, while the 6594 is four-wheel drive. Other giant log stackers from LeTourneau's past that compare to the model 6592/6594's capacity are the 70-ton 2894SS (1979), the 60-ton 2794 (1970), the 60-ton F-1204 (1968), the 65-ton F-1304 (1967), and the 60-ton F-60 (1956).

The log stackers are essentially giant forklifts, so it made sense for LeTourneau to market just such a machine. Referred to as FL-Lift Trucks, later changed to LeTro-Lifts, these forklifts utilized the same tractors found in the log stackers, minus the giant curved tusk hooks that typically held log loads. The main drive chassis could be configured strictly as a conventional forklift, or one with a single jib crane mounted on top of the hoist rack above the fork attachment. These models were referred to as LeTro-Jibs. The SP-Side Porter or LeTro-Porter was another model type. In this incarnation, the same tractor types found in the other model manifestations were equipped with electric-drive handlers, or grips, designed for picking up and transporting large bulk containers and piggyback trailers. The main grip attachment traveled on the same type of hoist tower as all other variations. From an engineering standpoint, LeTourneau sure got its money's worth out of the log stacker tractor's basic design.

The LeTro-Pik, whose concept dates back to the early 1930s, was the engineering basis for the LeTro-Stacker, LeTro-Lift, LeTro-Jib, and LeTro-Porter. The basic tractor design evolved from a crane unit towed by a single-axle Tournapull tractor to the diesel-electric-drive models of the 1950s. Over the years, models featured varying fixed-height steel tube-framed booms. These machines were the perfect choice for clearing crashed or disabled aircraft off runways or aircraft carriers. Their compact design made them the ideal choice. The LeTourneau 2754A Multi-Purpose Mobile Crane is the oldest model still in production today. It is strictly a special-order item. In 1998, the Egyptian Civil Aviation Authority placed the last order for this type of crane.

The LeTourneau 2754A Multi-Purpose Mobile Crane has changed very little since its introduction in the 1950s as the LeTro-Pik. The 70-ton-capacity crane is a special-order item. The last order for nine of these units was received from the Egyptian Civil Aviation Authority in 1998.

The Egyptians were impressed with the machines—so much so, that the aviation authority mandated that at least one of these specialized LeTourneau cranes be present at all of Egypt's major civilian airports.

Besides crash cranes, LeTourneau has manufactured lattice-boom cranes that can either be mounted on pedestals or mobile electric-drive wheeled chassis. These cranes are intended for marine and dockside port use. Marine application cranes are most often used on offshore drilling rigs, but are available for sale to other builders as well. The company's largest crane was a one-of-a-kind structure referred to as the RD-1600 Electric Deck Crane, which was built in 1959. Fitted with a 200-foot boom and rated at 250 tons, it was specifically built for use on a specially prepared floating crane platform (LeTourneau Offshore Hull No. 10). Christened the Elephante, it was delivered to Consorcio Puente Maracaibo of Caracas, Venezuela, for the construction of a bridge across Lake Maracaibo. The crane provided excellent service until August 1968, when it was destroyed by a fire off the coast of Louisiana. Though the crane was a total loss, Hull No. 10 was salvageable and was rebuilt as a drilling rig renamed the Little Bob.

The JC-40 Jib Crane is another highly specialized piece of logging equipment. First introduced in 1974, the towerlike crane is rated at 20 tons capacity for its traveling trolley grapple hook. The JC-40 comes in two overall height sizes of 92 feet and 118 feet. The total length of the main boom and counterweight assembly is 179 feet. ECO

LeTourneau discovered that specially designed and built machines sold for working in shipping and rail yards provided a good source of income. This group of machines included the Strad-L-Port and a Strad-L-Hoist, which were two kinds of custom-built lifting devices for handling various large containers and piggyback trailers. Both of these devices were constructed of large steel beams, supported by towerlike legs. The Strad-L-Port consisted of dual-beam gantries that spanned two rail lines and two roadways, to the left and right of each track. The Strad-L-Port utilized an additional traveling-beam support suspended from the main structure, which could be raised or lowered as needed. Long electrically controlled gripping tongs were connected to the main structure. These tongs were able to reach around and load or unload piggyback trailers from train railcars. In unloading the piggyback trailers, the Strad-L-Port was able to place them at 45 degree angles on either the right or left side of the tracks. This allowed trucks to quickly pick up their trailers for delivery. It took the unit an average of one minute per trailer during unloading. The entire structure traveled on rubber tires, and it was driven by four powerful LeTourneau wheel-traction motors placed on each corner. The Strad-L-Hoist was similar to the Strad-L-Port in design, but it did not have the extra suspended traveling-beam supports. Instead, its main grip was suspended and traveled on the main

support beams. The Strad-L-Hoist's working height was increased, and this allowed it to stack box containers in shipyards, or to pick up and travel with other large items, such as precast concrete structures. The Port was mainly confined to loading and unloading piggyback cars, because of the limited working height of the unit's traveling beam spans. Like the Strad-L-Port, the Strad-L-Hoist also traveled on wheels powered by traction motors. But unlike the Strad-L-Port, the Strad-L-Hoist could be configured as a single-span beam design, while the Strad-L-Port required two. Both units were diesel-electric drive and their operations were completely self-contained.

The Strad-L-Port was the first of these powered structures to be built, and it was shipped by LeTourneau in September 1964. The first Strad-L-Hoist was shipped in 1968. A few years after the introduction of these units, LeTourneau assigned the trade names of LeTro-port and LeTro-hoist. LeTourneau continues to offer one model of each of the following model lines as a special-order product: the ST-100 LeTro-port and the SST-100 Single Beam Straddle Hoist.

The JC-40 Jib Crane is another product line that shares some of the LeTourneau engineering know-how found in their pedestal-mounted lift cranes and straddle hoists. The JC-40 is a tower-crane-like structure with a revolving triangle, steel-tube

This is one of LeTourneau's Lectromelt furnaces in full operation at its Longview steel mill. These 25-ton electric arc furnaces can melt base steel and iron like butter. Extreme care must be taken by the mill's workers at all times when in the vicinity of these furnaces. As one would expect, the heat put off by one of these units is tremendous.

The largest of all offshore, self-elevating, platform drilling rigs designed and built by LeTourneau, Inc.'s Marine Group is the Super Gorilla class. The first unit was Hull #219, nicknamed "Gorilla V." Built for Rowan Companies, Inc.—the current owners of LeTourneau, Inc.—the Gorilla V launched in November 1998. It is shown here under construction at the company's Vicksburg, Mississippi, shipyard. The people working around the main hull structure give you an idea just how big the Super Gorilla really is.

boom assembly, mounted on a 9-foot-diameter steel column. A moving trolley attached to the main boom travels the length of the span with a Mack full-swiveling grapple hook. With this 40,000-pound-capacity grapple, the JC-40 is able to unload the largest logging trucks and stack the logs in a circular pattern around itself. The JC-40s can be found at logging mills and chipping plants in the southern United States and eastern Canada. The JC-40 Model line was first introduced in 1974 and is still in current production as of 2001.

During the 1960s and 1970s, LeTourneau continued to build the highly specialized LeTro-Crusher. First introduced in the mid-1950s, the LeTro-Crushers were primarily used to knock down dense wooded overgrowth in remote areas where there was no road access. Many contractors in the southern United States bought the machines for clearing mesquite on large, unproductive tracts of land. The LeTro-Crushers would knock down this vegetation, chop it up, and push it into the ground with

their large, bladed steel wheels. As the debris decayed in the ground, the soil would become more fertile and productive. The most popular models built were the G-40 and G-80 Tree Crushers from the 1960s, and the Marathon LeTourneau 3523 and 3723 LeTro-Crushers from the 1970s. These Marathon LeTourneau models were the last to be marketed by the company. Shipped from the factory in June 1981, the model 3523 was the last crusher built. The total production of all variations of tree crushers built by LeTourneau between 1953 and 1981, including prototypes, totaled 86 units.

Marathon LeTourneau would try to expand its mining equipment offerings even further when it purchased the Robbins MLR Tractor Series rotary blast hole drill product line from Robbins Manufacturing, Inc. of Birmingham, Alabama, in June 1990. But the mild economic recession in North America of the early 1990s slowed sales of the crawler-mounted mining drills. The Robbins MLR rotary blast hole drill product line joined the former Titan haul truck line—and are no longer openly marketed in the mining industry. Today, the drill line is a custom-built-to-order-only product offering.

Steel-plating production from LeTourneau's own Longview steel mill proved to be very profitable. Opened in 1951, the mill has been an important producer of steel plating, ranging from 3/4 inch to 10 inches in thickness. It cranks out steel for LeTourneau machines and vehicles and provides steel for several major distributors and service centers, fabricators, and manufacturers in various other types of industries. Its Mini-Mill melt shop utilizes 25-ton electric arc furnaces, which provide the flexibility of producing small quantities of specialty grades of steel, as well as larger volumes in other grades. Whether melting, pouring, plate rolling, heat-treating, cutting, and shipping, LeTourneau's steel mini-mill can do it all.

It is probably a good thing that LeTourneau, Inc. makes so much of its own steel, because the company's modern giant offshore drilling rig platforms use an enormous amount of the material. Since November 1955, the Marine Group has delivered 173 of these leviathans. Another two are under construction at the time of this writing. The Marine Group, with its vast experience designing and building offshore drilling platforms, is the main reason that Rowan bought LeTourneau. The large mining equipment was simply icing on the cake.

LeTourneau builds the largest self-elevating drilling rigs in the world, and the Super Gorilla class is the largest of these monstrous platform types. First launched in 1998, the Super Gorilla class of drilling rigs was designed for working in the most severe weather and ocean conditions imaginable, such as those found in the central North Sea, a key oil-drilling region of the world. The Super Gorilla is part of LeTourneau, Inc.'s Gorilla class of platforms utilizing the company's patented Slotilever design. This design allows the rig to be configured for slot or cantilever drilling modes. In previous hull configurations, the platform design had to be one or the other. A slot-drilling rig has a rectangular opening in the stern over which the drilling tower, or draw-works, is positioned. A cantilever design has the drilling tower moved aft of the platform itself and can be adjusted port or starboard to drill multiple production wells. The Gorilla class can do it all from one platform.

The first Gorilla (Hull #200) was launched in December 1983. Gorilla II followed in 1984, Gorilla III in 1985, and Gorilla IV in 1986. The first of the Super Gorilla class was Gorilla V (Hull #219), which was put out to sea in November 1998. Other Super Gorillas followed, including Gorilla VI in 2000, and Gorilla VII and VIII, both of which were under construction at the Vicksburg plant at the time of this writing. Most of the Gorilla platforms have been for one customer—Rowan. Rowan purchased LeTourneau to make sure that it would always be able to get the drilling rigs it wanted, in this case, giant self-elevating jack-up Gorillas.

A Gorilla platform is huge, but a Super Gorilla is even larger. The Super's hull length is 306 feet, its width is 300 feet, the depth

at the side is 36 feet, and the maximum leg length is 713 feet. The drilling elevated weight of the platform is 23,740 tons. The maximum water depth for the Super Gorilla is 550 feet. In 408 feet of water it can withstand 96-foot waves and 89-knot winds. It has its own 94x90-foot heliport, as well as crew quarters for 120 personnel at any one time. Quick-evacuation life pods are suspended on both sides of the rig and can hold and protect all of the rig's personnel when dropped into the water, even in a raging storm.

Whether it is building the world's largest self-elevating jack-up drilling platform, or the world's largest front-end loader for mining duties, LeTourneau has never backed down from a challenge. From its early days with R. G. at the helm to today, LeTourneau, Inc. will continue to innovate and push the boundaries of engineering and design. The legacy of R. G. LeTourneau lives on in the men and women working at the Longview and Vicksburg plants, who design and build these mechanized marvels. These fantastic machines utilize electric-motor systems first introduced by R. G. more than 50 years ago. If the past is any indication of what is to come from the Texas-based company, you can bet it will be big, and then some.

This is the Gorilla V as it makes its way across the Atlantic on the back of a gigantic semisubmersible transport ship heading to its first working contract in the North Sea. As of 2001, the Super Gorilla–class of jack-up rigs are the largest self-elevating drilling platforms in service around the world.

BIBLIOGRAPHY

Crismon, Fred W. U.S. Military Wheeled Vehicles. Sarasota, Florida: Crestline Publishing, 1983.

Gowenlock, Philip G. The LeTourneau Legend. Brisbane, Australia: Paddington Publications, 1996.

LeTourneau, R. G. Mover of Men and Mountains. Chicago, Illinois: Moody Press, 1970.

LeTourneau, Richard H. Edited by Louise LeTourneau Dick. R. G. Talks About . . . Longview, Texas: LeTourneau Press, 1985.

LeTourneau, Richard H. Success Without Succeeding. Grand Rapids, Michigan: Zondervan Publishing House, 1976.

LeTourneau, Richard H. The Earthensteel Report. Kearney, Nebraska: Morris Publishing, 2000.

Rodengen, Jeffrey L. The Legend of Rowan. Fort Lauderdale, Florida: Write Stuff Enterprises, Inc., 1998.

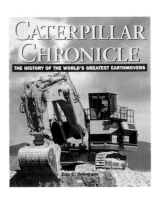
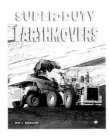

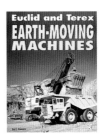

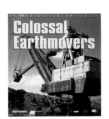
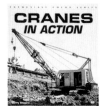